Teen Titans

TITANS AROUND THE WORLD

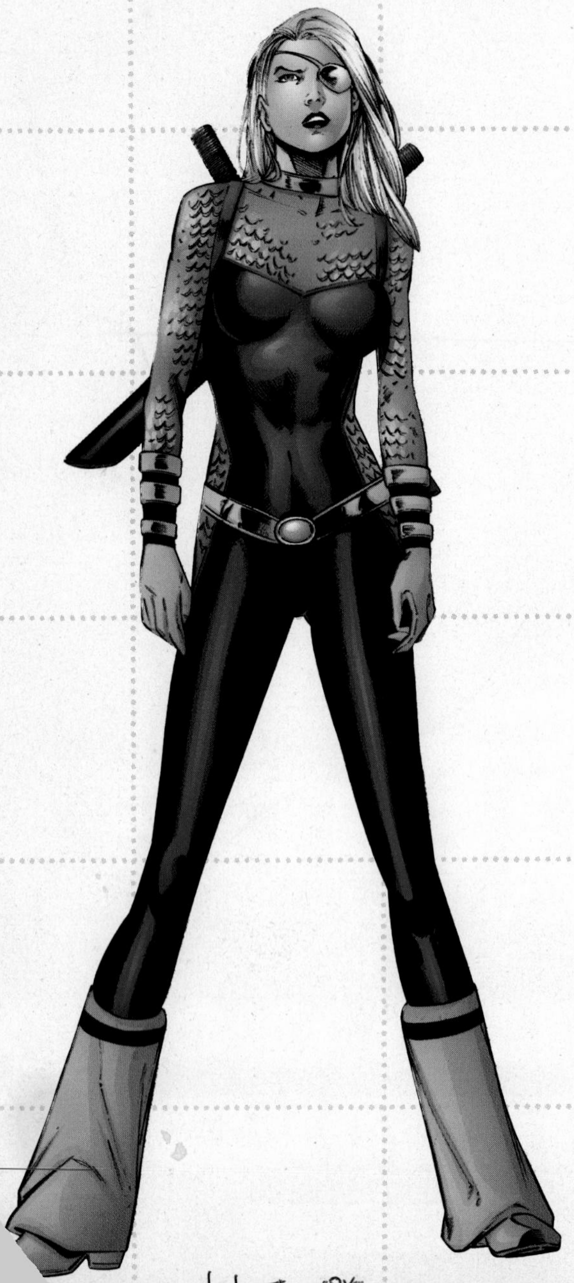

Dan DiDio Senior VP-Executive Editor
Eddie Berganza Editor-original series
Jeanine Schaefer Assistant Editor-original series
Bob Joy Editor-collected edition
Robbin Brosterman Senior Art Director
Paul Levitz President & Publisher
Georg Brewer VP-Design & DC Direct Creative
Richard Bruning Senior VP-Creative Director
Patrick Caldon Executive VP-Finance & Operations
Chris Caramalis VP-Finance
John Cunningham VP-Marketing
Terri Cunningham VP-Managing Editor
Stephanie Fierman Senior VP-Sales & Marketing
Alison Gill VP-Manufacturing
Hank Kanalz VP-General Manager, WildStorm
Jim Lee Editorial Director-WildStorm
Paula Lowitt Senior VP-Business & Legal Affairs
MaryEllen McLaughlin VP-Advertising & Custom Publishing
John Nee VP-Business Development
Gregory Noveck Senior VP-Creative Affairs
Cheryl Rubin Senior VP-Brand Management
Jeff Trojan VP-Business Development, DC Direct
Bob Wayne VP-Sales

Cover art by Tony Daniel and Kevin Conrad
Cover color by Richard & Tanya Horie
Logo designed by Terry Marks
Publication design by Robbie Biederman

TEEN TITANS: TITANS AROUND THE WORLD

DC Comics, 1700 Broadway, New York, NY 10019
A Warner Bros. Entertainment Company
Printed in Canada. First Printing.
ISBN: 1-4012-1217-4
ISBN 13: 978-1-4012-1217-9

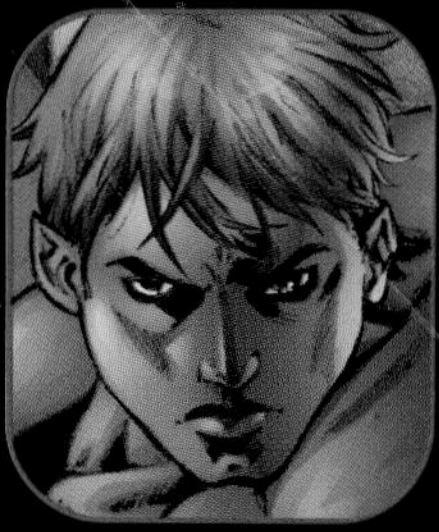

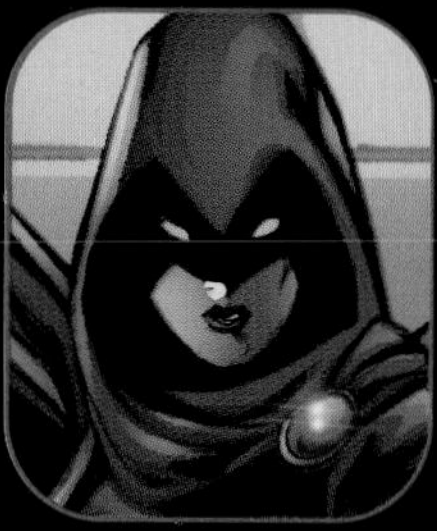

Teen Titans

TITANS AROUND THE WORLD

Written by Geoff Johns

olored by Tanya and Richard Horie

The cataclysmic Infinite Crisis left the Teen Titans physically and emotionally devastated. Even the
of numerous members didn't stop the team from continuing their legacy as the unsurpassable
assemblage of teenage super-heroes. In the year following the Crisis, more than twenty teen
adventurers joined their ranks. All of them looking to make the world a better place... except on

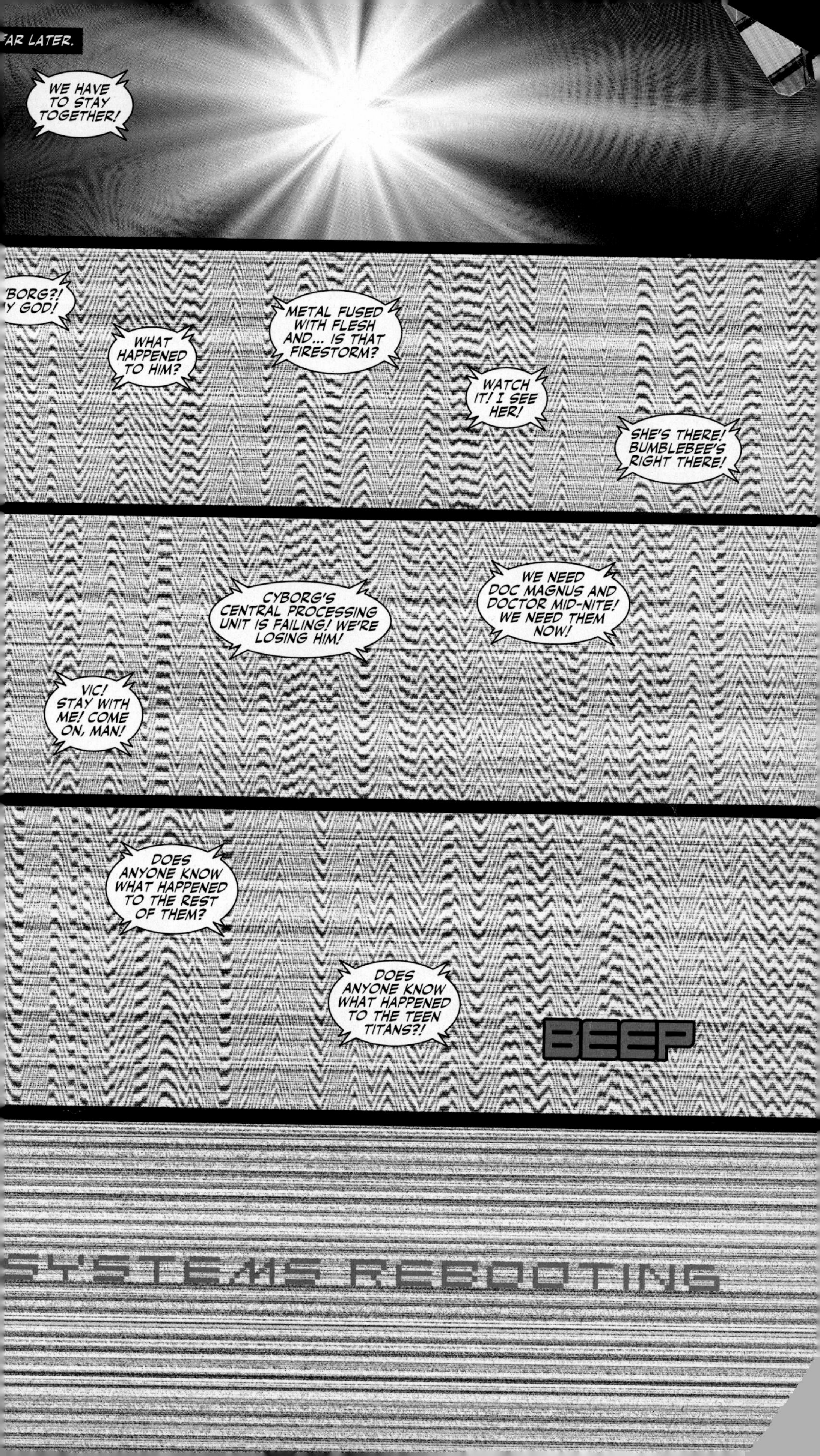
AR LATER.
WE HAVE TO STAY TOGETHER!
BORG?! Y GOD!
WHAT HAPPENED TO HIM?
METAL FUSED WITH FLESH AND... IS THAT FIRESTORM?
WATCH IT! I SEE HER!
SHE'S THERE! BUMBLEBEE'S RIGHT THERE!
CYBORG'S CENTRAL PROCESSING UNIT IS FAILING! WE'RE LOSING HIM!
WE NEED DOC MAGNUS AND DOCTOR MID-NITE! WE NEED THEM NOW!
VIC! STAY WITH ME! COME ON, MAN!
DOES ANYONE KNOW WHAT HAPPENED TO THE REST OF THEM?
DOES ANYONE KNOW WHAT HAPPENED TO THE TEEN TITANS?!
BEEP
SYSTEMS REBOOTING

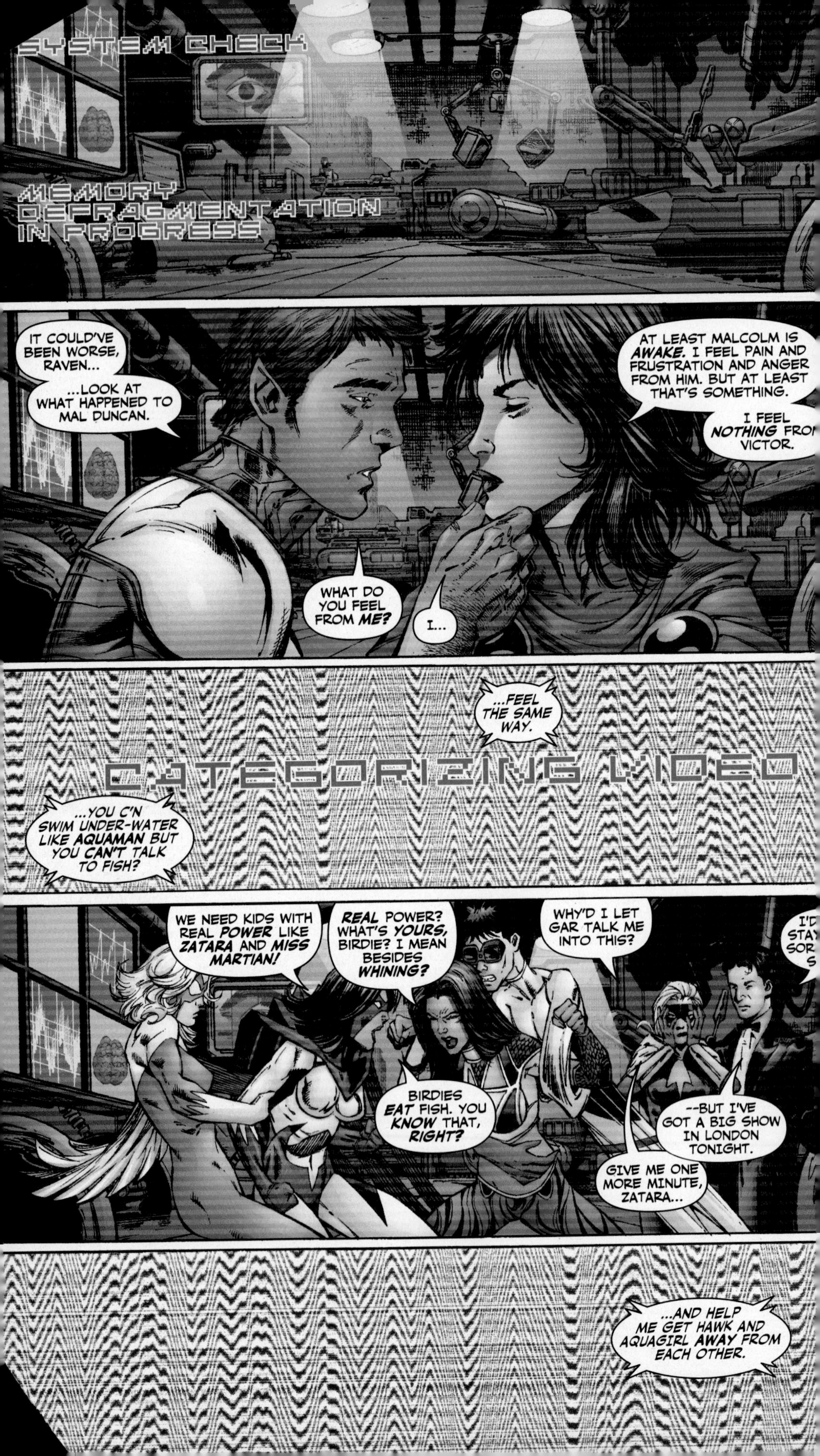
SYSTEM CHECK
MEMORY DEFRAGMENTATION IN PROGRESS
IT COULD'VE BEEN WORSE, RAVEN...
...LOOK AT WHAT HAPPENED TO MAL DUNCAN.
AT LEAST MALCOLM IS AWAKE. I FEEL PAIN AND FRUSTRATION AND ANGER FROM HIM. BUT AT LEAST THAT'S SOMETHING.
I FEEL NOTHING FROM VICTOR.
WHAT DO YOU FEEL FROM ME?
I...
...FEEL THE SAME WAY.
CATEGORIZING VIDEO
...YOU C'N SWIM UNDER-WATER LIKE AQUAMAN BUT YOU CAN'T TALK TO FISH?
WE NEED KIDS WITH REAL POWER LIKE ZATARA AND MISS MARTIAN!
REAL POWER? WHAT'S YOURS, BIRDIE? I MEAN BESIDES WHINING?
WHY'D I LET GAR TALK ME INTO THIS?
BIRDIES EAT FISH. YOU KNOW THAT, RIGHT?
--BUT I'VE GOT A BIG SHOW IN LONDON TONIGHT.
GIVE ME ONE MORE MINUTE, ZATARA...
...AND HELP ME GET HAWK AND AQUAGIRL AWAY FROM EACH OTHER.

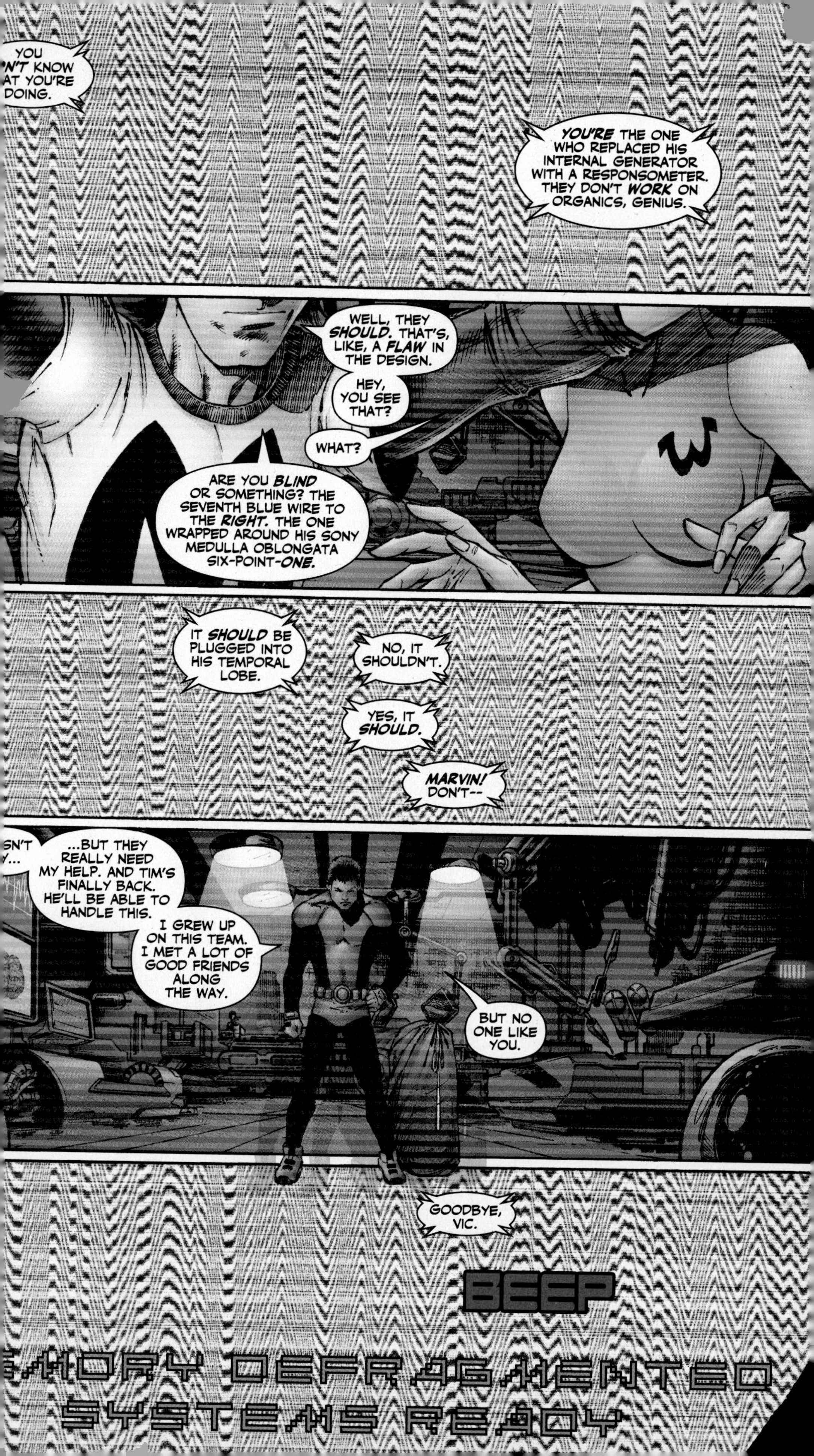
YOU N'T KNOW AT YOU'RE DOING.
YOU'RE THE ONE WHO REPLACED HIS INTERNAL GENERATOR WITH A RESPONSOMETER. THEY DON'T WORK ON ORGANICS, GENIUS.
WELL, THEY SHOULD. THAT'S, LIKE, A FLAW IN THE DESIGN.
HEY, YOU SEE THAT?
WHAT?
ARE YOU BLIND OR SOMETHING? THE SEVENTH BLUE WIRE TO THE RIGHT. THE ONE WRAPPED AROUND HIS SONY MEDULLA OBLONGATA SIX-POINT-ONE.
IT SHOULD BE PLUGGED INTO HIS TEMPORAL LOBE.
NO, IT SHOULDN'T.
YES, IT SHOULD.
MARVIN! DON'T--
SN'T
...BUT THEY REALLY NEED MY HELP. AND TIM'S FINALLY BACK. HE'LL BE ABLE TO HANDLE THIS.
I GREW UP ON THIS TEAM. I MET A LOT OF GOOD FRIENDS ALONG THE WAY.
BUT NO ONE LIKE YOU.
GOODBYE, VIC.
BEEP
MORY DEFRAGMENTED
SYSTEMS READY

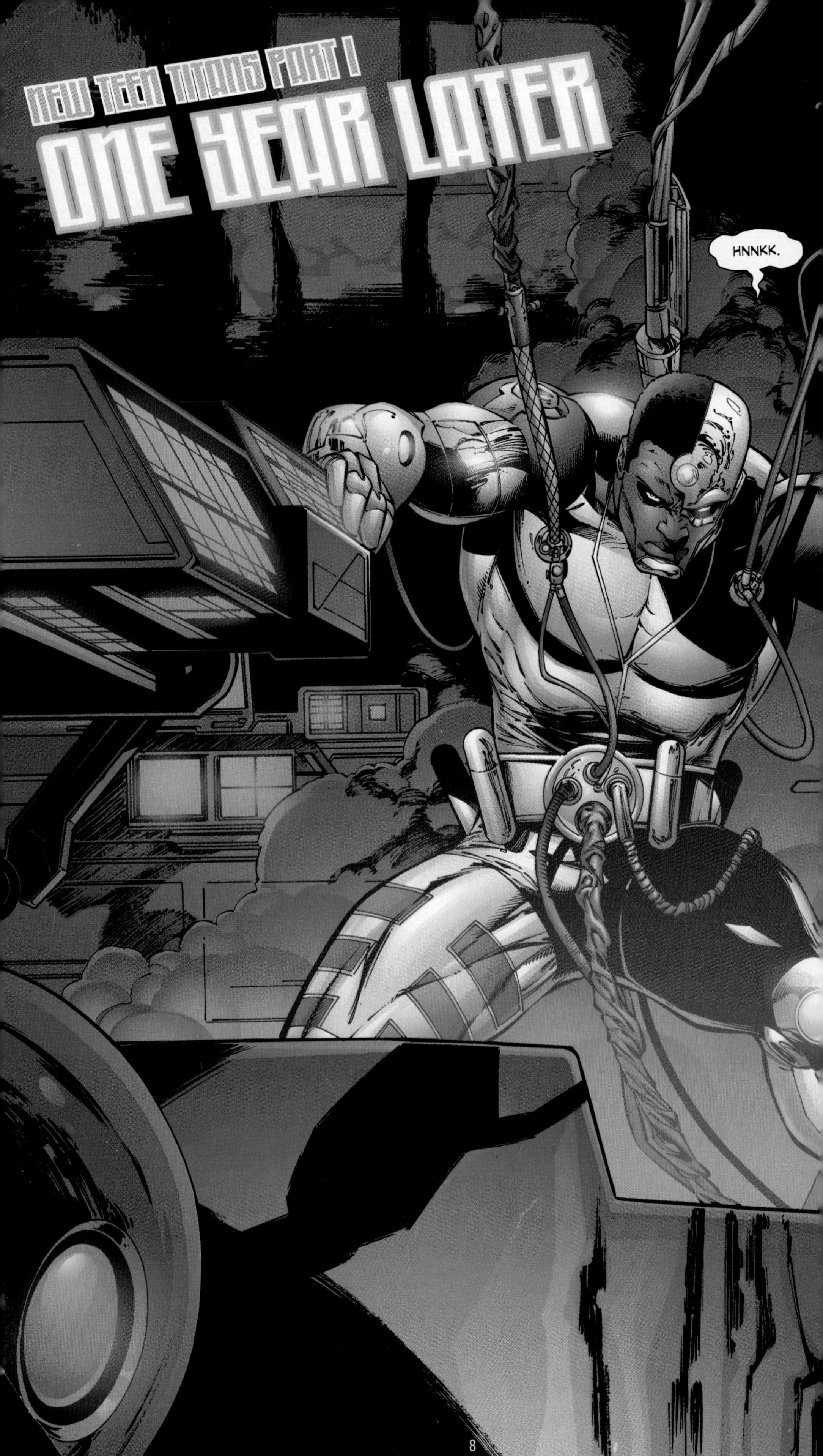
NEW TEEN TITANS PART 1
ONE YEAR LATER
HNNKK.

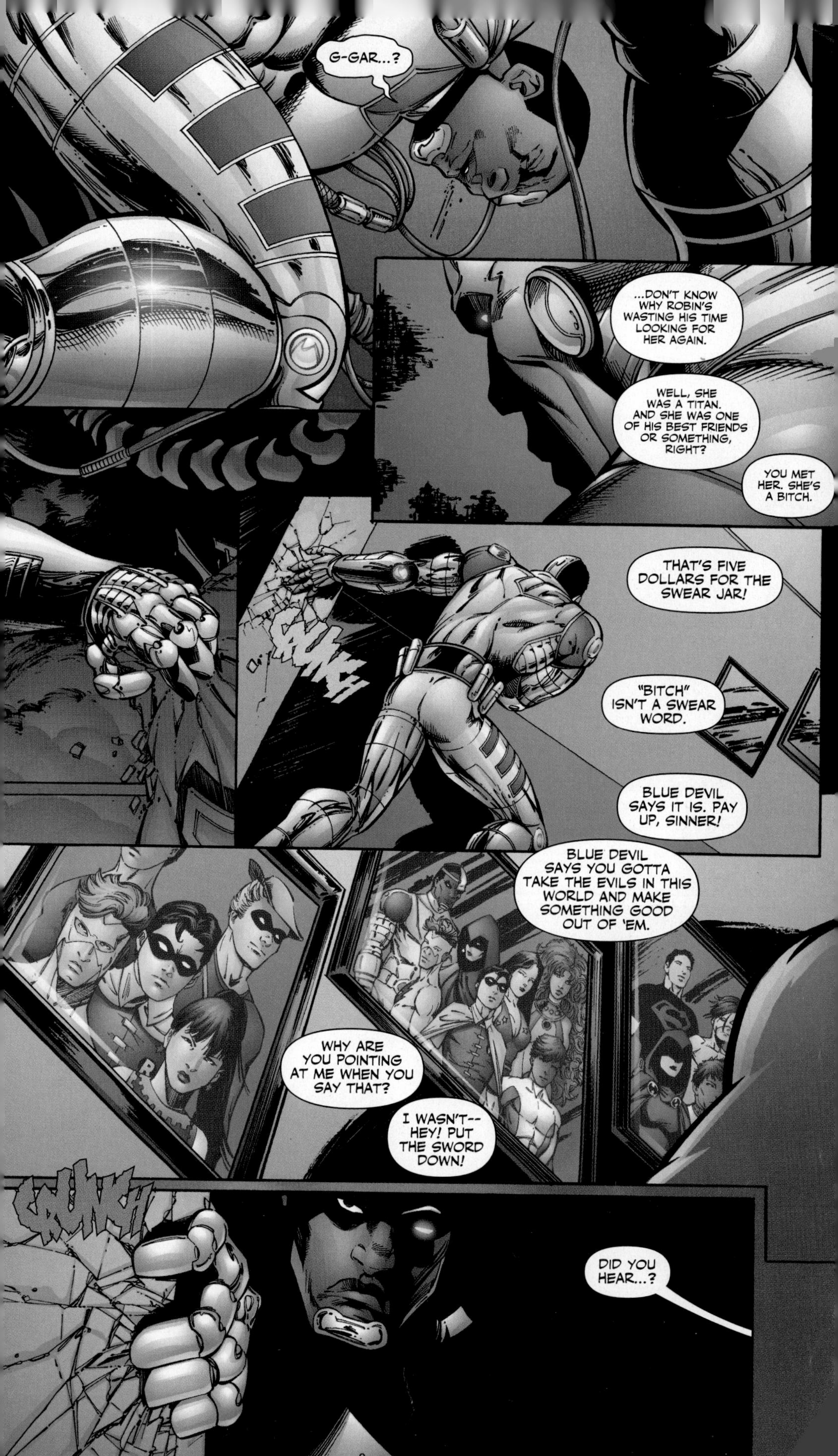
G-GAR...?
...DON'T KNOW WHY ROBIN'S WASTING HIS TIME LOOKING FOR HER AGAIN.
WELL, SHE WAS A TITAN. AND SHE WAS ONE OF HIS BEST FRIENDS OR SOMETHING, RIGHT?
YOU MET HER. SHE'S A BITCH.
CRUNK!
THAT'S FIVE DOLLARS FOR THE SWEAR JAR!
"BITCH" ISN'T A SWEAR WORD.
BLUE DEVIL SAYS IT IS. PAY UP, SINNER!
BLUE DEVIL SAYS YOU GOTTA TAKE THE EVILS IN THIS WORLD AND MAKE SOMETHING GOOD OUT OF 'EM.
WHY ARE YOU POINTING AT ME WHEN YOU SAY THAT?
I WASN'T-- HEY! PUT THE SWORD DOWN!
CRUNCH
DID YOU HEAR...?

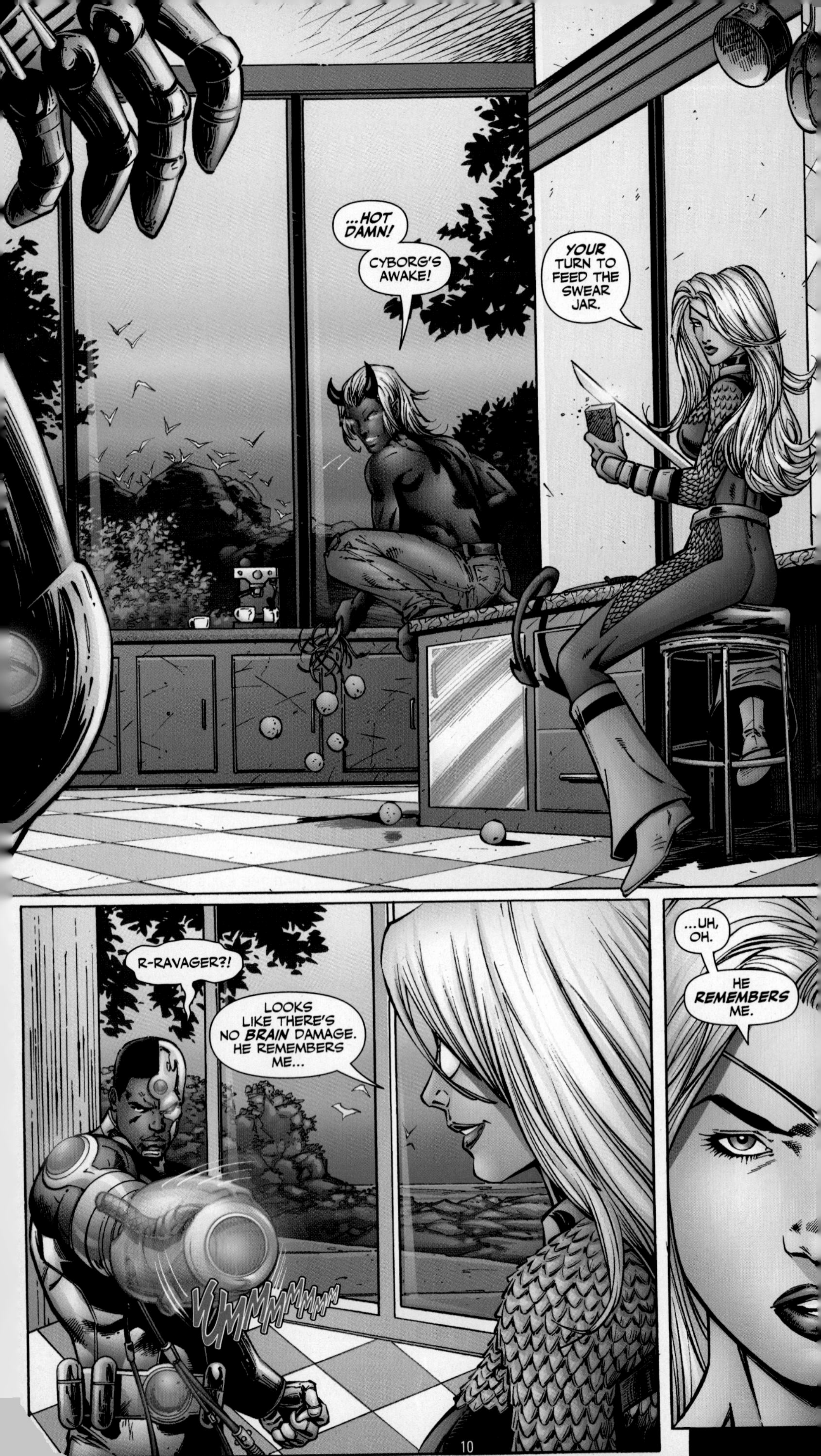
...HOT DAMN!
CYBORG'S AWAKE!
YOUR TURN TO FEED THE SWEAR JAR.
R-RAVAGER?!
LOOKS LIKE THERE'S NO BRAIN DAMAGE. HE REMEMBERS ME...
VUMMMMMMMM
...UH, OH.
HE REMEMBERS ME.

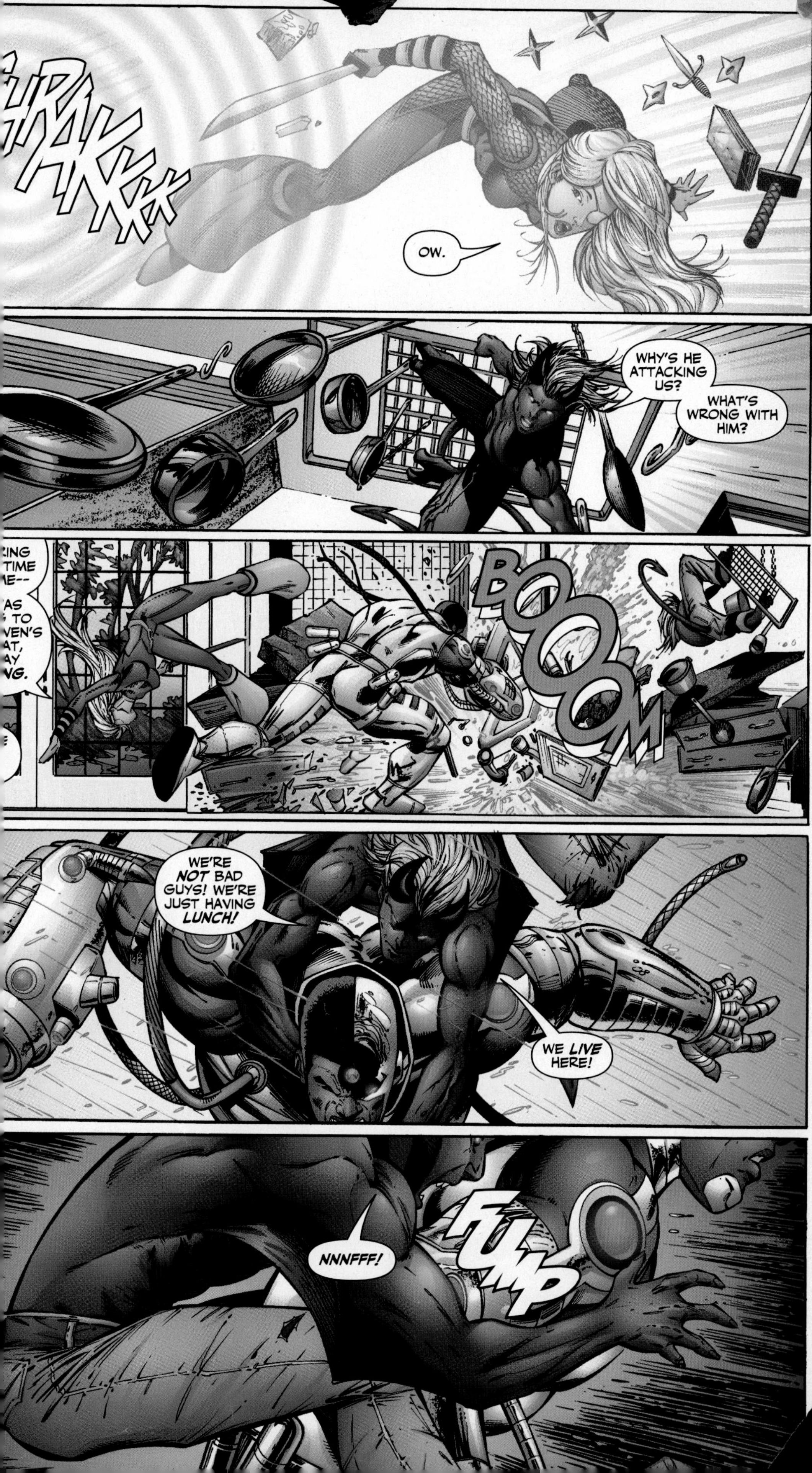
OW.
WHY'S HE ATTACKING US?
WHAT'S WRONG WITH HIM?
BOOOOM
WE'RE NOT BAD GUYS! WE'RE JUST HAVING LUNCH!
WE LIVE HERE!
NNNFFF!
FUMP

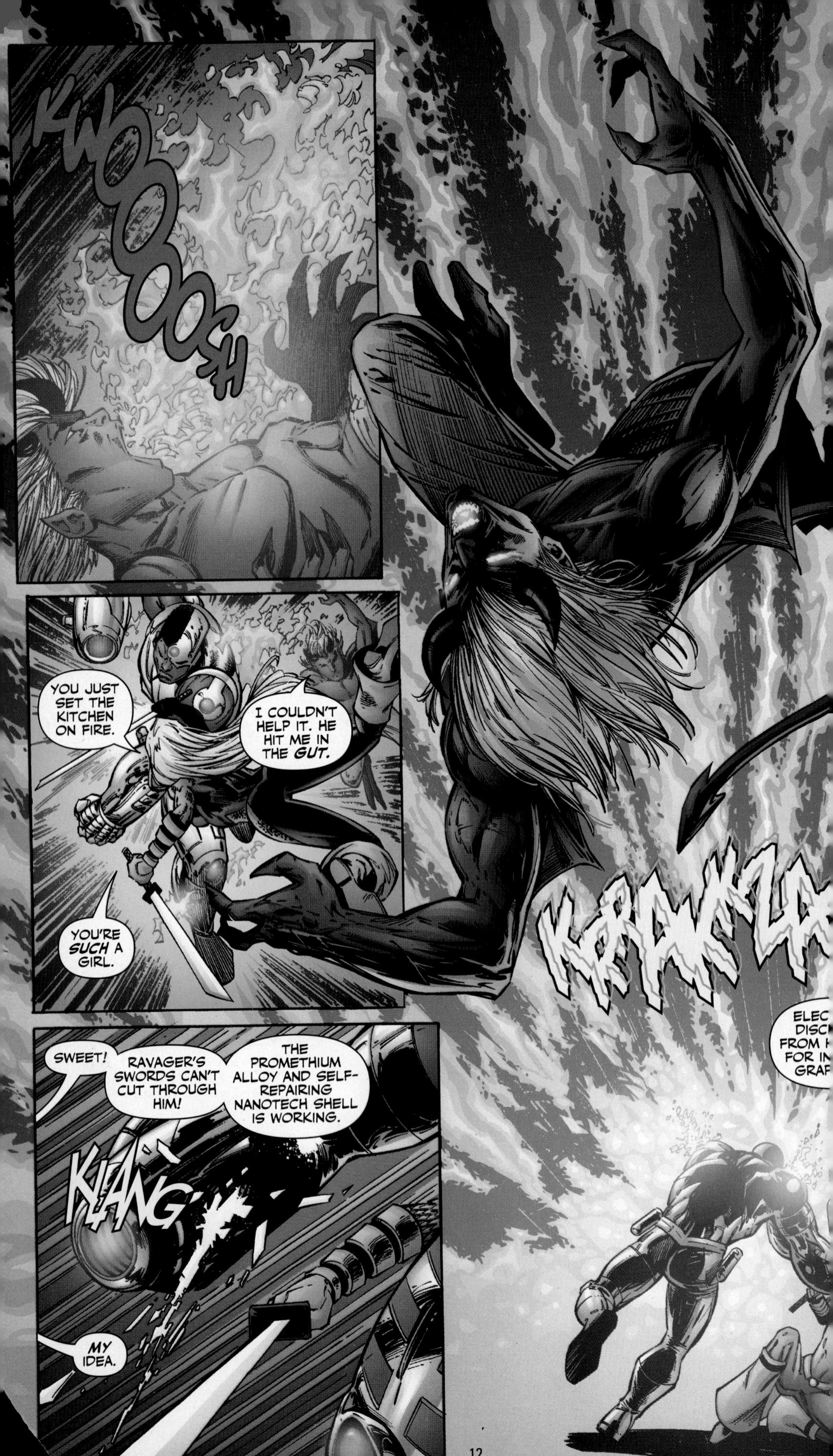
KWOOOOOOSH
YOU JUST SET THE KITCHEN ON FIRE.
I COULDN'T HELP IT. HE HIT ME IN THE *GUT*.
YOU'RE *SUCH* A GIRL.
KRAKZA
ELEC DISC FROM H FOR IN GRAP
SWEET!
RAVAGER'S SWORDS CAN'T CUT THROUGH HIM!
THE PROMETHIUM ALLOY AND SELF-REPAIRING NANOTECH SHELL IS WORKING.
KLANG
MY IDEA.

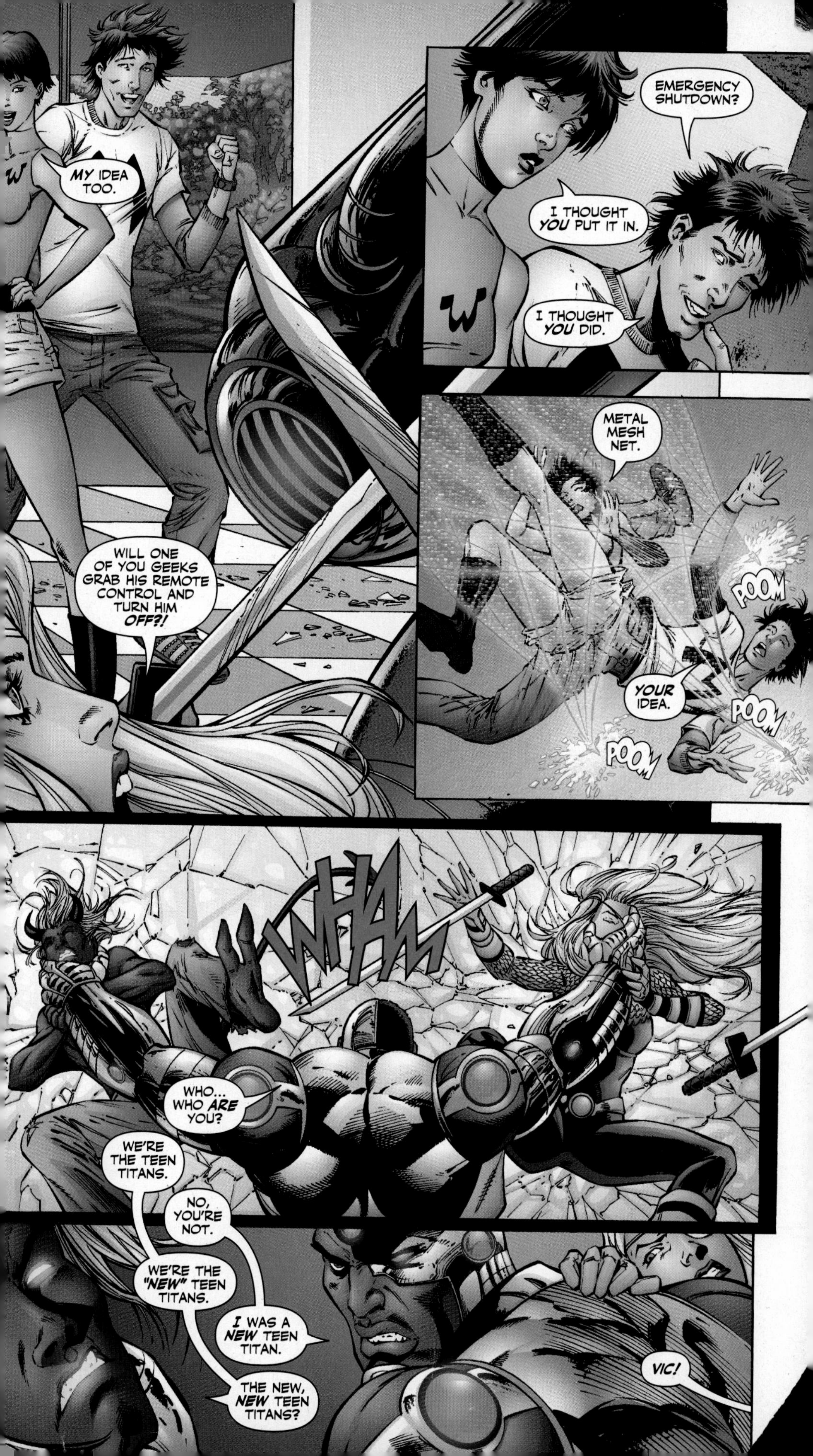
MY IDEA TOO.
EMERGENCY SHUTDOWN?
I THOUGHT YOU PUT IT IN.
I THOUGHT YOU DID.
WILL ONE OF YOU GEEKS GRAB HIS REMOTE CONTROL AND TURN HIM OFF?!
METAL MESH NET.
POOM
YOUR IDEA.
POOM
POOM
WHAM
WHO... WHO ARE YOU?
WE'RE THE TEEN TITANS.
NO, YOU'RE NOT.
WE'RE THE "NEW" TEEN TITANS.
I WAS A NEW TEEN TITAN.
VIC!
THE NEW, NEW TEEN TITANS?

WELCOME BACK.

WE KICKED *BUTT* ON YOU, *THAT'S* WHAT.

AND NOW WE NEED TO REMODEL THE KITCHEN.

THESE TWO ARE *MARVIN* AND *WENDY*.

TH... KIND O... CARET... OF... TOW...

TH... SPEN... LAS... MON... REBUI... YO...

DAD SENT US OVER TO HELP AFTER WE GRADUATED FROM M.I.T... ON OUR SIXTEENTH BIRTHDAY.

I'M THE OLDEST.

BY LIKE *FIVE* MINUTES.

THIS IS EDDIE BLOOMBERG.

KID DEVIL HERE. I'M *BLUE DEVIL'S* SIDEKICK.

I THOUGHT *BLUE DEVIL* WAS A SIDEKICK.

AND YOU ALREADY KNOW ROSE WILSON.

WHAT THE HELL IS SLADE'S DAUGHTER DOING HERE?

ROBIN?

WE ALL HOPED YOU'D BE AWAKE SOON.

WHAT'S GOING ON?

OH, DON'T WORRY, CYBORG, I'M NOT LIKE *TERRA...*

...I'M A *GOOD GIRL* NOW.

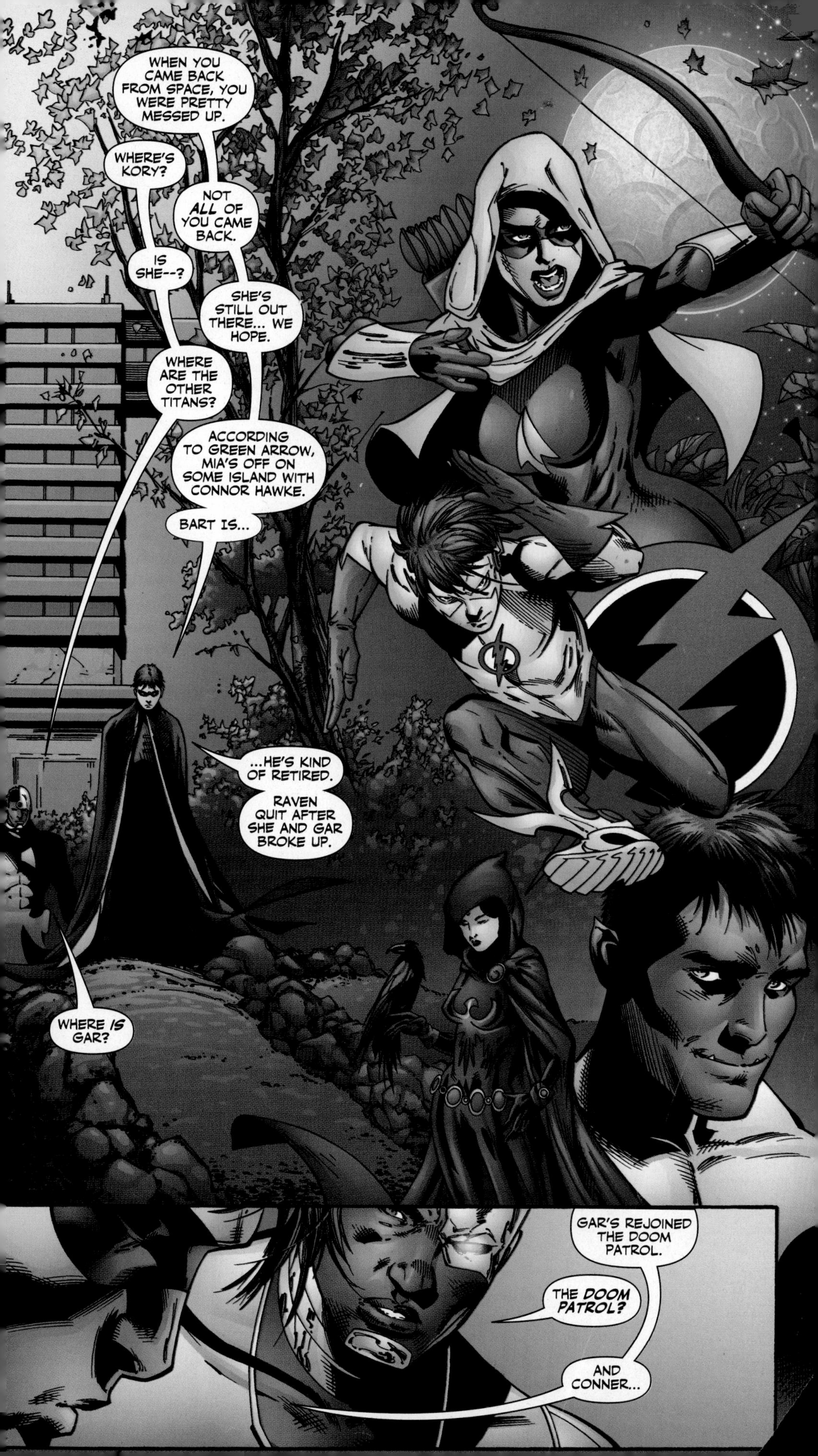

WHEN YOU CAME BACK FROM SPACE, YOU WERE PRETTY MESSED UP.
WHERE'S KORY?
NOT ALL OF YOU CAME BACK.
IS SHE--?
SHE'S STILL OUT THERE... WE HOPE.
WHERE ARE THE OTHER TITANS?
ACCORDING TO GREEN ARROW, MIA'S OFF ON SOME ISLAND WITH CONNOR HAWKE.
BART IS...
...HE'S KIND OF RETIRED.
RAVEN QUIT AFTER SHE AND GAR BROKE UP.
WHERE IS GAR?
GAR'S REJOINED THE DOOM PATROL.
THE DOOM PATROL?
AND CONNER...

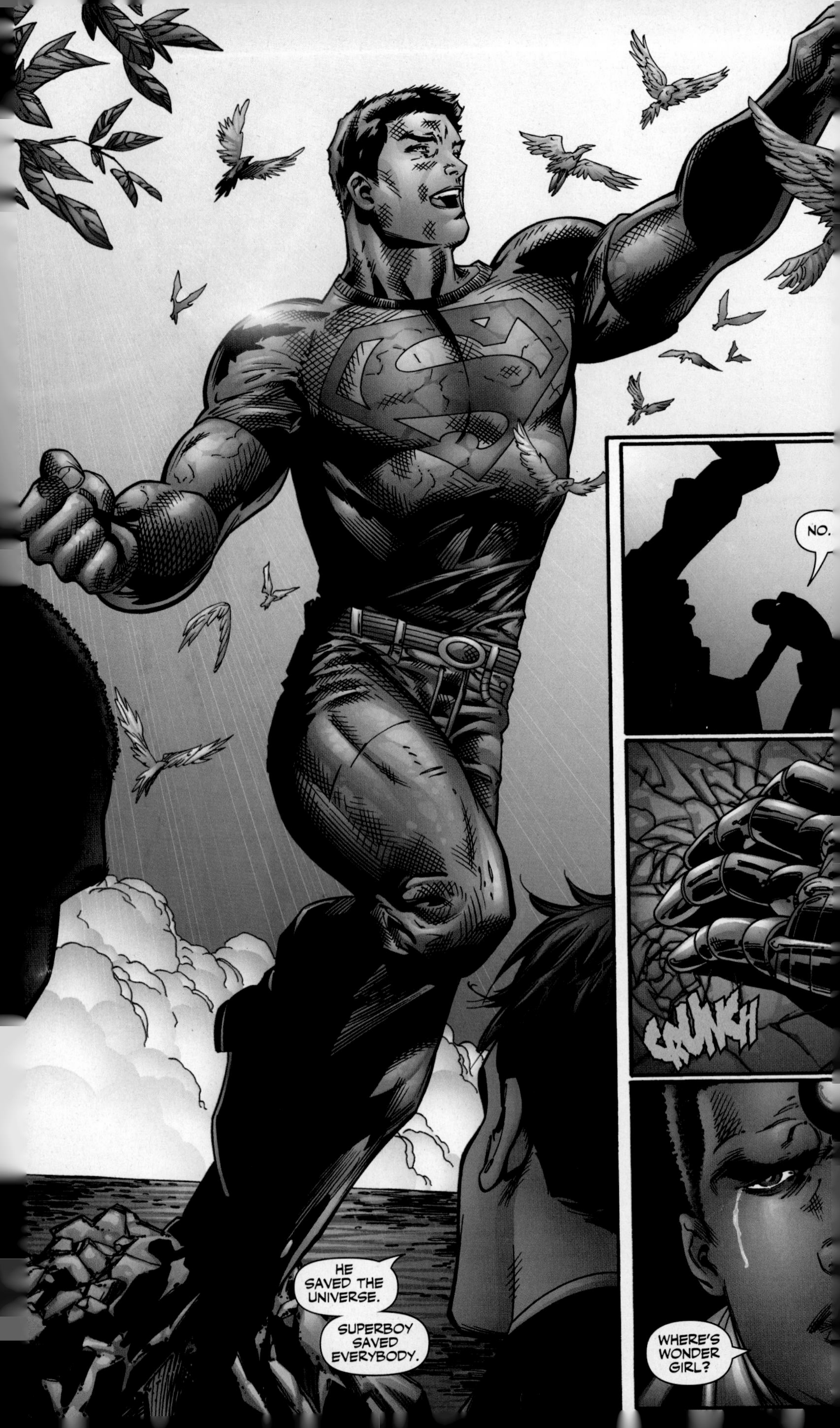
NO.
CRUNCH
HE SAVED THE UNIVERSE.
SUPERBOY SAVED EVERYBODY.
WHERE'S WONDER GIRL?

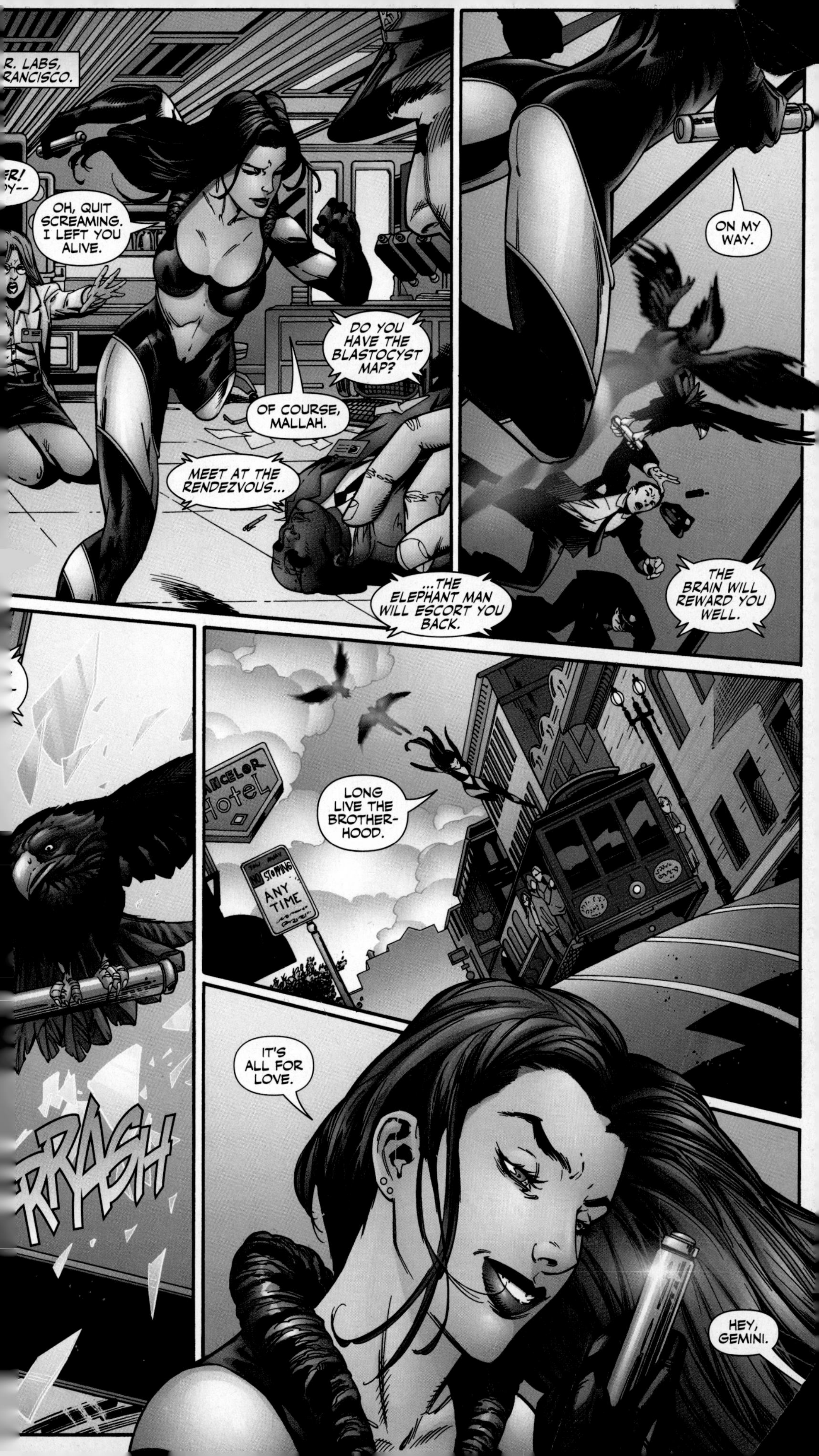
R. LABS,
RANCISCO.
ER!
DY--
OH, QUIT SCREAMING. I LEFT YOU ALIVE.
DO YOU HAVE THE BLASTOCYST MAP?
OF COURSE, MALLAH.
MEET AT THE RENDEZVOUS...
...THE ELEPHANT MAN WILL ESCORT YOU BACK.
ON MY WAY.
THE BRAIN WILL REWARD YOU WELL.
CRASH
ANCELOR
Hotel
NO STOPPING
ANY TIME
LONG LIVE THE BROTHER-HOOD.
IT'S ALL FOR LOVE.
HEY, GEMINI.

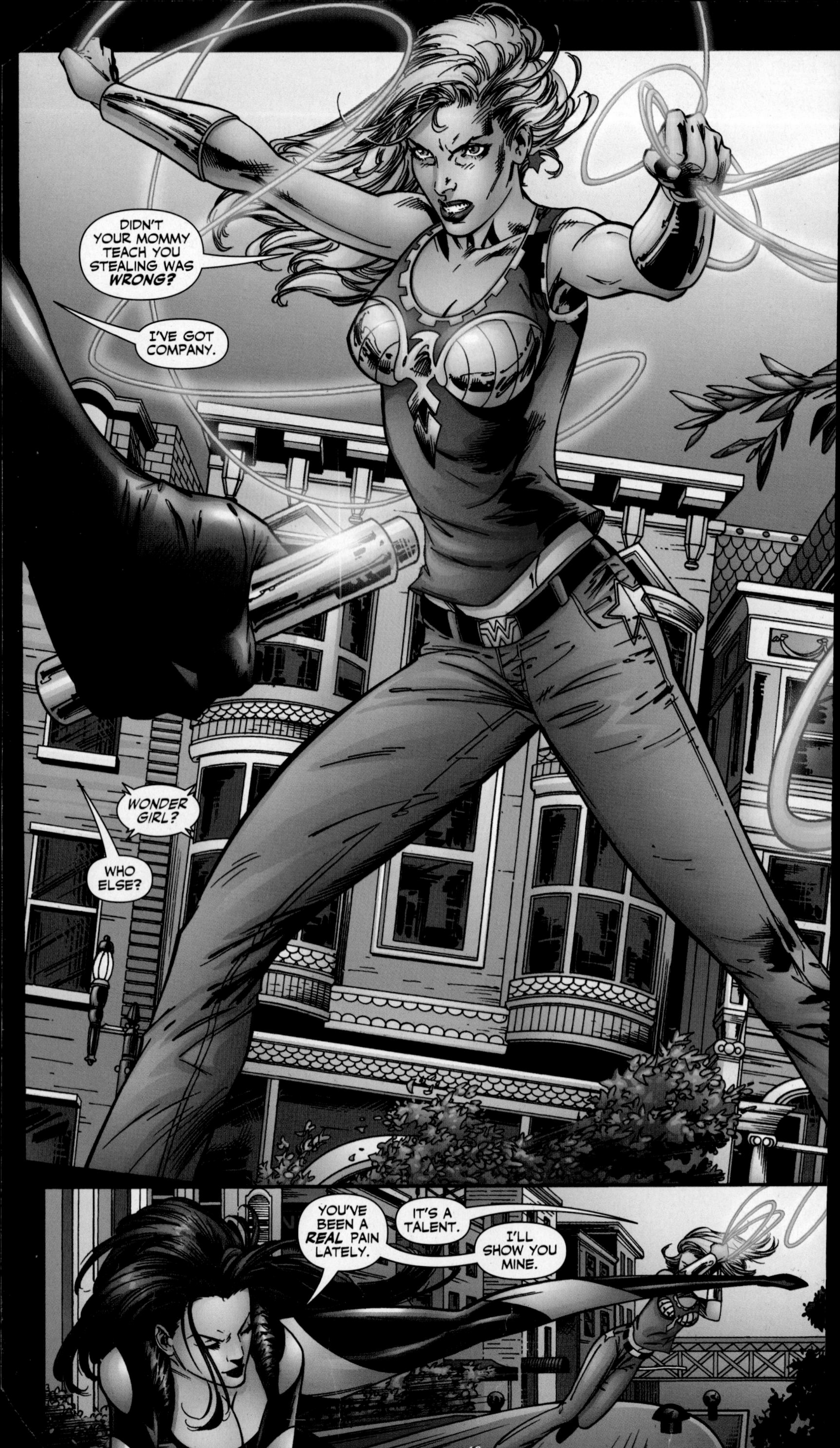
DIDN'T YOUR MOMMY TEACH YOU STEALING WAS WRONG?
I'VE GOT COMPANY.
WONDER GIRL?
WHO ELSE?
YOU'VE BEEN A REAL PAIN LATELY.
IT'S A TALENT.
I'LL SHOW YOU MINE.

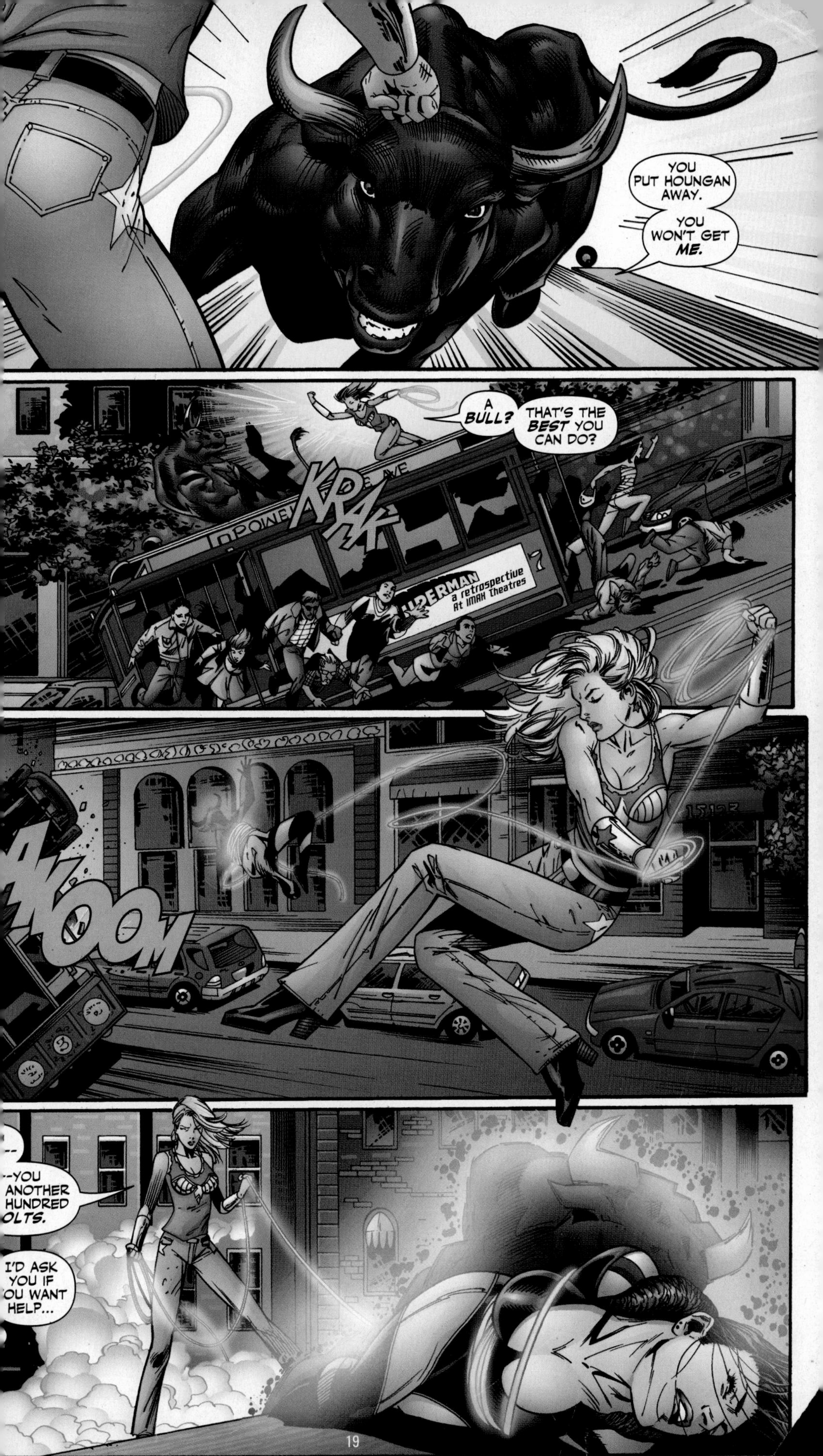

YOU PUT HOUNGAN AWAY.
YOU WON'T GET ME.
A BULL?
THAT'S THE BEST YOU CAN DO?
KRAK
POWELL & HYDE AVE
SUPERMAN a retrospective At IMAX Theatres
--
--YOU ANOTHER HUNDRED OLTS.
I'D ASK YOU IF OU WANT HELP...

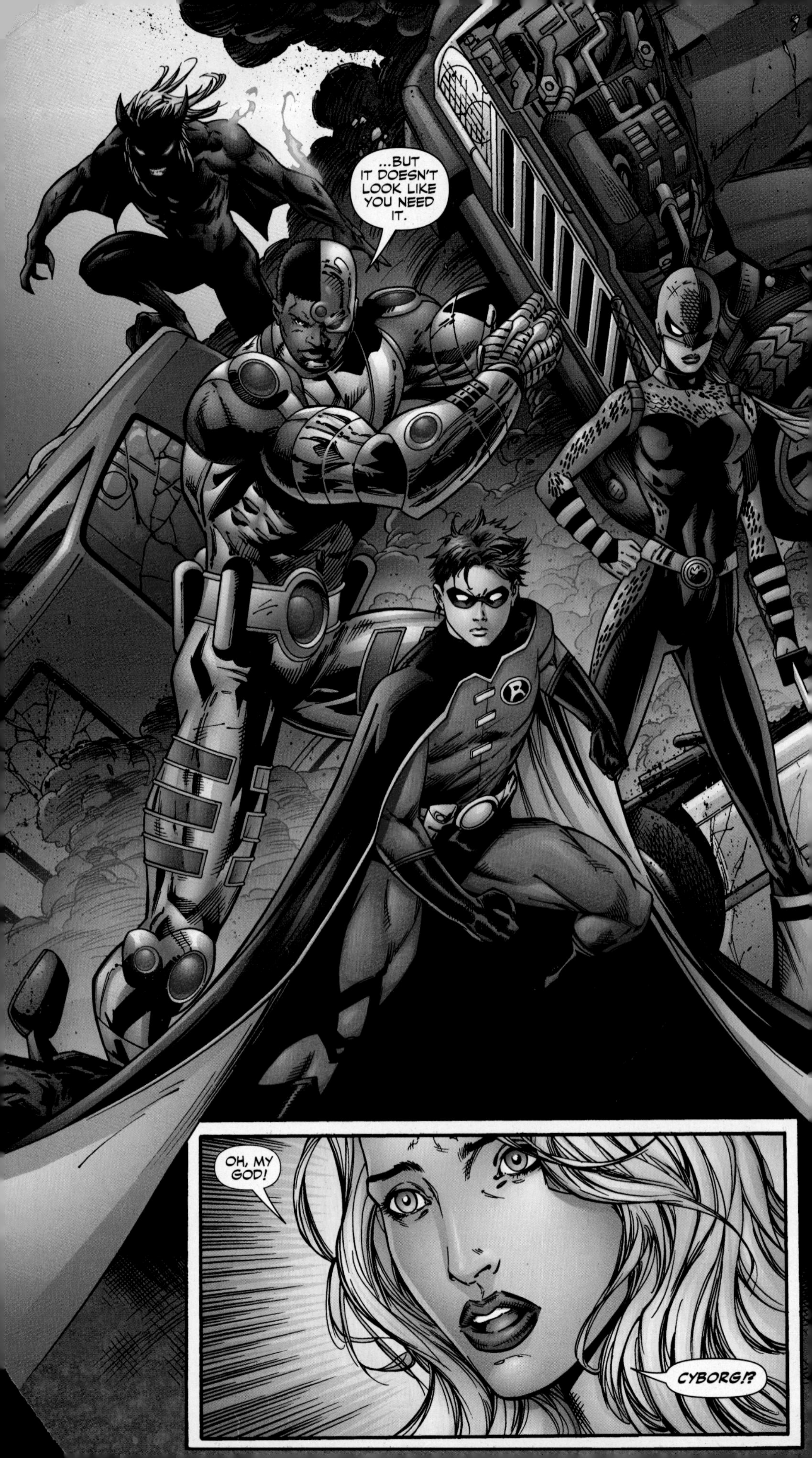
...BUT IT DOESN'T LOOK LIKE YOU NEED IT.
OH, MY GOD!
CYBORG!?

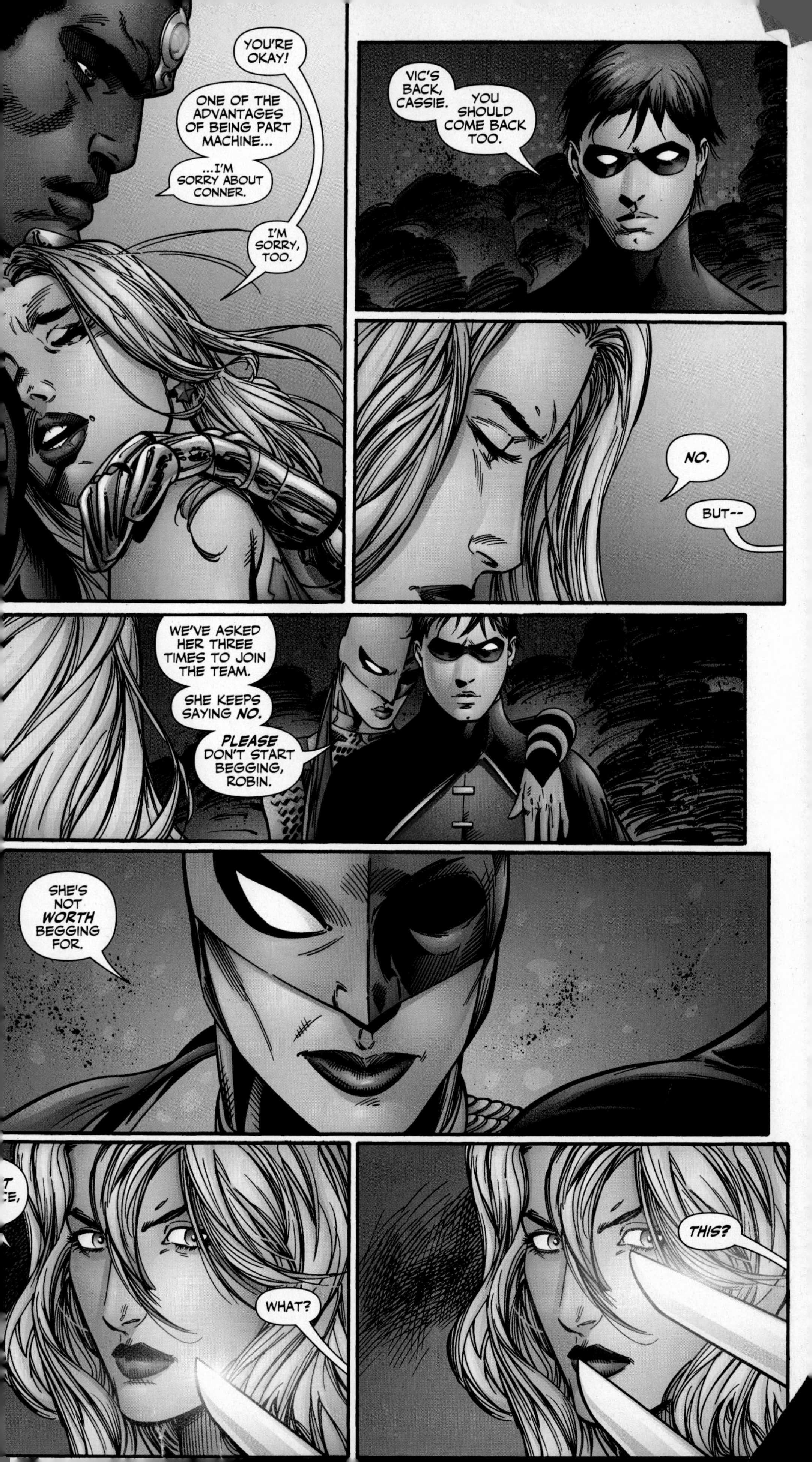
YOU'RE OKAY!
ONE OF THE ADVANTAGES OF BEING PART MACHINE...
...I'M SORRY ABOUT CONNER.
I'M SORRY, TOO.
VIC'S BACK, CASSIE.
YOU SHOULD COME BACK TOO.
NO.
BUT--
WE'VE ASKED HER THREE TIMES TO JOIN THE TEAM.
SHE KEEPS SAYING NO.
PLEASE DON'T START BEGGING, ROBIN.
SHE'S NOT WORTH BEGGING FOR.
WHAT?
THIS?

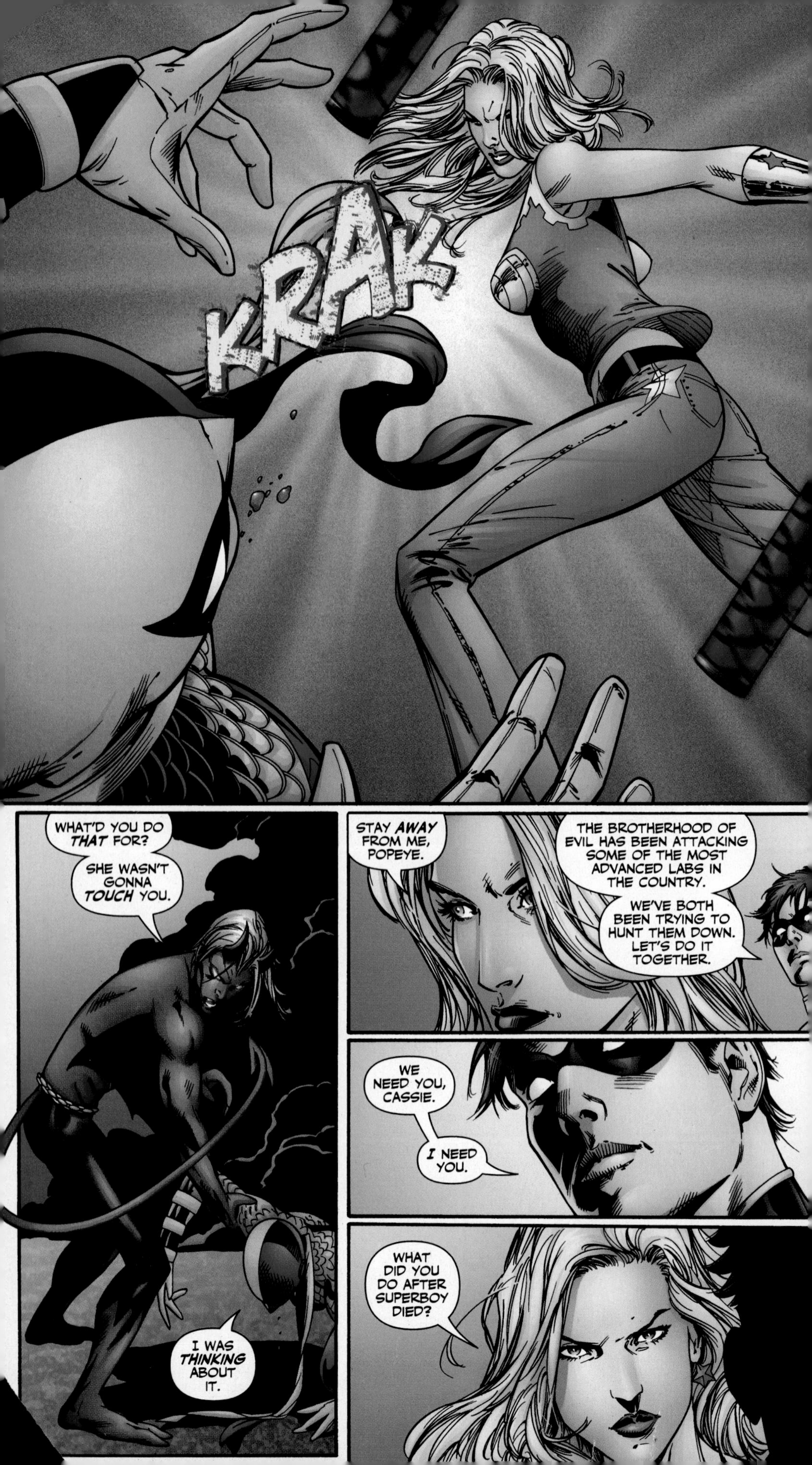

KRAK
WHAT'D YOU DO *THAT* FOR?
SHE WASN'T GONNA *TOUCH* YOU.
I WAS *THINKING* ABOUT IT.
STAY *AWAY* FROM ME, POPEYE.
THE BROTHERHOOD OF EVIL HAS BEEN ATTACKING SOME OF THE MOST ADVANCED LABS IN THE COUNTRY.
WE'VE BOTH BEEN TRYING TO HUNT THEM DOWN. LET'S DO IT TOGETHER.
WE NEED YOU, CASSIE.
I NEED YOU.
WHAT DID YOU DO AFTER SUPERBOY DIED?

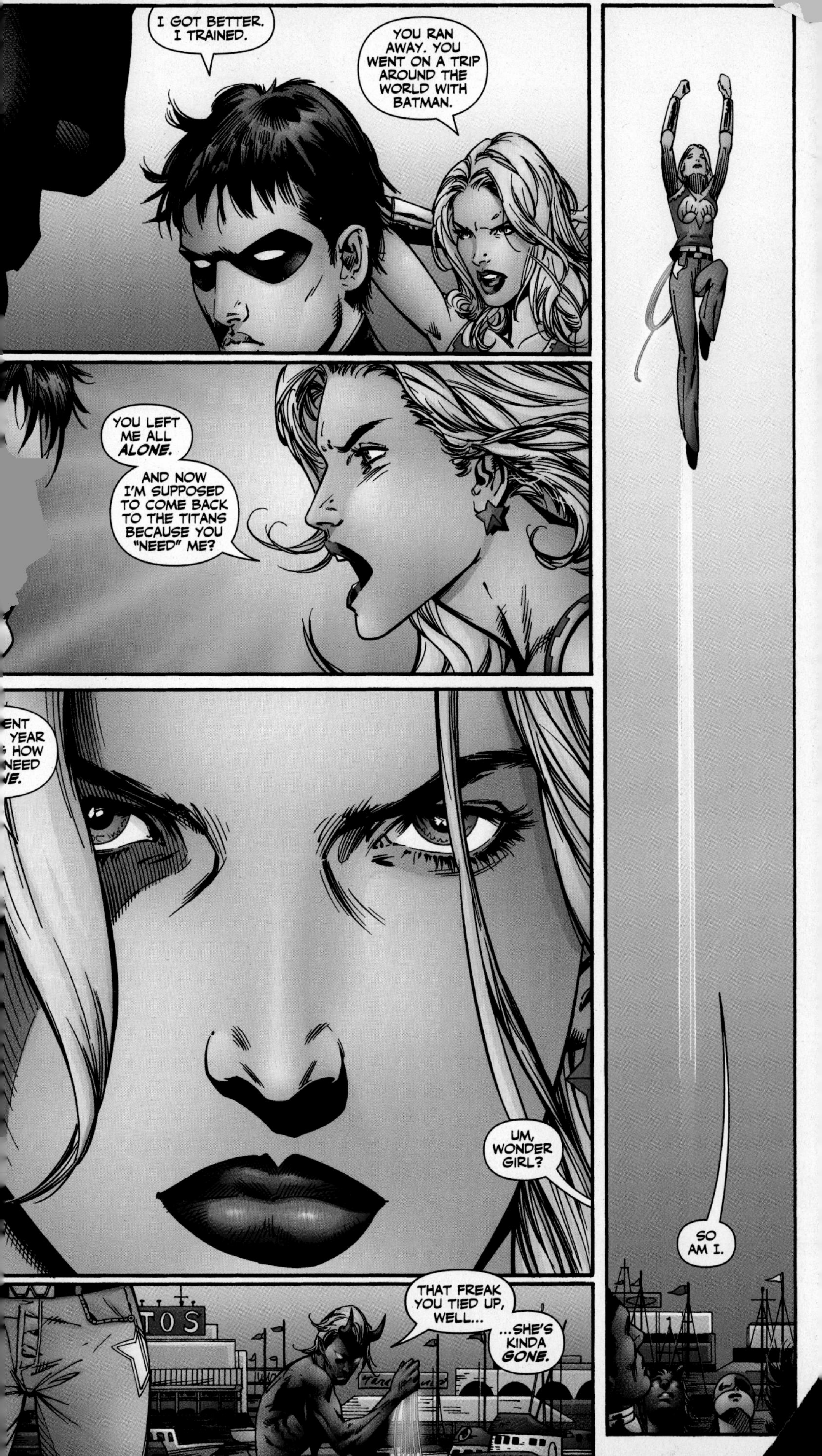
I GOT BETTER. I TRAINED.
YOU RAN AWAY. YOU WENT ON A TRIP AROUND THE WORLD WITH BATMAN.
YOU LEFT ME ALL *ALONE.*
AND NOW I'M SUPPOSED TO COME BACK TO THE TITANS BECAUSE YOU "NEED" ME?
UM, WONDER GIRL?
THAT FREAK YOU TIED UP, WELL...
...SHE'S KINDA *GONE.*
SO AM I.
TOS

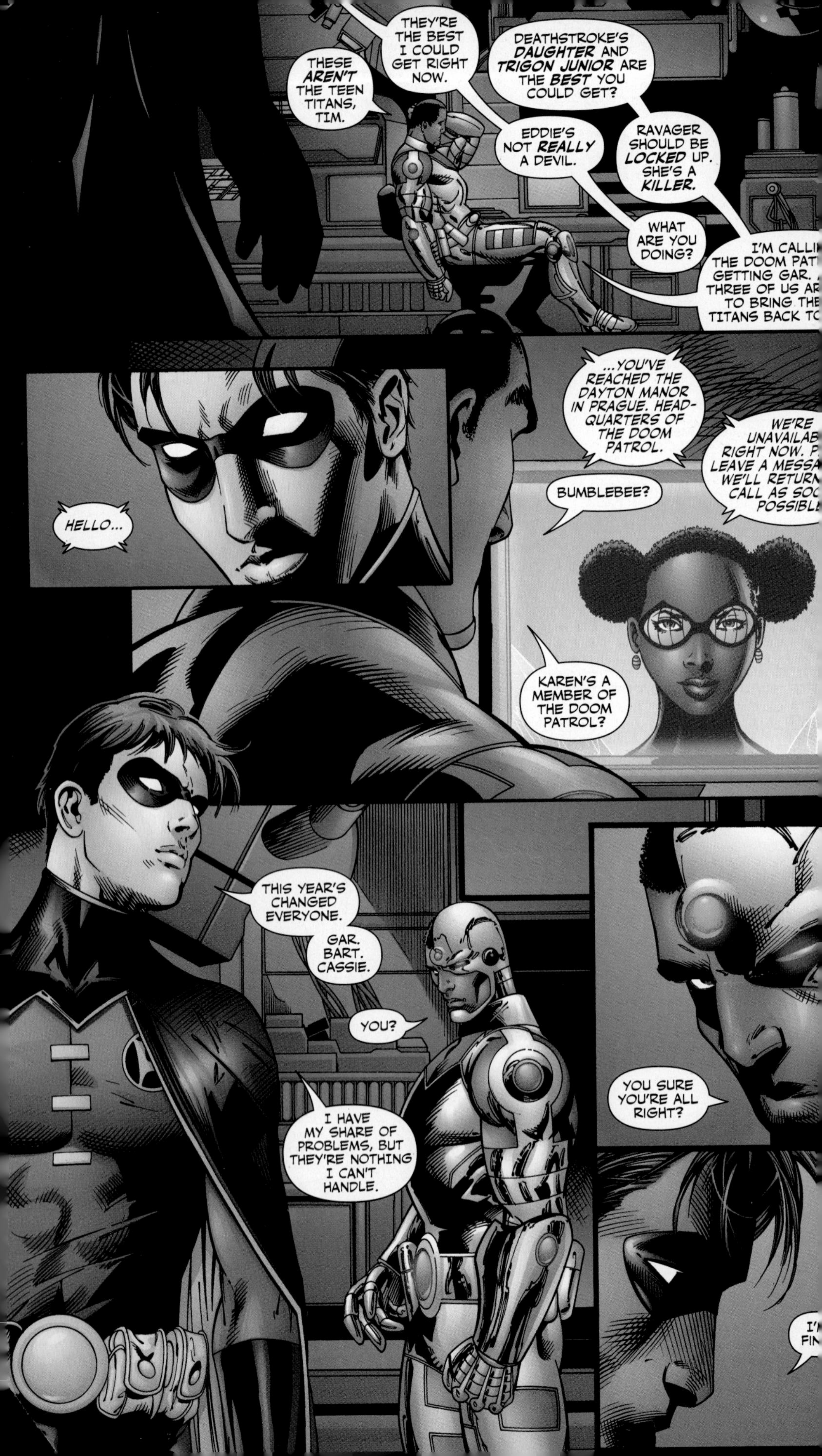

THESE AREN'T THE TEEN TITANS, TIM.
THEY'RE THE BEST I COULD GET RIGHT NOW.
DEATHSTROKE'S DAUGHTER AND TRIGON JUNIOR ARE THE BEST YOU COULD GET?
EDDIE'S NOT REALLY A DEVIL.
RAVAGER SHOULD BE LOCKED UP. SHE'S A KILLER.
WHAT ARE YOU DOING?
I'M CALLI
THE DOOM PAT
GETTING GAR.
THREE OF US AR
TO BRING THE
TITANS BACK TO
HELLO...
...YOU'VE REACHED THE DAYTON MANOR IN PRAGUE. HEAD-QUARTERS OF THE DOOM PATROL.
WE'RE
UNAVAILAB
RIGHT NOW. P
LEAVE A MESSA
WE'LL RETURN
CALL AS SOO
POSSIBL
BUMBLEBEE?
KAREN'S A MEMBER OF THE DOOM PATROL?
THIS YEAR'S CHANGED EVERYONE.
GAR. BART. CASSIE.
YOU?
I HAVE MY SHARE OF PROBLEMS, BUT THEY'RE NOTHING I CAN'T HANDLE.
YOU SURE YOU'RE ALL RIGHT?
I'
FIN

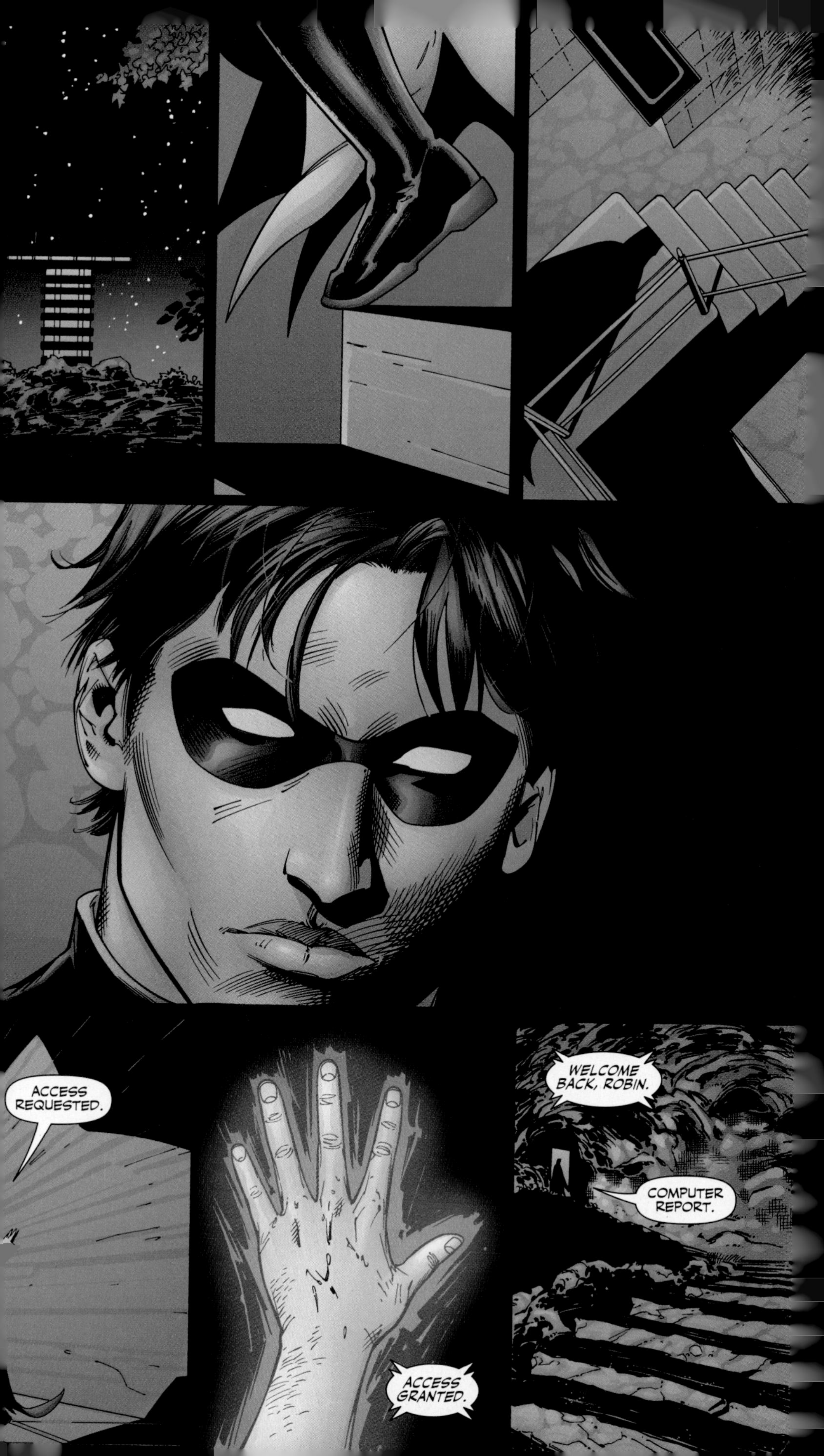
ACCESS REQUESTED.
ACCESS GRANTED.
WELCOME BACK, ROBIN.
COMPUTER REPORT.

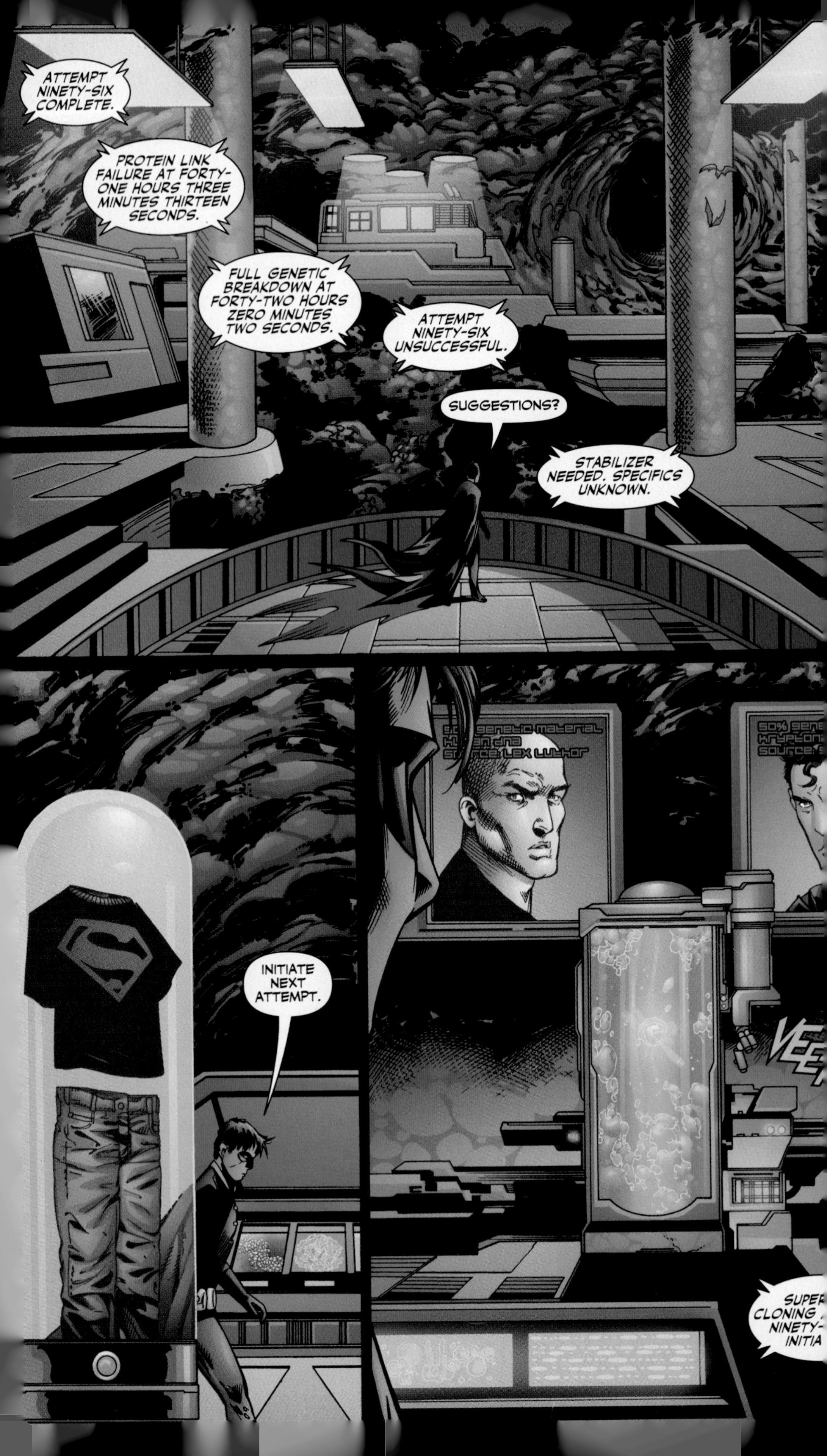
ATTEMPT NINETY-SIX COMPLETE.
PROTEIN LINK FAILURE AT FORTY-ONE HOURS THREE MINUTES THIRTEEN SECONDS.
FULL GENETIC BREAKDOWN AT FORTY-TWO HOURS ZERO MINUTES TWO SECONDS.
ATTEMPT NINETY-SIX UNSUCCESSFUL.
SUGGESTIONS?
STABILIZER NEEDED. SPECIFICS UNKNOWN.
INITIATE NEXT ATTEMPT.
SUPER
CLONING
NINETY-
INITIA

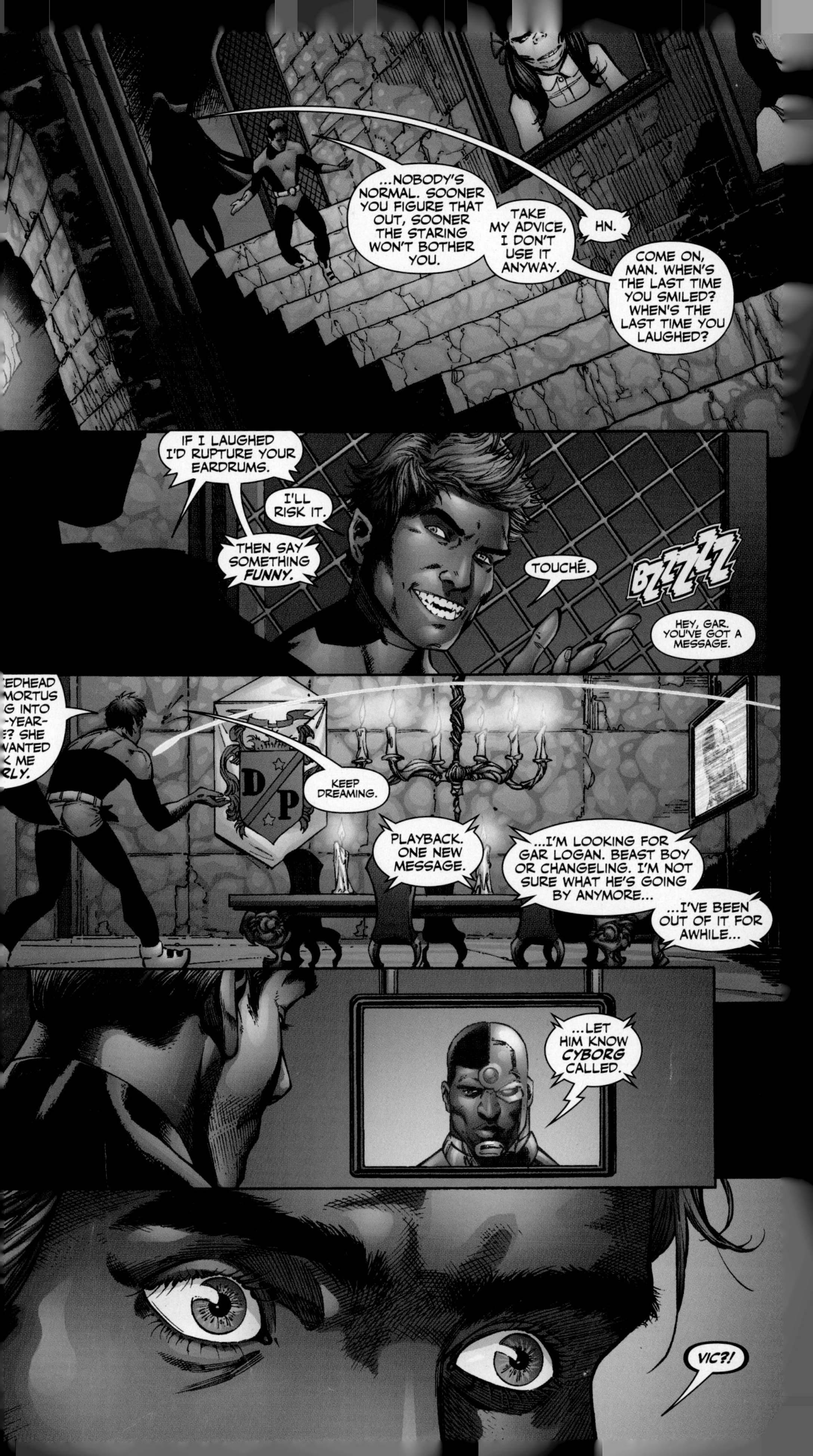
...NOBODY'S NORMAL. SOONER YOU FIGURE THAT OUT, SOONER THE STARING WON'T BOTHER YOU.
TAKE MY ADVICE, I DON'T USE IT ANYWAY.
HN.
COME ON, MAN. WHEN'S THE LAST TIME YOU SMILED? WHEN'S THE LAST TIME YOU LAUGHED?
IF I LAUGHED I'D RUPTURE YOUR EARDRUMS.
I'LL RISK IT.
THEN SAY SOMETHING FUNNY.
TOUCHÉ.
BZZZZZ
HEY, GAR. YOU'VE GOT A MESSAGE.
KEEP DREAMING.
D P
PLAYBACK. ONE NEW MESSAGE.
...I'M LOOKING FOR GAR LOGAN. BEAST BOY OR CHANGELING. I'M NOT SURE WHAT HE'S GOING BY ANYMORE...
...I'VE BEEN OUT OF IT FOR AWHILE...
...LET HIM KNOW CYBORG CALLED.
VIC?!

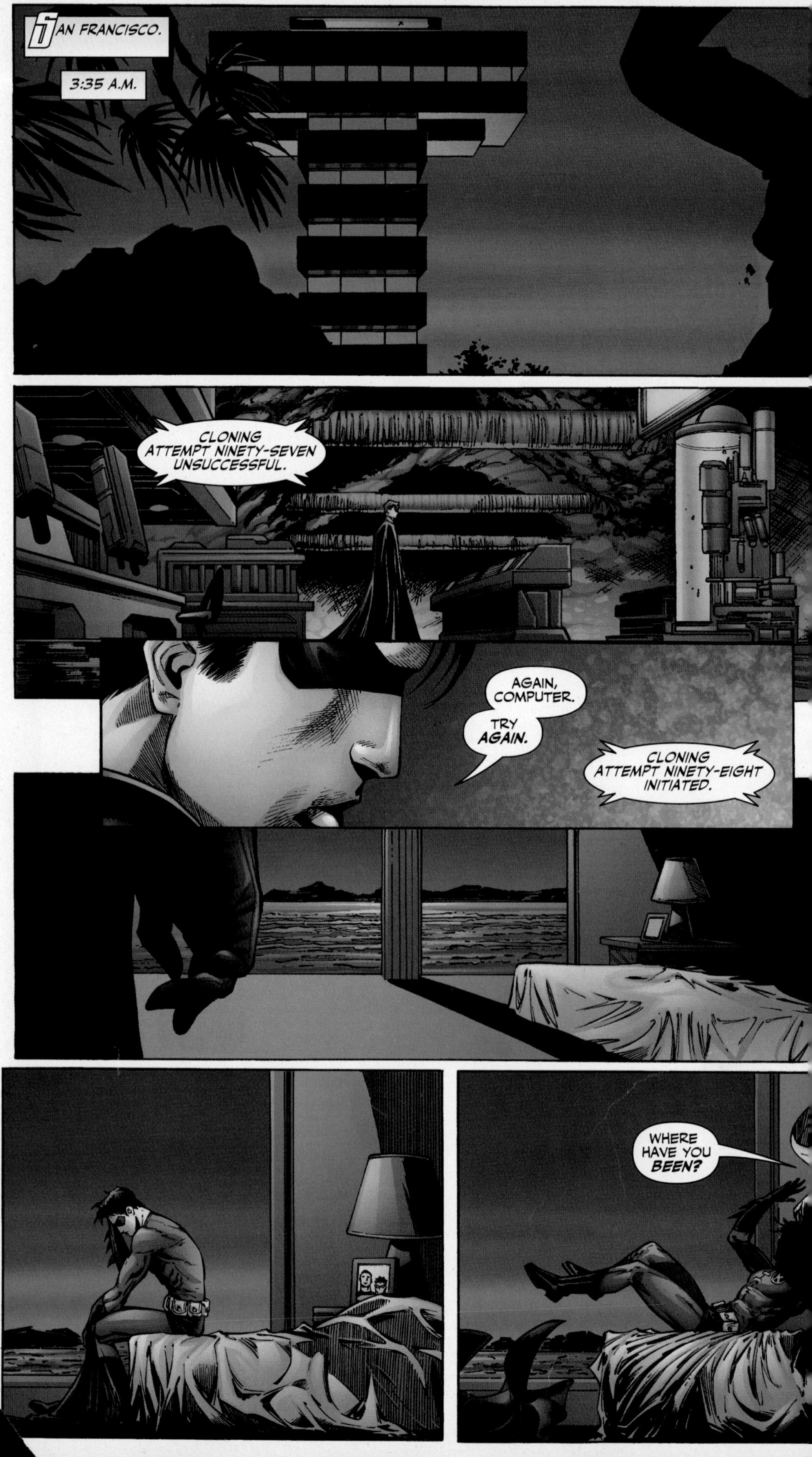
SAN FRANCISCO.
3:35 A.M.
CLONING ATTEMPT NINETY-SEVEN UNSUCCESSFUL.
AGAIN, COMPUTER.
TRY AGAIN.
CLONING ATTEMPT NINETY-EIGHT INITIATED.
WHERE HAVE YOU BEEN?

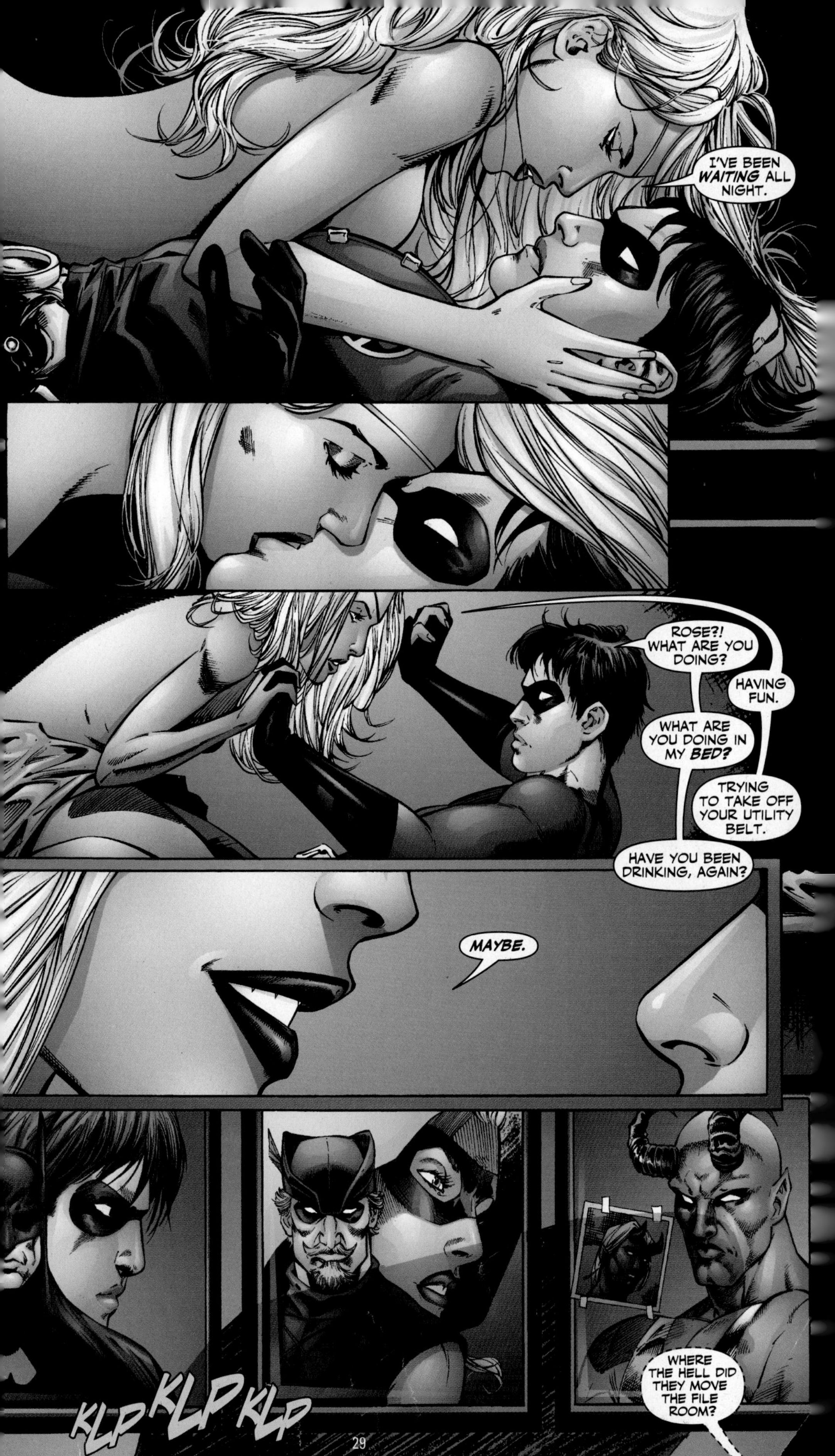
I'VE BEEN WAITING ALL NIGHT.
ROSE?! WHAT ARE YOU DOING?
HAVING FUN.
WHAT ARE YOU DOING IN MY BED?
TRYING TO TAKE OFF YOUR UTILITY BELT.
HAVE YOU BEEN DRINKING, AGAIN?
MAYBE.
KLP KLP KLP
WHERE THE HELL DID THEY MOVE THE FILE ROOM?

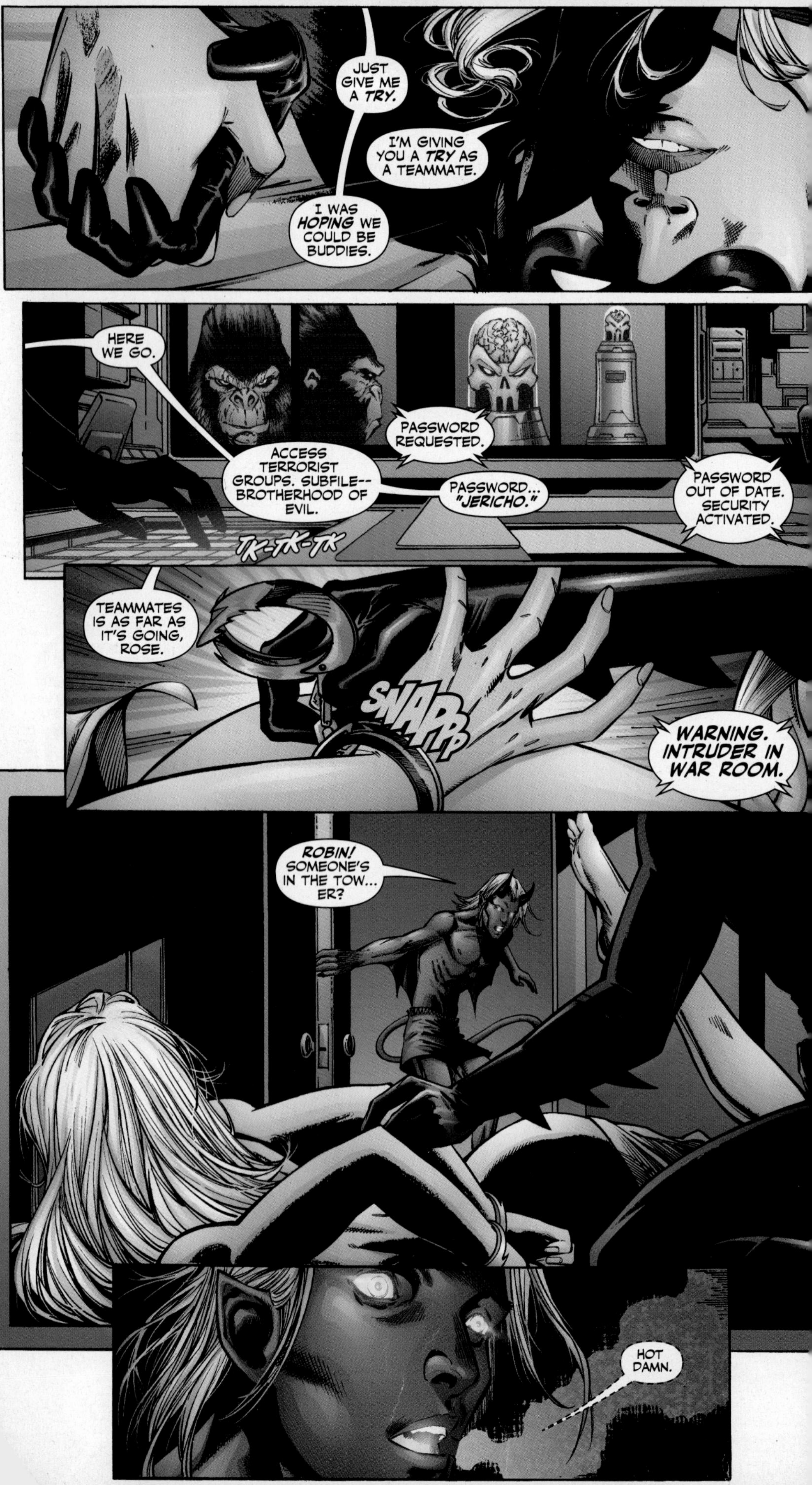
JUST GIVE ME A *TRY.*
I'M GIVING YOU A *TRY* AS A TEAMMATE.
I WAS *HOPING* WE COULD BE BUDDIES.
HERE WE GO.
ACCESS TERRORIST GROUPS. SUBFILE-- BROTHERHOOD OF EVIL.
TK-TK-TK
PASSWORD REQUESTED.
PASSWORD... *"JERICHO."*
PASSWORD OUT OF DATE. SECURITY ACTIVATED.
TEAMMATES IS AS FAR AS IT'S GOING, ROSE.
SNAPPP
WARNING. INTRUDER IN WAR ROOM.
ROBIN! SOMEONE'S IN THE TOW... ER?
HOT DAMN.

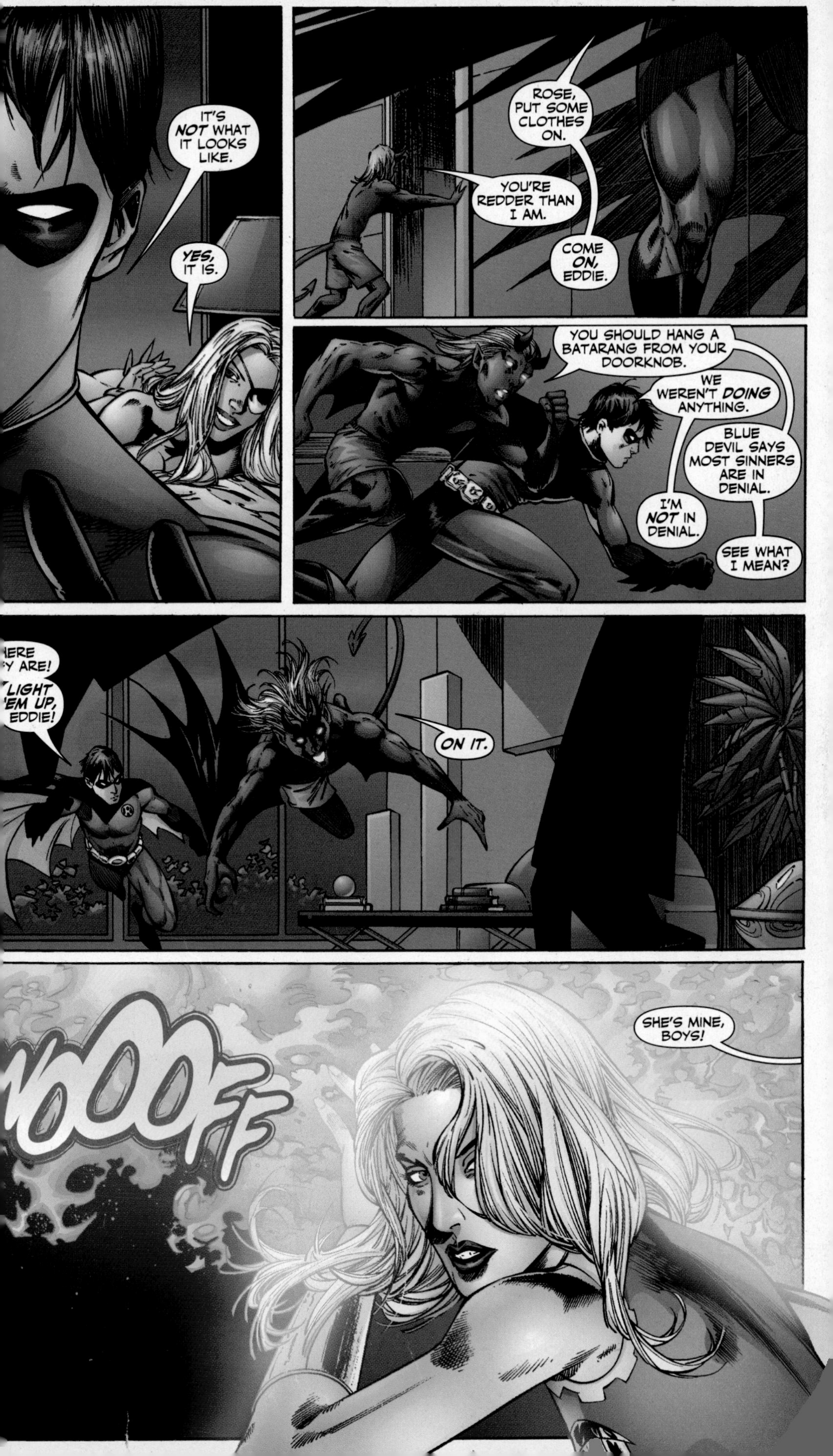
IT'S *NOT* WHAT IT LOOKS LIKE.
YES, IT IS.
ROSE, PUT SOME CLOTHES ON.
YOU'RE REDDER THAN I AM.
COME *ON,* EDDIE.
YOU SHOULD HANG A BATARANG FROM YOUR DOORKNOB.
WE WEREN'T *DOING* ANYTHING.
BLUE DEVIL SAYS MOST SINNERS ARE IN DENIAL.
I'M *NOT* IN DENIAL.
SEE WHAT I MEAN?
HERE
Y ARE!
LIGHT
'EM UP,
EDDIE!
ON IT.
SHE'S MINE, BOYS!

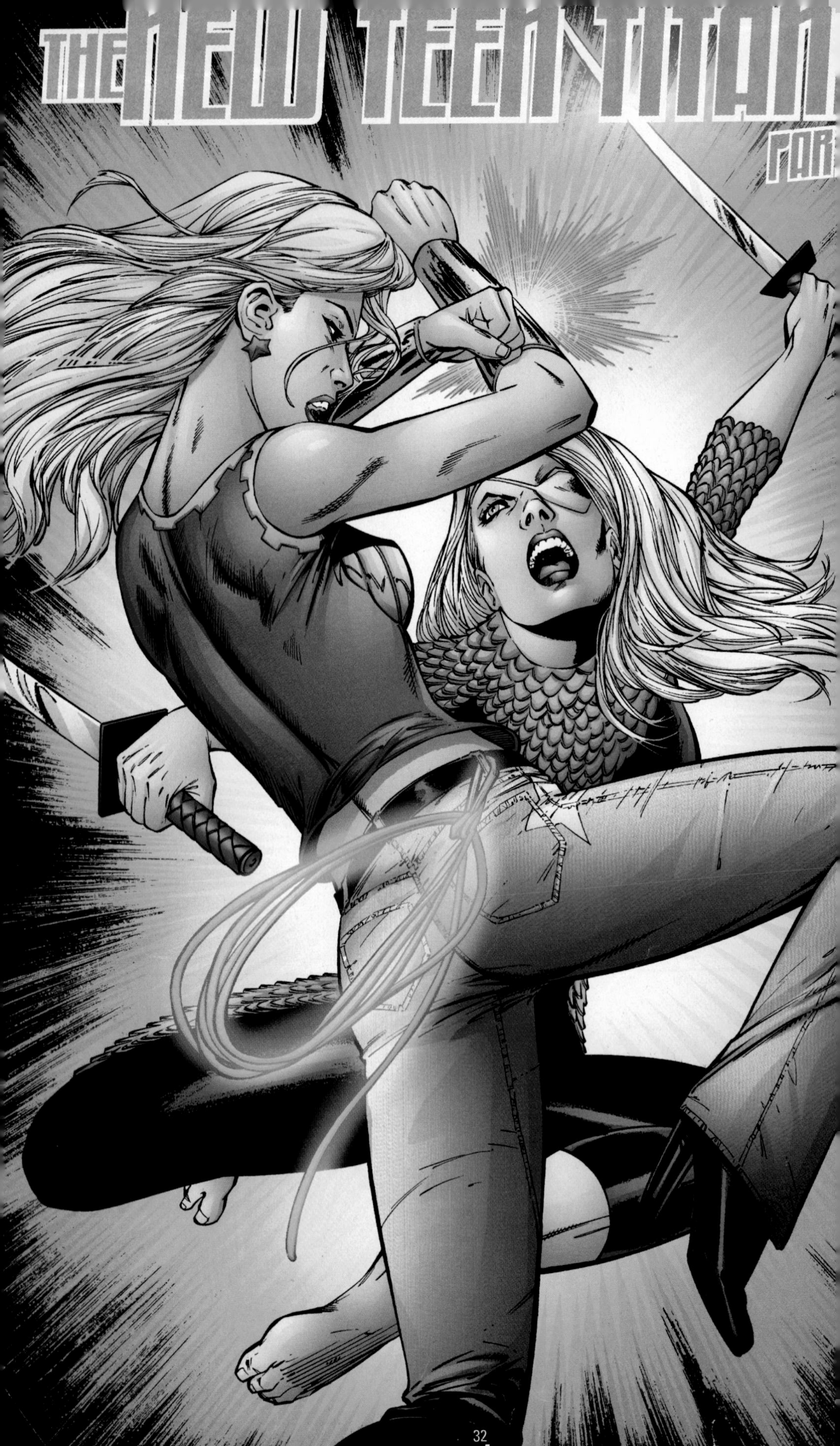
THE NEW TEEN TITAN
PAR

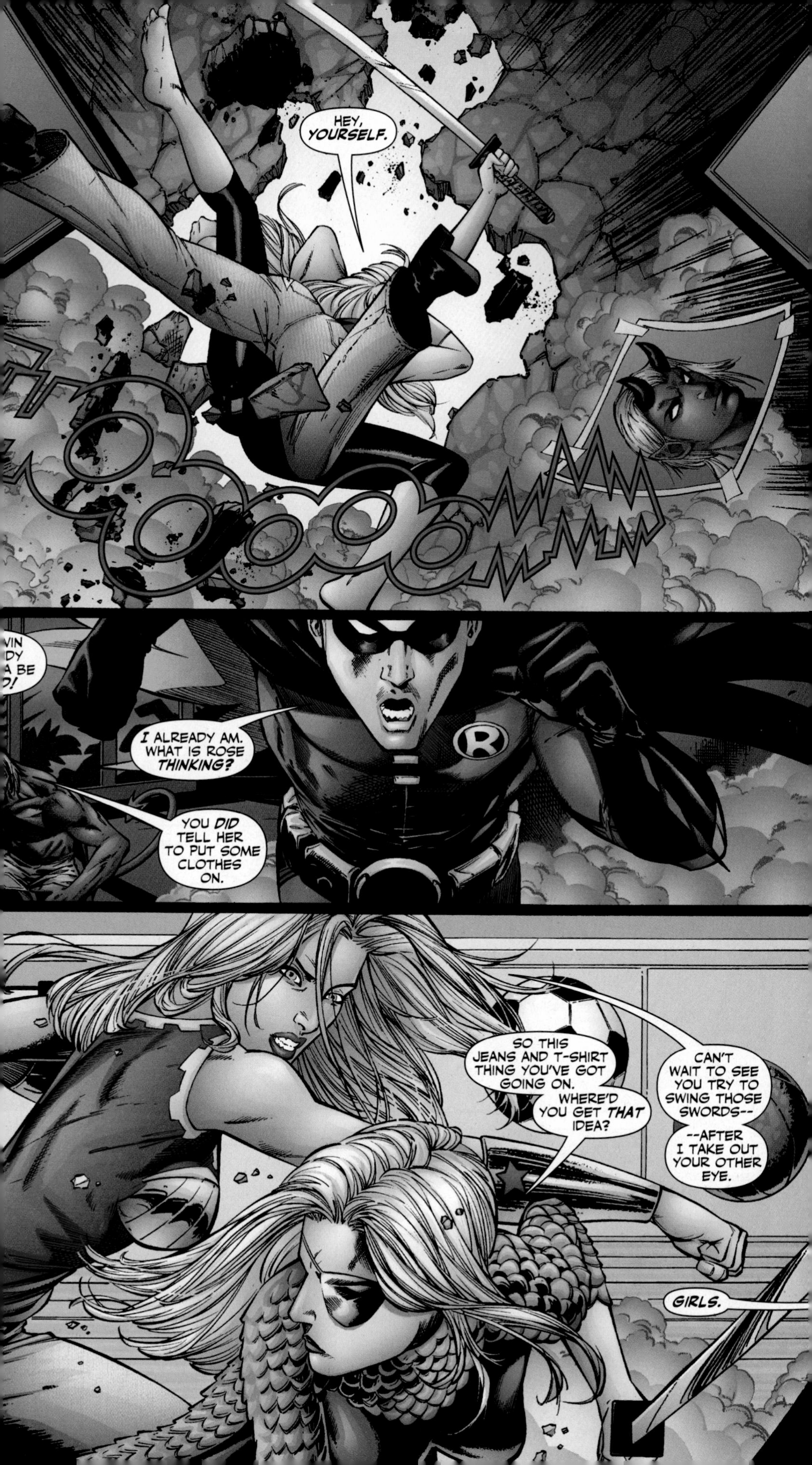
HEY, YOURSELF.
I ALREADY AM. WHAT IS ROSE THINKING?
YOU DID TELL HER TO PUT SOME CLOTHES ON.
SO THIS JEANS AND T-SHIRT THING YOU'VE GOT GOING ON. WHERE'D YOU GET THAT IDEA?
CAN'T WAIT TO SEE YOU TRY TO SWING THOSE SWORDS--
--AFTER I TAKE OUT YOUR OTHER EYE.
GIRLS.

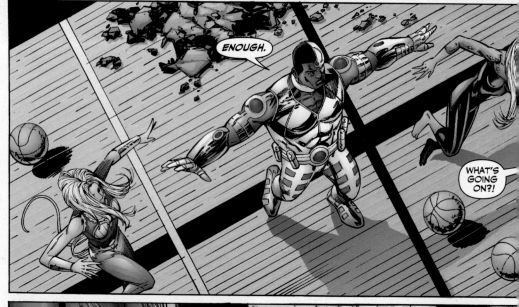

ENOUGH.

WHAT'S GOING ON?!

WONDER GIRL?! SWEET.

WHO MADE THIS HOLE IN THE WALL? WE JUST FIXED THE KITCHEN!

DON'T LOOK AT US.

I'M NO DO YOU HOW TIGHT JEANS A

HONEST MARVIN

EVERYBODY CALM DOWN.

WONDER GIRL'S THE ONE TRESPASSING.

I HAVE MORE RIGHT TO BE HERE THAN YOU.

YOU DON'T WANT TO BE HERE, PRINCESS, REMEMBER?

IT'S TIME WE HAD A TALK, CASSIE.

RAVAGER. KID DEVIL.

GIVE THE TITANS A MINUTE.

THE TITANS? BUT WE'RE--

W

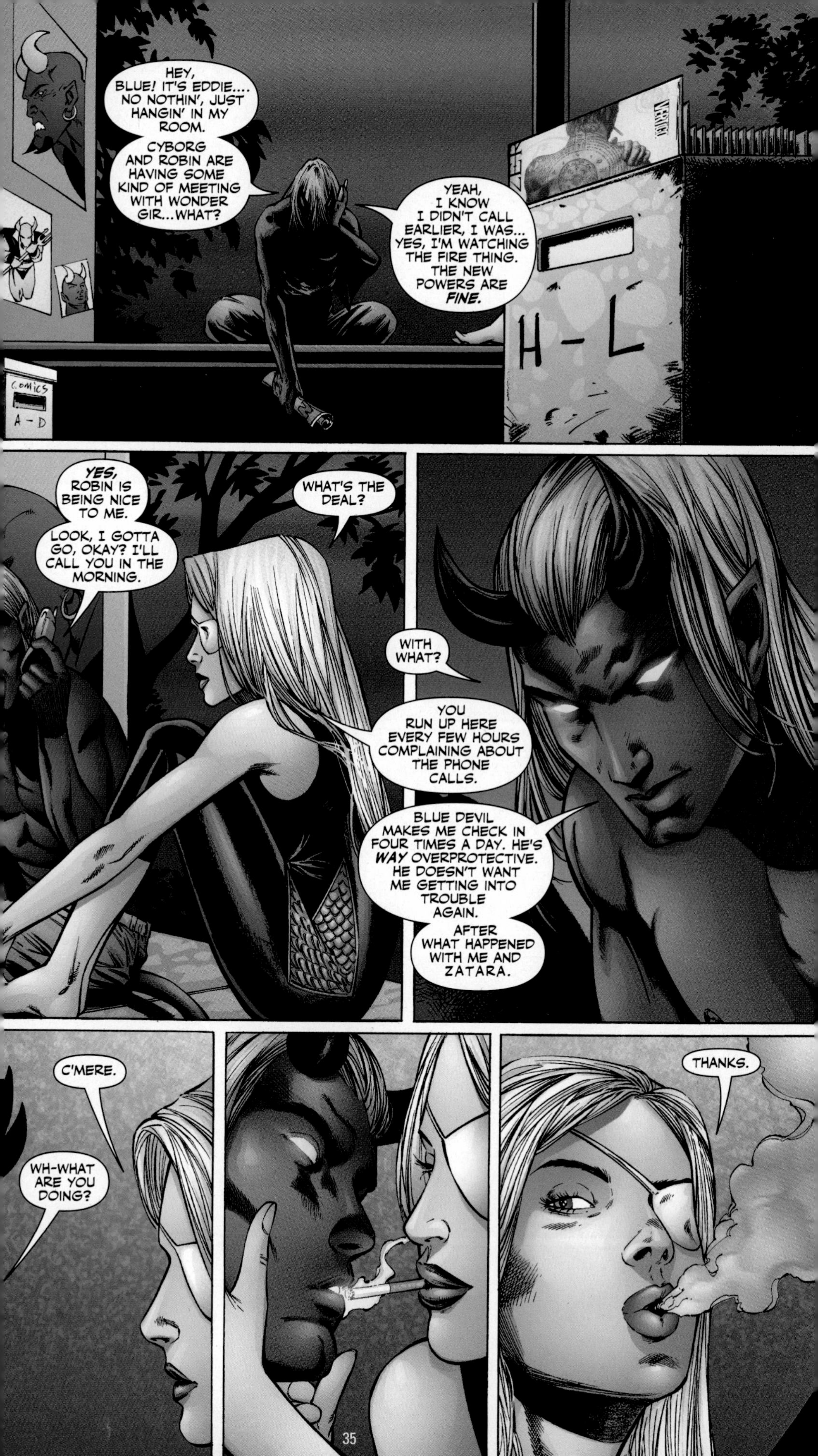
HEY, BLUE! IT'S EDDIE.... NO NOTHIN', JUST HANGIN' IN MY ROOM.
CYBORG AND ROBIN ARE HAVING SOME KIND OF MEETING WITH WONDER GIR...WHAT?
YEAH, I KNOW I DIDN'T CALL EARLIER, I WAS... YES, I'M WATCHING THE FIRE THING. THE NEW POWERS ARE *FINE.*
COMICS
A - D
H - L
YES, ROBIN IS BEING NICE TO ME.
LOOK, I GOTTA GO, OKAY? I'LL CALL YOU IN THE MORNING.
WHAT'S THE DEAL?
WITH WHAT?
YOU RUN UP HERE EVERY FEW HOURS COMPLAINING ABOUT THE PHONE CALLS.
BLUE DEVIL MAKES ME CHECK IN FOUR TIMES A DAY. HE'S *WAY* OVERPROTECTIVE. HE DOESN'T WANT ME GETTING INTO TROUBLE AGAIN.
AFTER WHAT HAPPENED WITH ME AND ZATARA.
C'MERE.
WH-WHAT ARE YOU DOING?
THANKS.

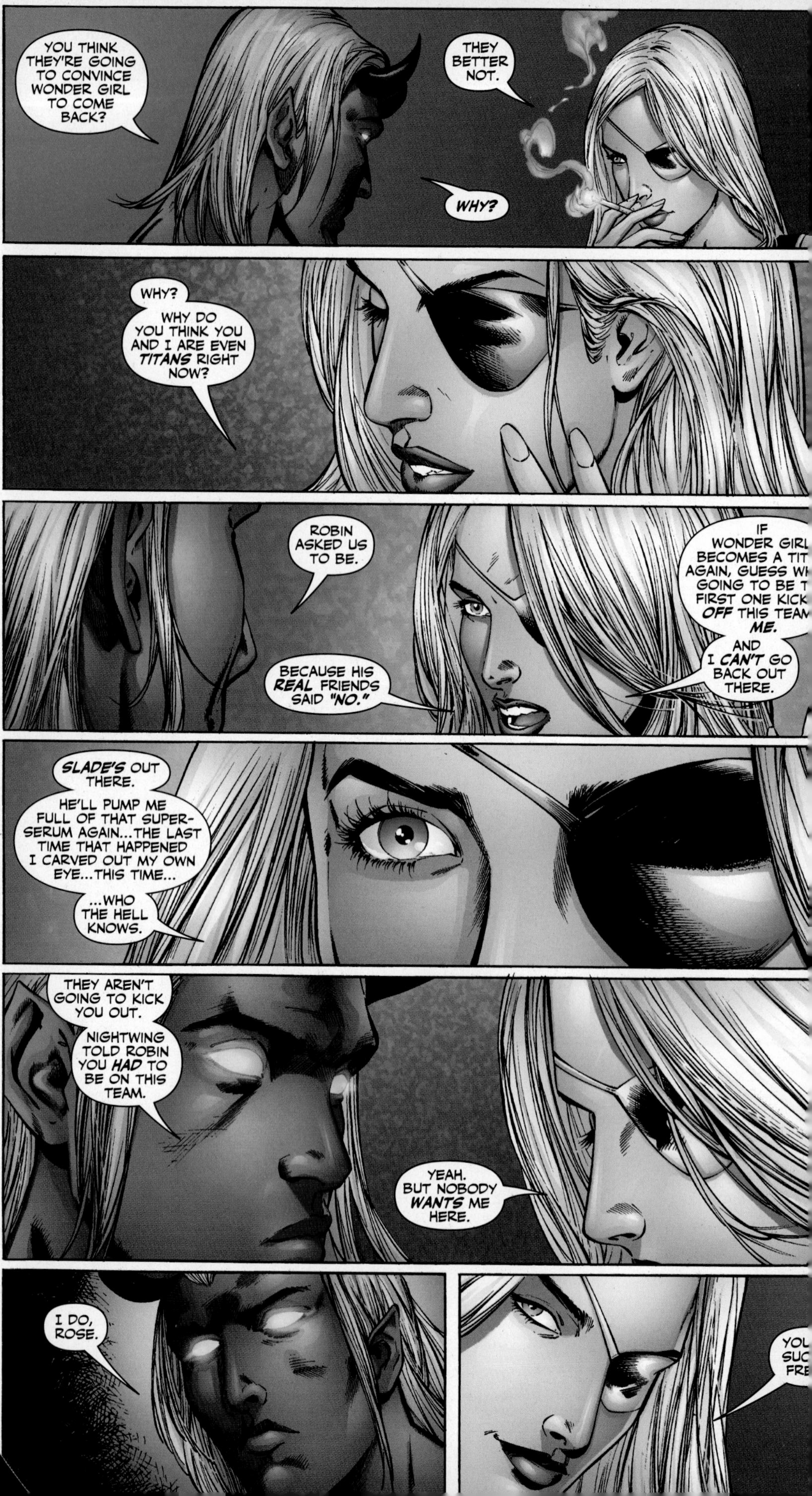

YOU THINK THEY'RE GOING TO CONVINCE WONDER GIRL TO COME BACK?
THEY BETTER NOT.
WHY?
WHY?
WHY DO YOU THINK YOU AND I ARE EVEN TITANS RIGHT NOW?
ROBIN ASKED US TO BE.
BECAUSE HIS REAL FRIENDS SAID "NO."
IF WONDER GIRL BECOMES A TIT AGAIN, GUESS W GOING TO BE T FIRST ONE KICK OFF THIS TEAM ME.
AND I CAN'T GO BACK OUT THERE.
SLADE'S OUT THERE.
HE'LL PUMP ME FULL OF THAT SUPER-SERUM AGAIN...THE LAST TIME THAT HAPPENED I CARVED OUT MY OWN EYE...THIS TIME...
...WHO THE HELL KNOWS.
THEY AREN'T GOING TO KICK YOU OUT.
NIGHTWING TOLD ROBIN YOU HAD TO BE ON THIS TEAM.
YEAH. BUT NOBODY WANTS ME HERE.
I DO, ROSE.

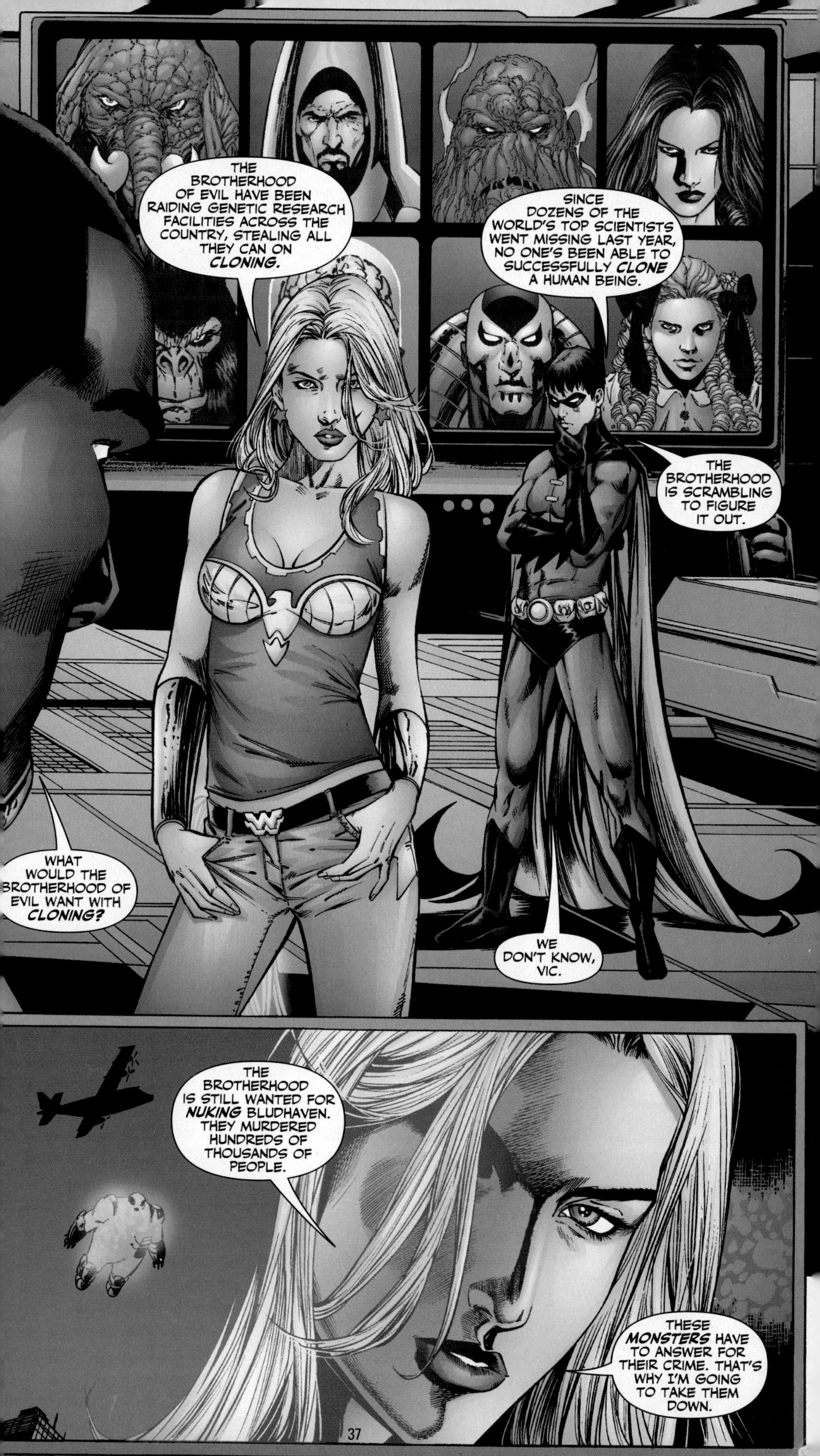
THE BROTHERHOOD OF EVIL HAVE BEEN RAIDING GENETIC RESEARCH FACILITIES ACROSS THE COUNTRY, STEALING ALL THEY CAN ON CLONING.
SINCE DOZENS OF THE WORLD'S TOP SCIENTISTS WENT MISSING LAST YEAR, NO ONE'S BEEN ABLE TO SUCCESSFULLY CLONE A HUMAN BEING.
THE BROTHERHOOD IS SCRAMBLING TO FIGURE IT OUT.
WHAT WOULD THE BROTHERHOOD OF EVIL WANT WITH CLONING?
WE DON'T KNOW, VIC.
THE BROTHERHOOD IS STILL WANTED FOR NUKING BLUDHAVEN. THEY MURDERED HUNDREDS OF THOUSANDS OF PEOPLE.
THESE MONSTERS HAVE TO ANSWER FOR THEIR CRIME. THAT'S WHY I'M GOING TO TAKE THEM DOWN.

WHY'D YOU COME HERE IF YOU DIDN'T WANT OUR HELP?

I WANTED TO SEE IF YOU HAD ANY NEW INFORMATION ON WHERE THEY MIGHT BE HIDING OUT.

WHY DIDN'T YOU JUST *ASK*?

WHEN DID YOU SUDDENLY GET SO INTERESTED IN *STOPPING* THEM?

YOU DON'T THINK I CAN HANDLE THIS MYSELF.

I NEVER SAID YOU COULDN'T HANDLE THIS YOURSELF.

YOU DIDN'T HAVE TO *SAY* IT.

I SEE HOW YOU LOOK AT ME, TIM.

I TRIED *SO* HARD.

I TRIED SO HARD TO SAVE HIM.

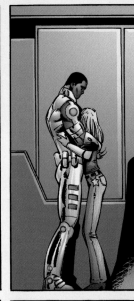

I KNOW YOU DID.

THE TITANS HAVEN'T BEEN HERE FOR YOU LATELY, BUT WE ARE *NOW*.

TAKE DOWN THE BROTHERHOOD WITH US. AFTERWARDS, YOU CAN DECIDE IF YOU WANT TO COME BACK TO THIS TEAM. AND IF YOU DO--

--YOU'LL HELP US BRING THE REST OF THEM BACK. GAR. RAVEN. BART. MIA.

THE *REAL* TITANS.

VEET VEET

META-HUMAN POLICE REPORTS ARE COMING IN.

THE BROTHER IN NEW YOR ABANDONED CLO THAT BELONGE WILDEBEEST

YOU GUYS STILL HAVE THAT *JET*?

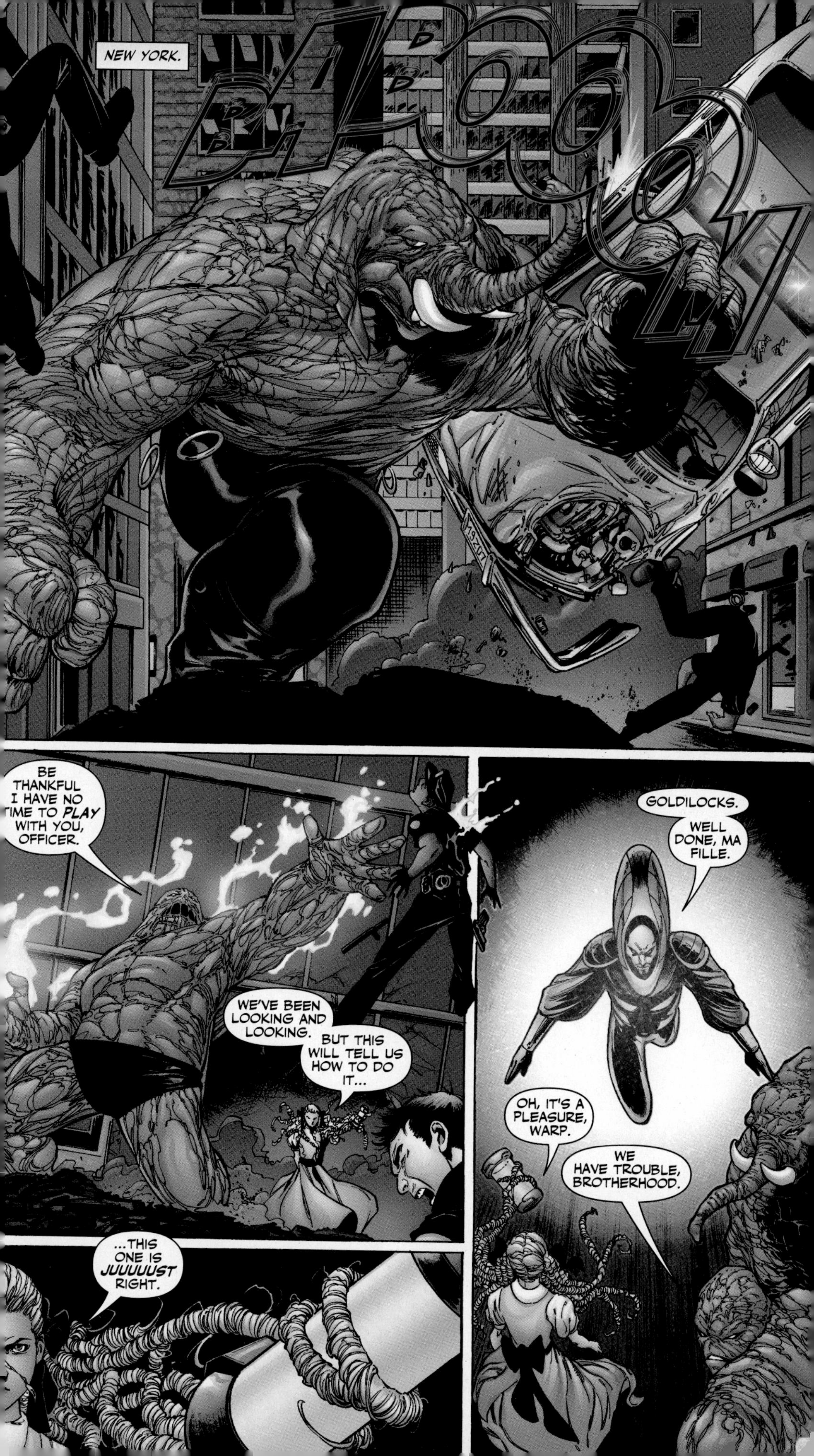
NEW YORK.
BE THANKFUL I HAVE NO TIME TO PLAY WITH YOU, OFFICER.
WE'VE BEEN LOOKING AND LOOKING.
BUT THIS WILL TELL US HOW TO DO IT...
...THIS ONE IS JUUUUUST RIGHT.
GOLDILOCKS.
WELL DONE, MA FILLE.
OH, IT'S A PLEASURE, WARP.
WE HAVE TROUBLE, BROTHERHOOD.

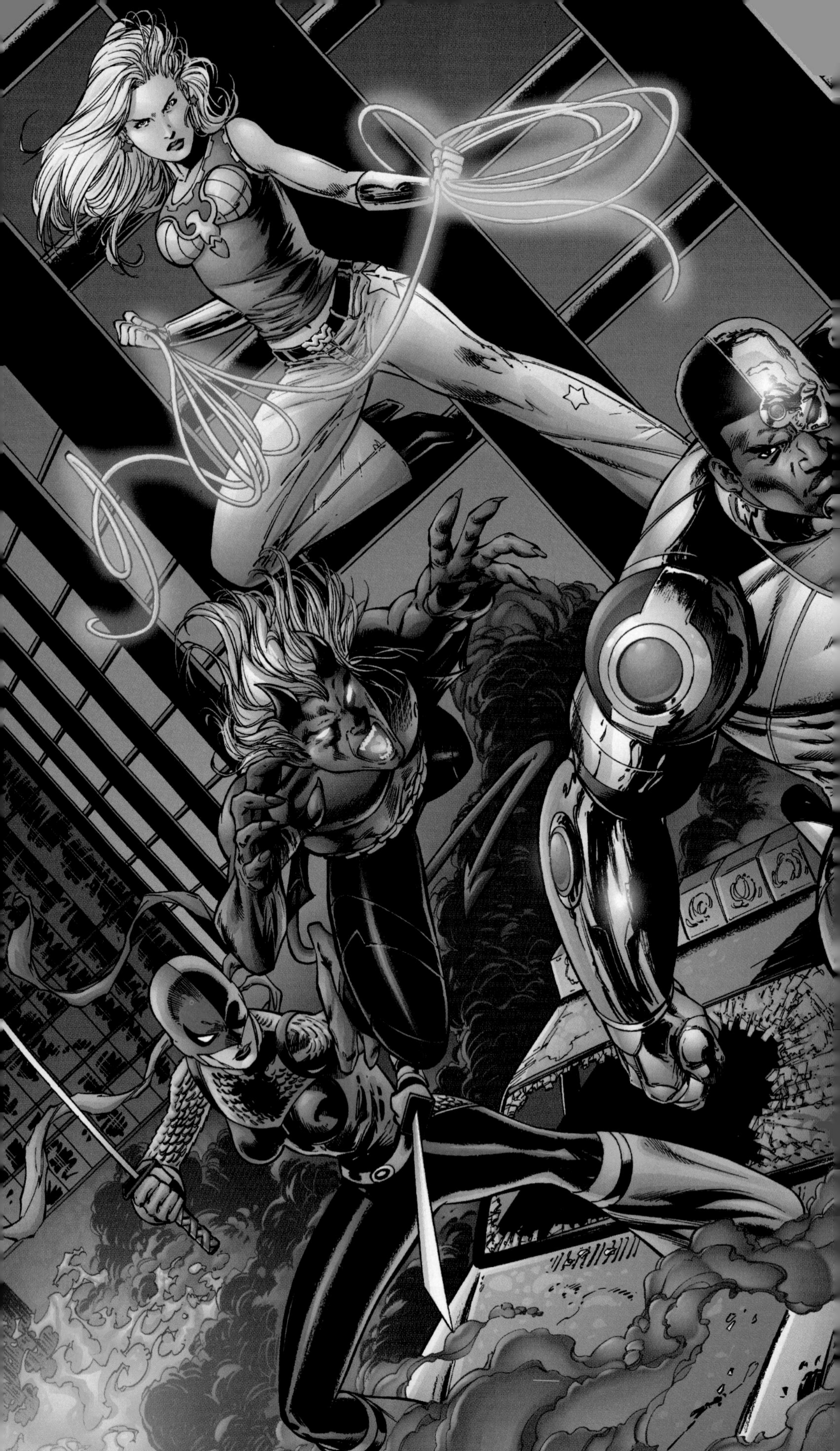

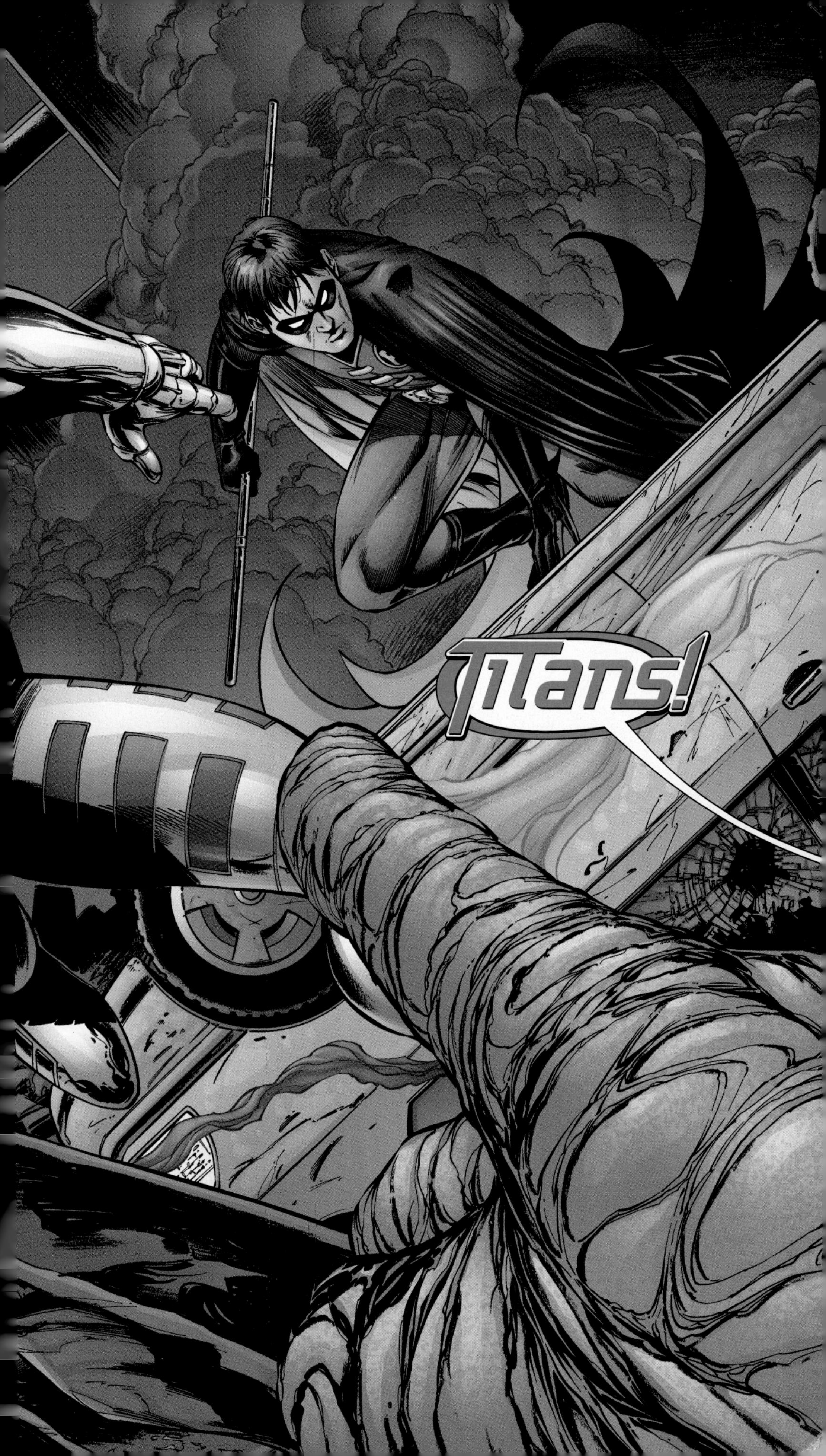
TITANS!

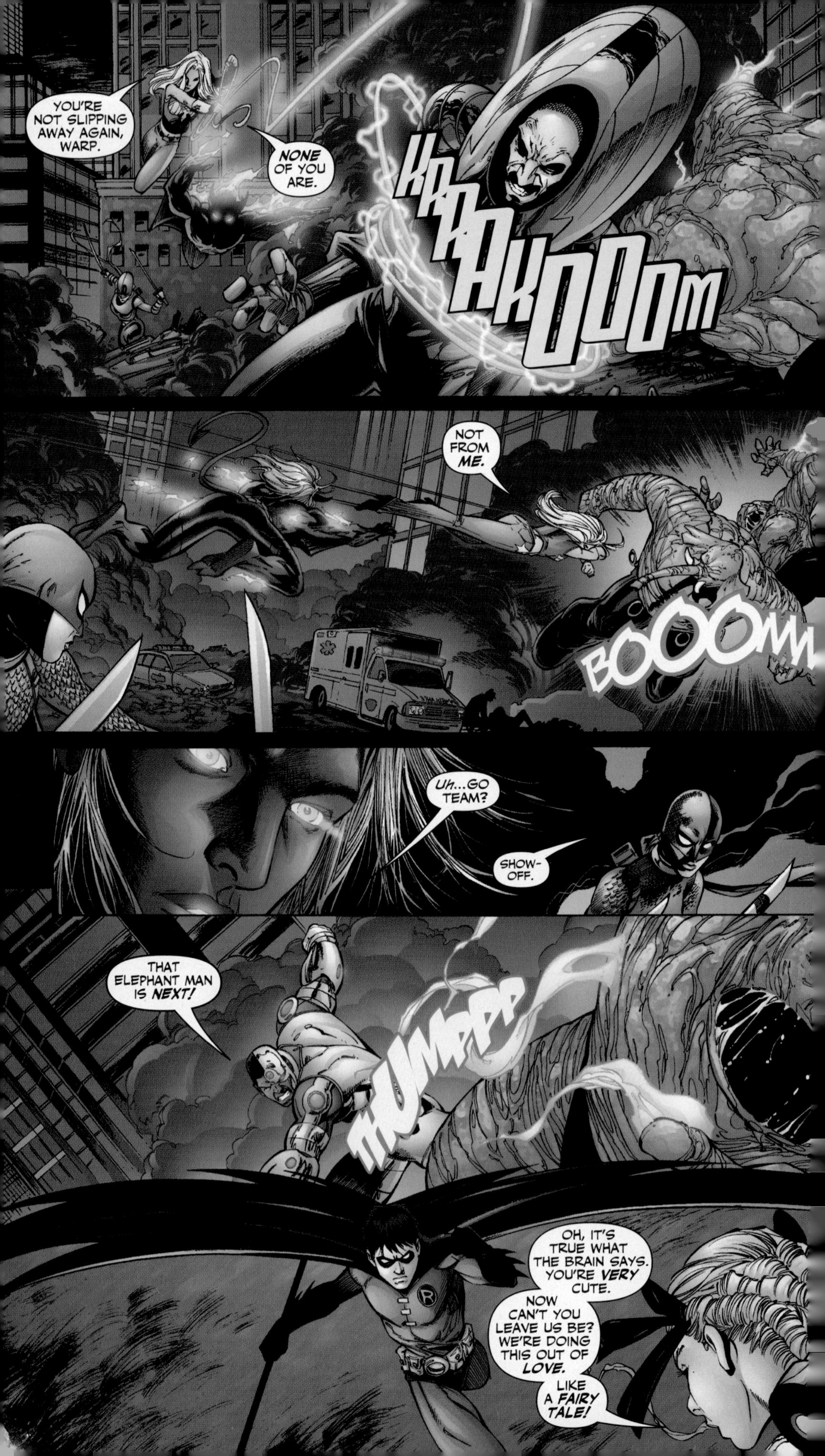
YOU'RE NOT SLIPPING AWAY AGAIN, WARP.
NONE OF YOU ARE.
KRRRAKOOOM
NOT FROM ME.
BOOOM
Uh...GO TEAM?
SHOW-OFF.
THAT ELEPHANT MAN IS NEXT!
THUMPP
OH, IT'S TRUE WHAT THE BRAIN SAYS. YOU'RE VERY CUTE.
NOW CAN'T YOU LEAVE US BE? WE'RE DOING THIS OUT OF LOVE.
LIKE A FAIRY TALE!

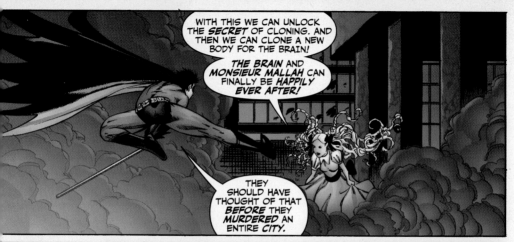

WITH THIS WE CAN UNLOCK THE *SECRET* OF CLONING. AND THEN WE CAN CLONE A NEW BODY FOR THE BRAIN!

THE BRAIN AND MONSIEUR MALLAH CAN FINALLY BE *HAPPILY EVER AFTER!*

THEY SHOULD HAVE THOUGHT OF THAT *BEFORE* THEY *MURDERED* AN ENTIRE *CITY.*

Mmff.

SO *VERY* CUTE.

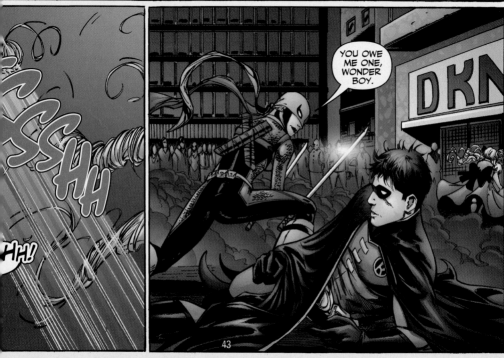

SSSHH

HH!

YOU OWE ME ONE, WONDER BOY.

DKN

43

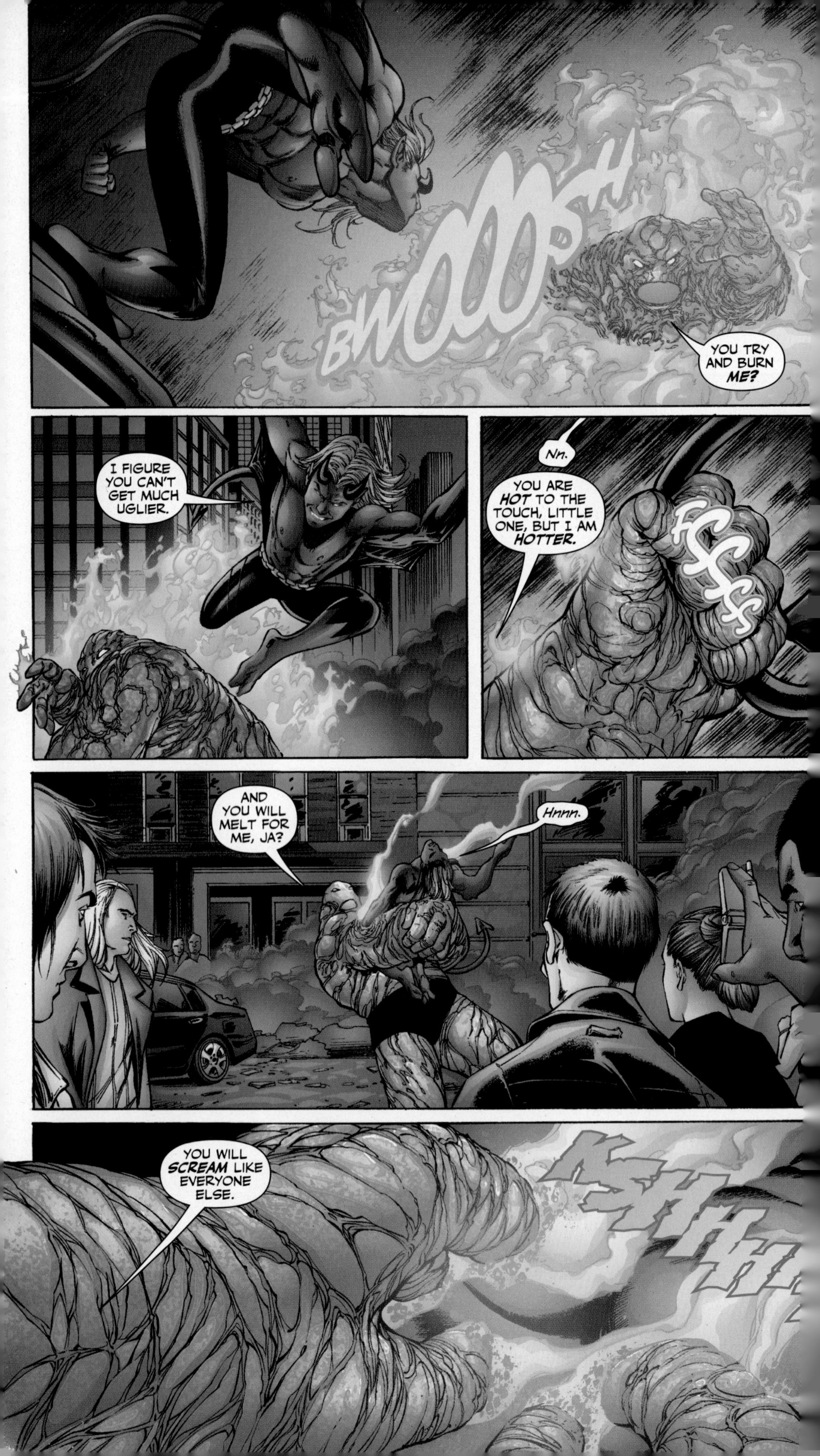
BWOOSH
YOU TRY AND BURN ME?
I FIGURE YOU CAN'T GET MUCH UGLIER.
Nn.
YOU ARE HOT TO THE TOUCH, LITTLE ONE, BUT I AM HOTTER.
FSSSS
AND YOU WILL MELT FOR ME, JA?
Hnnn.
YOU WILL SCREAM LIKE EVERYONE ELSE.

ARRGHHH!!

KRE-AK-TCH

HAHAHA. NOW WHO IS THE UGLY ONE?

LET HIM GO!

VHMM

RRR.

PLASMUS!

WE HAVE WHAT WE NEED.

THE BRAIN'S DREAM WILL SOON BE REALIZED. LONG LIVE THE BROTHERHOOD.

LONG LIVE THE BROTHERHOOD.

FW OOOoo

GGG.

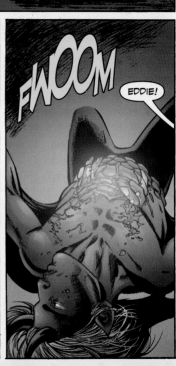

FWOOM

EDDIE!

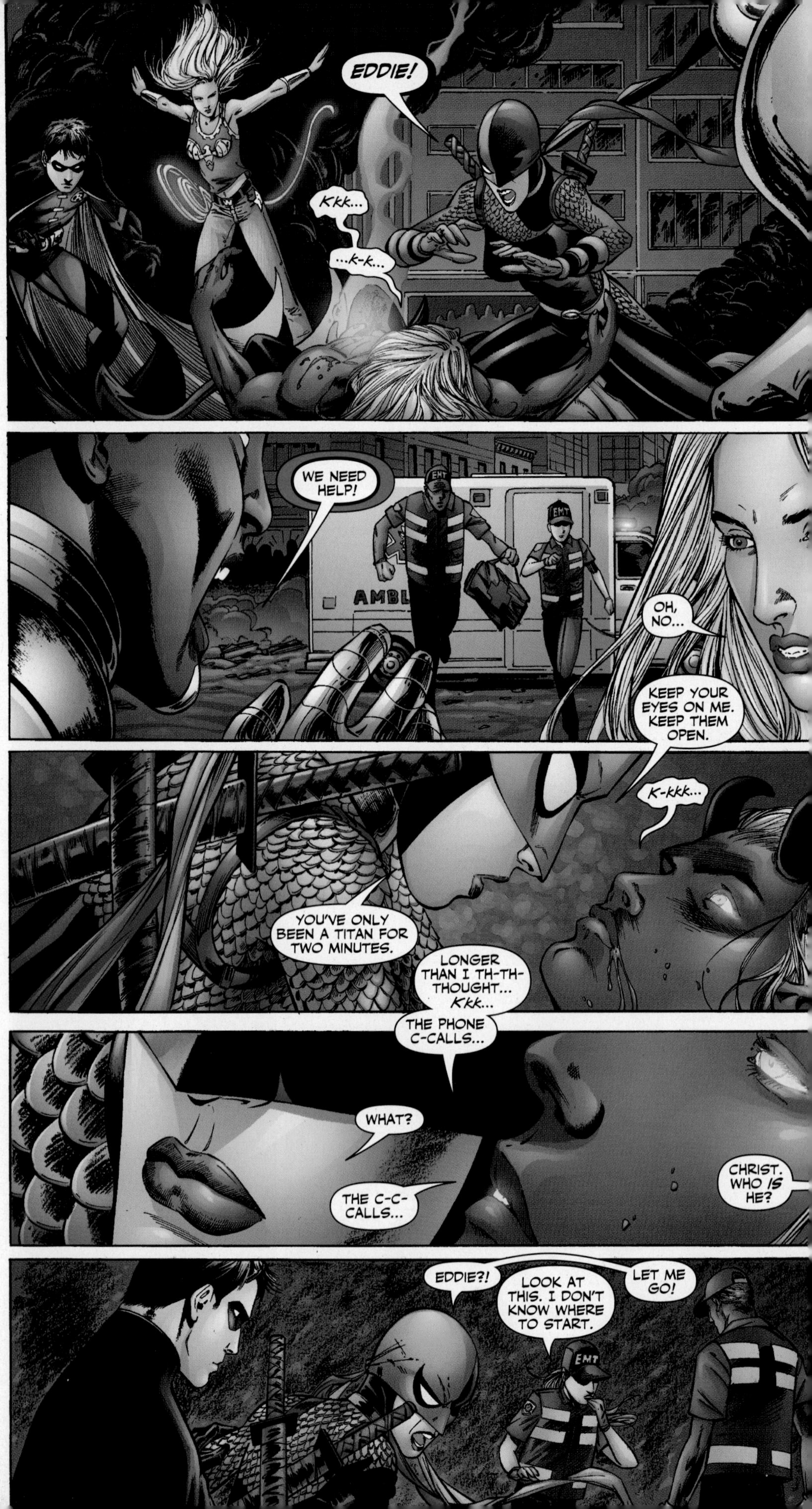
EDDIE!
Kkk...
...k-k...
WE NEED HELP!
OH, NO...
KEEP YOUR EYES ON ME. KEEP THEM OPEN.
K-kkk...
YOU'VE ONLY BEEN A TITAN FOR TWO MINUTES.
LONGER THAN I TH-TH-THOUGHT... Kkk...
THE PHONE C-CALLS...
WHAT?
THE C-C-CALLS...
CHRIST. WHO IS HE?
EDDIE?!
LOOK AT THIS. I DON'T KNOW WHERE TO START.
LET ME GO!

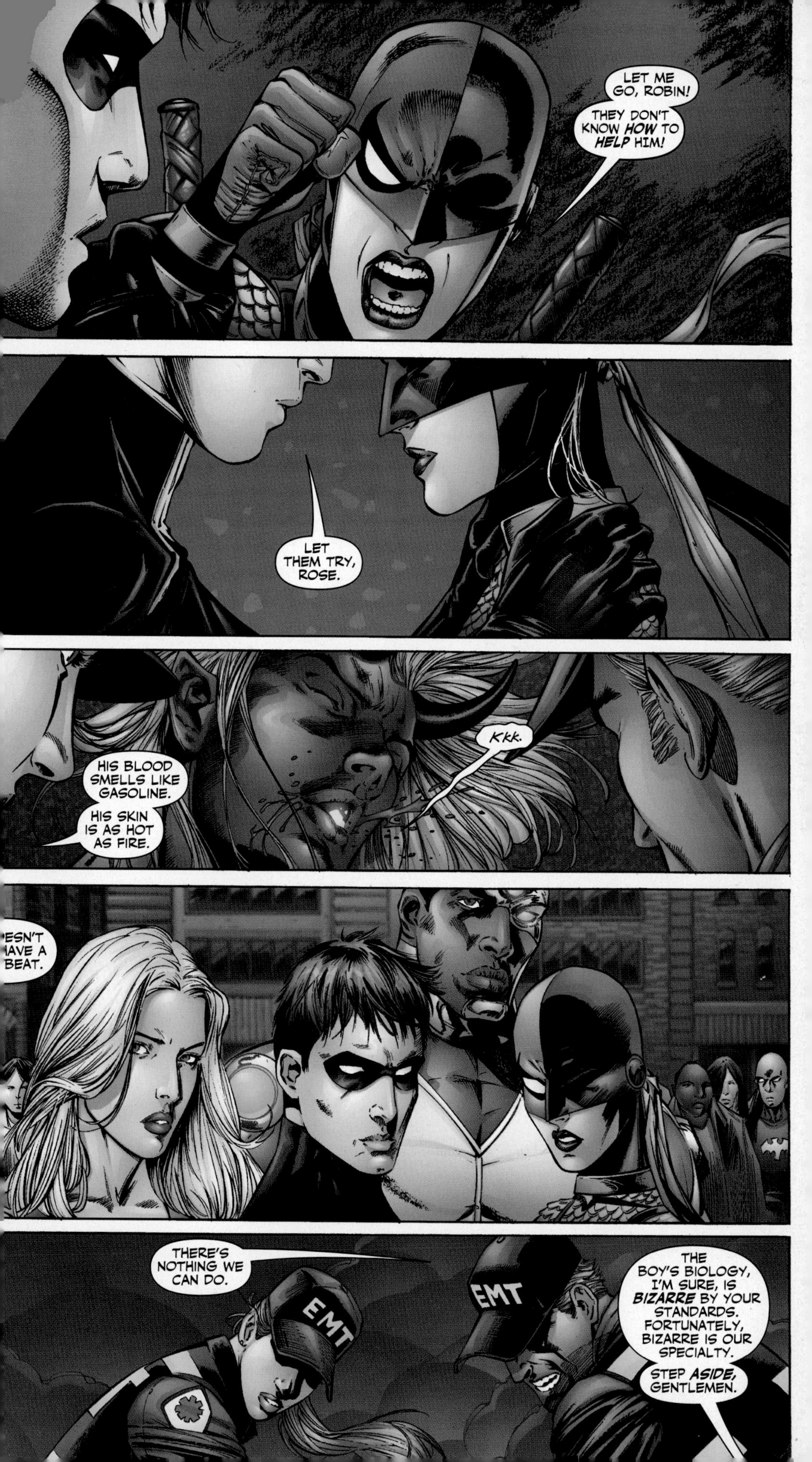
LET ME GO, ROBIN!
THEY DON'T KNOW HOW TO HELP HIM!
LET THEM TRY, ROSE.
HIS BLOOD SMELLS LIKE GASOLINE.
HIS SKIN IS AS HOT AS FIRE.
Kkk.
ESN'T IAVE A BEAT.
THERE'S NOTHING WE CAN DO.
THE BOY'S BIOLOGY, I'M SURE, IS BIZARRE BY YOUR STANDARDS. FORTUNATELY, BIZARRE IS OUR SPECIALTY.
STEP ASIDE, GENTLEMEN.
EMT
EMT

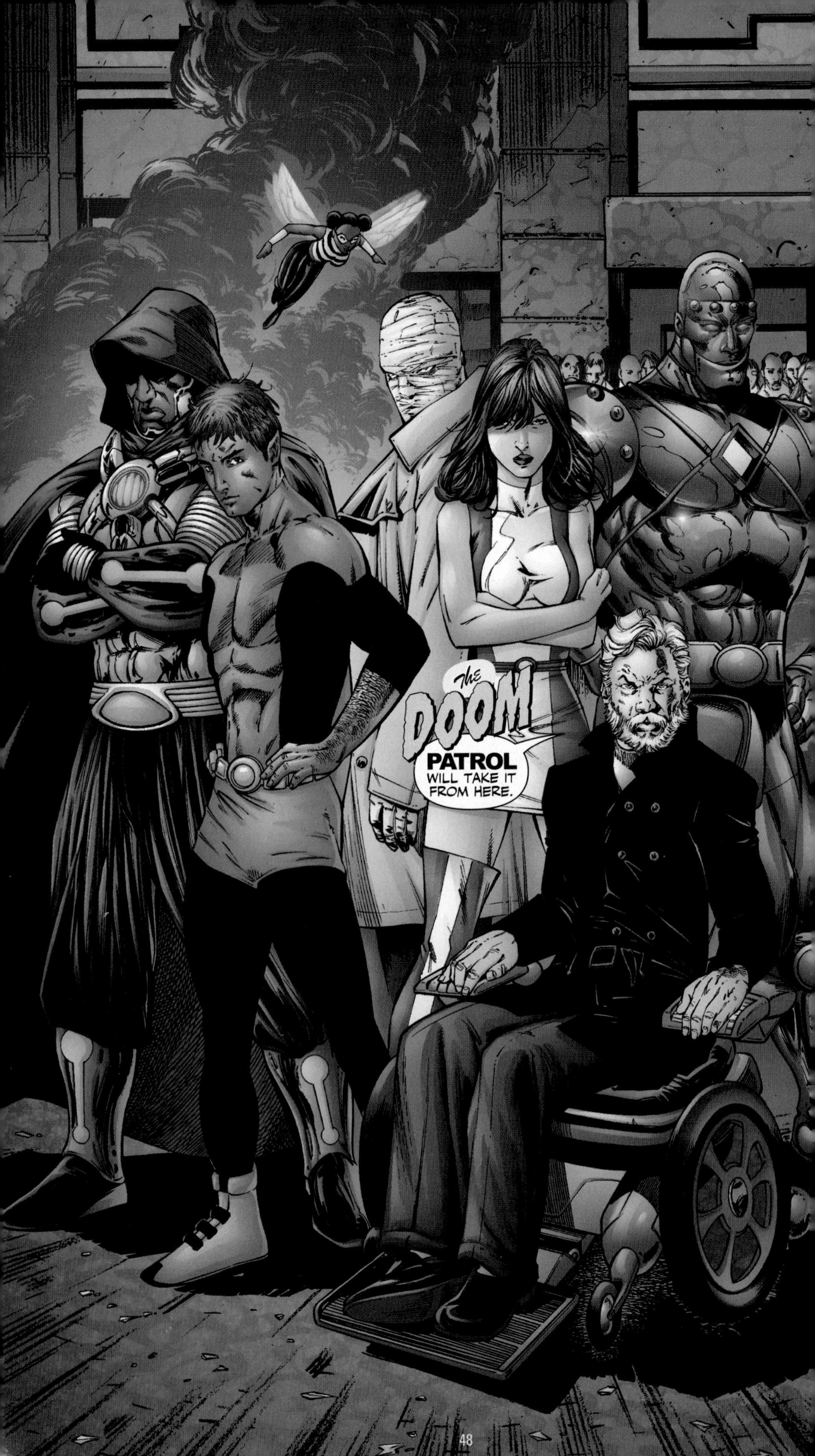
THE DOOM PATROL WILL TAKE IT FROM HERE.

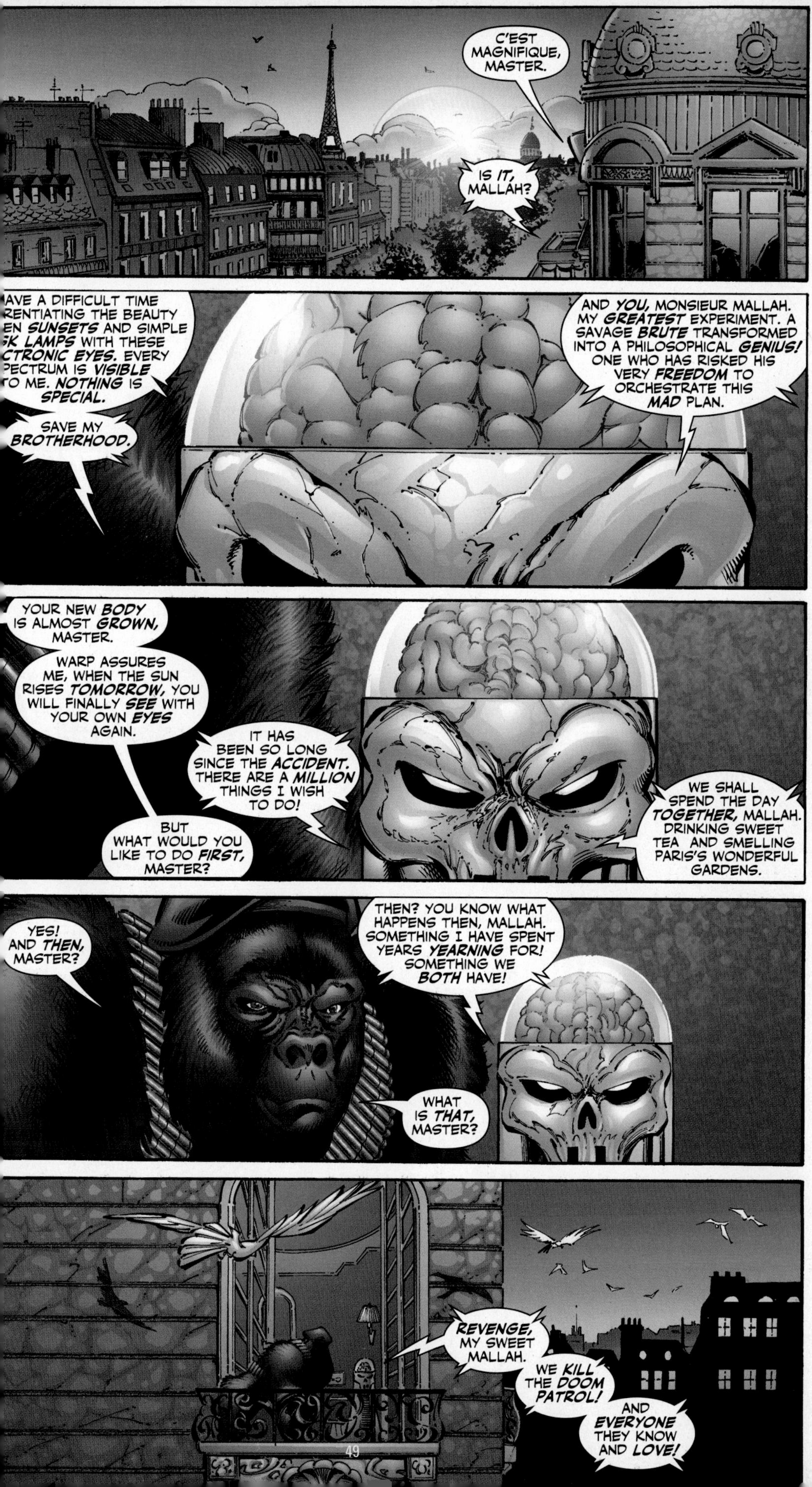
C'EST MAGNIFIQUE, MASTER.
IS IT, MALLAH?
AVE A DIFFICULT TIME RENTIATING THE BEAUTY EN SUNSETS AND SIMPLE SK LAMPS WITH THESE CTRONIC EYES. EVERY PECTRUM IS VISIBLE TO ME. NOTHING IS SPECIAL.
SAVE MY BROTHERHOOD.
AND YOU, MONSIEUR MALLAH. MY GREATEST EXPERIMENT. A SAVAGE BRUTE TRANSFORMED INTO A PHILOSOPHICAL GENIUS! ONE WHO HAS RISKED HIS VERY FREEDOM TO ORCHESTRATE THIS MAD PLAN.
YOUR NEW BODY IS ALMOST GROWN, MASTER.
WARP ASSURES ME, WHEN THE SUN RISES TOMORROW, YOU WILL FINALLY SEE WITH YOUR OWN EYES AGAIN.
IT HAS BEEN SO LONG SINCE THE ACCIDENT. THERE ARE A MILLION THINGS I WISH TO DO!
BUT WHAT WOULD YOU LIKE TO DO FIRST, MASTER?
WE SHALL SPEND THE DAY TOGETHER, MALLAH. DRINKING SWEET TEA AND SMELLING PARIS'S WONDERFUL GARDENS.
YES! AND THEN, MASTER?
THEN? YOU KNOW WHAT HAPPENS THEN, MALLAH. SOMETHING I HAVE SPENT YEARS YEARNING FOR! SOMETHING WE BOTH HAVE!
WHAT IS THAT, MASTER?
REVENGE, MY SWEET MALLAH.
WE KILL THE DOOM PATROL!
AND EVERYONE THEY KNOW AND LOVE!

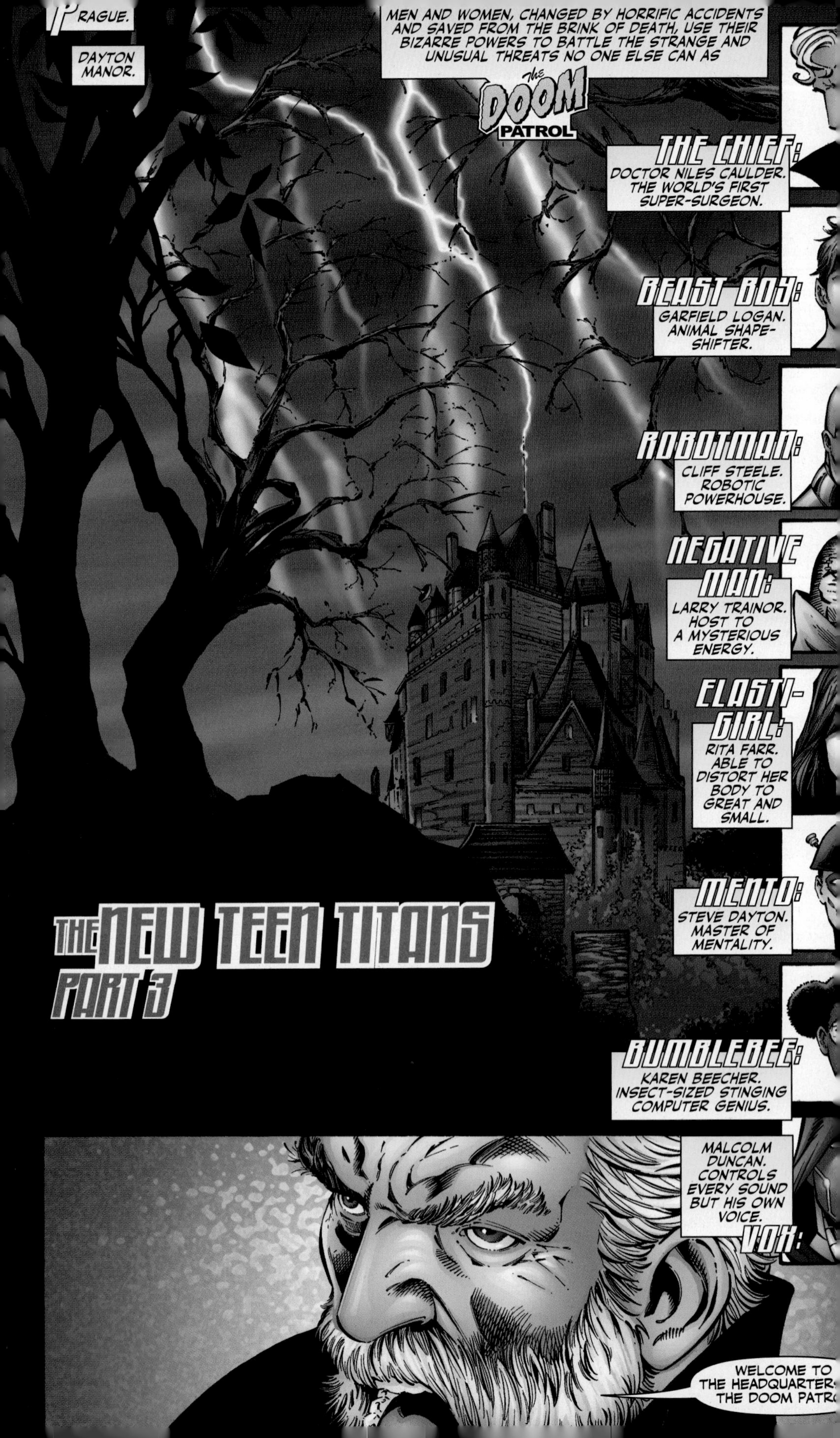
PRAGUE.
DAYTON MANOR.
MEN AND WOMEN, CHANGED BY HORRIFIC ACCIDENTS AND SAVED FROM THE BRINK OF DEATH, USE THEIR BIZARRE POWERS TO BATTLE THE STRANGE AND UNUSUAL THREATS NO ONE ELSE CAN AS
THE DOOM PATROL
THE CHIEF: DOCTOR NILES CAULDER. THE WORLD'S FIRST SUPER-SURGEON.
BEAST BOY: GARFIELD LOGAN. ANIMAL SHAPE-SHIFTER.
ROBOTMAN: CLIFF STEELE. ROBOTIC POWERHOUSE.
NEGATIVE MAN: LARRY TRAINOR. HOST TO A MYSTERIOUS ENERGY.
ELASTI-GIRL: RITA FARR. ABLE TO DISTORT HER BODY TO GREAT AND SMALL.
MENTO: STEVE DAYTON. MASTER OF MENTALITY.
THE NEW TEEN TITANS PART 3
BUMBLEBEE: KAREN BEECHER. INSECT-SIZED STINGING COMPUTER GENIUS.
VOX: MALCOLM DUNCAN. CONTROLS EVERY SOUND BUT HIS OWN VOICE.
WELCOME TO THE HEADQUARTERS THE DOOM PATR

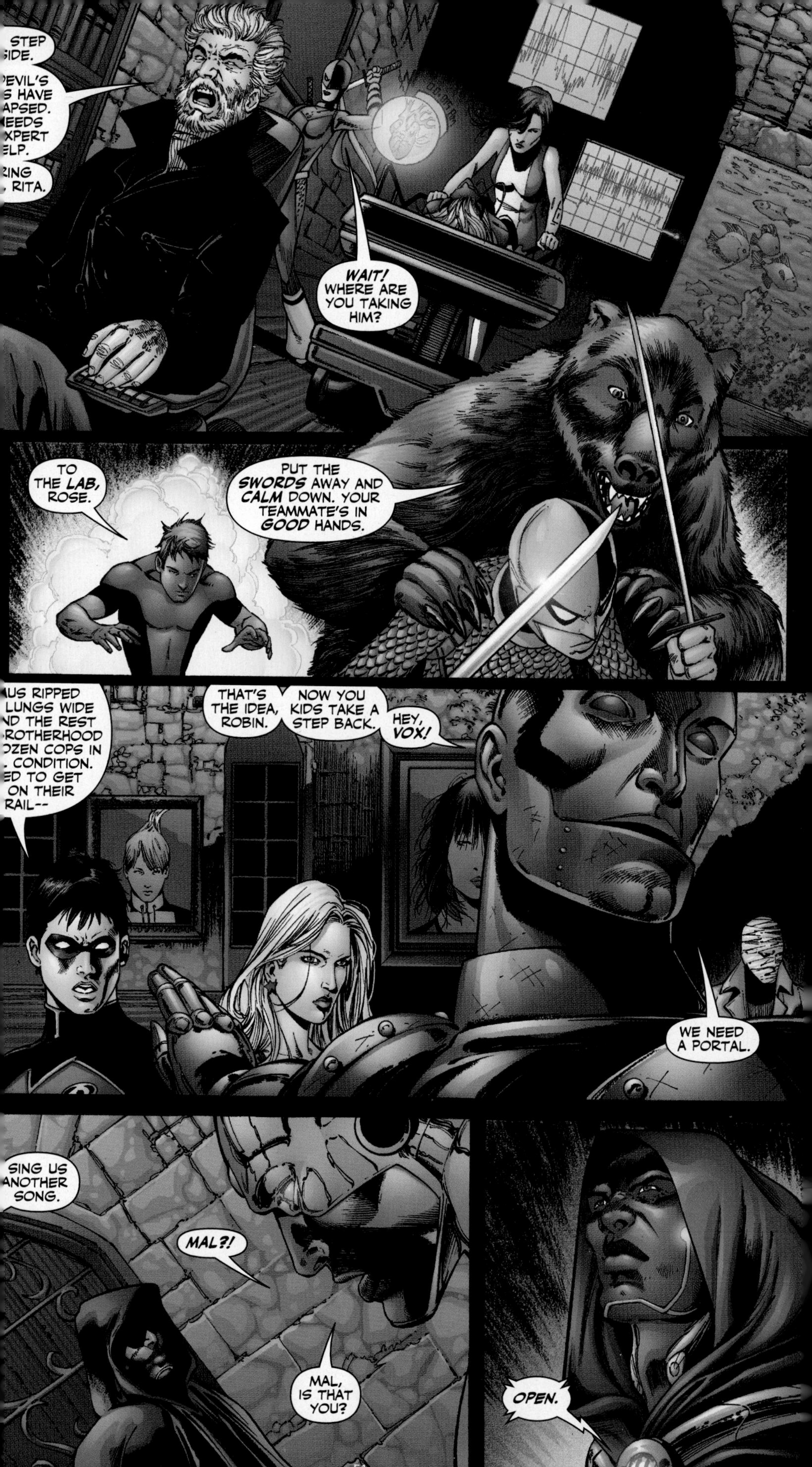
STEP
SIDE.
EVIL'S
S HAVE
APSED.
EEDS
XPERT
ELP.
ZING
, RITA.
WAIT! WHERE ARE YOU TAKING HIM?
TO THE LAB, ROSE.
PUT THE SWORDS AWAY AND CALM DOWN. YOUR TEAMMATE'S IN GOOD HANDS.
US RIPPED
LUNGS WIDE
ND THE REST
ROTHERHOOD
OZEN COPS IN
. CONDITION.
ED TO GET
ON THEIR
RAIL--
THAT'S THE IDEA, ROBIN.
NOW YOU KIDS TAKE A STEP BACK.
HEY, VOX!
WE NEED A PORTAL.
SING US ANOTHER SONG.
MAL?!
MAL, IS THAT YOU?
OPEN.

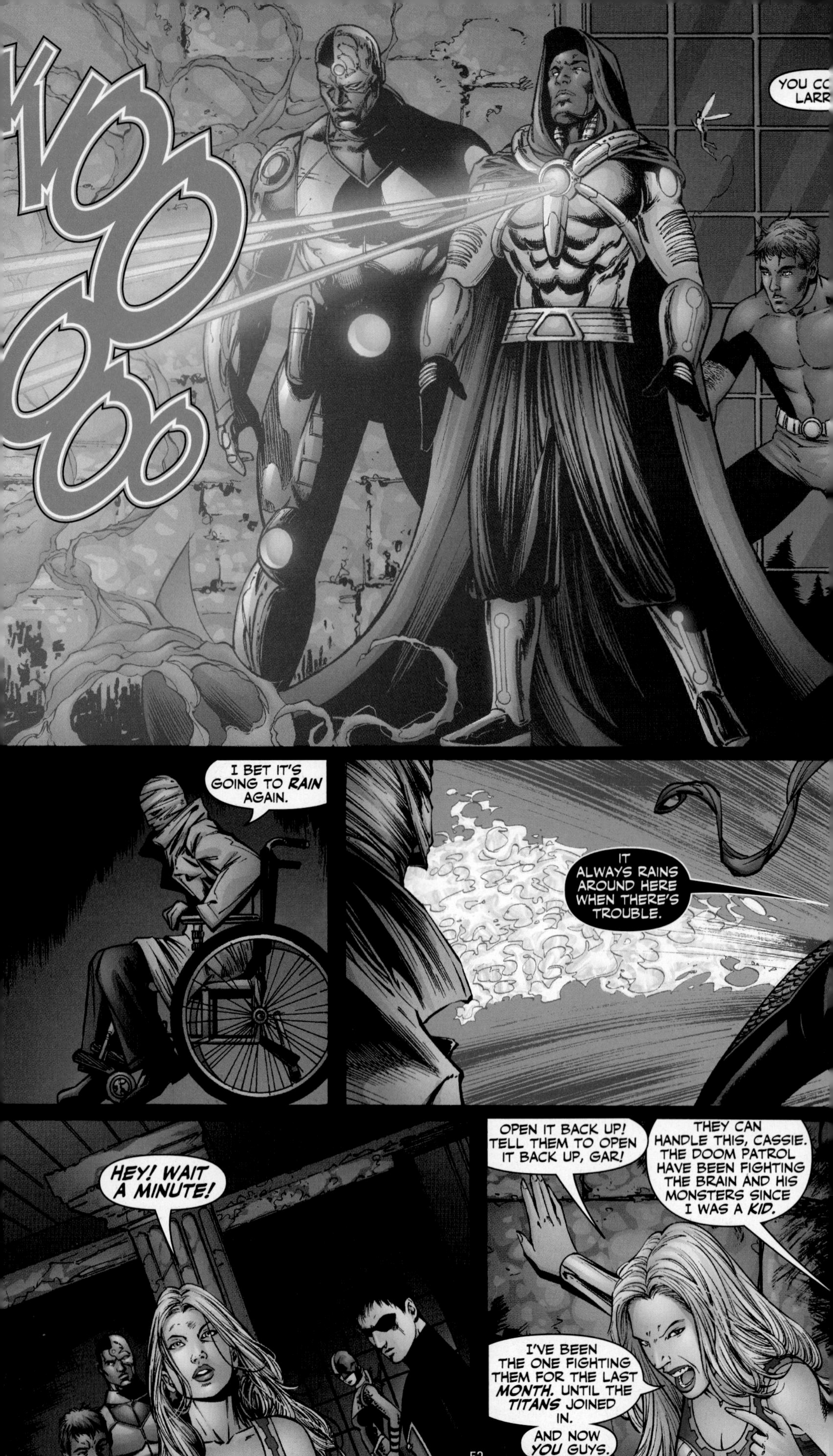

YOOOOOO
YOU CO
LARR
I BET IT'S GOING TO RAIN AGAIN.
IT ALWAYS RAINS AROUND HERE WHEN THERE'S TROUBLE.
HEY! WAIT A MINUTE!
OPEN IT BACK UP! TELL THEM TO OPEN IT BACK UP, GAR!
THEY CAN HANDLE THIS, CASSIE. THE DOOM PATROL HAVE BEEN FIGHTING THE BRAIN AND HIS MONSTERS SINCE I WAS A KID.
I'VE BEEN THE ONE FIGHTING THEM FOR THE LAST MONTH. UNTIL THE TITANS JOINED IN.
AND NOW YOU GUYS.

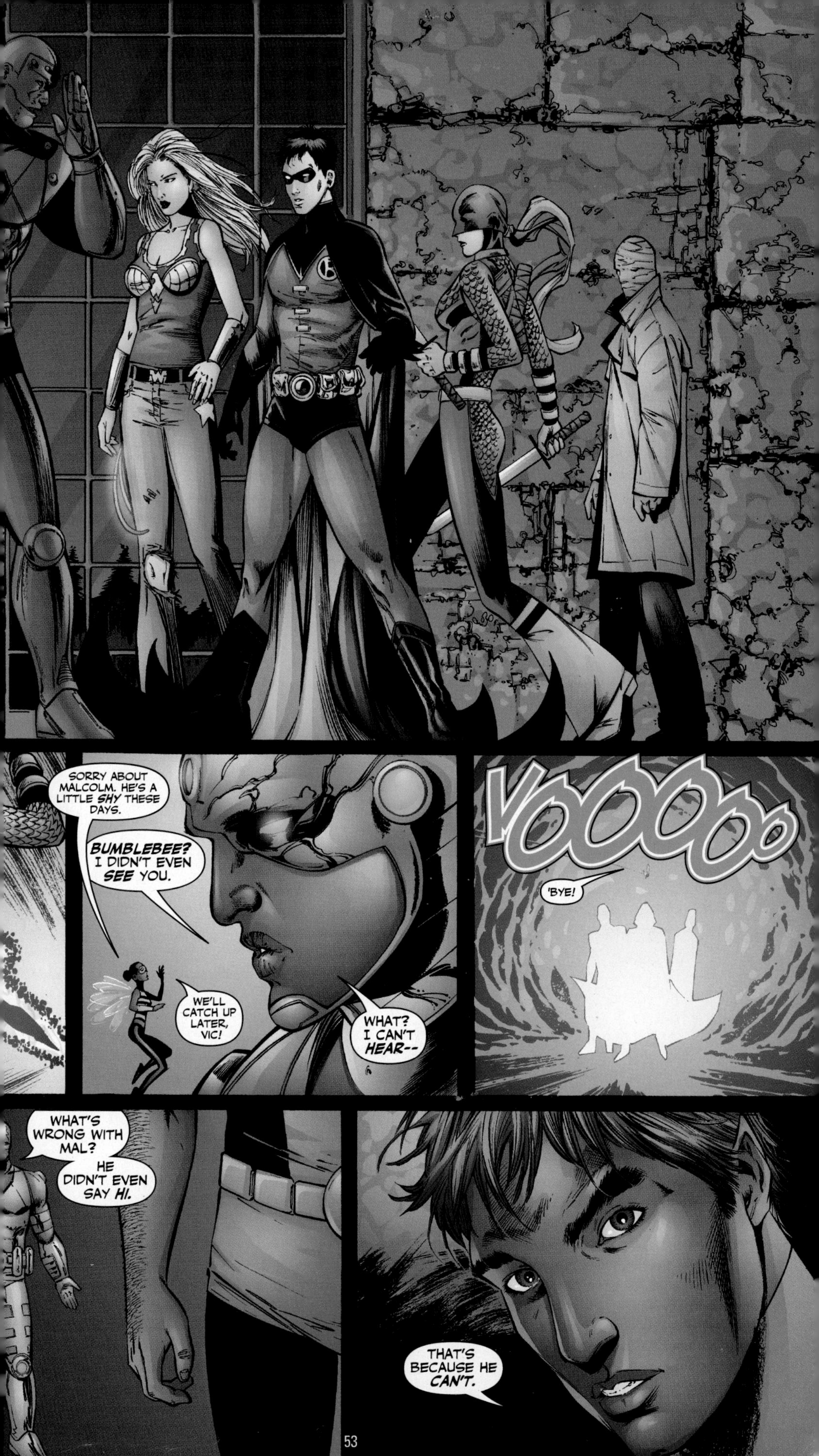
SORRY ABOUT MALCOLM. HE'S A LITTLE SHY THESE DAYS.
BUMBLEBEE? I DIDN'T EVEN SEE YOU.
WE'LL CATCH UP LATER, VIC!
WHAT? I CAN'T HEAR--
VOOOOoo
'BYE!
WHAT'S WRONG WITH MAL?
HE DIDN'T EVEN SAY HI.
THAT'S BECAUSE HE CAN'T.

WHO THE HELL'S *MAL?*

MALCOLM DUNCAN. WE CALL HIM *VOX* NOW. HE AND HIS WIFE, *BUMBLEBEE,* USED TO BE *TITANS.*

LAST YEAR, THEY WERE LOST IN DEEP SPACE ALONG WITH VIC.

WHEN YOU ALL CAME BACK, THERE WERE SOME *COMPLICATIONS.*

I DON'T REMEMBER--

BECAUSE YOU WERE *SHUT DOWN.* YOU GOT OFF *EASY* COMPARED TO THE OTHERS.

"MALCOLM'S SUB-SONIC WEAPONS BLEW *UP* IN HIS FACE.

"HIS LUNGS AND VOCAL CORDS HAD TO BE REPLACED.

"BUMBLEBEE WAS IRRADIATED WITH SOME KIND OF ENERGY AND SHRANK *DOWN* TO A SIX-INCH HEIGHT.

"NOW SHE'S ON SPECIAL MEDS THE CHIEF DEVELOPED THAT KEEP HER DIMINUTIVE HEART FROM GOING INTO CARDIAC ARREST."

AFTER THE OPERATIONS, THE CHIEF OFFERED THEM BOTH A PLACE ON THIS TEAM. RESCUED FROM DISASTER. LIKE THE *REST* OF THE DOOM PATROL.

THE CHIEF TOLD ME A DOZEN TIMES, WHEN YOU WOKE UP, HE'D MAKE *CYBORG* THE SAME OFFER.

THAT IS, UNLESS YOU'RE HAPP BEING WITH T TEEN TITAN

THE T TITAN

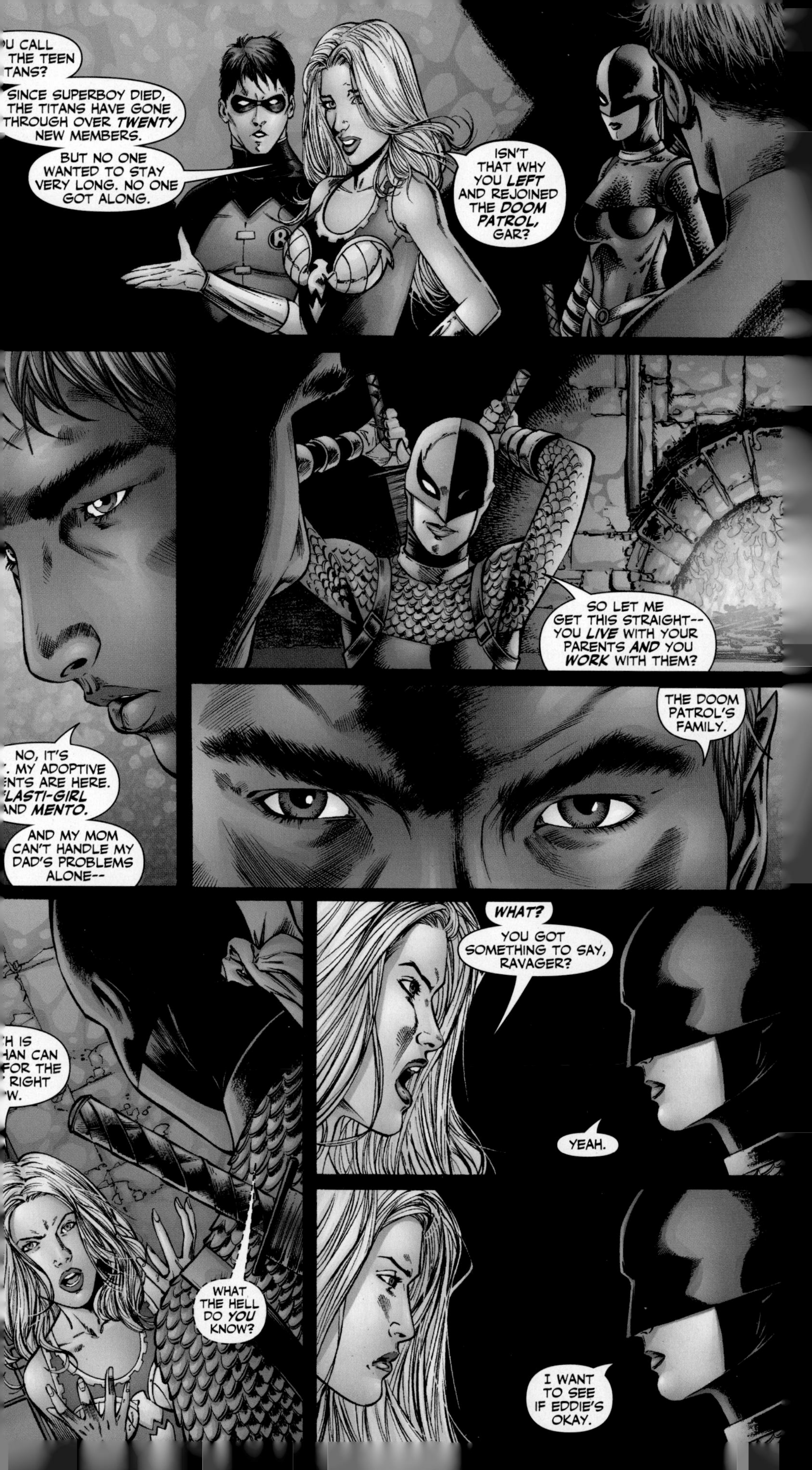
U CALL THE TEEN TANS?
SINCE SUPERBOY DIED, THE TITANS HAVE GONE THROUGH OVER TWENTY NEW MEMBERS.
BUT NO ONE WANTED TO STAY VERY LONG. NO ONE GOT ALONG.
ISN'T THAT WHY YOU LEFT AND REJOINED THE DOOM PATROL, GAR?
SO LET ME GET THIS STRAIGHT-- YOU LIVE WITH YOUR PARENTS AND YOU WORK WITH THEM?
NO, IT'S . MY ADOPTIVE NTS ARE HERE. LASTI-GIRL AND MENTO.
AND MY MOM CAN'T HANDLE MY DAD'S PROBLEMS ALONE--
THE DOOM PATROL'S FAMILY.
H IS HAN CAN FOR THE RIGHT W.
WHAT THE HELL DO YOU KNOW?
WHAT? YOU GOT SOMETHING TO SAY, RAVAGER?
YEAH.
I WANT TO SEE IF EDDIE'S OKAY.

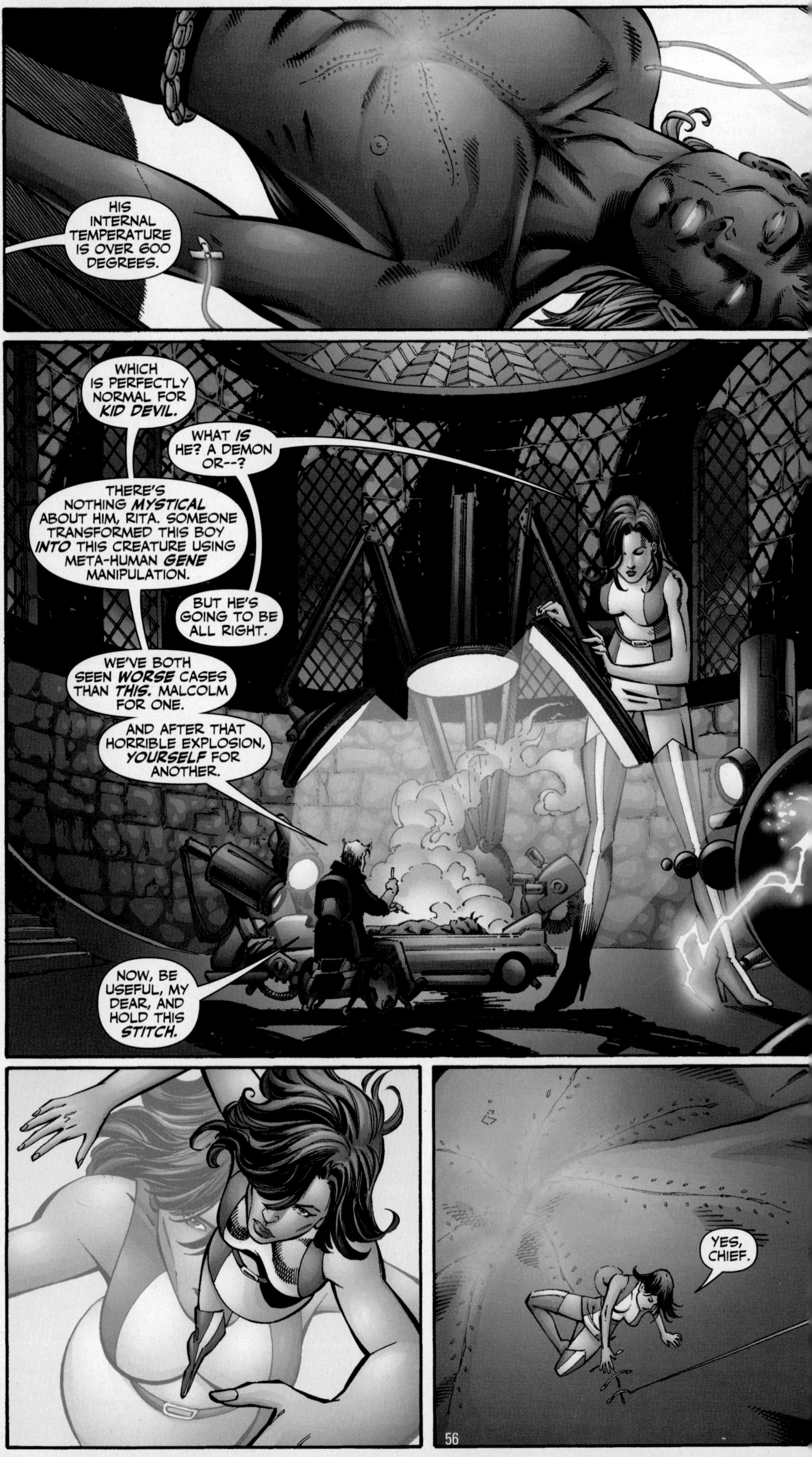
HIS INTERNAL TEMPERATURE IS OVER 600 DEGREES.
WHICH IS PERFECTLY NORMAL FOR KID DEVIL.
WHAT IS HE? A DEMON OR--?
THERE'S NOTHING MYSTICAL ABOUT HIM, RITA. SOMEONE TRANSFORMED THIS BOY INTO THIS CREATURE USING META-HUMAN GENE MANIPULATION.
BUT HE'S GOING TO BE ALL RIGHT.
WE'VE BOTH SEEN WORSE CASES THAN THIS. MALCOLM FOR ONE.
AND AFTER THAT HORRIBLE EXPLOSION, YOURSELF FOR ANOTHER.
NOW, BE USEFUL, MY DEAR, AND HOLD THIS STITCH.
YES, CHIEF.

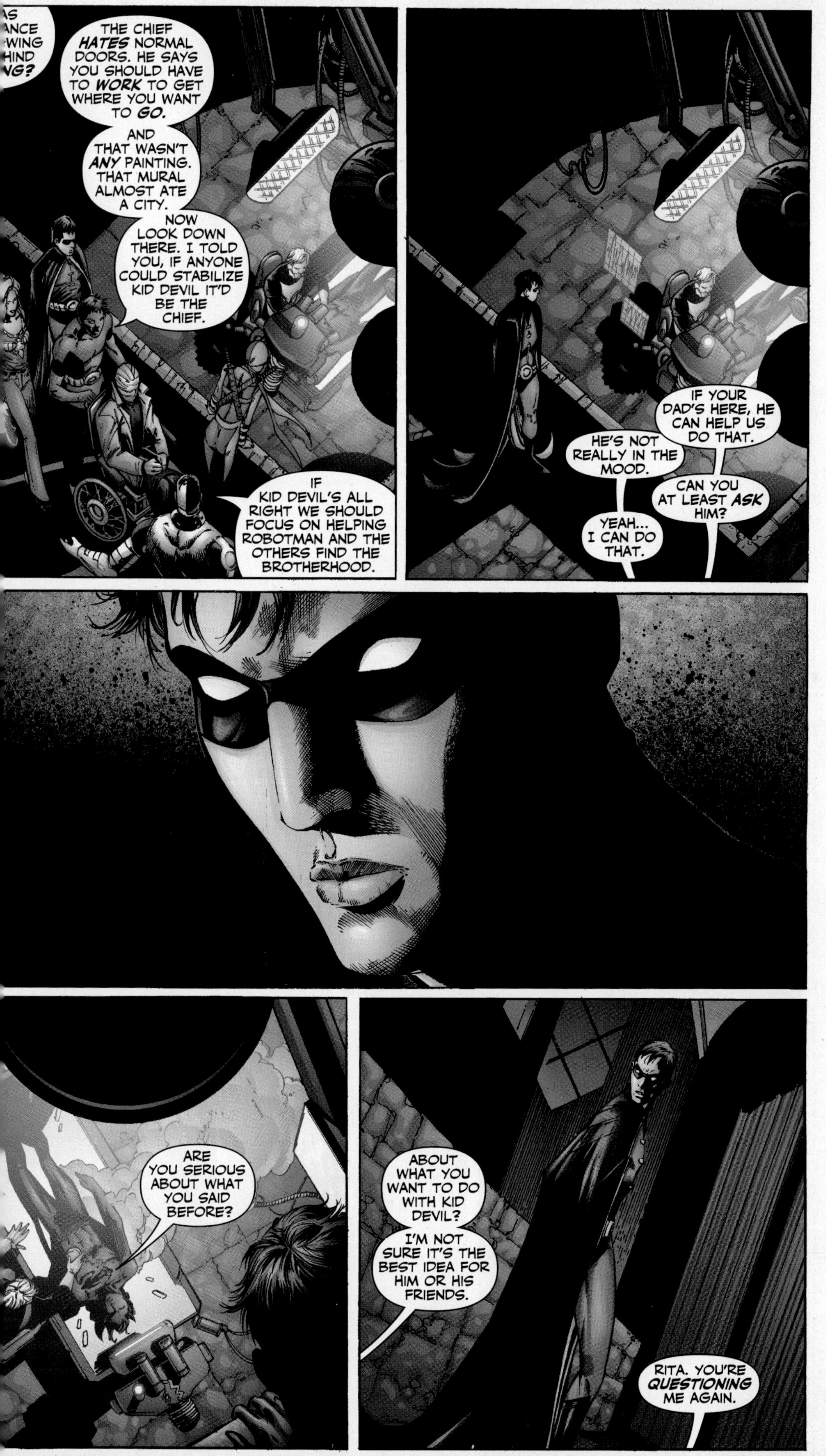
AS ...ANCE ...WING ...HIND ...NG?
THE CHIEF HATES NORMAL DOORS. HE SAYS YOU SHOULD HAVE TO WORK TO GET WHERE YOU WANT TO GO.
AND THAT WASN'T ANY PAINTING. THAT MURAL ALMOST ATE A CITY.
NOW LOOK DOWN THERE. I TOLD YOU, IF ANYONE COULD STABILIZE KID DEVIL IT'D BE THE CHIEF.
IF KID DEVIL'S ALL RIGHT WE SHOULD FOCUS ON HELPING ROBOTMAN AND THE OTHERS FIND THE BROTHERHOOD.
IF YOUR DAD'S HERE, HE CAN HELP US DO THAT.
HE'S NOT REALLY IN THE MOOD.
CAN YOU AT LEAST ASK HIM?
YEAH... I CAN DO THAT.
ARE YOU SERIOUS ABOUT WHAT YOU SAID BEFORE?
ABOUT WHAT YOU WANT TO DO WITH KID DEVIL?
I'M NOT SURE IT'S THE BEST IDEA FOR HIM OR HIS FRIENDS.
RITA. YOU'RE QUESTIONING ME AGAIN.

I WAS ONLY--

IMAGINE IF I HAD LISTENED TO EVERYONE *ELSE* WHEN YOU WERE SUPPOSED TO BE *DEAD.*

I TOOK YOUR *SKULL* FROM THE WATERS OF THAT ISLAND WHERE COLONEL ZAHL AND THE BROTHERHOOD TRIED TO BLOW US TO *KINGDOM COME.*

I TREATED IT WITH SYNTHETIC PROTEINS FOR *YEARS,* UNTIL YOU WERE ABLE TO *REGROW* YOUR MALLEABLE BODY.

BACK INT ELASTI-G

YOU *SHOULD* BE DEAD. *ALL* OF YOU SHOULD BE *DEAD* TEN TIMES OVER.

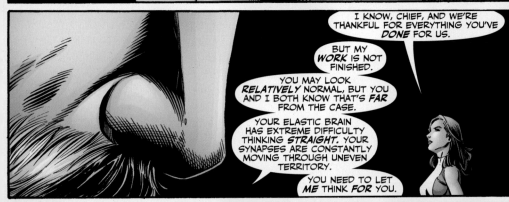

I KNOW, CHIEF, AND WE'RE THANKFUL FOR EVERYTHING YOU'VE *DONE* FOR US.

BUT MY *WORK* IS NOT FINISHED.

YOU MAY LOOK *RELATIVELY* NORMAL, BUT YOU AND I BOTH KNOW THAT'S *FAR* FROM THE CASE.

YOUR ELASTIC BRAIN HAS EXTREME DIFFICULTY THINKING *STRAIGHT.* YOUR SYNAPSES ARE CONSTANTLY MOVING THROUGH UNEVEN TERRITORY.

YOU NEED TO LET *ME* THINK *FOR* YOU.

YOU FOLLOW MY ORDERS LIKE THE OTHERS AND MAYBE-- *MAYBE* ONE DAY YOU WON'T BE A *FREAK* ANYMORE.

AND PEOPLE WILL *LOVE* YOU LIKE THEY USED TO, MY *STARLET.*

YOU'RE RIGHT, CHIEF.

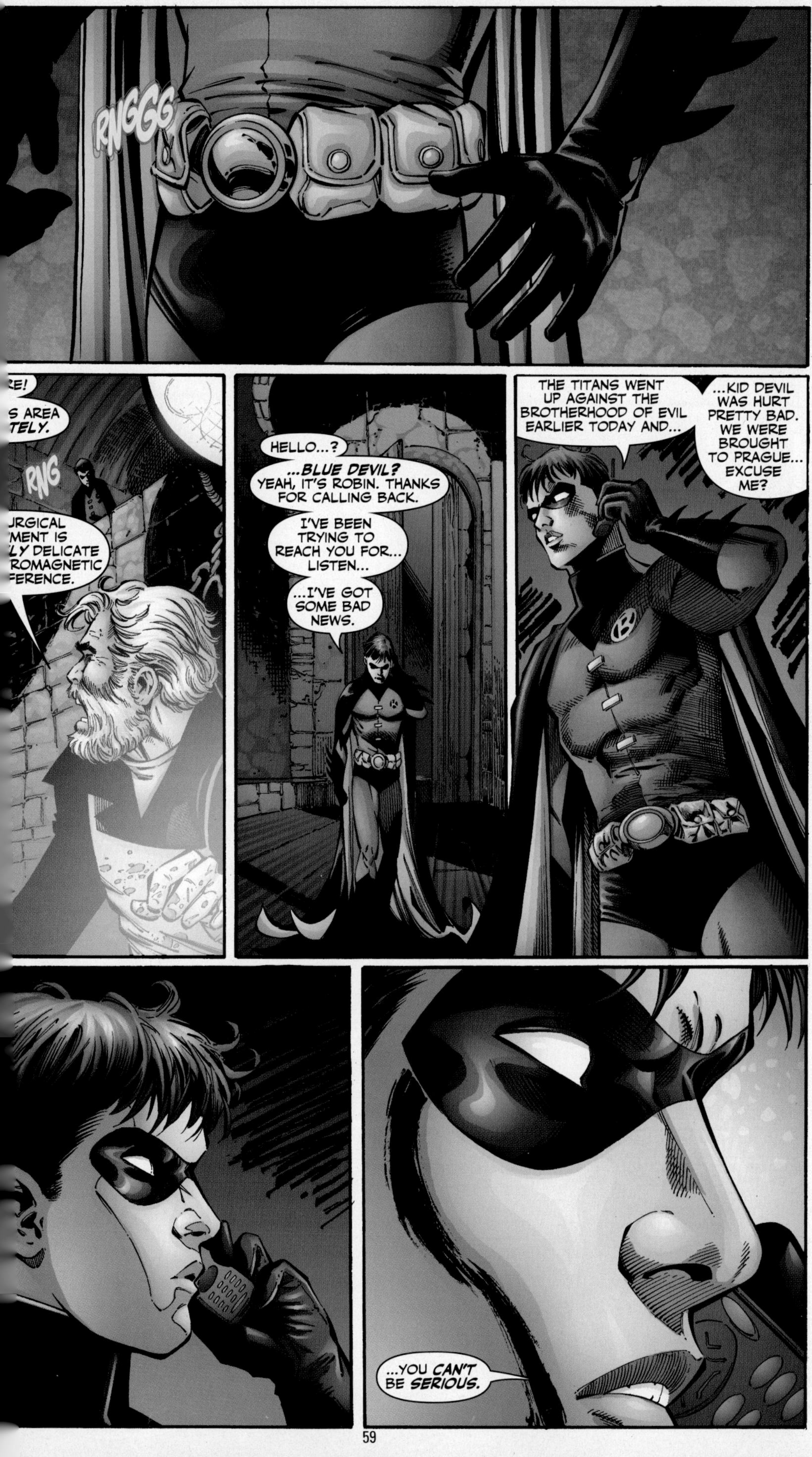
RNGGG
RE!
S AREA
TELY.
RNG
URGICAL
MENT IS
LY DELICATE
ROMAGNETIC
FERENCE.
HELLO...?
...BLUE DEVIL? YEAH, IT'S ROBIN. THANKS FOR CALLING BACK.
I'VE BEEN TRYING TO REACH YOU FOR... LISTEN...
...I'VE GOT SOME BAD NEWS.
THE TITANS WENT UP AGAINST THE BROTHERHOOD OF EVIL EARLIER TODAY AND...
...KID DEVIL WAS HURT PRETTY BAD. WE WERE BROUGHT TO PRAGUE... EXCUSE ME?
...YOU CAN'T BE SERIOUS.

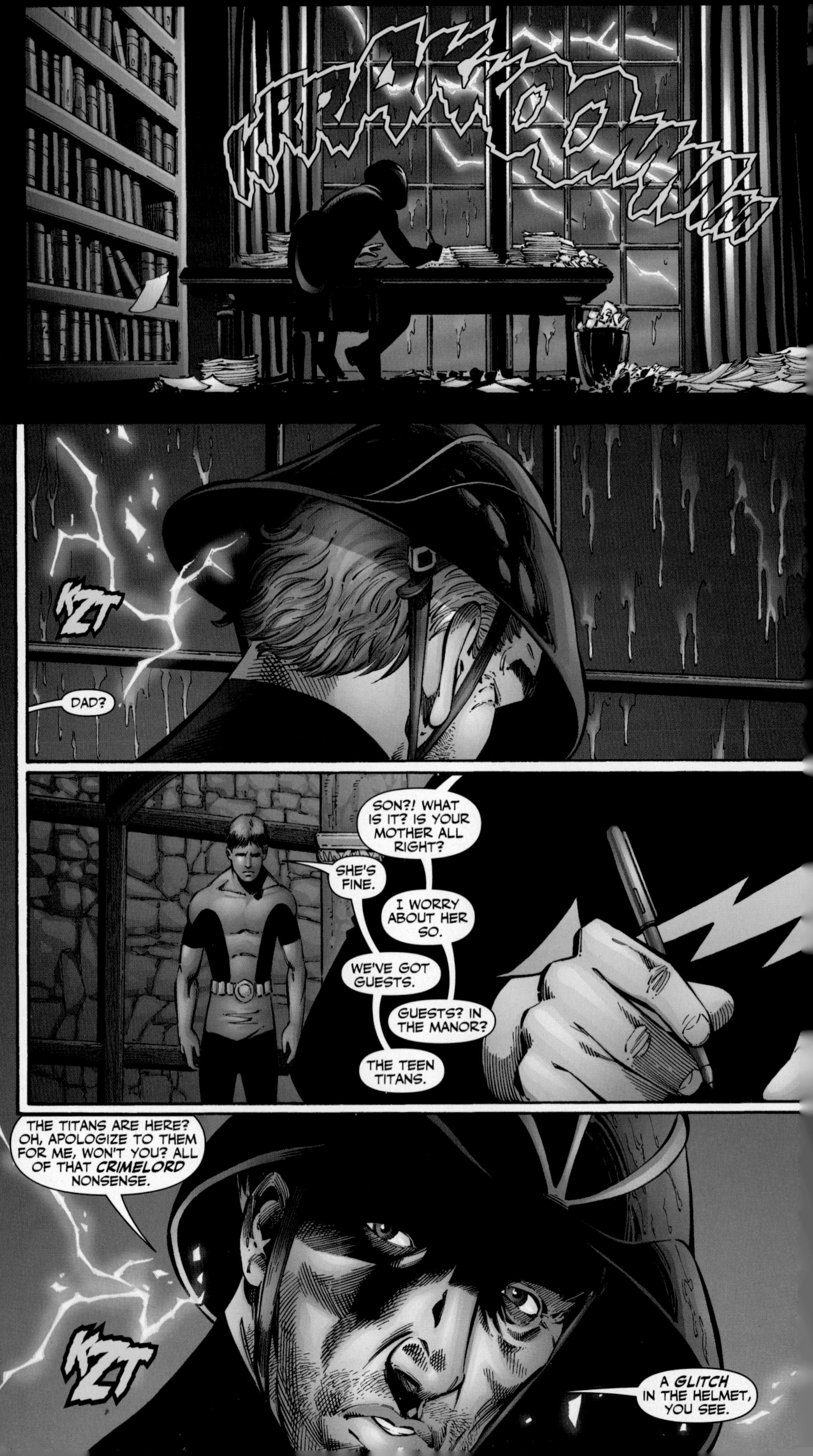
KZT
DAD?
SON?! WHAT IS IT? IS YOUR MOTHER ALL RIGHT?
SHE'S FINE.
I WORRY ABOUT HER SO.
WE'VE GOT GUESTS.
GUESTS? IN THE MANOR?
THE TEEN TITANS.
THE TITANS ARE HERE? OH, APOLOGIZE TO THEM FOR ME, WON'T YOU? ALL OF THAT *CRIMELORD* NONSENSE.
KZT
A *GLITCH* IN THE HELMET, YOU SEE.

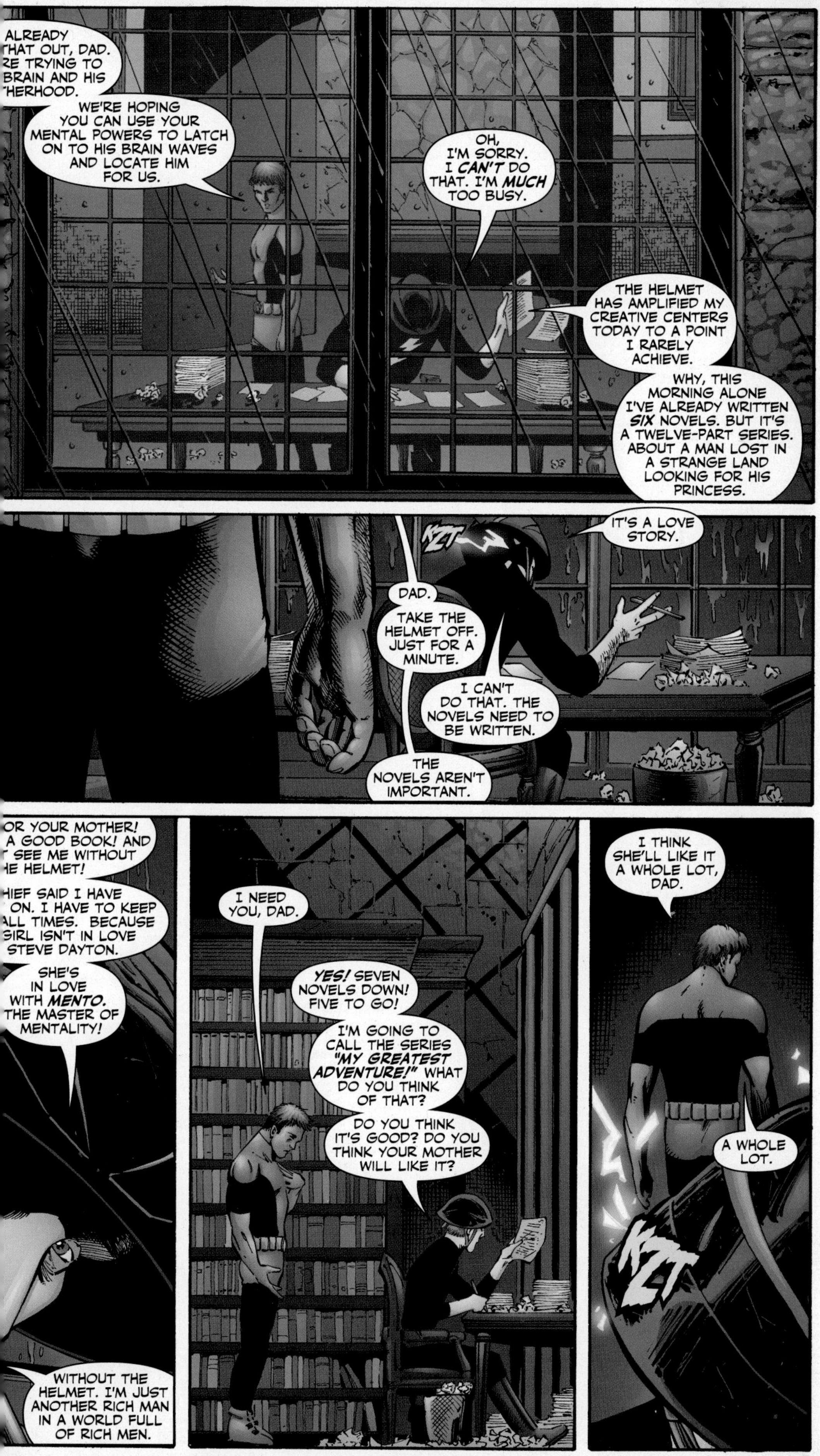
ALREADY
THAT OUT, DAD.
RE TRYING TO
BRAIN AND HIS
HERHOOD.
WE'RE HOPING YOU CAN USE YOUR MENTAL POWERS TO LATCH ON TO HIS BRAIN WAVES AND LOCATE HIM FOR US.
OH, I'M SORRY. I CAN'T DO THAT. I'M MUCH TOO BUSY.
THE HELMET HAS AMPLIFIED MY CREATIVE CENTERS TODAY TO A POINT I RARELY ACHIEVE.
WHY, THIS MORNING ALONE I'VE ALREADY WRITTEN SIX NOVELS. BUT IT'S A TWELVE-PART SERIES. ABOUT A MAN LOST IN A STRANGE LAND LOOKING FOR HIS PRINCESS.
KZT
IT'S A LOVE STORY.
DAD.
TAKE THE HELMET OFF. JUST FOR A MINUTE.
I CAN'T DO THAT. THE NOVELS NEED TO BE WRITTEN.
THE NOVELS AREN'T IMPORTANT.
OR YOUR MOTHER!
A GOOD BOOK! AND
SEE ME WITHOUT
E HELMET!
HIEF SAID I HAVE
ON. I HAVE TO KEEP
LL TIMES. BECAUSE
GIRL ISN'T IN LOVE
STEVE DAYTON.
SHE'S IN LOVE WITH MENTO. THE MASTER OF MENTALITY!
WITHOUT THE HELMET. I'M JUST ANOTHER RICH MAN IN A WORLD FULL OF RICH MEN.
I NEED YOU, DAD.
YES! SEVEN NOVELS DOWN! FIVE TO GO!
I'M GOING TO CALL THE SERIES "MY GREATEST ADVENTURE!" WHAT DO YOU THINK OF THAT?
DO YOU THINK IT'S GOOD? DO YOU THINK YOUR MOTHER WILL LIKE IT?
I THINK SHE'LL LIKE IT A WHOLE LOT, DAD.
A WHOLE LOT.
KZT

DID ANYONE ELSE NOTICE IT WAS *SNOWING* IN THE BALLROOM?

HOW CAN THEY *LIVE* IN A PLACE LIKE *THIS*?

BECAUSE THEY'RE TOTALLY INSANE.

SAYS THE GIRL WHO CARVED OUT HER OWN *EYE* FOR "DADDY."

THAT WAS *TEMPORARY* INSANITY. ASK THE *JUDGE.*

YOU KNOW, I NEVER REALLY UNDERSTOOD WHAT NEGATIVE MAN WAS.

IS TH-- ENER-- LIVING-- OR /S--

LARR-- A LITTL-- OF *BO*-- FRIEND-- CAN R-- TO T--

CHIEF. HOW'S--?

I'M HAPPY TO ANNOUNCE THAT MY EFFORTS WERE A *SUCCESS.*

KID DEVIL IS OUT OF SURGERY AND HEALING REMARKABLY WELL. TEN TIMES FASTER THAN NORMAL. RIGHT NOW, I'D LIKE YOU ALL TO COME TO THE MEETING ROOM WITH ME.

I'D LIKE TO DISCUSS HIS *FUTURE.*

BEFORE WE GO TALK ABOUT HIM--

--I WANT TO TALK *TO* HIM.

OF COURSE, ROBIN.

OF COURSE.

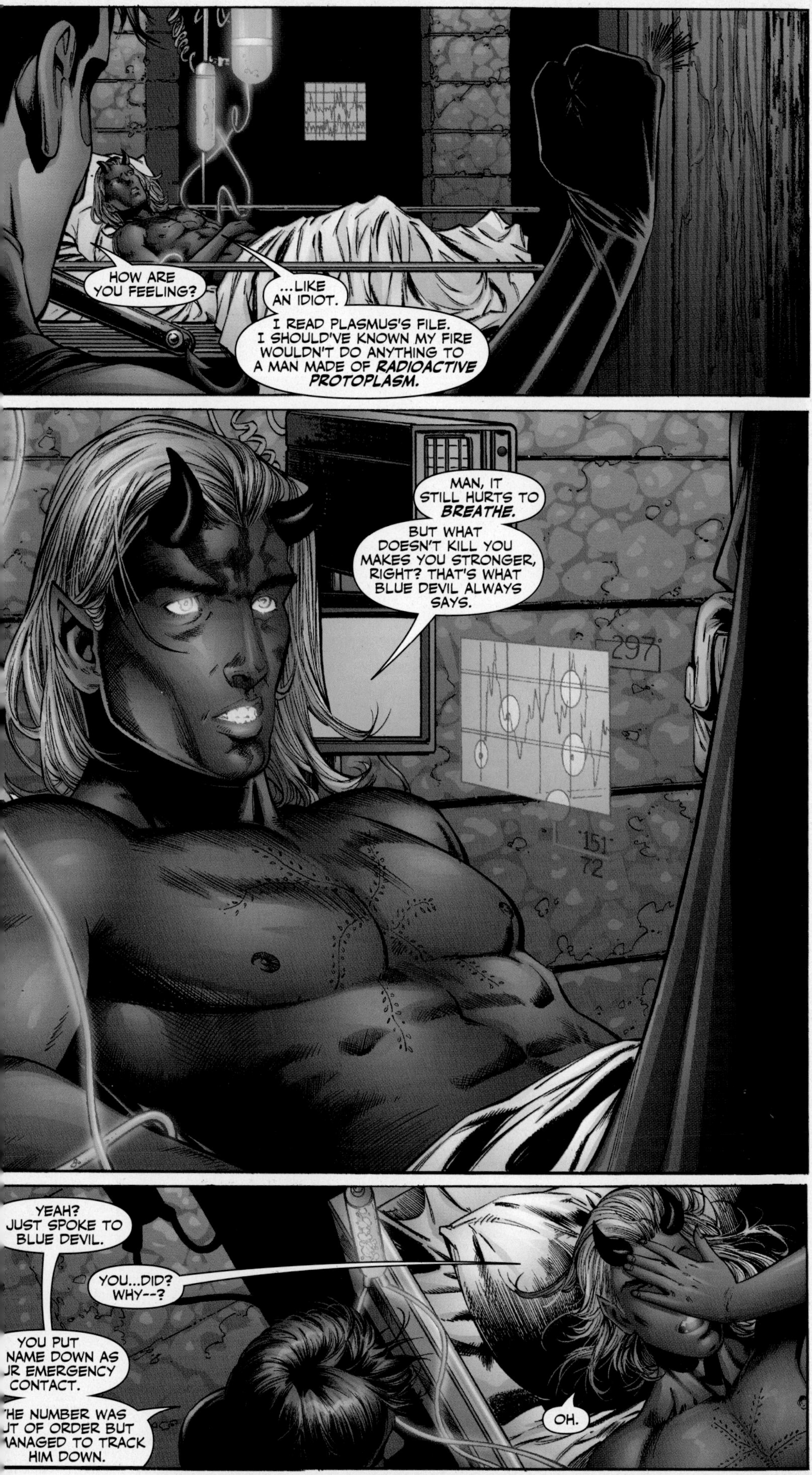
HOW ARE YOU FEELING?
...LIKE AN IDIOT.
I READ PLASMUS'S FILE. I SHOULD'VE KNOWN MY FIRE WOULDN'T DO ANYTHING TO A MAN MADE OF RADIOACTIVE PROTOPLASM.
MAN, IT STILL HURTS TO BREATHE.
BUT WHAT DOESN'T KILL YOU MAKES YOU STRONGER, RIGHT? THAT'S WHAT BLUE DEVIL ALWAYS SAYS.
297
151
72
YEAH? JUST SPOKE TO BLUE DEVIL.
YOU...DID? WHY--?
YOU PUT NAME DOWN AS UR EMERGENCY CONTACT.
HE NUMBER WAS UT OF ORDER BUT ANAGED TO TRACK HIM DOWN.
OH.

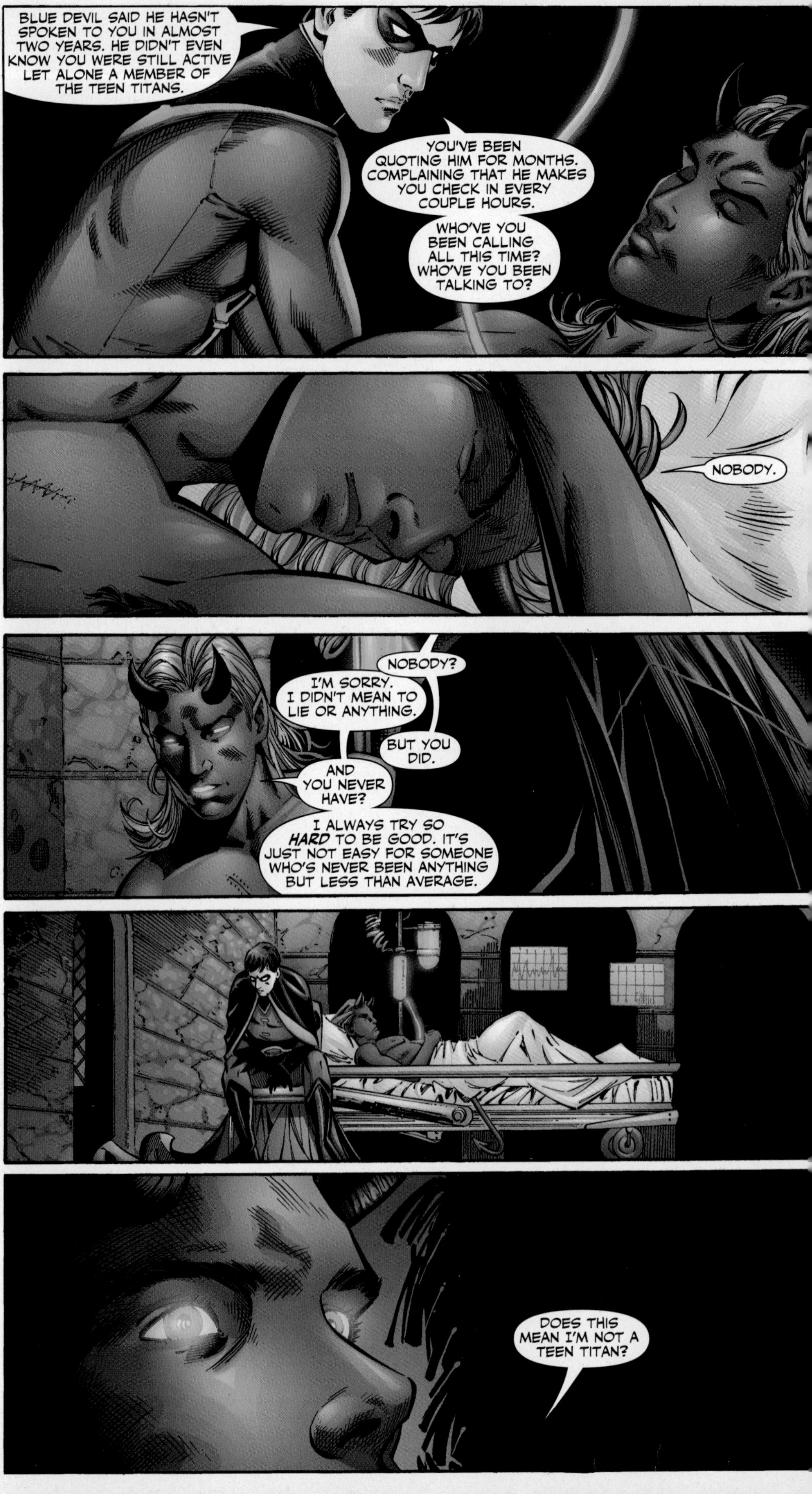
BLUE DEVIL SAID HE HASN'T SPOKEN TO YOU IN ALMOST TWO YEARS. HE DIDN'T EVEN KNOW YOU WERE STILL ACTIVE LET ALONE A MEMBER OF THE TEEN TITANS.
YOU'VE BEEN QUOTING HIM FOR MONTHS. COMPLAINING THAT HE MAKES YOU CHECK IN EVERY COUPLE HOURS.
WHO'VE YOU BEEN CALLING ALL THIS TIME? WHO'VE YOU BEEN TALKING TO?
NOBODY.
NOBODY?
I'M SORRY. I DIDN'T MEAN TO LIE OR ANYTHING.
BUT YOU DID.
AND YOU NEVER HAVE?
I ALWAYS TRY SO HARD TO BE GOOD. IT'S JUST NOT EASY FOR SOMEONE WHO'S NEVER BEEN ANYTHING BUT LESS THAN AVERAGE.
DOES THIS MEAN I'M NOT A TEEN TITAN?

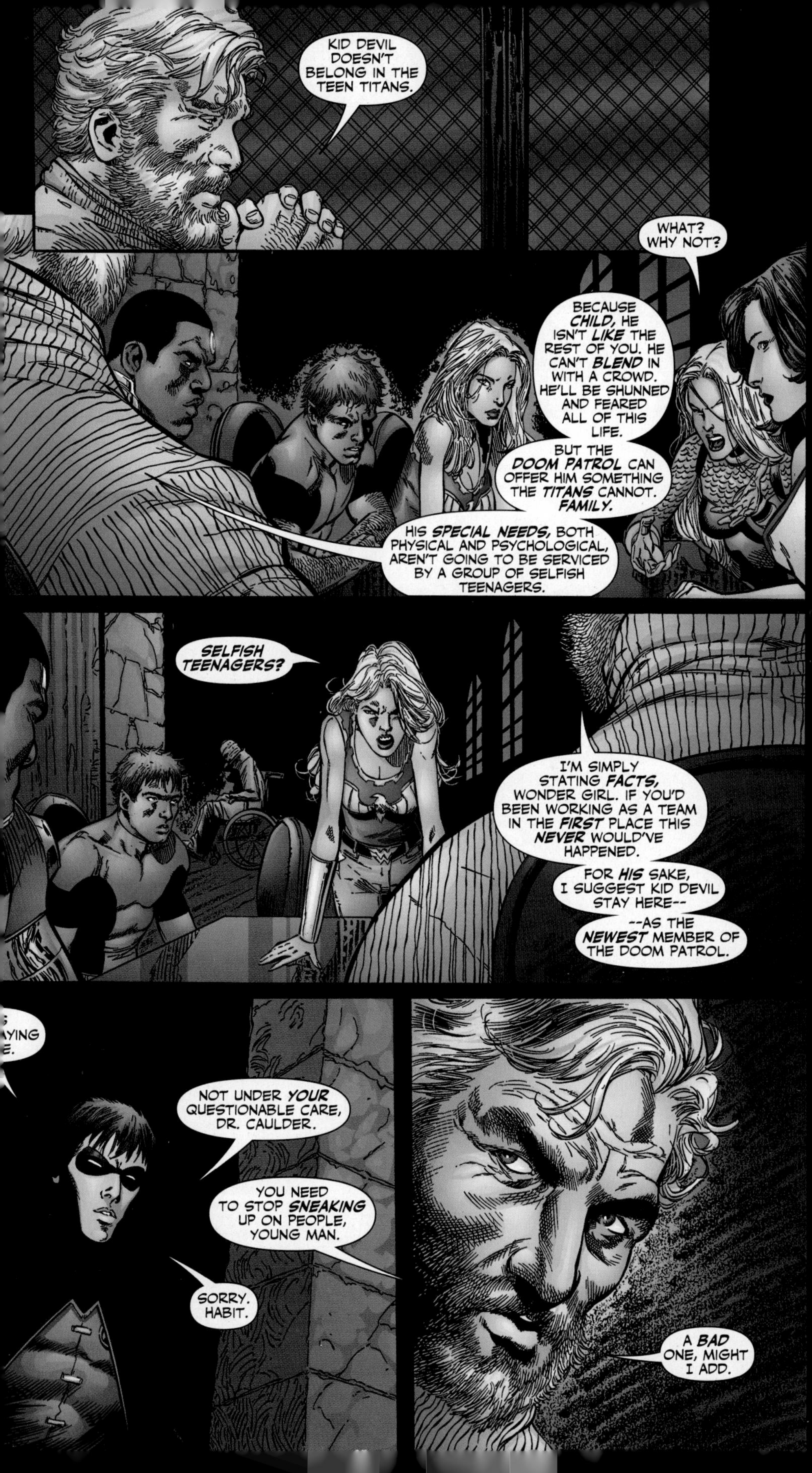
KID DEVIL DOESN'T BELONG IN THE TEEN TITANS.
WHAT? WHY NOT?
BECAUSE CHILD, HE ISN'T LIKE THE REST OF YOU. HE CAN'T BLEND IN WITH A CROWD. HE'LL BE SHUNNED AND FEARED ALL OF THIS LIFE.
BUT THE DOOM PATROL CAN OFFER HIM SOMETHING THE TITANS CANNOT. FAMILY.
HIS SPECIAL NEEDS, BOTH PHYSICAL AND PSYCHOLOGICAL, AREN'T GOING TO BE SERVICED BY A GROUP OF SELFISH TEENAGERS.
SELFISH TEENAGERS?
I'M SIMPLY STATING FACTS, WONDER GIRL. IF YOU'D BEEN WORKING AS A TEAM IN THE FIRST PLACE THIS NEVER WOULD'VE HAPPENED.
FOR HIS SAKE, I SUGGEST KID DEVIL STAY HERE--
--AS THE NEWEST MEMBER OF THE DOOM PATROL.
NOT UNDER YOUR QUESTIONABLE CARE, DR. CAULDER.
YOU NEED TO STOP SNEAKING UP ON PEOPLE, YOUNG MAN.
SORRY. HABIT.
A BAD ONE, MIGHT I ADD.

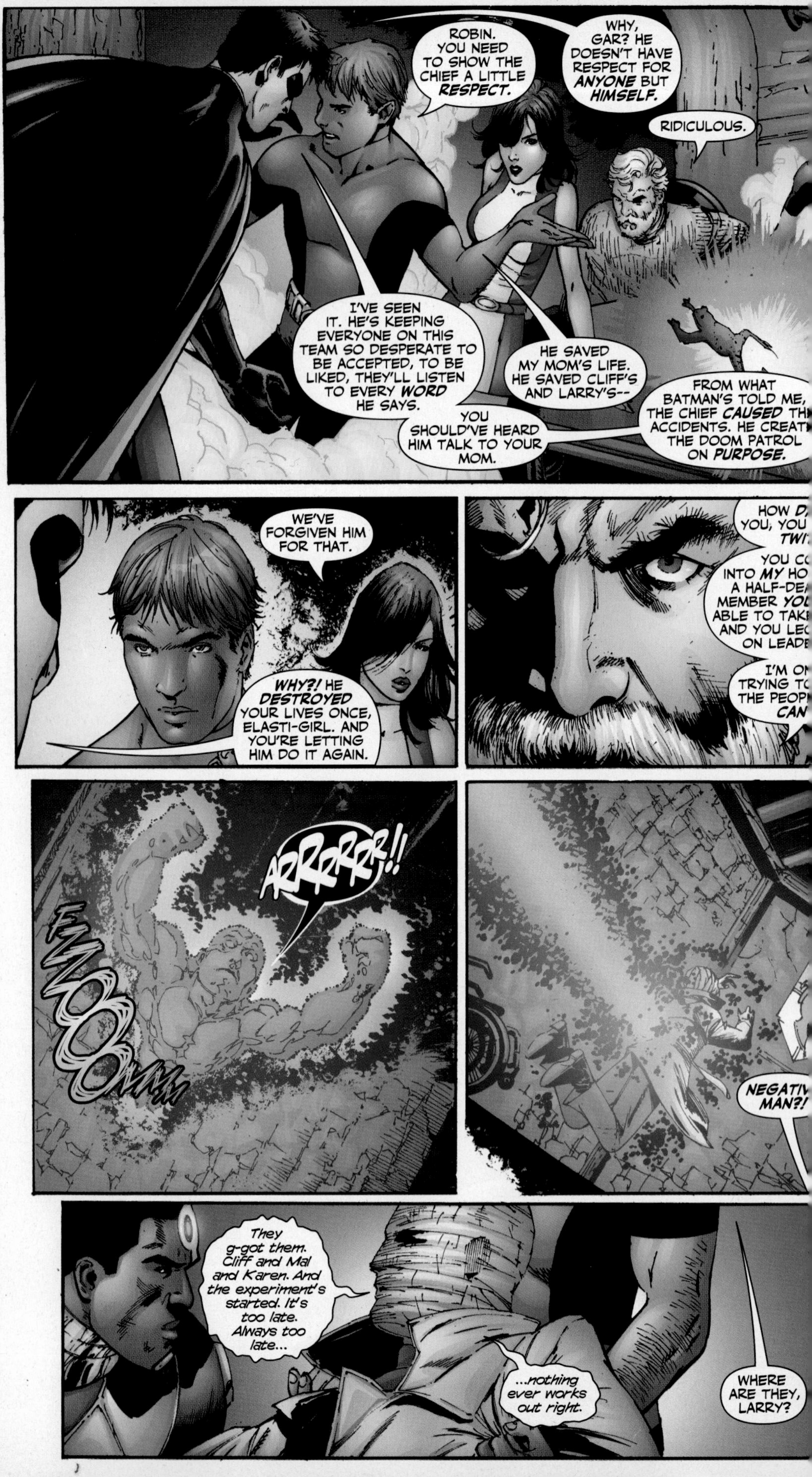
ROBIN. YOU NEED TO SHOW THE CHIEF A LITTLE RESPECT.
WHY, GAR? HE DOESN'T HAVE RESPECT FOR ANYONE BUT HIMSELF.
RIDICULOUS.
I'VE SEEN IT. HE'S KEEPING EVERYONE ON THIS TEAM SO DESPERATE TO BE ACCEPTED, TO BE LIKED, THEY'LL LISTEN TO EVERY WORD HE SAYS.
YOU SHOULD'VE HEARD HIM TALK TO YOUR MOM.
HE SAVED MY MOM'S LIFE. HE SAVED CLIFF'S AND LARRY'S--
FROM WHAT BATMAN'S TOLD ME, THE CHIEF CAUSED TH ACCIDENTS. HE CREAT THE DOOM PATROL ON PURPOSE.
WE'VE FORGIVEN HIM FOR THAT.
WHY?! HE DESTROYED YOUR LIVES ONCE, ELASTI-GIRL. AND YOU'RE LETTING HIM DO IT AGAIN.
HOW D YOU, YOU TWI
YOU C INTO MY HO A HALF-DEA MEMBER YOU ABLE TO TAK AND YOU LEC ON LEADE
I'M O TRYING T THE PEOP CAN
ARRRRRR!!
NEGATIV MAN?!
They g-got them. Cliff and Mal and Karen. And the experiment's started. It's too late. Always too late...
...nothing ever works out right.
WHERE ARE THEY, LARRY?

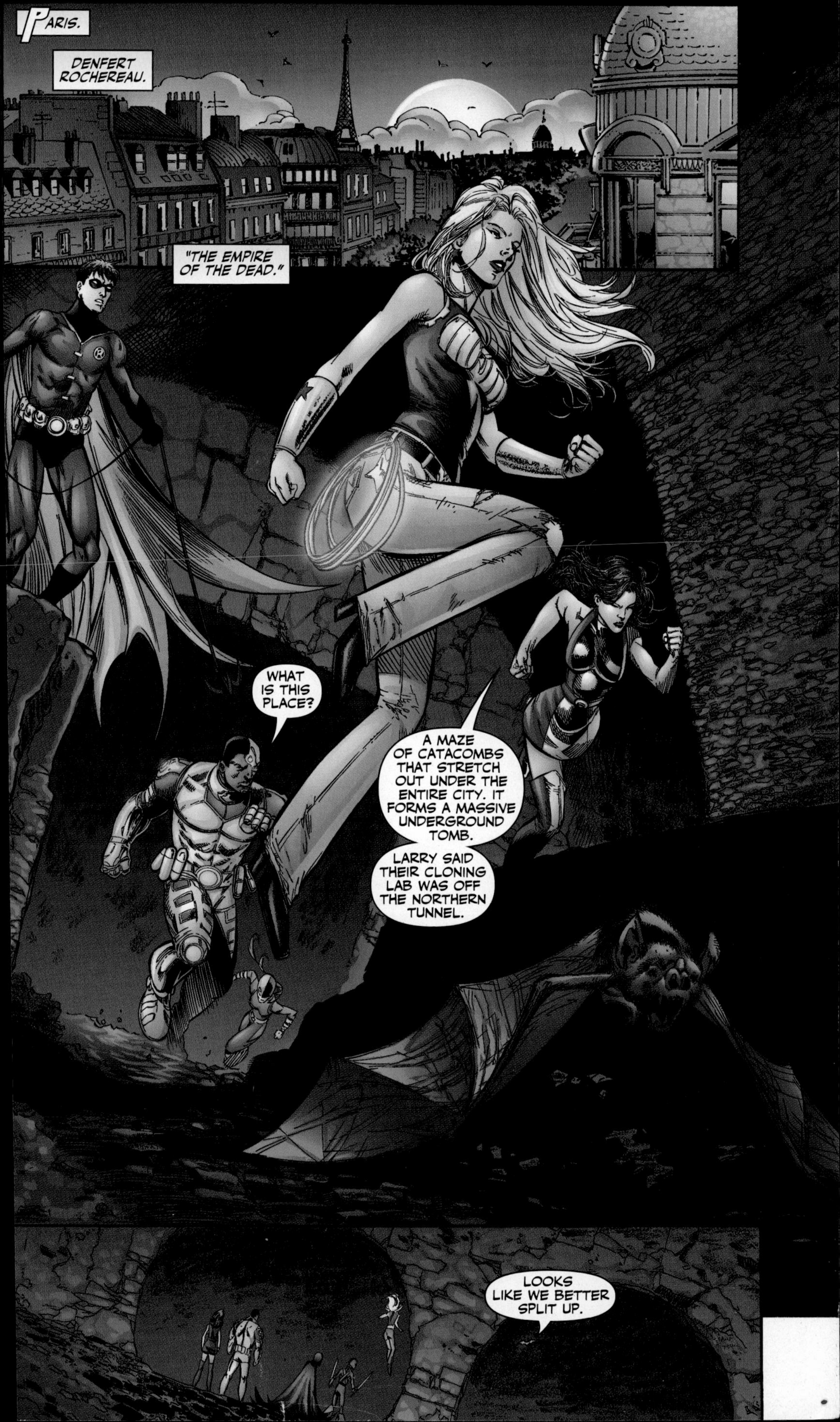
PARIS.
DENFERT ROCHEREAU.
"THE EMPIRE OF THE DEAD."
WHAT IS THIS PLACE?
A MAZE OF CATACOMBS THAT STRETCH OUT UNDER THE ENTIRE CITY. IT FORMS A MASSIVE UNDERGROUND TOMB.
LARRY SAID THEIR CLONING LAB WAS OFF THE NORTHERN TUNNEL.
LOOKS LIKE WE BETTER SPLIT UP.

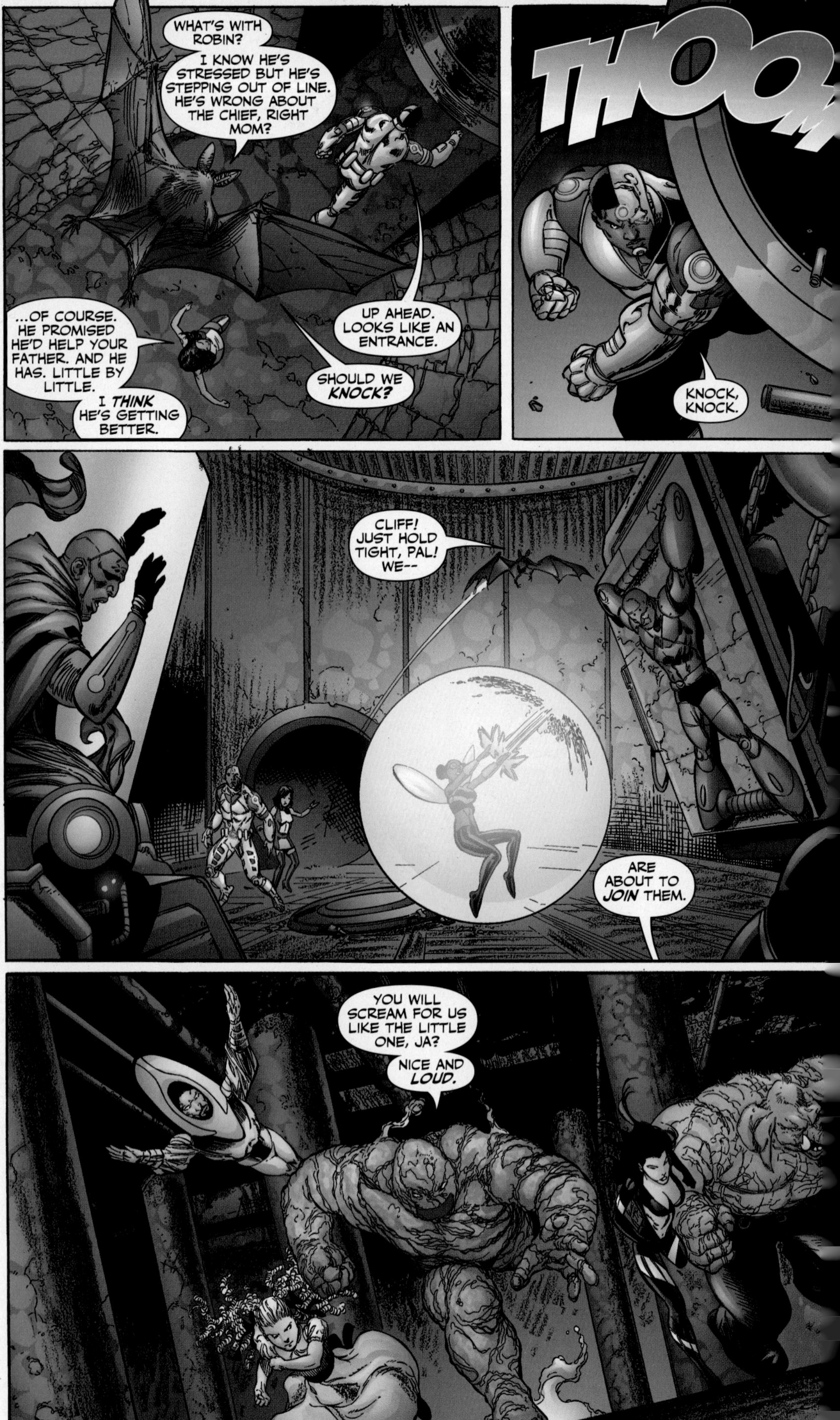
WHAT'S WITH ROBIN?
I KNOW HE'S STRESSED BUT HE'S STEPPING OUT OF LINE. HE'S WRONG ABOUT THE CHIEF, RIGHT MOM?
...OF COURSE. HE PROMISED HE'D HELP YOUR FATHER. AND HE HAS. LITTLE BY LITTLE.
I THINK HE'S GETTING BETTER.
UP AHEAD. LOOKS LIKE AN ENTRANCE.
SHOULD WE KNOCK?
THOOM
KNOCK, KNOCK.
CLIFF! JUST HOLD TIGHT, PAL! WE--
ARE ABOUT TO JOIN THEM.
YOU WILL SCREAM FOR US LIKE THE LITTLE ONE, JA?
NICE AND LOUD.

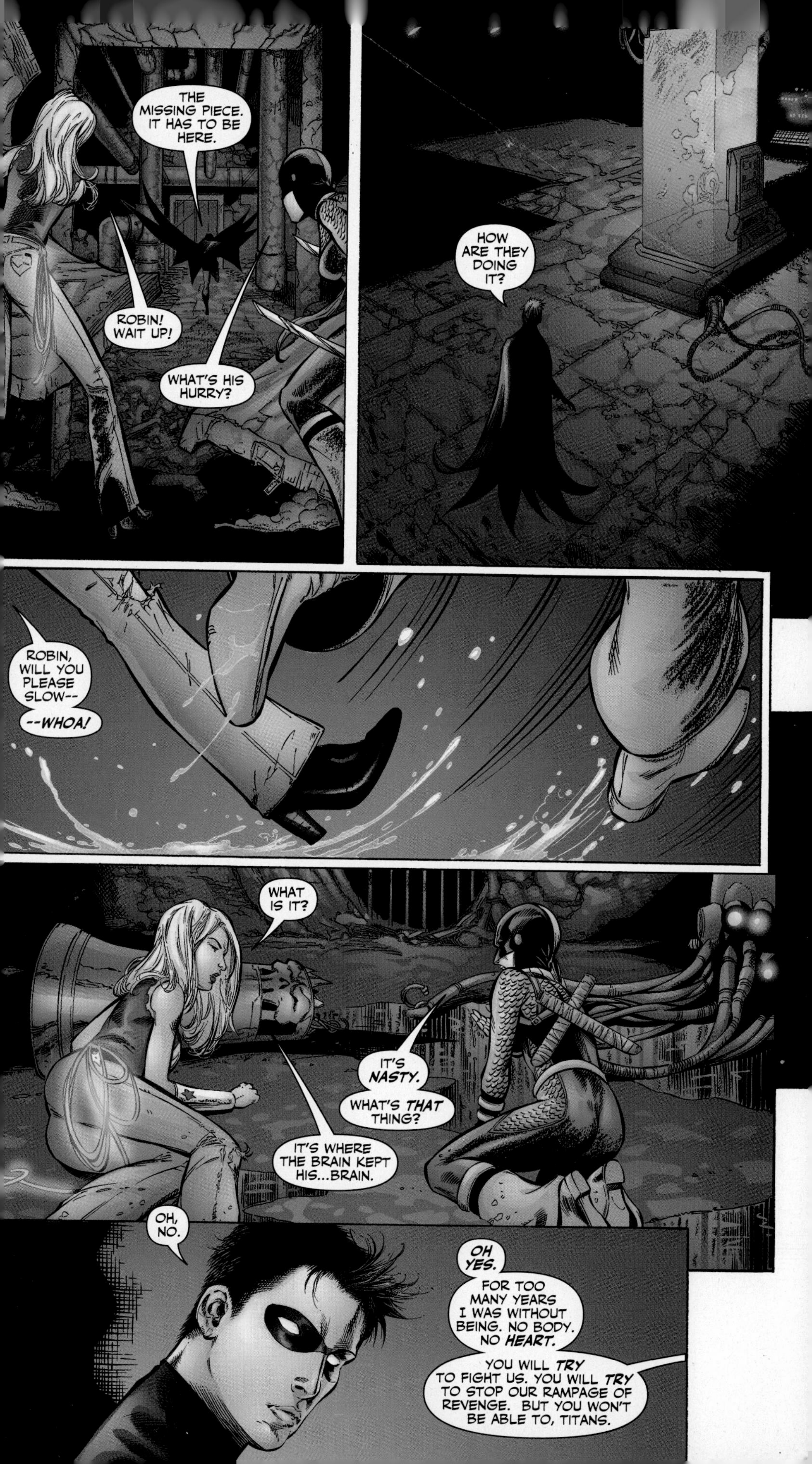

THE MISSING PIECE. IT HAS TO BE HERE.
ROBIN! WAIT UP!
WHAT'S HIS HURRY?
HOW ARE THEY DOING IT?
ROBIN, WILL YOU PLEASE SLOW--
--WHOA!
WHAT IS IT?
IT'S NASTY.
WHAT'S THAT THING?
IT'S WHERE THE BRAIN KEPT HIS...BRAIN.
OH, NO.
OH YES.
FOR TOO MANY YEARS I WAS WITHOUT BEING. NO BODY. NO HEART.
YOU WILL TRY TO FIGHT US. YOU WILL TRY TO STOP OUR RAMPAGE OF REVENGE. BUT YOU WON'T BE ABLE TO, TITANS.

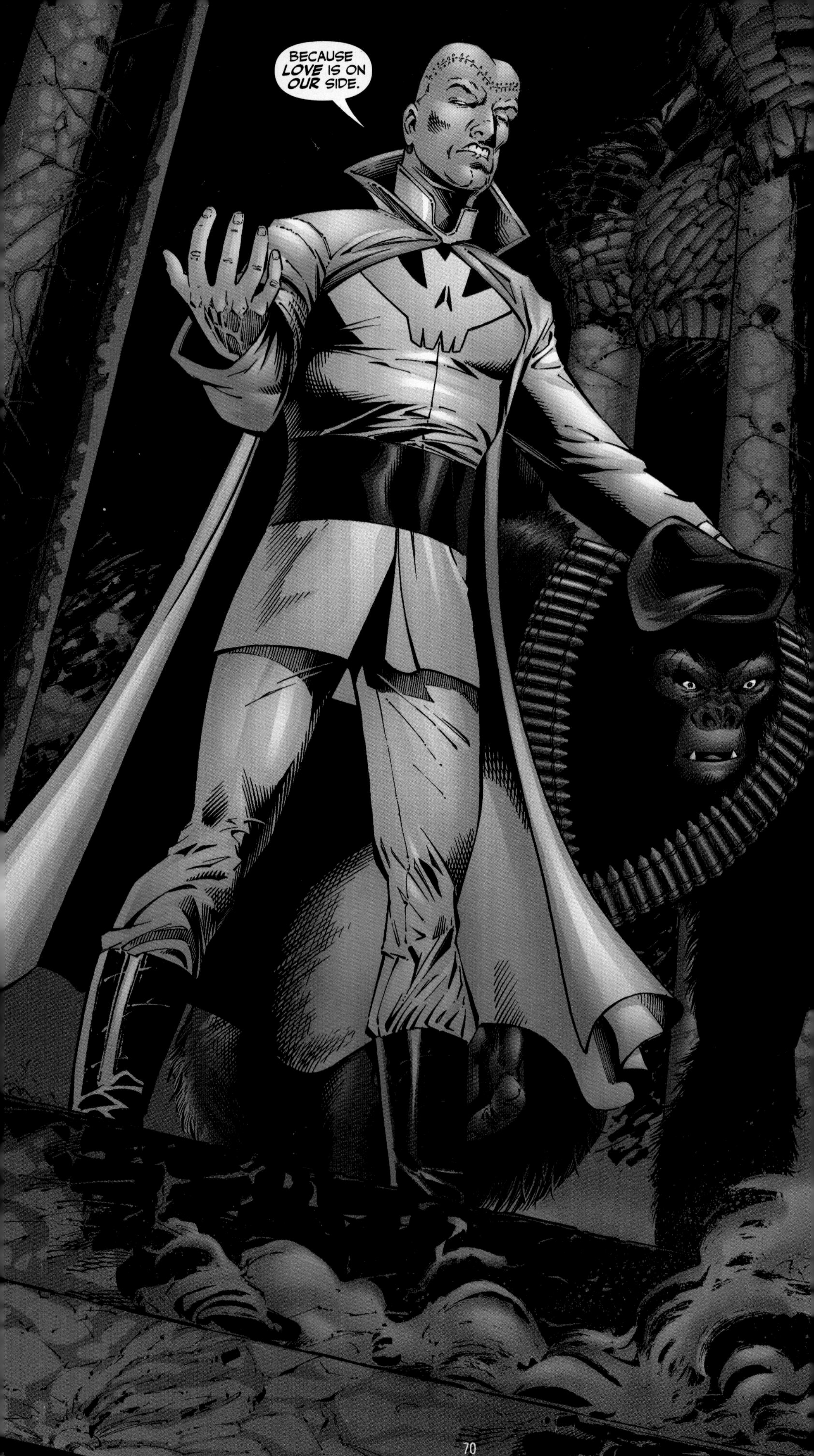
BECAUSE LOVE IS ON OUR SIDE.

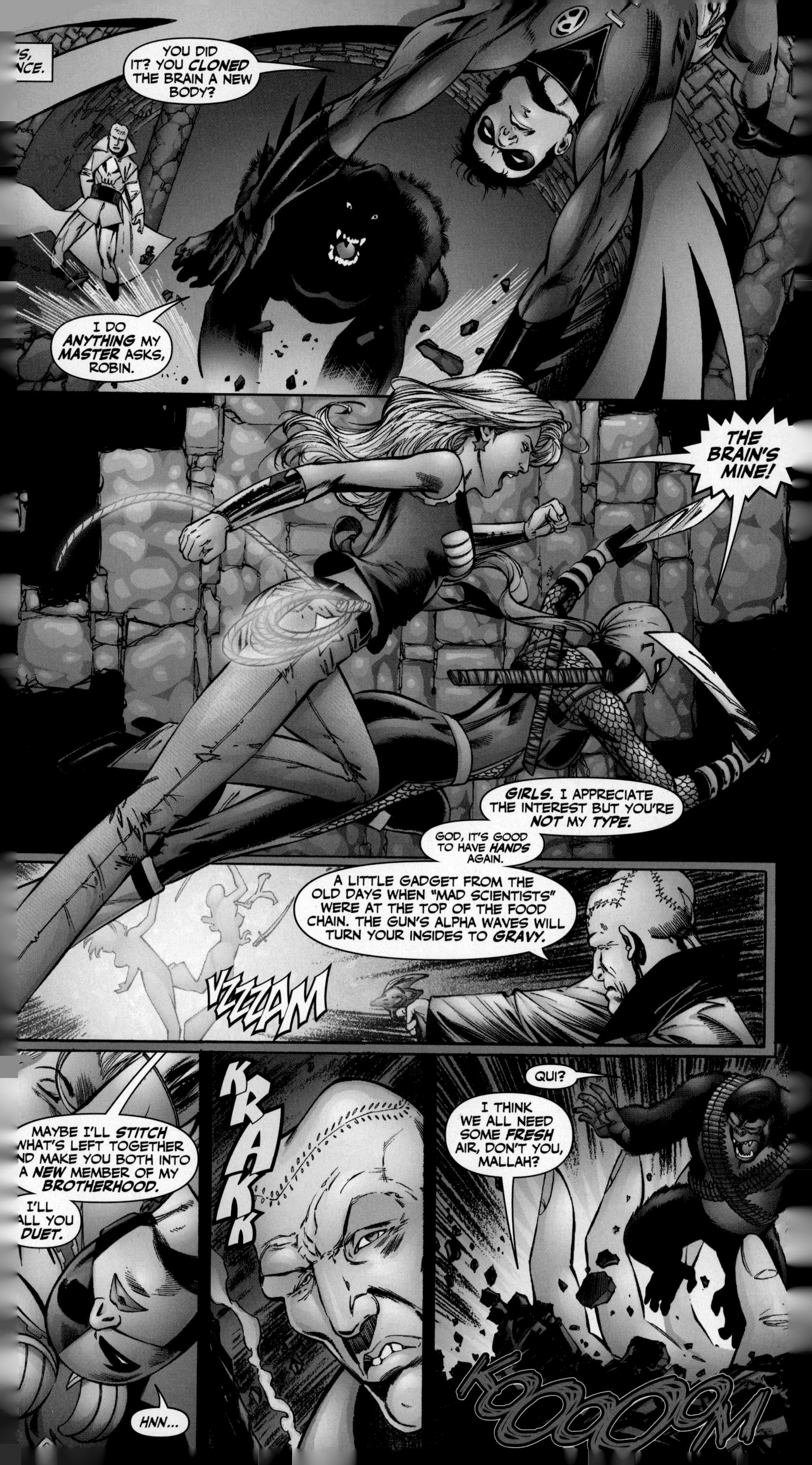
YOU DID IT? YOU CLONED THE BRAIN A NEW BODY?
I DO ANYTHING MY MASTER ASKS, ROBIN.
THE BRAIN'S MINE!
GIRLS. I APPRECIATE THE INTEREST BUT YOU'RE NOT MY TYPE.
GOD, IT'S GOOD TO HAVE HANDS AGAIN.
A LITTLE GADGET FROM THE OLD DAYS WHEN "MAD SCIENTISTS" WERE AT THE TOP OF THE FOOD CHAIN. THE GUN'S ALPHA WAVES WILL TURN YOUR INSIDES TO GRAVY.
VZZZAM
MAYBE I'LL STITCH WHAT'S LEFT TOGETHER ND MAKE YOU BOTH INTO A NEW MEMBER OF MY BROTHERHOOD.
I'LL ALL YOU DUET.
HNN...
KRAKK
QUI?
I THINK WE ALL NEED SOME FRESH AIR, DON'T YOU, MALLAH?
KOOOOOM

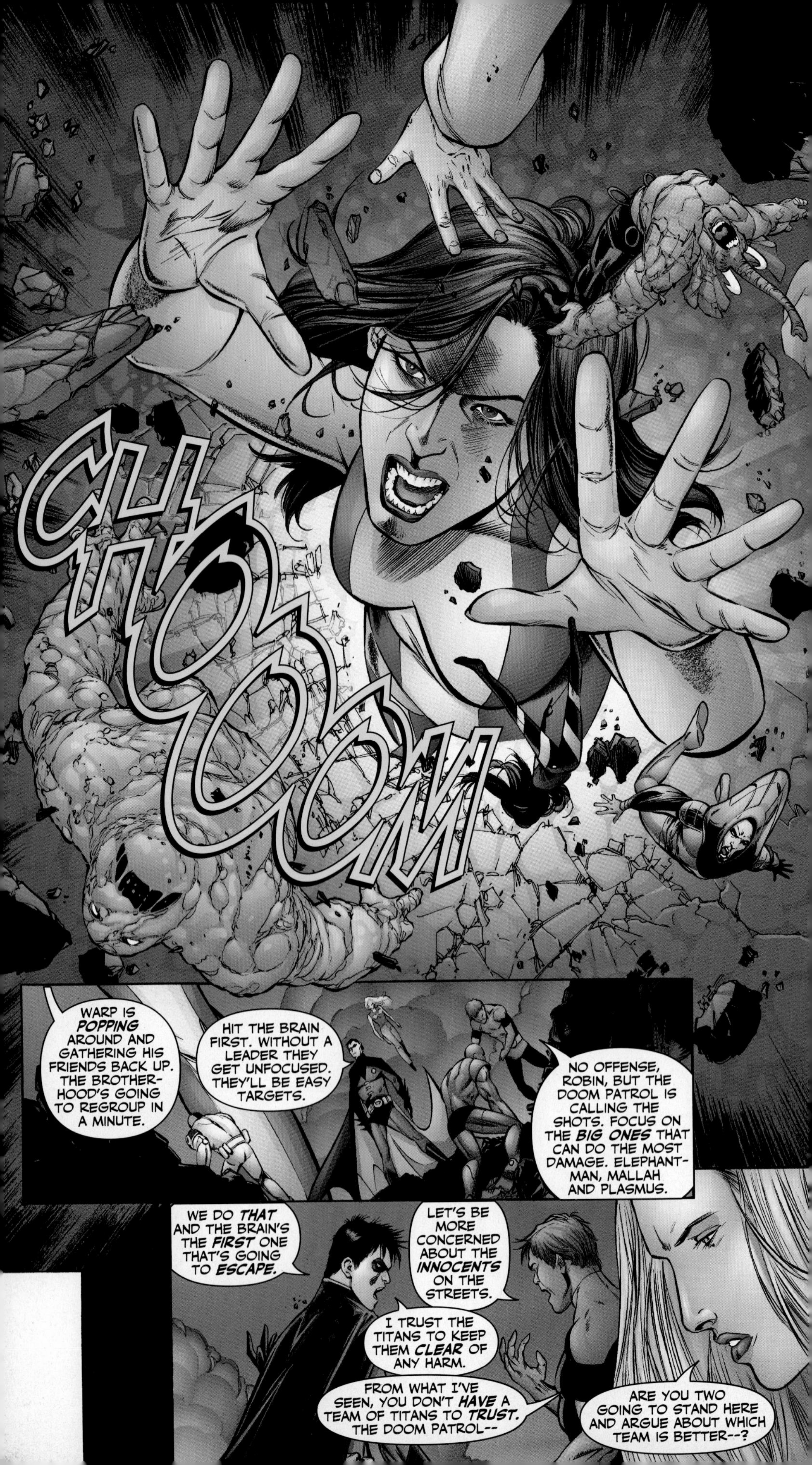
CHOOOM
WARP IS POPPING AROUND AND GATHERING HIS FRIENDS BACK UP. THE BROTHER-HOOD'S GOING TO REGROUP IN A MINUTE.
HIT THE BRAIN FIRST. WITHOUT A LEADER THEY GET UNFOCUSED. THEY'LL BE EASY TARGETS.
NO OFFENSE, ROBIN, BUT THE DOOM PATROL IS CALLING THE SHOTS. FOCUS ON THE BIG ONES THAT CAN DO THE MOST DAMAGE. ELEPHANT-MAN, MALLAH AND PLASMUS.
WE DO THAT AND THE BRAIN'S THE FIRST ONE THAT'S GOING TO ESCAPE.
LET'S BE MORE CONCERNED ABOUT THE INNOCENTS ON THE STREETS.
I TRUST THE TITANS TO KEEP THEM CLEAR OF ANY HARM.
FROM WHAT I'VE SEEN, YOU DON'T HAVE A TEAM OF TITANS TO TRUST. THE DOOM PATROL--
ARE YOU TWO GOING TO STAND HERE AND ARGUE ABOUT WHICH TEAM IS BETTER--?

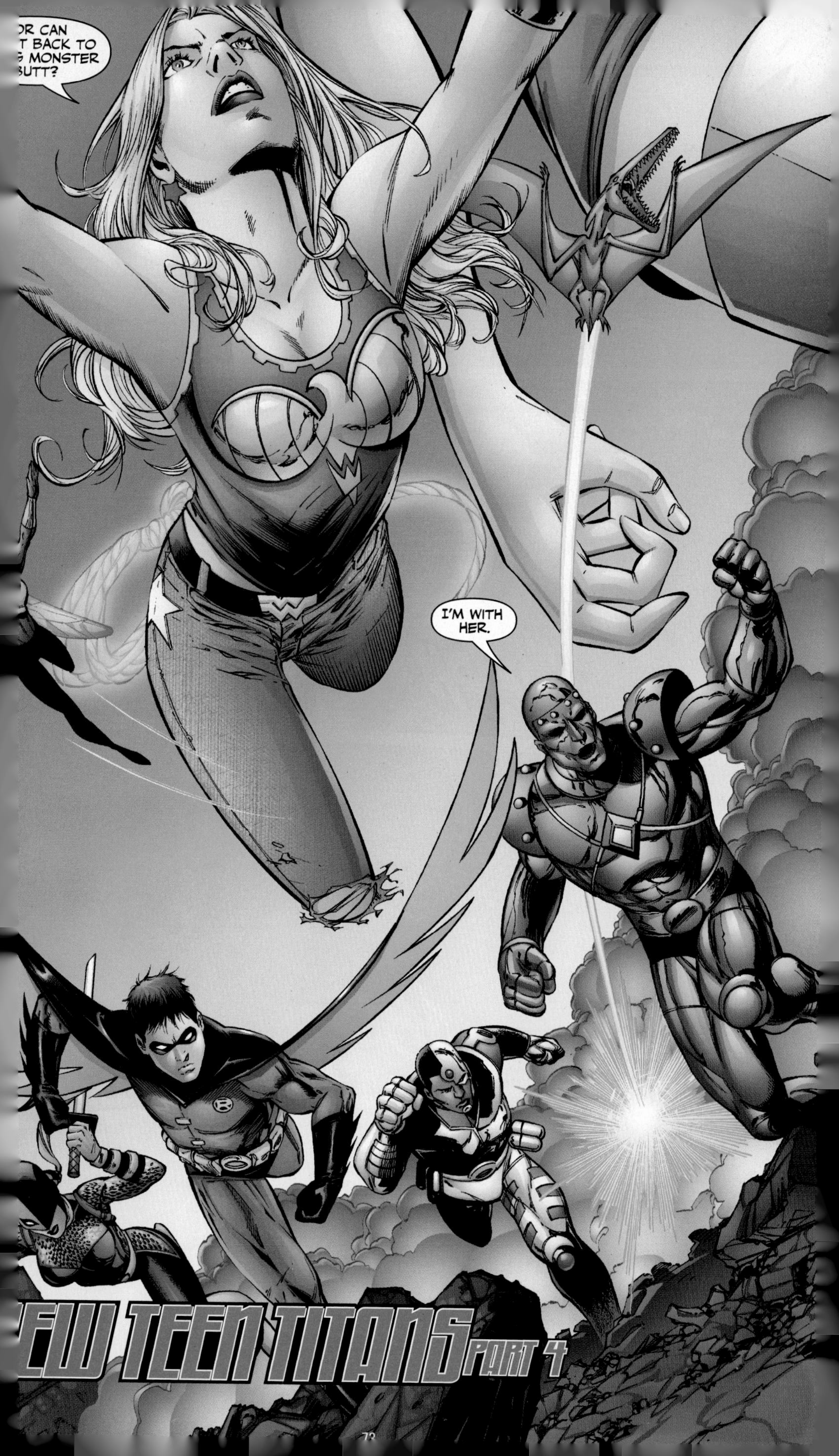
OR CAN
T BACK TO
G MONSTER
BUTT?
I'M WITH HER.
EW TEEN TITANS PART 4

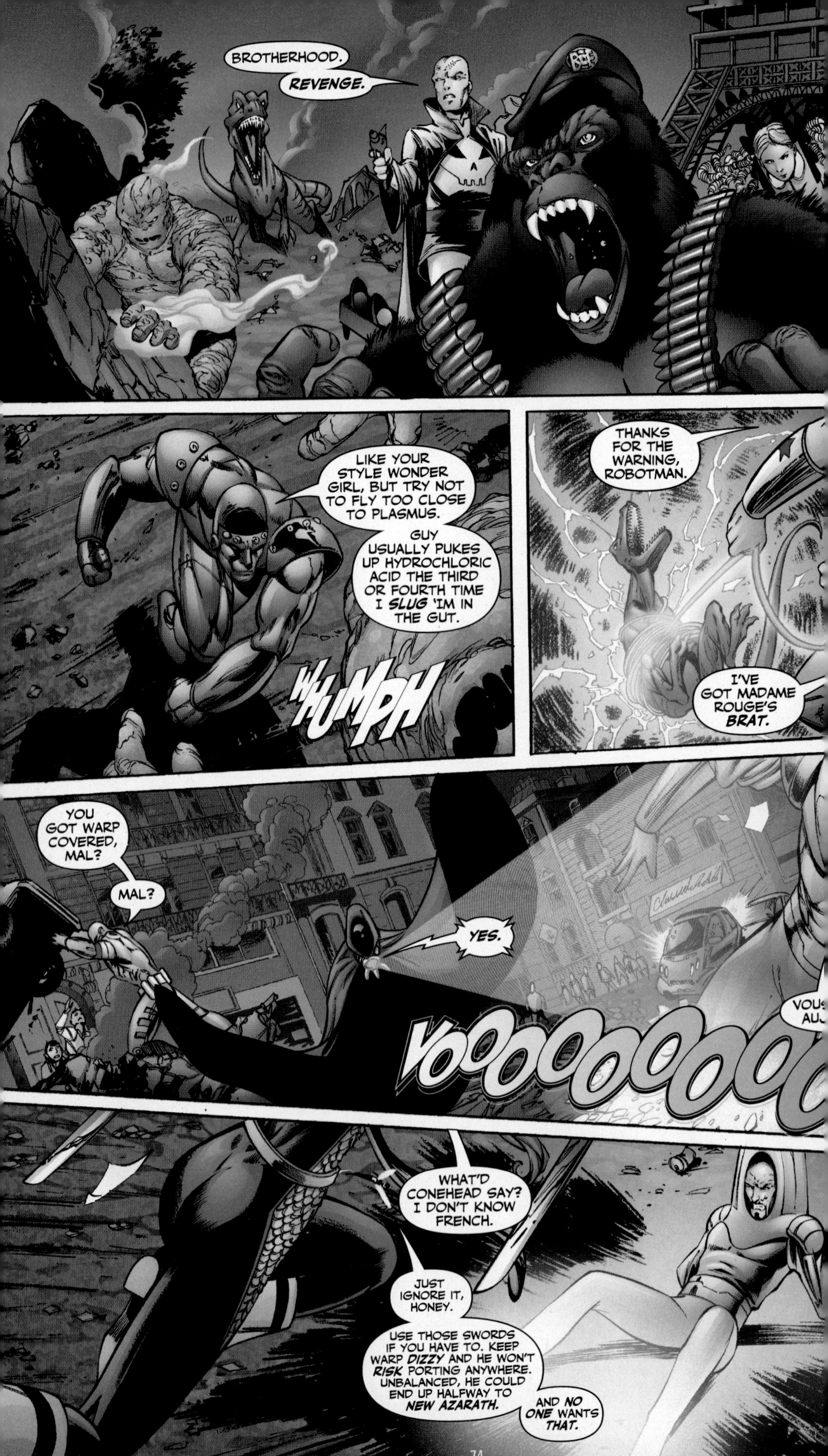

BROTHERHOOD.
REVENGE.
LIKE YOUR STYLE WONDER GIRL, BUT TRY NOT TO FLY TOO CLOSE TO PLASMUS.
GUY USUALLY PUKES UP HYDROCHLORIC ACID THE THIRD OR FOURTH TIME I SLUG 'IM IN THE GUT.
WHUMPH
THANKS FOR THE WARNING, ROBOTMAN.
I'VE GOT MADAME ROUGE'S BRAT.
YOU GOT WARP COVERED, MAL?
MAL?
YES.
YOOOOOOOOOO
WHAT'D CONEHEAD SAY? I DON'T KNOW FRENCH.
JUST IGNORE IT, HONEY.
USE THOSE SWORDS IF YOU HAVE TO. KEEP WARP DIZZY AND HE WON'T RISK PORTING ANYWHERE. UNBALANCED, HE COULD END UP HALFWAY TO NEW AZARATH.
AND NO ONE WANTS THAT.

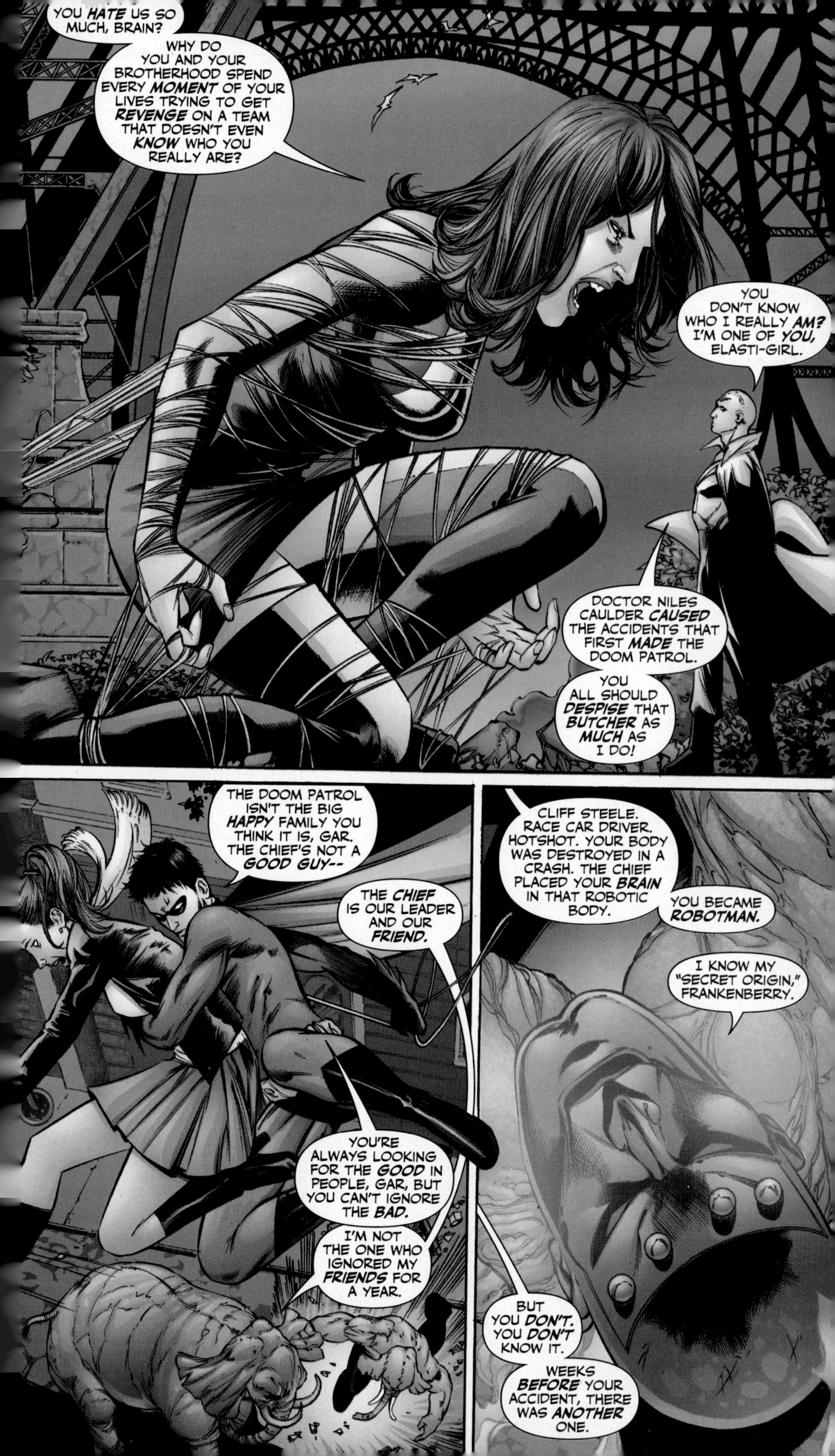

YOU HATE US SO MUCH, BRAIN?
WHY DO YOU AND YOUR BROTHERHOOD SPEND EVERY MOMENT OF YOUR LIVES TRYING TO GET REVENGE ON A TEAM THAT DOESN'T EVEN KNOW WHO YOU REALLY ARE?
YOU DON'T KNOW WHO I REALLY AM? I'M ONE OF YOU, ELASTI-GIRL.
DOCTOR NILES CAULDER CAUSED THE ACCIDENTS THAT FIRST MADE THE DOOM PATROL.
YOU ALL SHOULD DESPISE THAT BUTCHER AS MUCH AS I DO!
THE DOOM PATROL ISN'T THE BIG HAPPY FAMILY YOU THINK IT IS, GAR. THE CHIEF'S NOT A GOOD GUY--
THE CHIEF IS OUR LEADER AND OUR FRIEND.
YOU'RE ALWAYS LOOKING FOR THE GOOD IN PEOPLE, GAR, BUT YOU CAN'T IGNORE THE BAD.
I'M NOT THE ONE WHO IGNORED MY FRIENDS FOR A YEAR.
CLIFF STEELE. RACE CAR DRIVER. HOTSHOT. YOUR BODY WAS DESTROYED IN A CRASH. THE CHIEF PLACED YOUR BRAIN IN THAT ROBOTIC BODY.
YOU BECAME ROBOTMAN.
I KNOW MY "SECRET ORIGIN," FRANKENBERRY.
BUT YOU DON'T. YOU DON'T KNOW IT.
WEEKS BEFORE YOUR ACCIDENT, THERE WAS ANOTHER ONE.

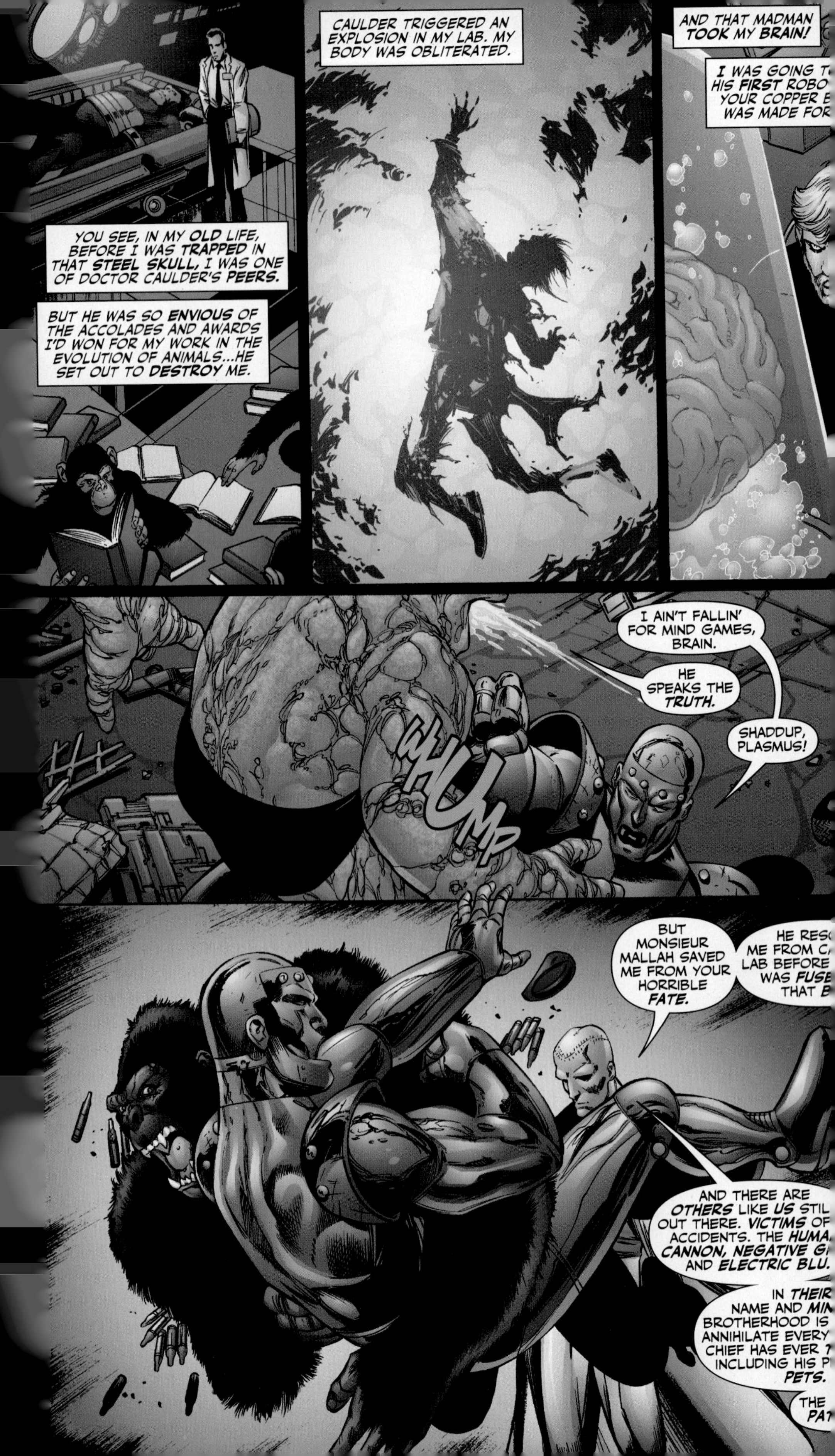
YOU SEE, IN MY OLD LIFE, BEFORE I WAS TRAPPED IN THAT STEEL SKULL, I WAS ONE OF DOCTOR CAULDER'S PEERS.
BUT HE WAS SO ENVIOUS OF THE ACCOLADES AND AWARDS I'D WON FOR MY WORK IN THE EVOLUTION OF ANIMALS...HE SET OUT TO DESTROY ME.
CAULDER TRIGGERED AN EXPLOSION IN MY LAB. MY BODY WAS OBLITERATED.
AND THAT MADMAN TOOK MY BRAIN!
I WAS GOING T HIS FIRST ROBO YOUR COPPER B WAS MADE FOR
I AIN'T FALLIN' FOR MIND GAMES, BRAIN.
HE SPEAKS THE TRUTH.
SHADDUP, PLASMUS!
WHUMP
BUT MONSIEUR MALLAH SAVED ME FROM YOUR HORRIBLE FATE.
HE RESC ME FROM C LAB BEFORE WAS FUSE THAT B
AND THERE ARE OTHERS LIKE US STIL OUT THERE. VICTIMS OF ACCIDENTS. THE HUMA CANNON, NEGATIVE G AND ELECTRIC BLU
IN THEIR NAME AND MIN BROTHERHOOD IS ANNIHILATE EVERY CHIEF HAS EVER INCLUDING HIS P PETS.
THE PAT

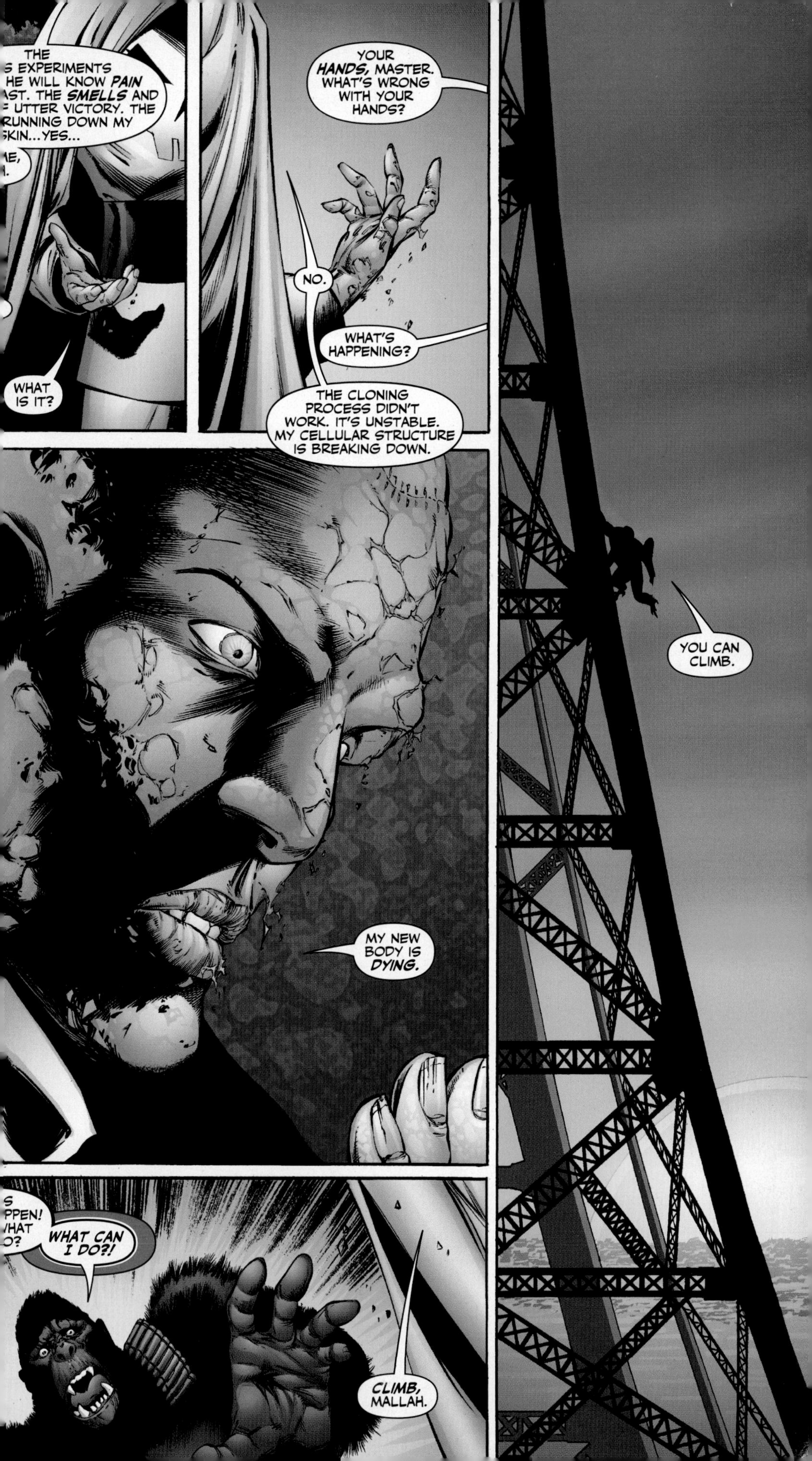
THE
S EXPERIMENTS
HE WILL KNOW *PAIN*
AST. THE *SMELLS* AND
F UTTER VICTORY. THE
RUNNING DOWN MY
SKIN...YES...
YOUR *HANDS,* MASTER. WHAT'S WRONG WITH YOUR HANDS?
NO.
WHAT'S HAPPENING?
WHAT IS IT?
THE CLONING PROCESS DIDN'T WORK. IT'S UNSTABLE. MY CELLULAR STRUCTURE IS BREAKING DOWN.
MY NEW BODY IS *DYING.*
YOU CAN CLIMB.
PPEN!
WHAT CAN I DO?!
CLIMB, MALLAH.

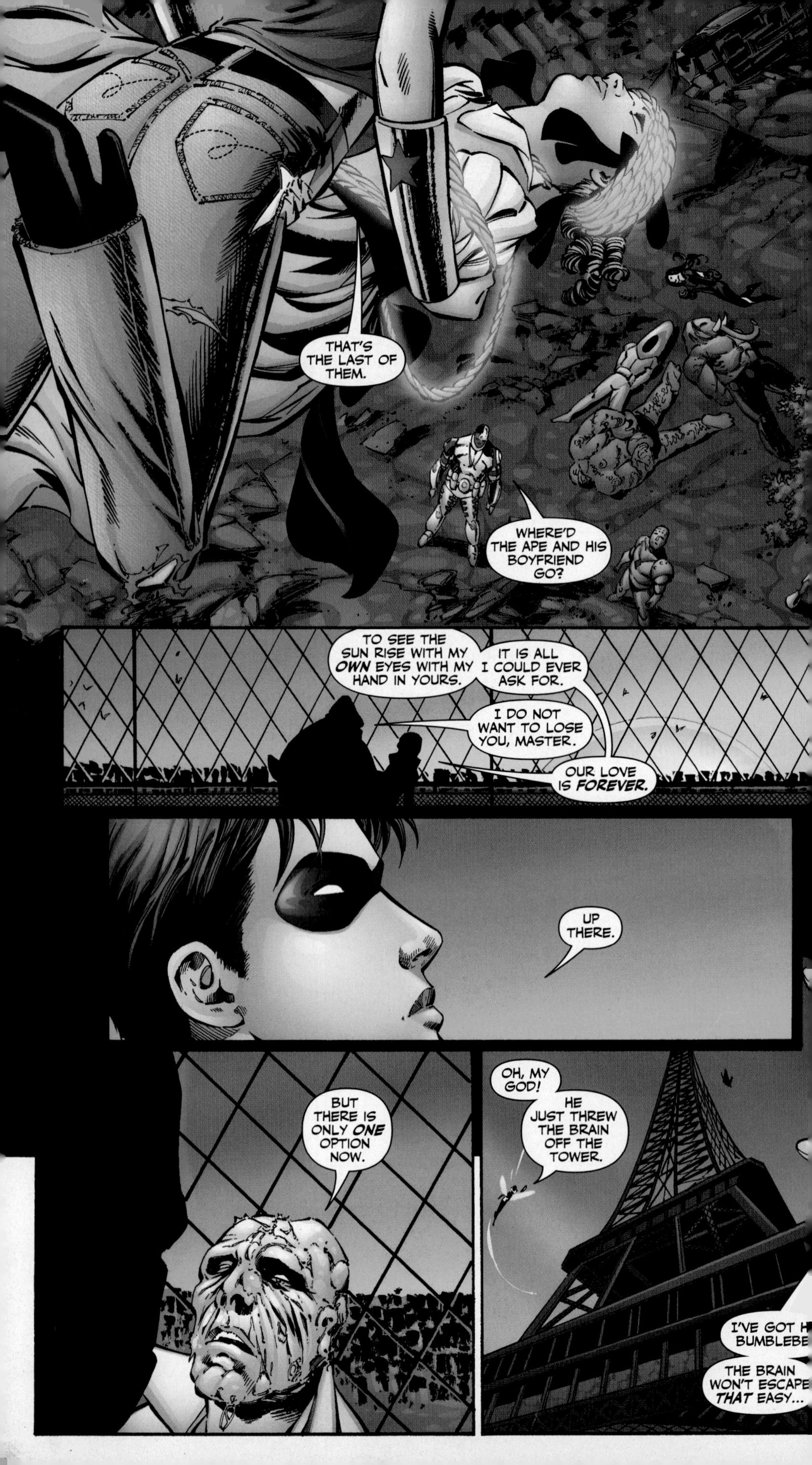
THAT'S THE LAST OF THEM.
WHERE'D THE APE AND HIS BOYFRIEND GO?
TO SEE THE SUN RISE WITH MY *OWN* EYES WITH MY HAND IN YOURS.
IT IS ALL I COULD EVER ASK FOR.
I DO NOT WANT TO LOSE YOU, MASTER.
OUR LOVE IS ***FOREVER.***
UP THERE.
BUT THERE IS ONLY *ONE* OPTION NOW.
OH, MY GOD!
HE JUST THREW THE BRAIN OFF THE TOWER.
THE BRAIN WON'T ESCAPE *THAT* EASY...

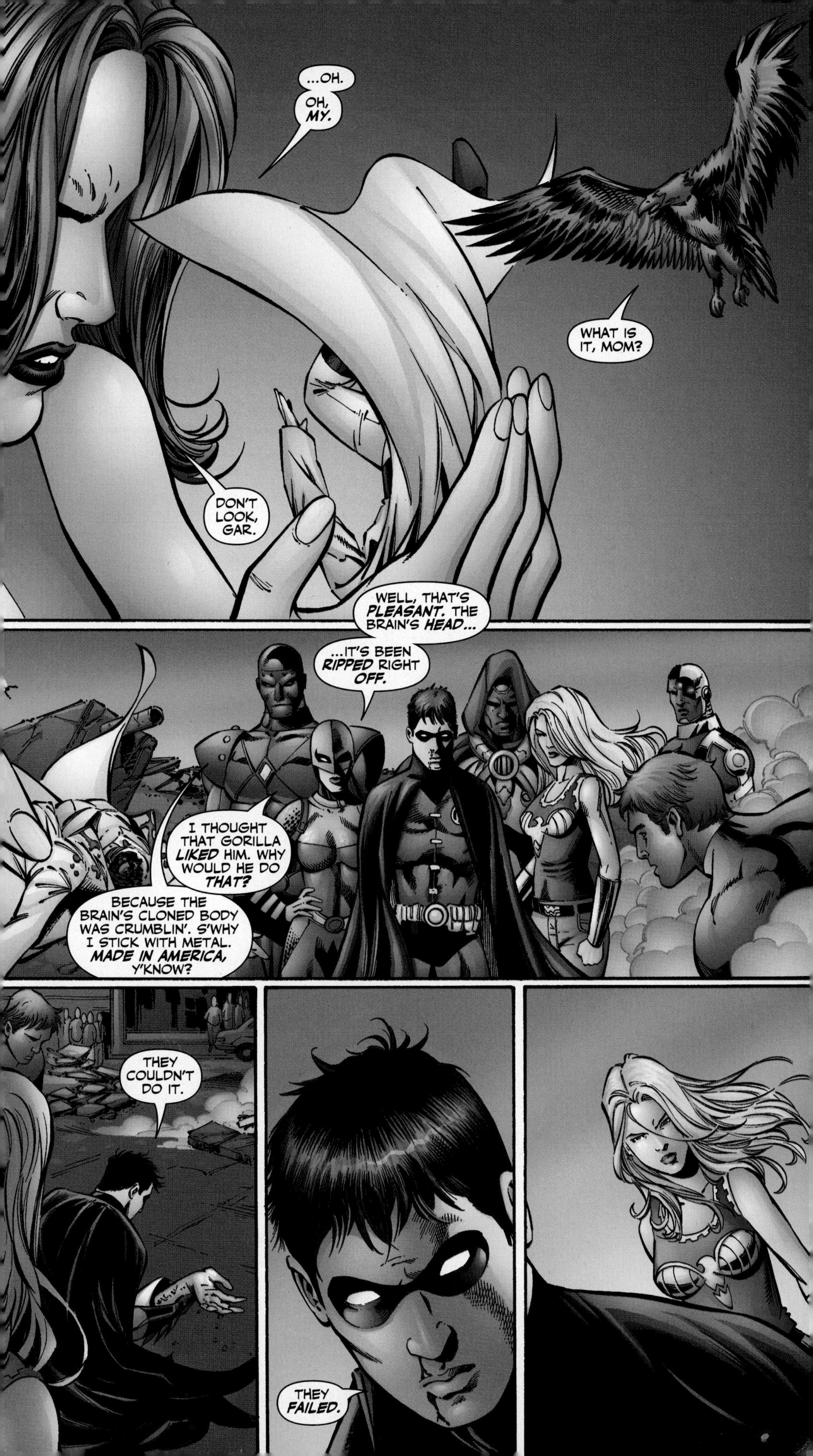
...OH.
OH, MY.
WHAT IS IT, MOM?
DON'T LOOK, GAR.
WELL, THAT'S PLEASANT. THE BRAIN'S HEAD...
...IT'S BEEN RIPPED RIGHT OFF.
I THOUGHT THAT GORILLA LIKED HIM. WHY WOULD HE DO THAT?
BECAUSE THE BRAIN'S CLONED BODY WAS CRUMBLIN'. S'WHY I STICK WITH METAL. MADE IN AMERICA, Y'KNOW?
THEY COULDN'T DO IT.
THEY FAILED.

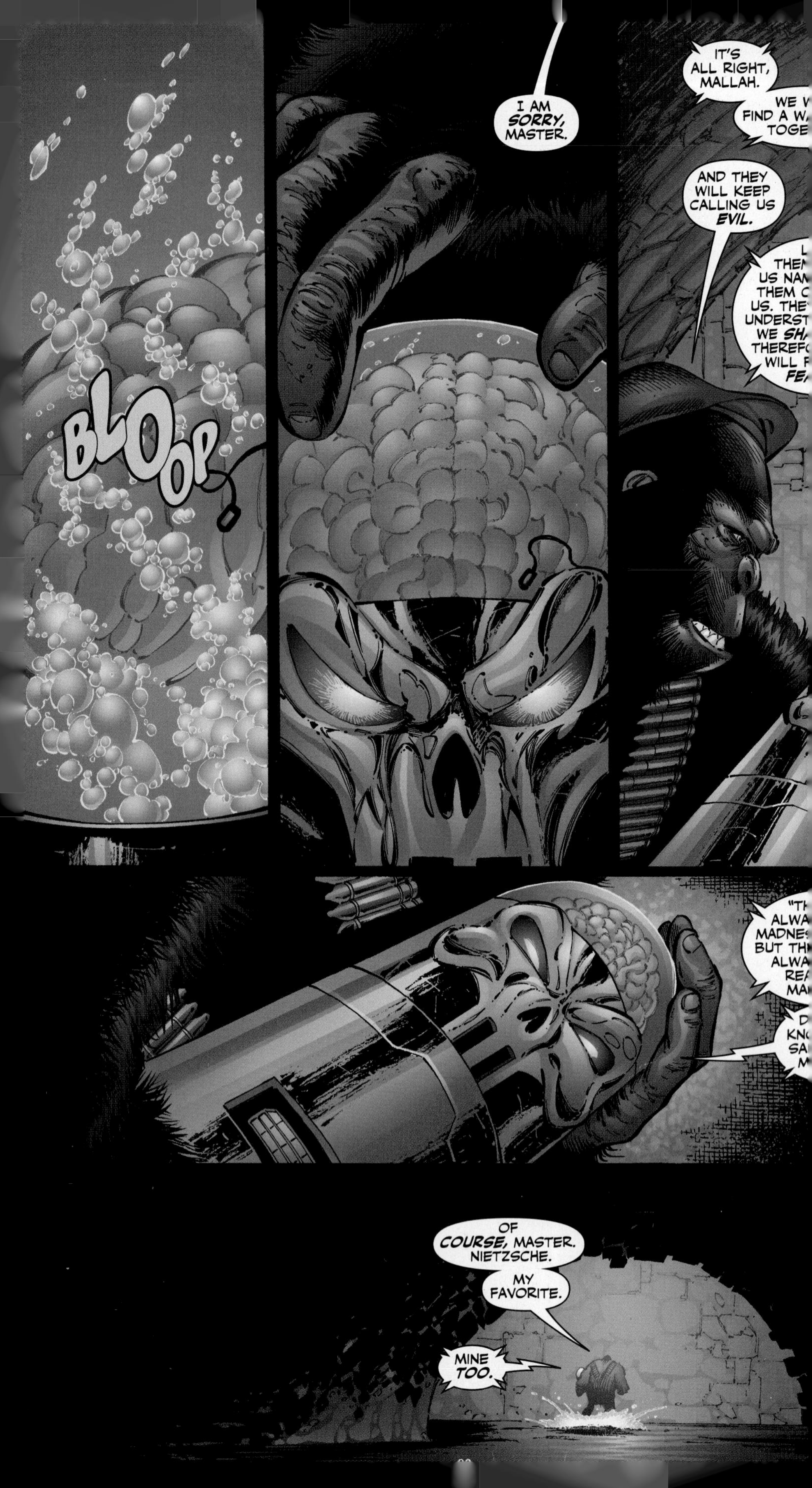
BLOOP
I AM *SORRY,* MASTER.
IT'S ALL RIGHT, MALLAH.
AND THEY WILL KEEP CALLING US *EVIL.*
OF *COURSE,* MASTER. NIETZSCHE.
MY FAVORITE.
MINE *TOO.*

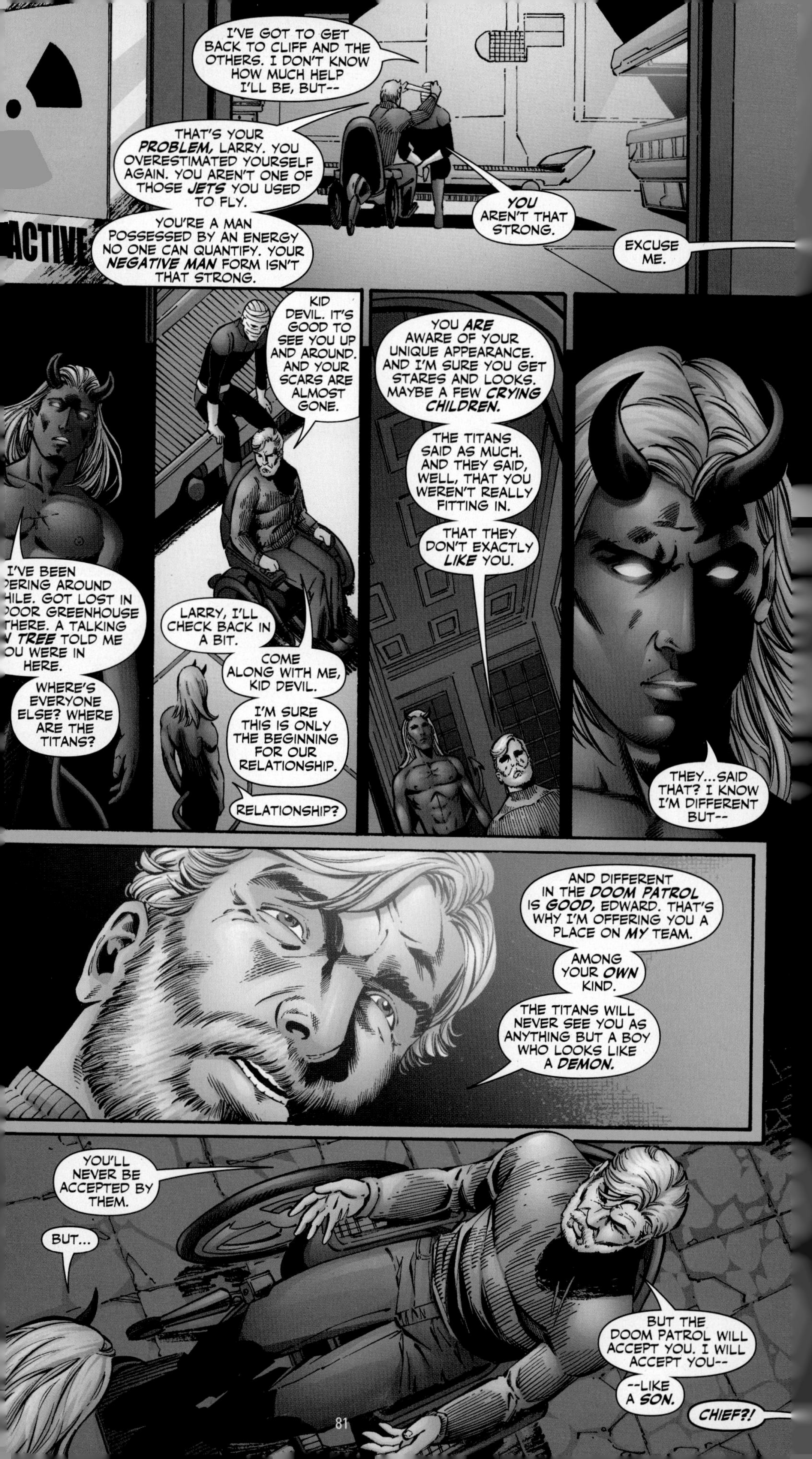

I'VE GOT TO GET BACK TO CLIFF AND THE OTHERS. I DON'T KNOW HOW MUCH HELP I'LL BE, BUT--
THAT'S YOUR PROBLEM, LARRY. YOU OVERESTIMATED YOURSELF AGAIN. YOU AREN'T ONE OF THOSE JETS YOU USED TO FLY.
YOU'RE A MAN POSSESSED BY AN ENERGY NO ONE CAN QUANTIFY. YOUR NEGATIVE MAN FORM ISN'T THAT STRONG.
YOU AREN'T THAT STRONG.
EXCUSE ME.
ACTIVE
I'VE BEEN PERING AROUND HILE. GOT LOST IN DOOR GREENHOUSE THERE. A TALKING TREE TOLD ME OU WERE IN HERE.
WHERE'S EVERYONE ELSE? WHERE ARE THE TITANS?
KID DEVIL. IT'S GOOD TO SEE YOU UP AND AROUND. AND YOUR SCARS ARE ALMOST GONE.
LARRY, I'LL CHECK BACK IN A BIT.
COME ALONG WITH ME, KID DEVIL.
I'M SURE THIS IS ONLY THE BEGINNING FOR OUR RELATIONSHIP.
RELATIONSHIP?
YOU ARE AWARE OF YOUR UNIQUE APPEARANCE. AND I'M SURE YOU GET STARES AND LOOKS. MAYBE A FEW CRYING CHILDREN.
THE TITANS SAID AS MUCH. AND THEY SAID, WELL, THAT YOU WEREN'T REALLY FITTING IN.
THAT THEY DON'T EXACTLY LIKE YOU.
THEY...SAID THAT? I KNOW I'M DIFFERENT BUT--
AND DIFFERENT IN THE DOOM PATROL IS GOOD, EDWARD. THAT'S WHY I'M OFFERING YOU A PLACE ON MY TEAM.
AMONG YOUR OWN KIND.
THE TITANS WILL NEVER SEE YOU AS ANYTHING BUT A BOY WHO LOOKS LIKE A DEMON.
YOU'LL NEVER BE ACCEPTED BY THEM.
BUT...
BUT THE DOOM PATROL WILL ACCEPT YOU. I WILL ACCEPT YOU--
--LIKE A SON.
CHIEF?!

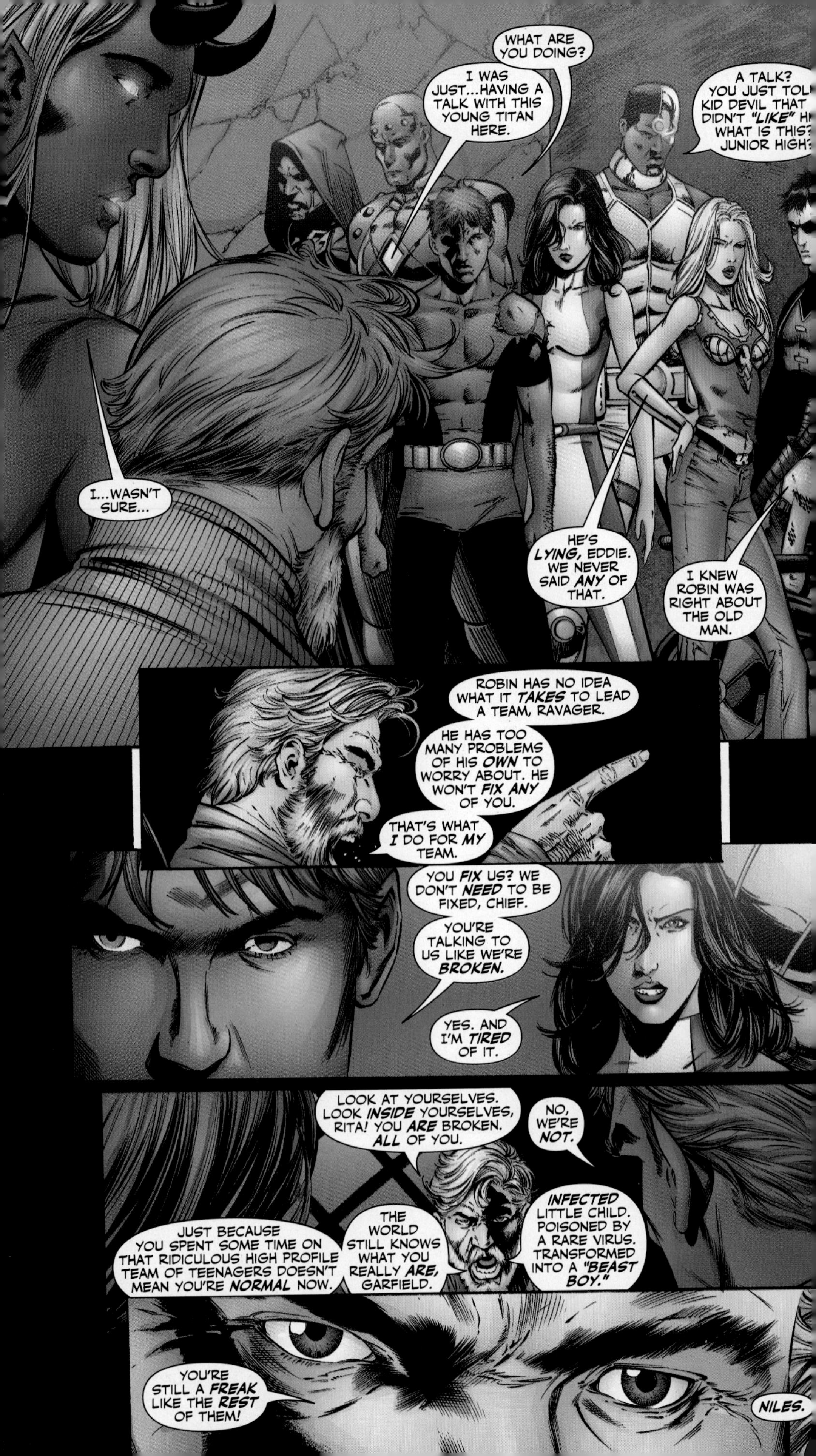

I WAS JUST...HAVING A TALK WITH THIS YOUNG TITAN HERE.
WHAT ARE YOU DOING?
A TALK? YOU JUST TOL KID DEVIL THAT DIDN'T "LIKE" H WHAT IS THIS? JUNIOR HIGH?
I...WASN'T SURE...
HE'S LYING, EDDIE. WE NEVER SAID ANY OF THAT.
I KNEW ROBIN WAS RIGHT ABOUT THE OLD MAN.
ROBIN HAS NO IDEA WHAT IT TAKES TO LEAD A TEAM, RAVAGER.
HE HAS TOO MANY PROBLEMS OF HIS OWN TO WORRY ABOUT. HE WON'T FIX ANY OF YOU.
THAT'S WHAT I DO FOR MY TEAM.
YOU FIX US? WE DON'T NEED TO BE FIXED, CHIEF.
YOU'RE TALKING TO US LIKE WE'RE BROKEN.
YES. AND I'M TIRED OF IT.
LOOK AT YOURSELVES. LOOK INSIDE YOURSELVES, RITA! YOU ARE BROKEN. ALL OF YOU.
NO, WE'RE NOT.
JUST BECAUSE YOU SPENT SOME TIME ON THAT RIDICULOUS HIGH PROFILE TEAM OF TEENAGERS DOESN'T MEAN YOU'RE NORMAL NOW.
THE WORLD STILL KNOWS WHAT YOU REALLY ARE, GARFIELD.
INFECTED LITTLE CHILD. POISONED BY A RARE VIRUS. TRANSFORMED INTO A "BEAST BOY."
YOU'RE STILL A FREAK LIKE THE REST OF THEM!
NILES.

NILES, THAT'S QUITE *ENOUGH*.

I'M THINKING A LITTLE BIT *CLEARER*.

?
NTO-
YOU
T HAVE
OFF.
T

DAD?

IF YOU WANT TO *STAY* ON THIS TEAM, AND IN *MY* HOUSE, AS A *MEMBER* OF THE DOOM PATROL, FINE. BUT YOU'RE NOT THE *LEADER* HERE ANYMORE.

AND IF YOU EVER, *EVER* SPEAK TO MY SON OR WIFE OR *ANY* OF US LIKE THAT AGAIN, I'LL DOWNGRADE YOUR I.Q. INTO A CHIMP'S.

ND
AVE
D TO
AND
THE
THEIR
SN'T
OU
RE,
S.

I...

DO YOU *UNDERSTAND* ME?

...IF YOU NEED ME I'LL BE IN MY LAB.

83

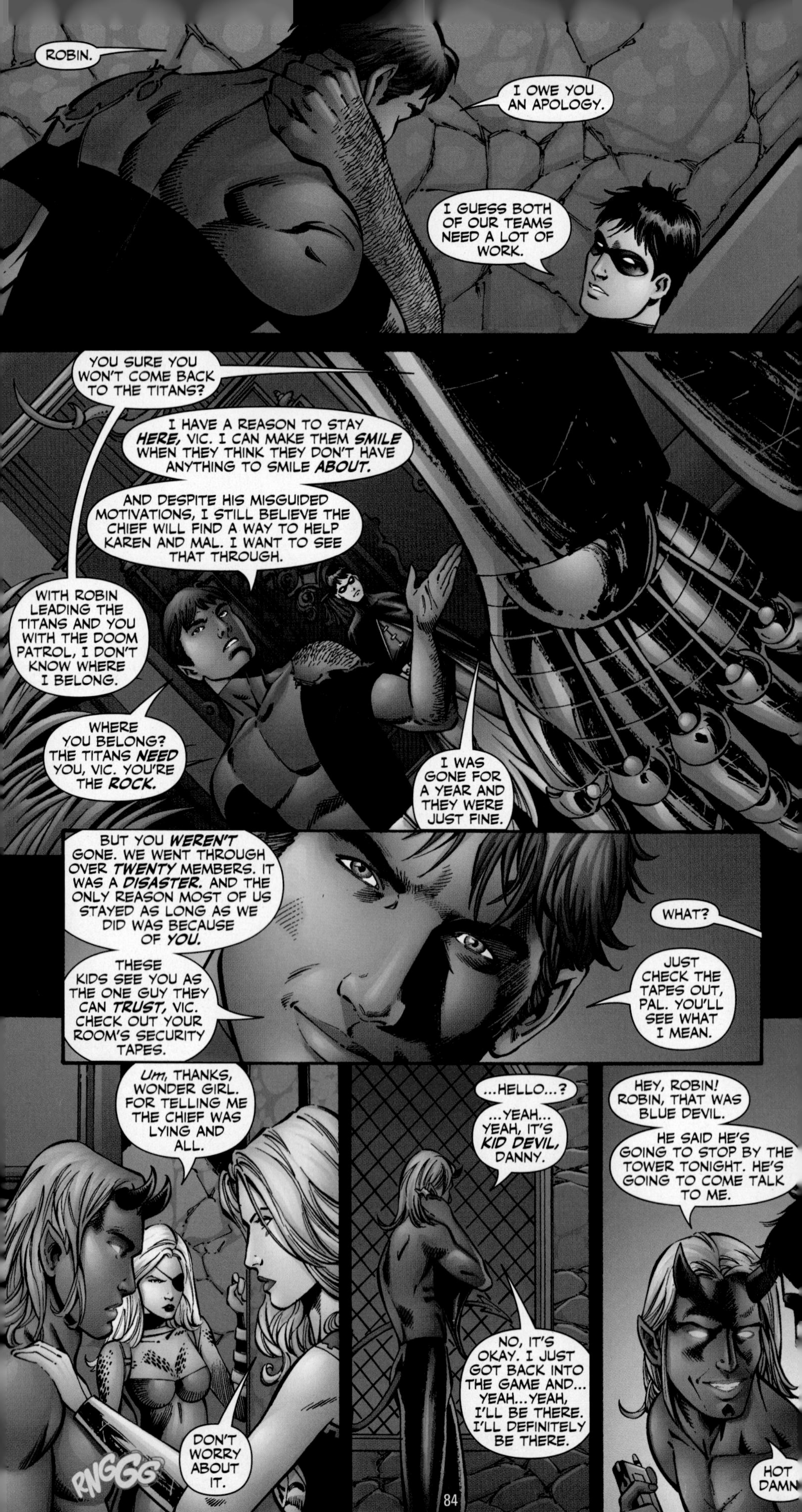
ROBIN.
I OWE YOU AN APOLOGY.
I GUESS BOTH OF OUR TEAMS NEED A LOT OF WORK.
YOU SURE YOU WON'T COME BACK TO THE TITANS?
I HAVE A REASON TO STAY HERE, VIC. I CAN MAKE THEM SMILE WHEN THEY THINK THEY DON'T HAVE ANYTHING TO SMILE ABOUT.
AND DESPITE HIS MISGUIDED MOTIVATIONS, I STILL BELIEVE THE CHIEF WILL FIND A WAY TO HELP KAREN AND MAL. I WANT TO SEE THAT THROUGH.
WITH ROBIN LEADING THE TITANS AND YOU WITH THE DOOM PATROL, I DON'T KNOW WHERE I BELONG.
WHERE YOU BELONG? THE TITANS NEED YOU, VIC. YOU'RE THE ROCK.
I WAS GONE FOR A YEAR AND THEY WERE JUST FINE.
BUT YOU WEREN'T GONE. WE WENT THROUGH OVER TWENTY MEMBERS. IT WAS A DISASTER. AND THE ONLY REASON MOST OF US STAYED AS LONG AS WE DID WAS BECAUSE OF YOU.
THESE KIDS SEE YOU AS THE ONE GUY THEY CAN TRUST, VIC. CHECK OUT YOUR ROOM'S SECURITY TAPES.
WHAT?
JUST CHECK THE TAPES OUT, PAL. YOU'LL SEE WHAT I MEAN.
Um, THANKS, WONDER GIRL. FOR TELLING ME THE CHIEF WAS LYING AND ALL.
DON'T WORRY ABOUT IT.
RNGGG
...HELLO...?
...YEAH... YEAH, IT'S KID DEVIL, DANNY.
NO, IT'S OKAY. I JUST GOT BACK INTO THE GAME AND... YEAH...YEAH, I'LL BE THERE. I'LL DEFINITELY BE THERE.
HEY, ROBIN! ROBIN, THAT WAS BLUE DEVIL.
HE SAID HE'S GOING TO STOP BY THE TOWER TONIGHT. HE'S GOING TO COME TALK TO ME.
HOT DAMN

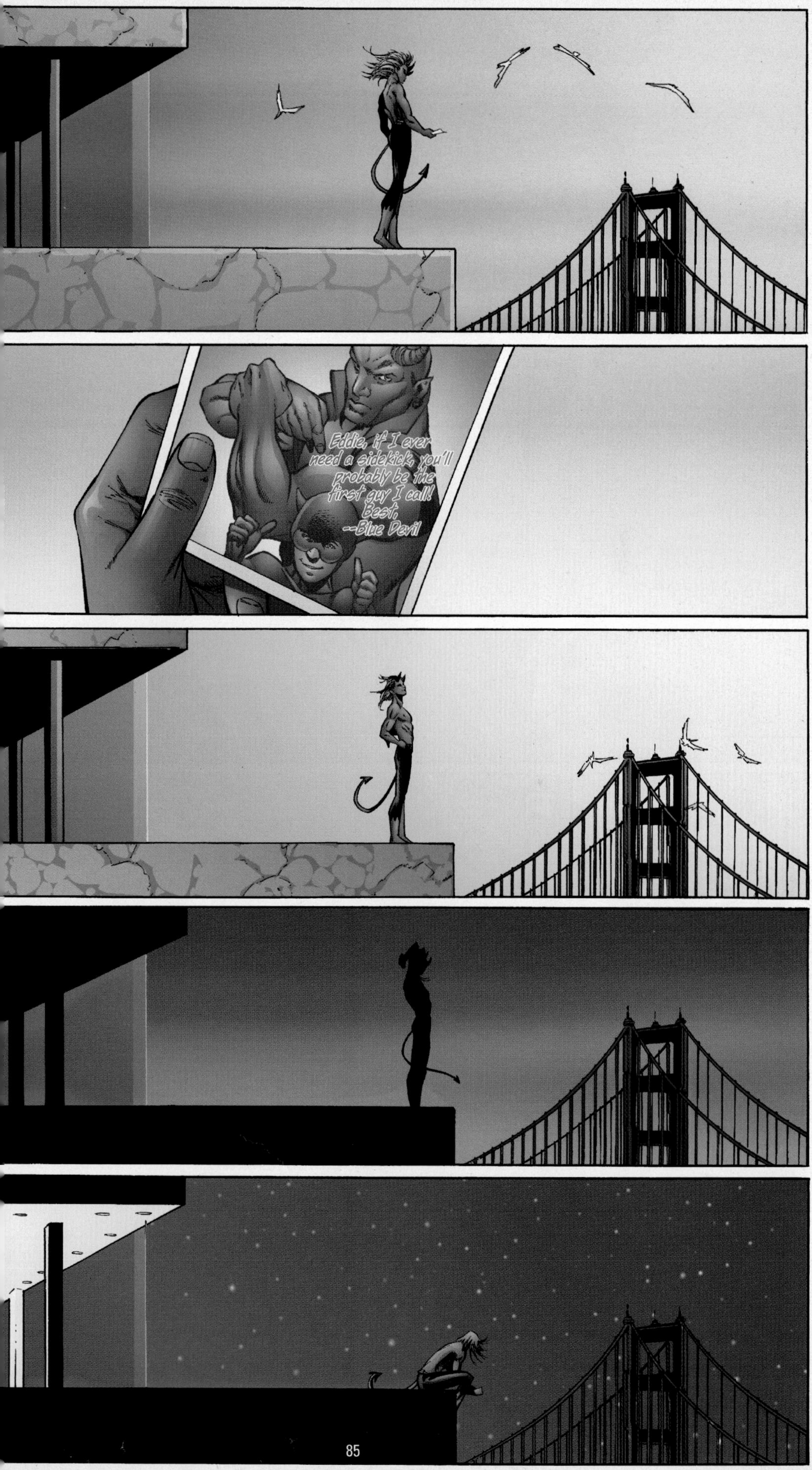
Eddie, if I ever need a sidekick, you'll probably be the first guy I call! Best, --Blue Devil

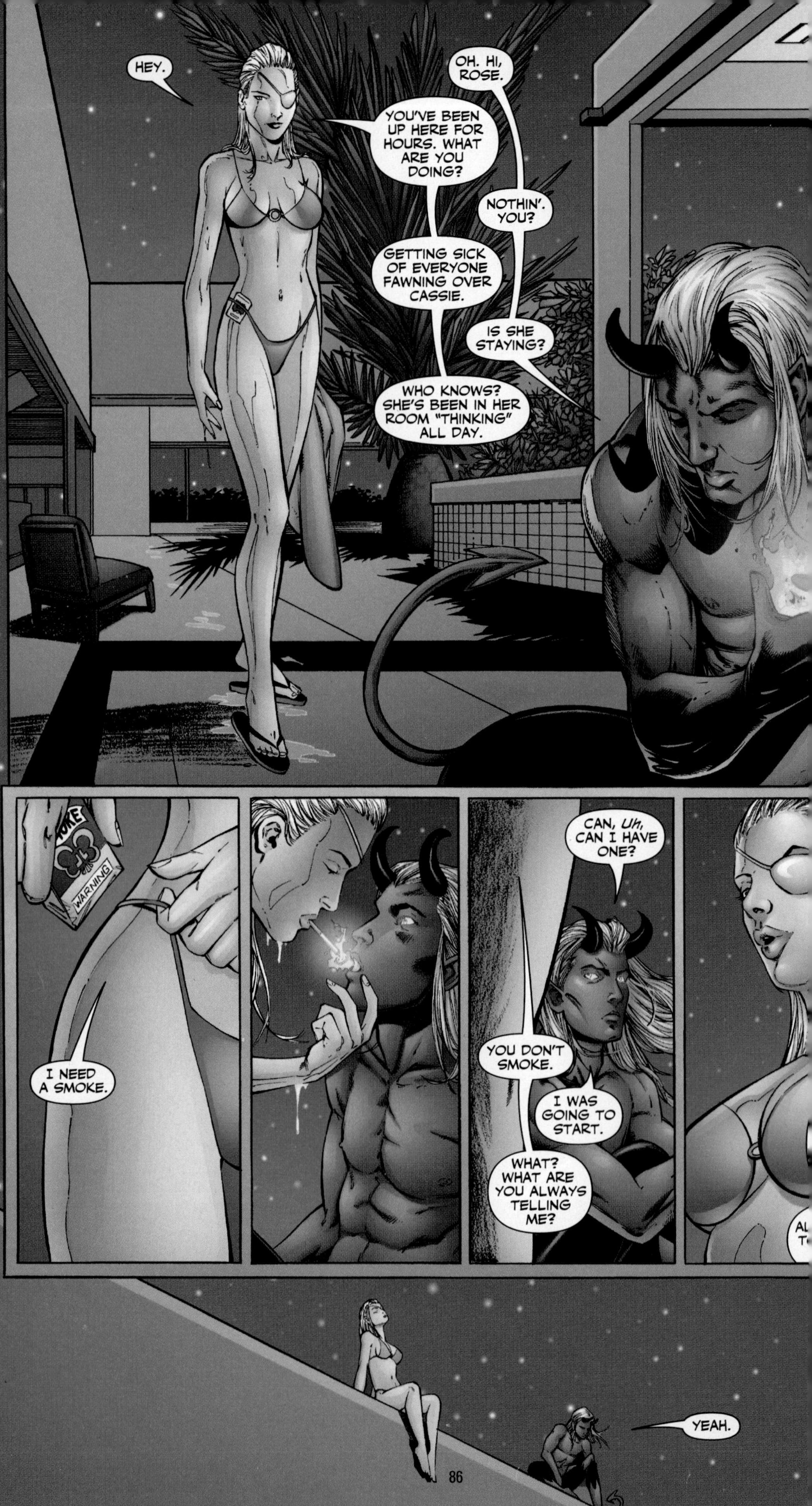
HEY.
OH. HI, ROSE.
YOU'VE BEEN UP HERE FOR HOURS. WHAT ARE YOU DOING?
NOTHIN'. YOU?
GETTING SICK OF EVERYONE FAWNING OVER CASSIE.
IS SHE STAYING?
WHO KNOWS? SHE'S BEEN IN HER ROOM "THINKING" ALL DAY.
WARNING
I NEED A SMOKE.
CAN, *UH*, CAN I HAVE ONE?
YOU DON'T SMOKE.
I WAS GOING TO START.
WHAT? WHAT ARE YOU ALWAYS TELLING ME?
YEAH.

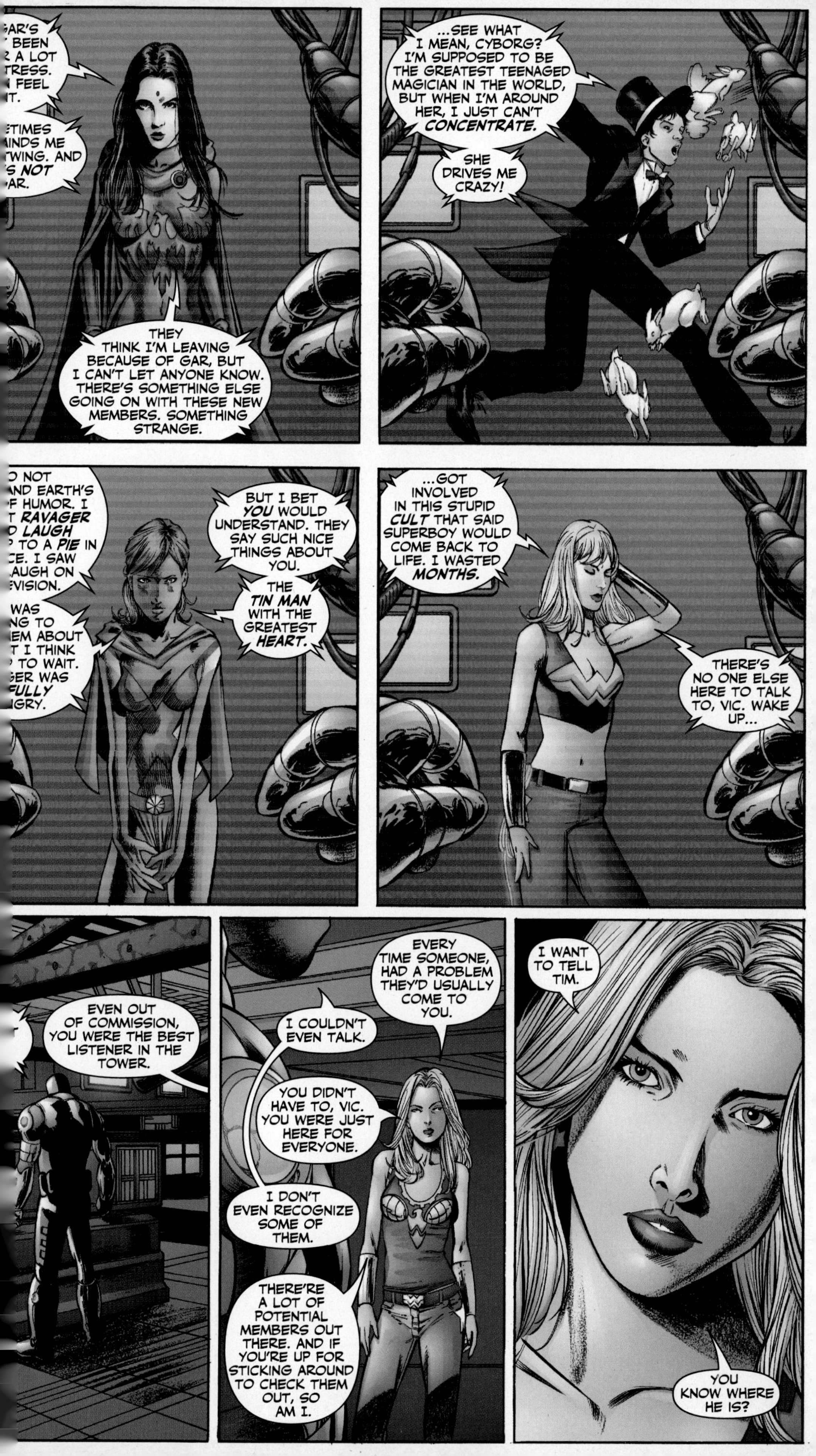

GAR'S BEEN A LOT TRESS. FEEL T.
ETIMES MINDS ME TWING. AND 'S NOT AR.
THEY THINK I'M LEAVING BECAUSE OF GAR, BUT I CAN'T LET ANYONE KNOW. THERE'S SOMETHING ELSE GOING ON WITH THESE NEW MEMBERS. SOMETHING STRANGE.
...SEE WHAT I MEAN, CYBORG? I'M SUPPOSED TO BE THE GREATEST TEENAGED MAGICIAN IN THE WORLD, BUT WHEN I'M AROUND HER, I JUST CAN'T CONCENTRATE.
SHE DRIVES ME CRAZY!
O NOT AND EARTH'S F HUMOR. I T RAVAGER D LAUGH P TO A PIE IN CE. I SAW AUGH ON EVISION.
WAS NG TO EM ABOUT T I THINK P TO WAIT. GER WAS FULLY NGRY.
BUT I BET YOU WOULD UNDERSTAND. THEY SAY SUCH NICE THINGS ABOUT YOU.
THE TIN MAN WITH THE GREATEST HEART.
...GOT INVOLVED IN THIS STUPID CULT THAT SAID SUPERBOY WOULD COME BACK TO LIFE. I WASTED MONTHS.
THERE'S NO ONE ELSE HERE TO TALK TO, VIC. WAKE UP...
EVEN OUT OF COMMISSION, YOU WERE THE BEST LISTENER IN THE TOWER.
EVERY TIME SOMEONE, HAD A PROBLEM THEY'D USUALLY COME TO YOU.
I COULDN'T EVEN TALK.
YOU DIDN'T HAVE TO, VIC. YOU WERE JUST HERE FOR EVERYONE.
I DON'T EVEN RECOGNIZE SOME OF THEM.
THERE'RE A LOT OF POTENTIAL MEMBERS OUT THERE. AND IF YOU'RE UP FOR STICKING AROUND TO CHECK THEM OUT, SO AM I.
I WANT TO TELL TIM.
YOU KNOW WHERE HE IS?

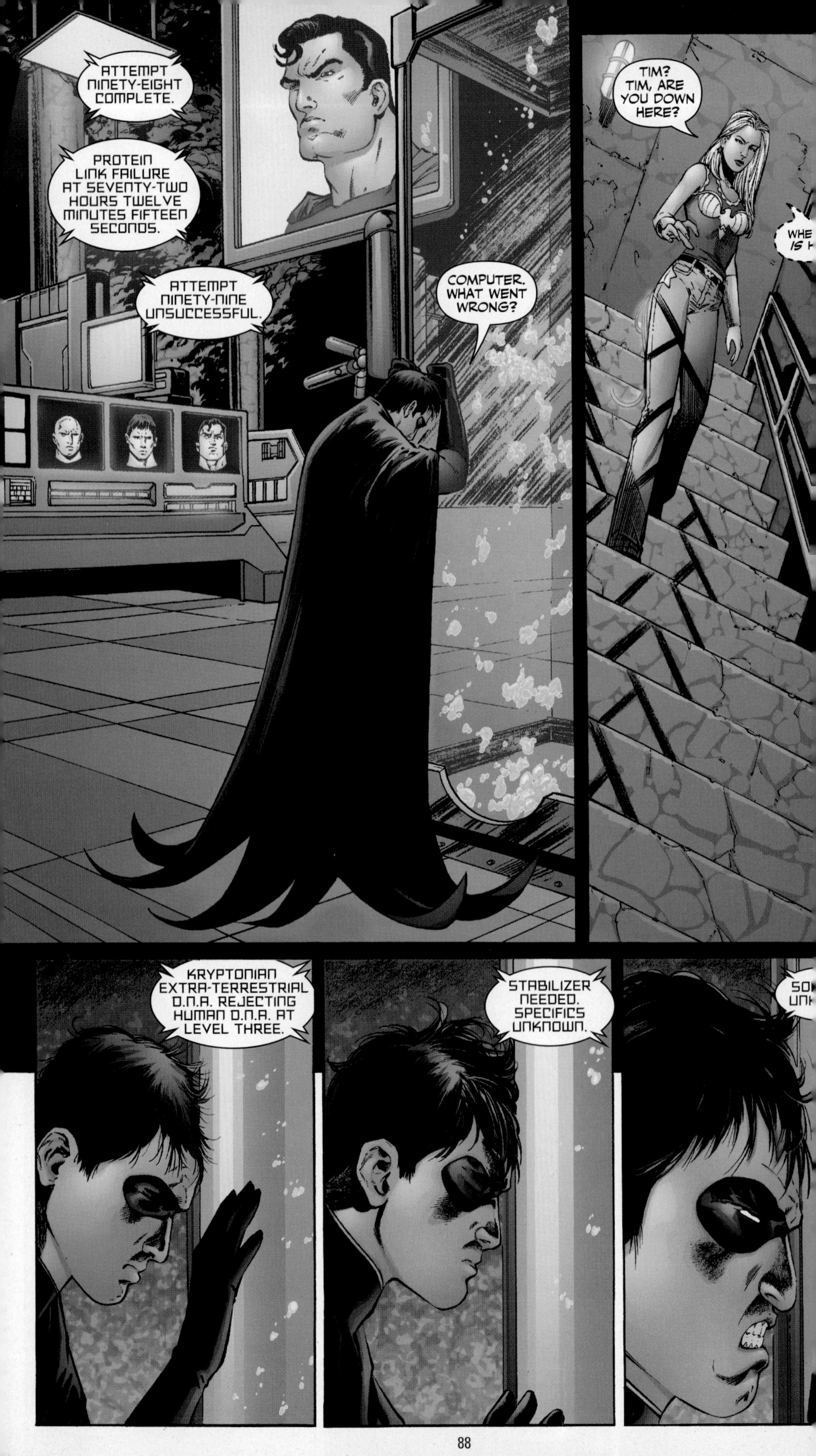

ATTEMPT NINETY-EIGHT COMPLETE.
PROTEIN LINK FAILURE AT SEVENTY-TWO HOURS TWELVE MINUTES FIFTEEN SECONDS.
ATTEMPT NINETY-NINE UNSUCCESSFUL.
COMPUTER. WHAT WENT WRONG?
TIM? TIM, ARE YOU DOWN HERE?
KRYPTONIAN EXTRA-TERRESTRIAL D.N.A. REJECTING HUMAN D.N.A. AT LEVEL THREE.
STABILIZER NEEDED. SPECIFICS UNKNOWN.

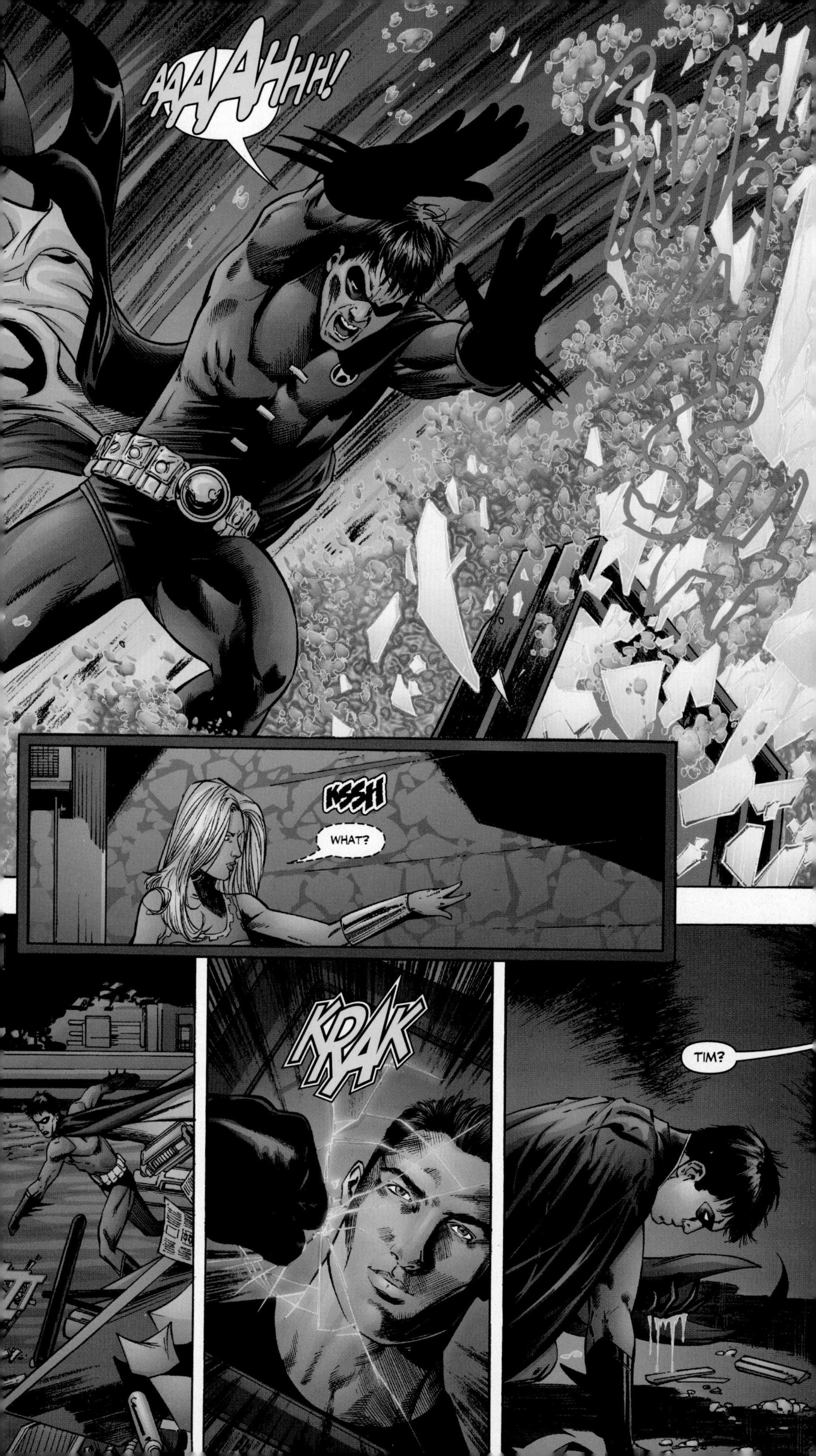
AAAAAHHH!
SMASH
KSSH
WHAT?
KRAK
TIM?

WHAT *IS* THIS? TIM. WHAT *IS* THIS PLACE?

WHAT ARE YOU DOING HERE?

WHAT'S IT LOOK LIKE?

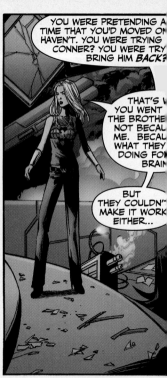

YOU WERE PRETENDING A TIME THAT YOU'D MOVED ON HAVEN'T. YOU WERE TRYING CONNER? YOU WERE TRY BRING HIM *BACK*?

THAT'S W YOU WENT THE BROTHE NOT BECAU ME. BECAU WHAT THEY DOING FO BRAIN

BUT THEY COULDN" MAKE IT WORK EITHER...

...WHY DIDN'T YOU *TELL* ME?!

WHY DIDN'T YOU TELL ME YOU WERE DOING THIS?

BECAUSE I CAN'T DO IT. BECAUSE I'M *FAILING* MY BEST FRIEND.

FAILING HIM? YOU CAN'T BRING HIM BACK LIKE THIS. EVEN IF YOU COULD, HE WOULDN'T BE CONNER. HE WOULDN'T BE THE SAME.

YOU *CAN'T*! HE WOULDN'T BE THE SUPERBOY WE KNEW!

HE'D BE CLOS ENOUGH

WE COULD *MAK* HIM CLOSE ENOUGH!

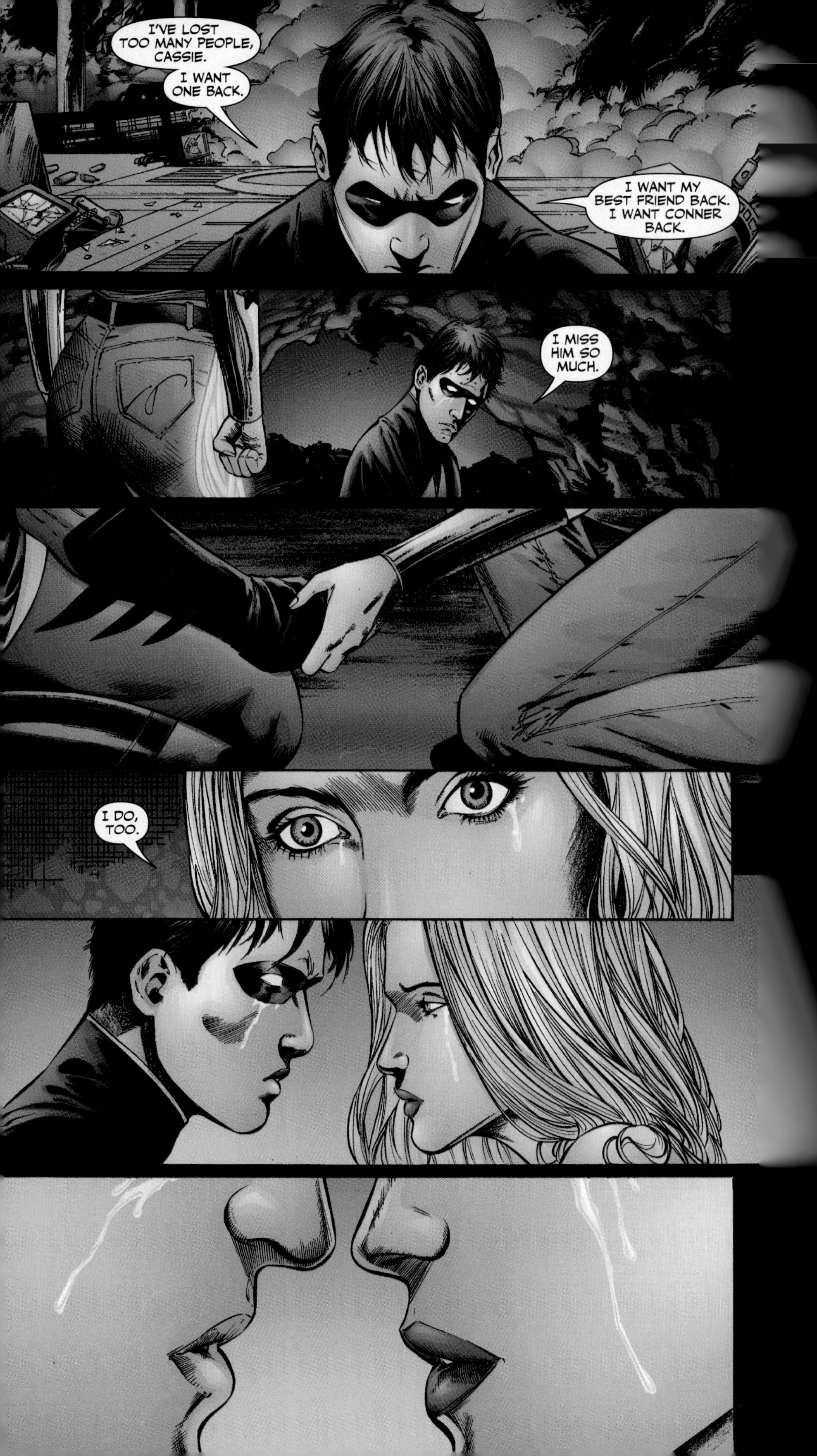
I'VE LOST TOO MANY PEOPLE, CASSIE.
I WANT ONE BACK.
I WANT MY BEST FRIEND BACK. I WANT CONNER BACK.
I MISS HIM SO MUCH.
I DO, TOO.

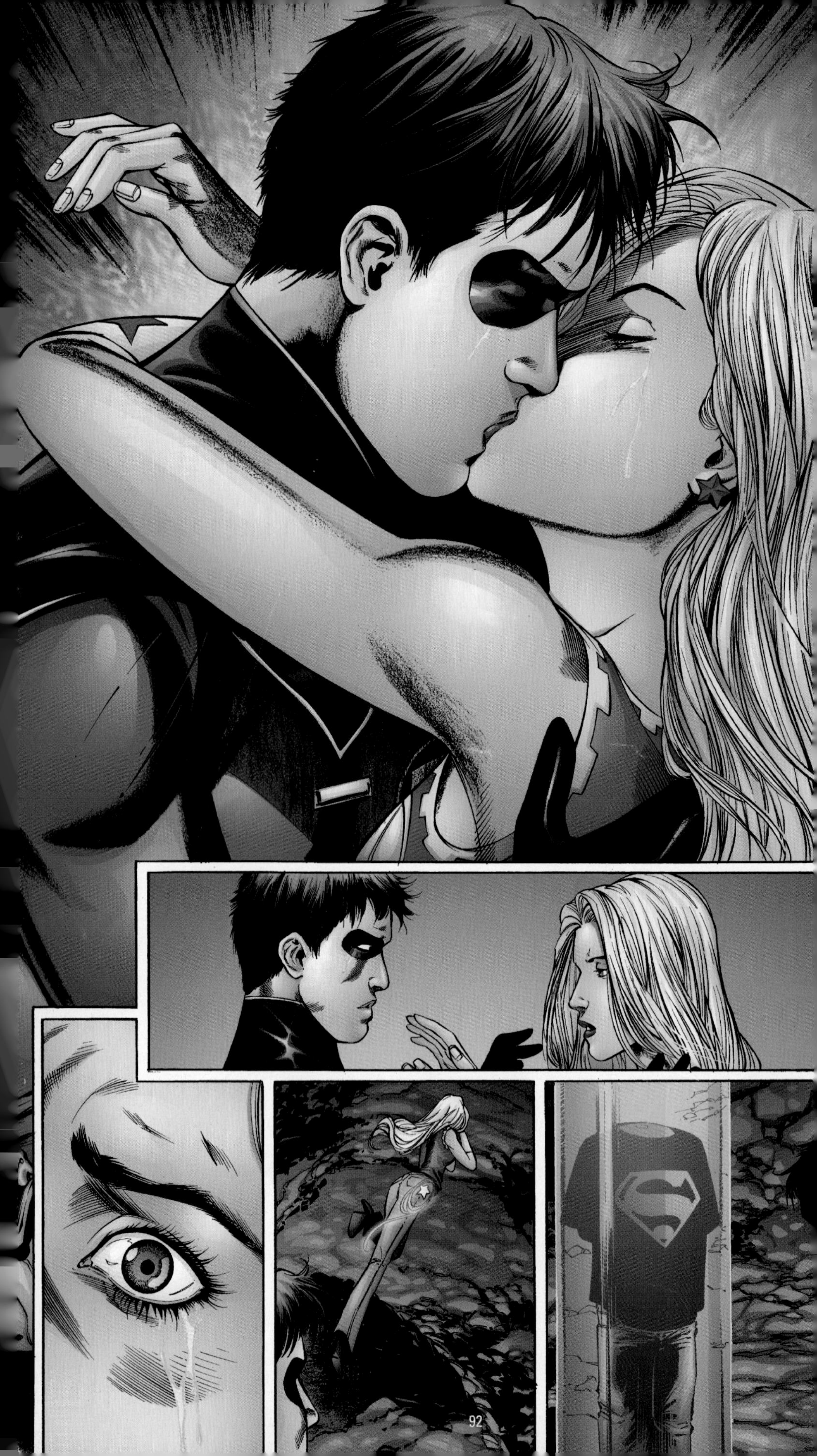

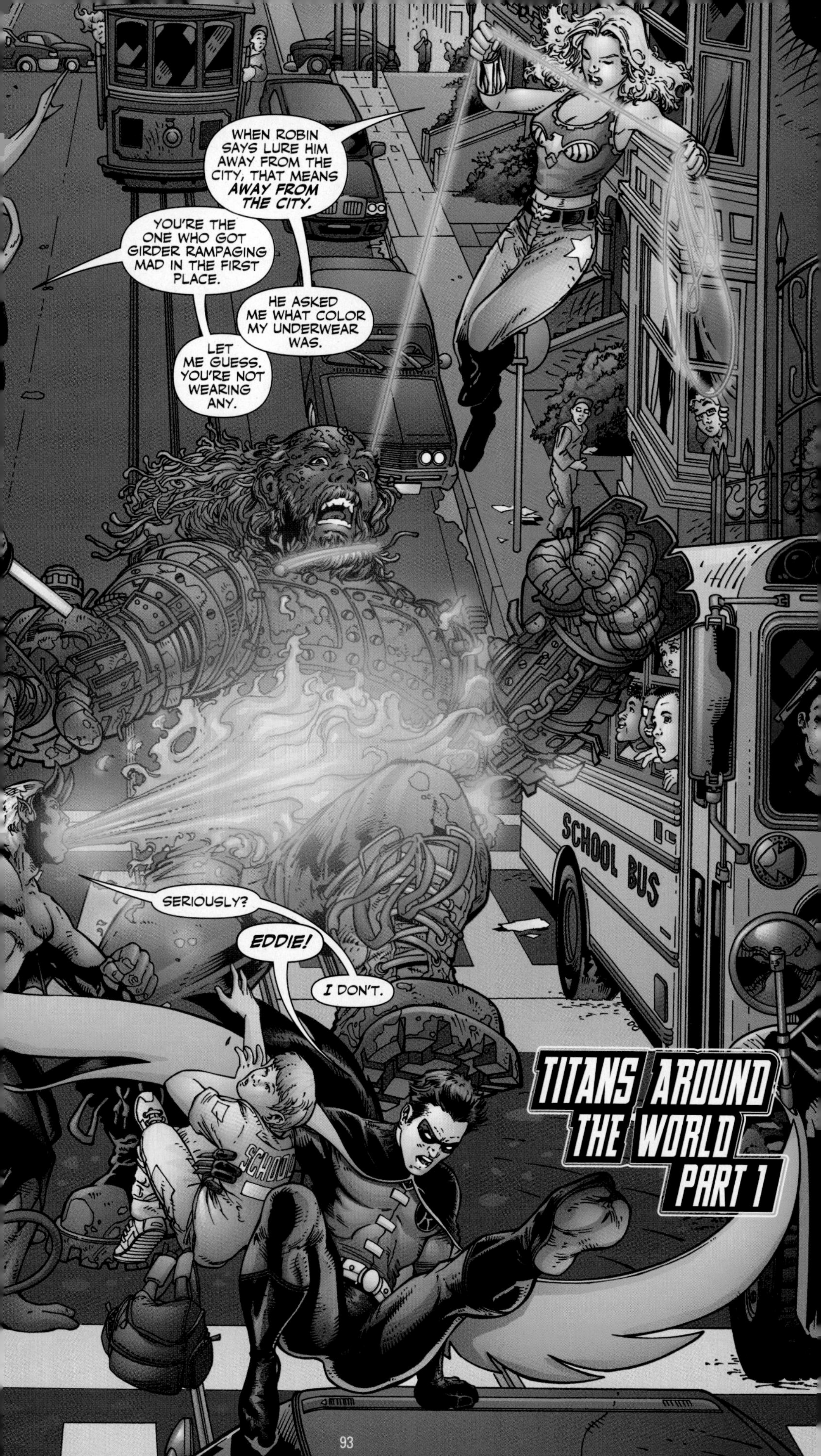
WHEN ROBIN SAYS LURE HIM AWAY FROM THE CITY, THAT MEANS *AWAY FROM THE CITY.*
YOU'RE THE ONE WHO GOT GIRDER RAMPAGING MAD IN THE FIRST PLACE.
HE ASKED ME WHAT COLOR MY UNDERWEAR WAS.
LET ME GUESS. YOU'RE NOT WEARING ANY.
SCHOOL BUS
SERIOUSLY?
EDDIE!
I DON'T.
TITANS AROUND THE WORLD PART 1

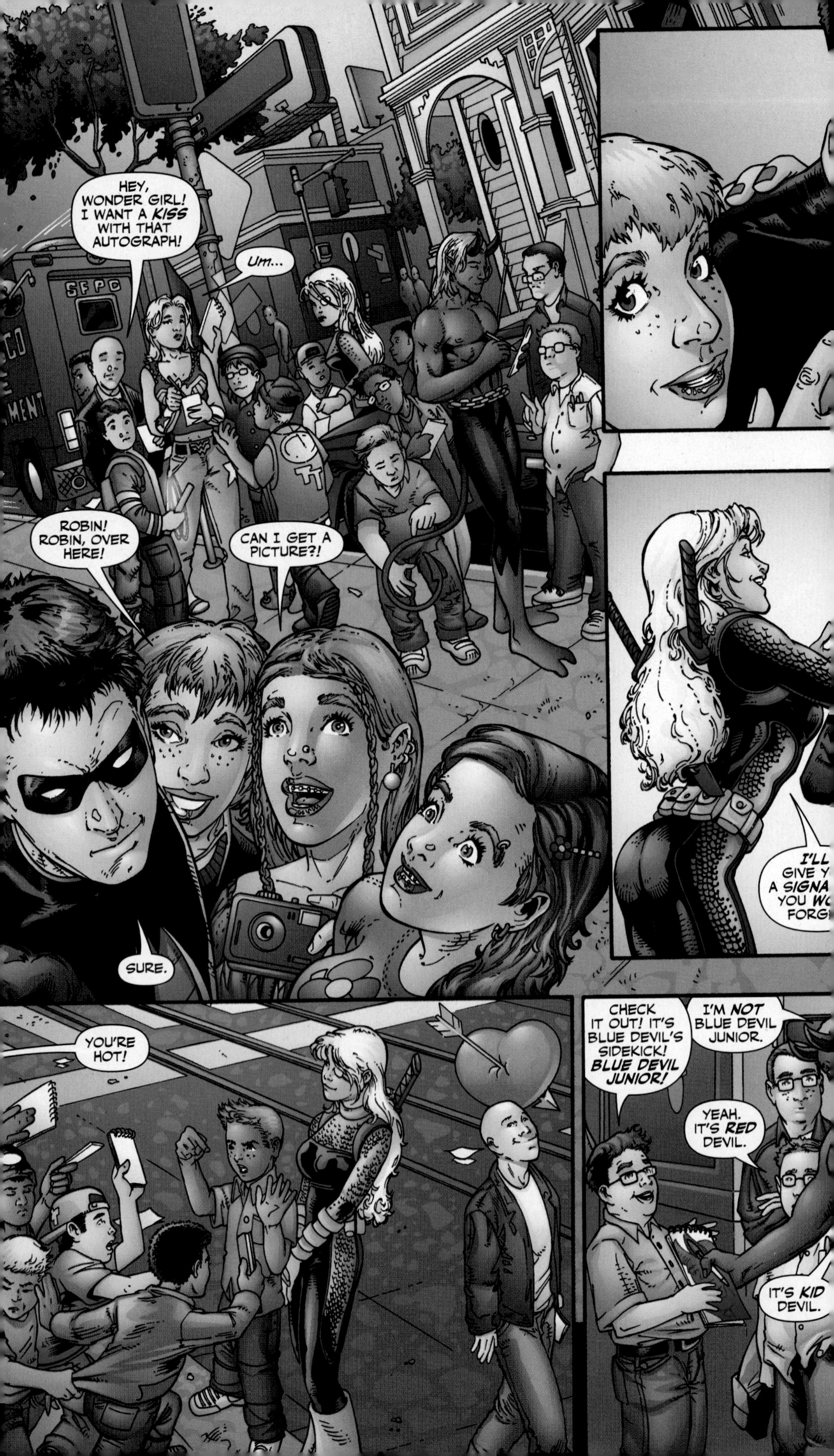
HEY, WONDER GIRL! I WANT A *KISS* WITH THAT AUTOGRAPH!
Um...
SFPD
ROBIN! ROBIN, OVER HERE!
CAN I GET A PICTURE?!
SURE.
I'LL GIVE Y A *SIGNA* YOU *W* FORG
YOU'RE HOT!
CHECK IT OUT! IT'S BLUE DEVIL'S SIDEKICK! *BLUE DEVIL JUNIOR!*
I'M *NOT* BLUE DEVIL JUNIOR.
YEAH. IT'S *RED* DEVIL.
IT'S *KID* DEVIL.

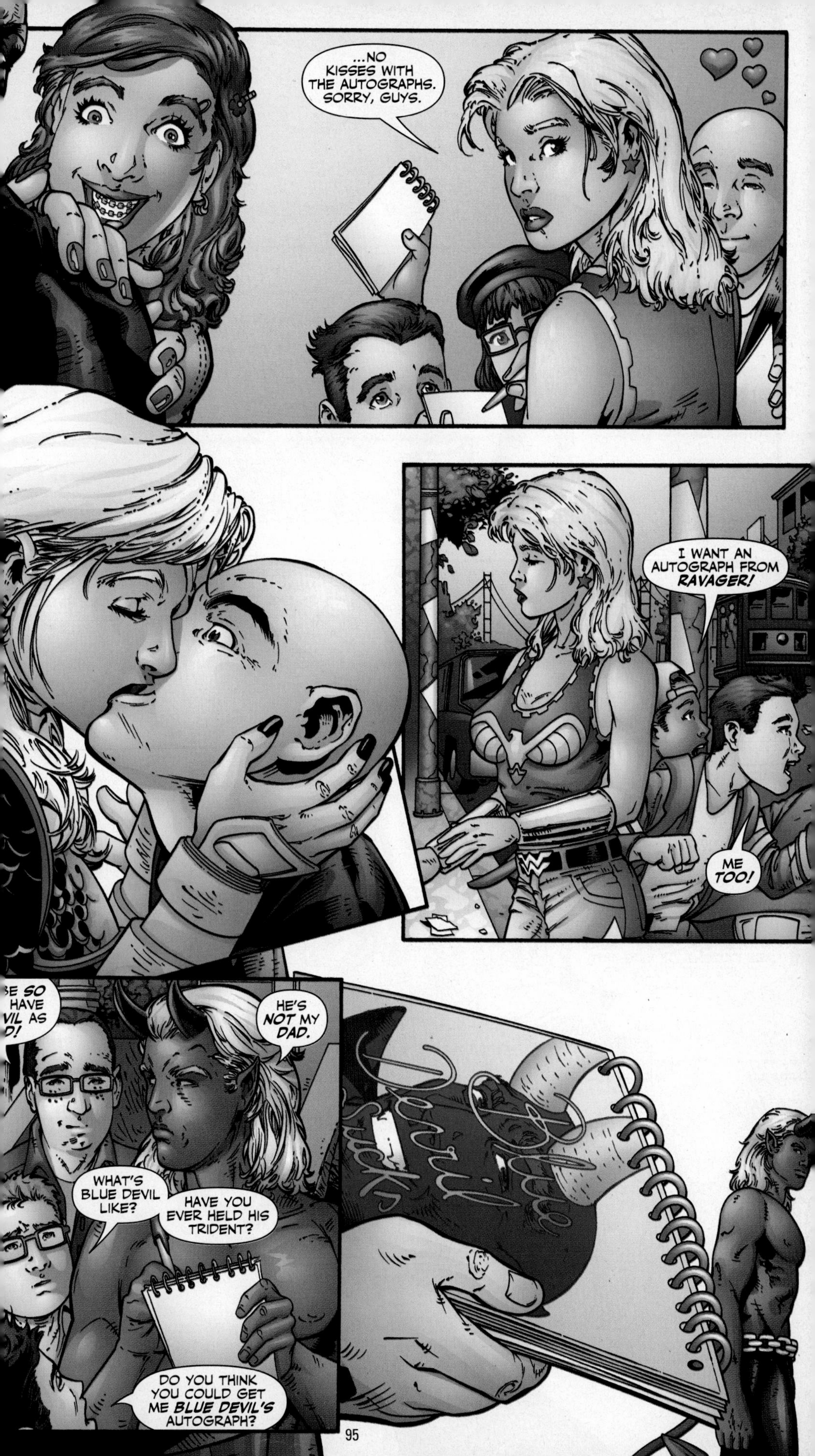
...NO KISSES WITH THE AUTOGRAPHS. SORRY, GUYS.
I WANT AN AUTOGRAPH FROM RAVAGER!
ME TOO!
HE'S NOT MY DAD.
WHAT'S BLUE DEVIL LIKE?
HAVE YOU EVER HELD HIS TRIDENT?
DO YOU THINK YOU COULD GET ME BLUE DEVIL'S AUTOGRAPH?

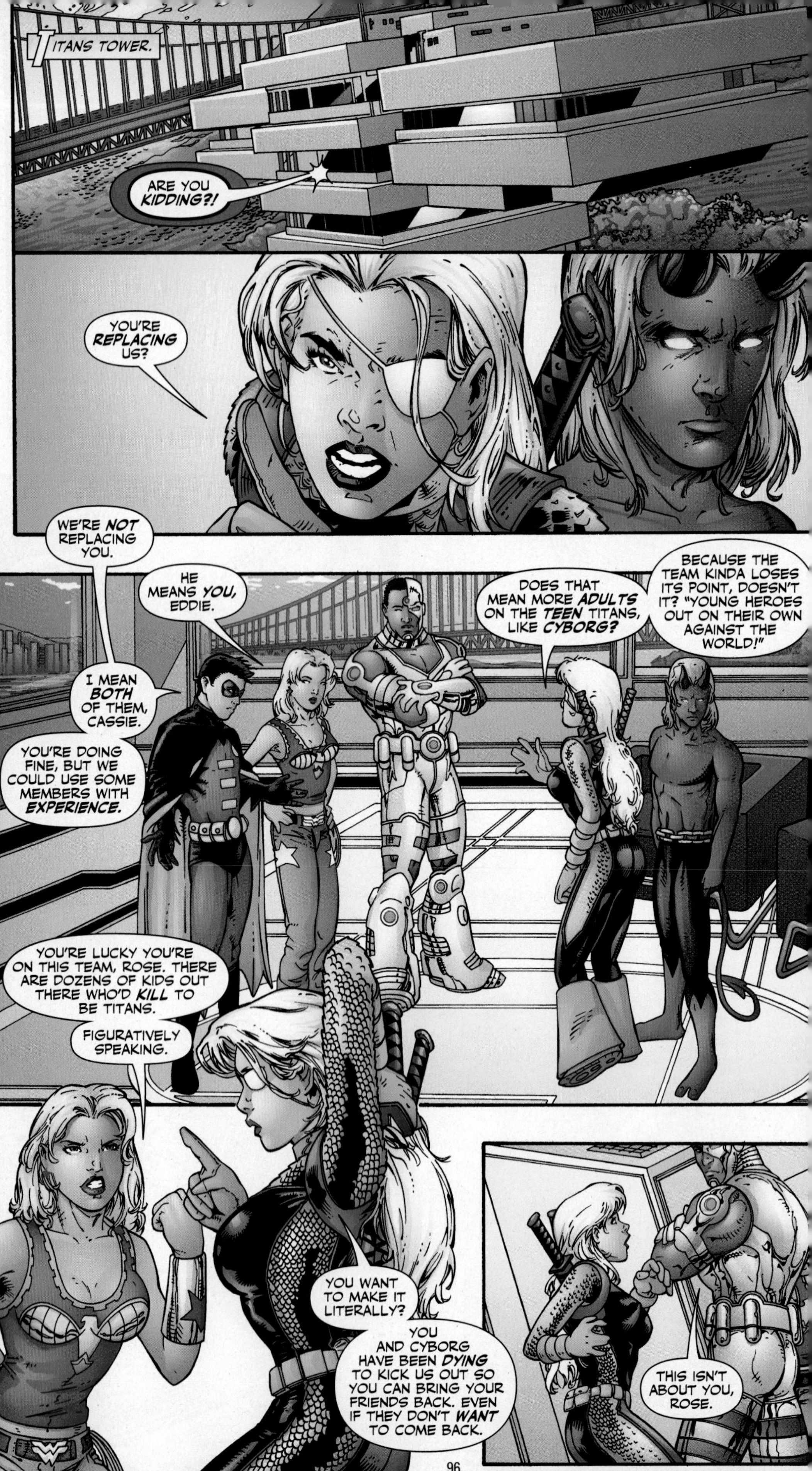
TITANS TOWER.
ARE YOU KIDDING?!
YOU'RE REPLACING US?
WE'RE NOT REPLACING YOU.
HE MEANS YOU, EDDIE.
I MEAN BOTH OF THEM, CASSIE.
YOU'RE DOING FINE, BUT WE COULD USE SOME MEMBERS WITH EXPERIENCE.
DOES THAT MEAN MORE ADULTS ON THE TEEN TITANS, LIKE CYBORG?
BECAUSE THE TEAM KINDA LOSES ITS POINT, DOESN'T IT? "YOUNG HEROES OUT ON THEIR OWN AGAINST THE WORLD!"
YOU'RE LUCKY YOU'RE ON THIS TEAM, ROSE. THERE ARE DOZENS OF KIDS OUT THERE WHO'D KILL TO BE TITANS.
FIGURATIVELY SPEAKING.
YOU WANT TO MAKE IT LITERALLY?
YOU AND CYBORG HAVE BEEN DYING TO KICK US OUT SO YOU CAN BRING YOUR FRIENDS BACK. EVEN IF THEY DON'T WANT TO COME BACK.
THIS ISN'T ABOUT YOU, ROSE.

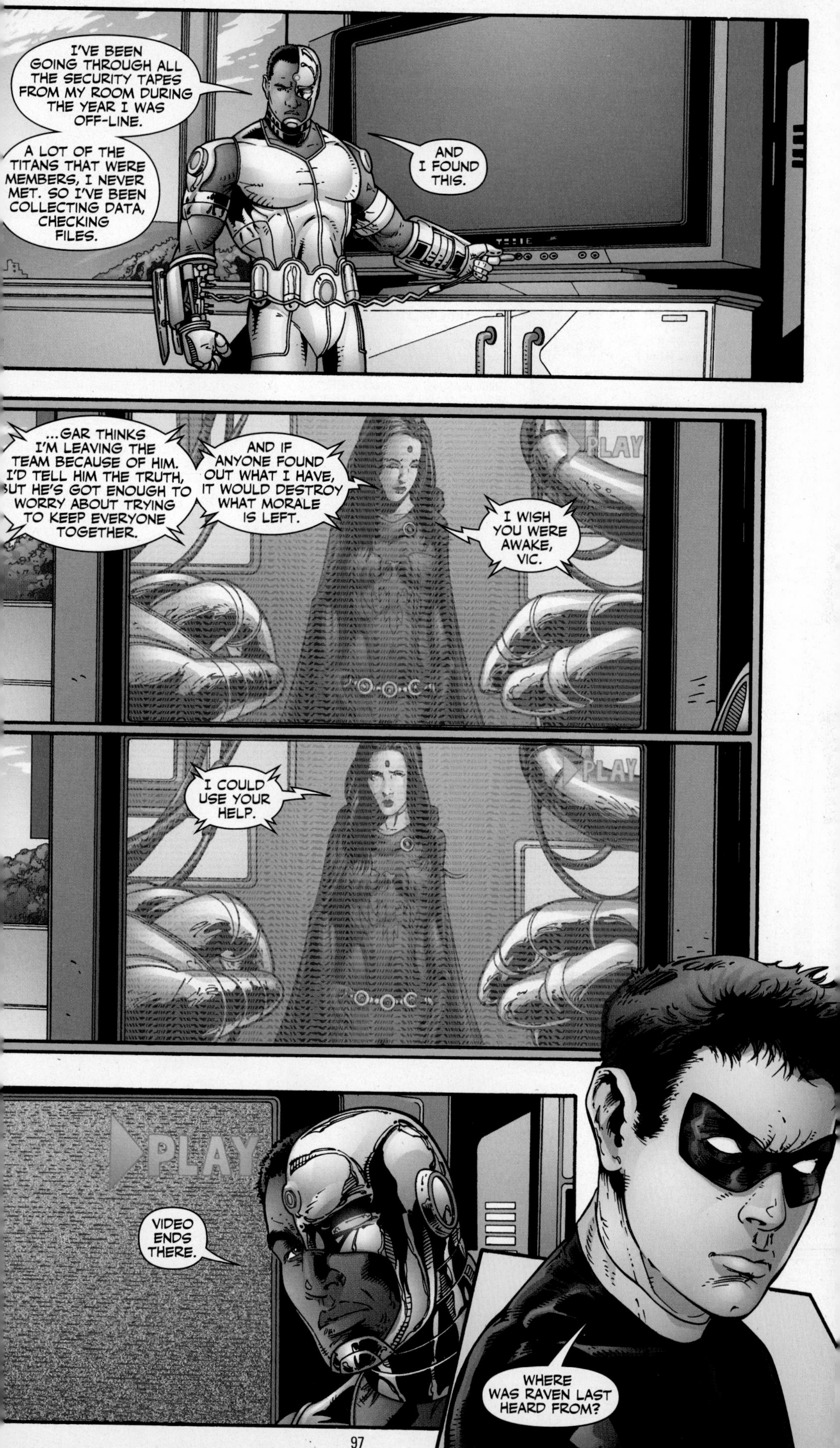

I'VE BEEN GOING THROUGH ALL THE SECURITY TAPES FROM MY ROOM DURING THE YEAR I WAS OFF-LINE.
A LOT OF THE TITANS THAT WERE MEMBERS, I NEVER MET. SO I'VE BEEN COLLECTING DATA, CHECKING FILES.
AND I FOUND THIS.
PLAY
...GAR THINKS I'M LEAVING THE TEAM BECAUSE OF HIM. I'D TELL HIM THE TRUTH, BUT HE'S GOT ENOUGH TO WORRY ABOUT TRYING TO KEEP EVERYONE TOGETHER.
AND IF ANYONE FOUND OUT WHAT I HAVE, IT WOULD DESTROY WHAT MORALE IS LEFT.
I WISH YOU WERE AWAKE, VIC.
PLAY
I COULD USE YOUR HELP.
PLAY
VIDEO ENDS THERE.
WHERE WAS RAVEN LAST HEARD FROM?

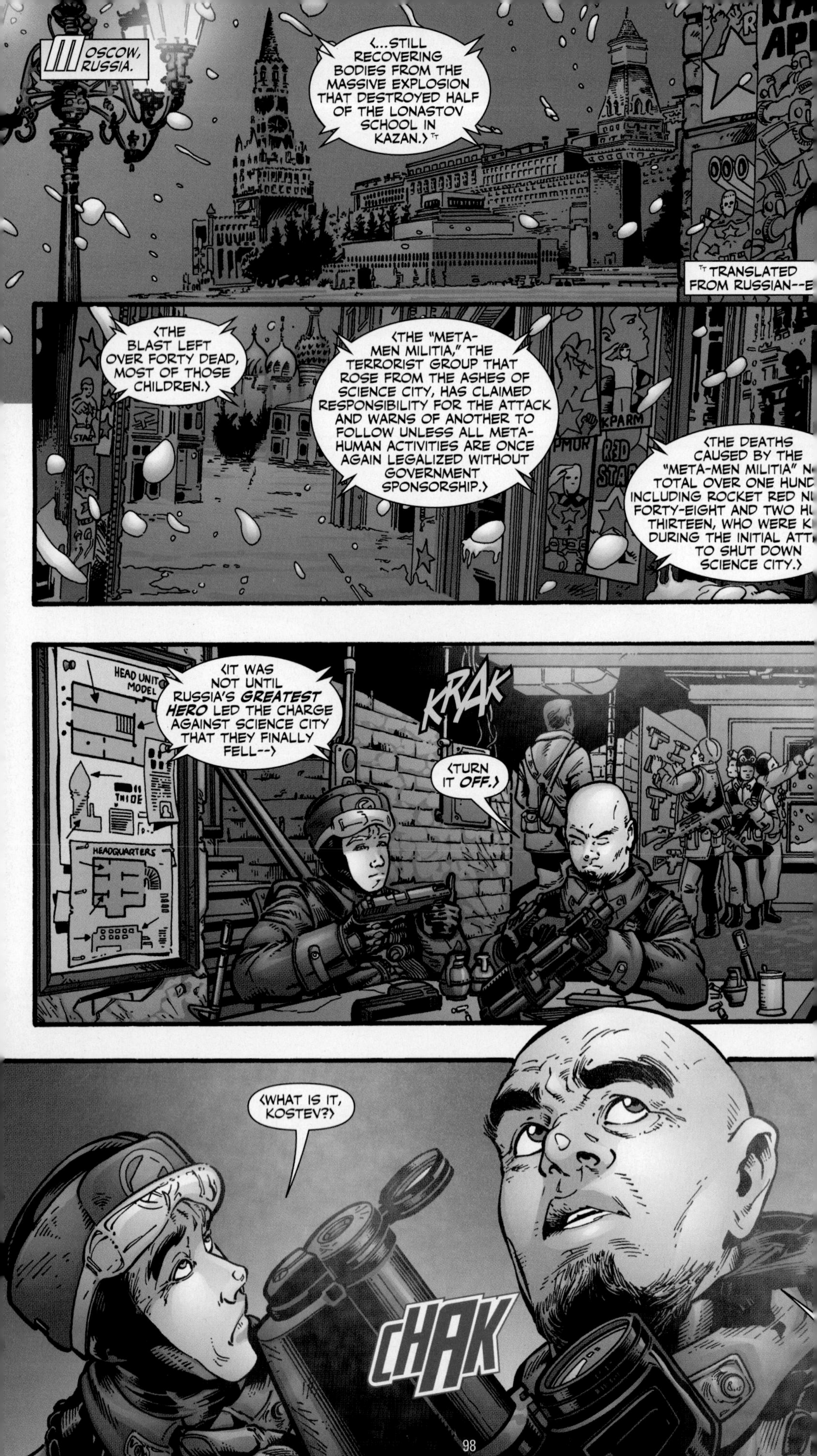
MOSCOW, RUSSIA.
‹...STILL RECOVERING BODIES FROM THE MASSIVE EXPLOSION THAT DESTROYED HALF OF THE LONASTOV SCHOOL IN KAZAN.› TT
TT TRANSLATED FROM RUSSIAN--E
‹THE BLAST LEFT OVER FORTY DEAD, MOST OF THOSE CHILDREN.›
‹THE "META-MEN MILITIA," THE TERRORIST GROUP THAT ROSE FROM THE ASHES OF SCIENCE CITY, HAS CLAIMED RESPONSIBILITY FOR THE ATTACK AND WARNS OF ANOTHER TO FOLLOW UNLESS ALL META-HUMAN ACTIVITIES ARE ONCE AGAIN LEGALIZED WITHOUT GOVERNMENT SPONSORSHIP.›
‹THE DEATHS CAUSED BY THE "META-MEN MILITIA" N TOTAL OVER ONE HUND INCLUDING ROCKET RED NI FORTY-EIGHT AND TWO HU THIRTEEN, WHO WERE K DURING THE INITIAL ATT TO SHUT DOWN SCIENCE CITY.›
HEAD UNIT MODEL
HEADQUARTERS
‹IT WAS NOT UNTIL RUSSIA'S GREATEST HERO LED THE CHARGE AGAINST SCIENCE CITY THAT THEY FINALLY FELL--›
KRAK
‹TURN IT OFF.›
‹WHAT IS IT, KOSTEV?›
CHAK

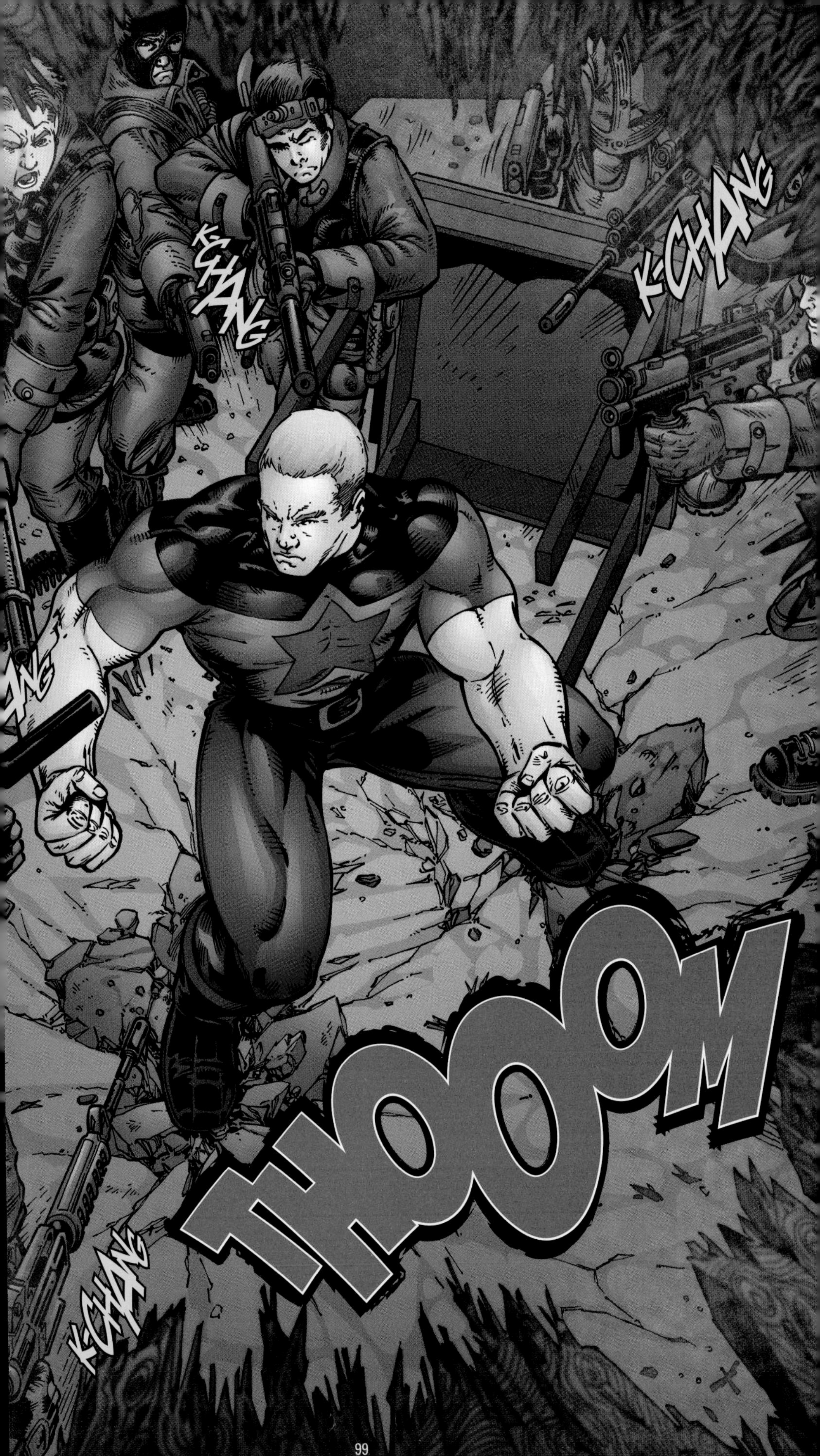
K-CHANG
K-CHANG
THOOOM
K-CHANG

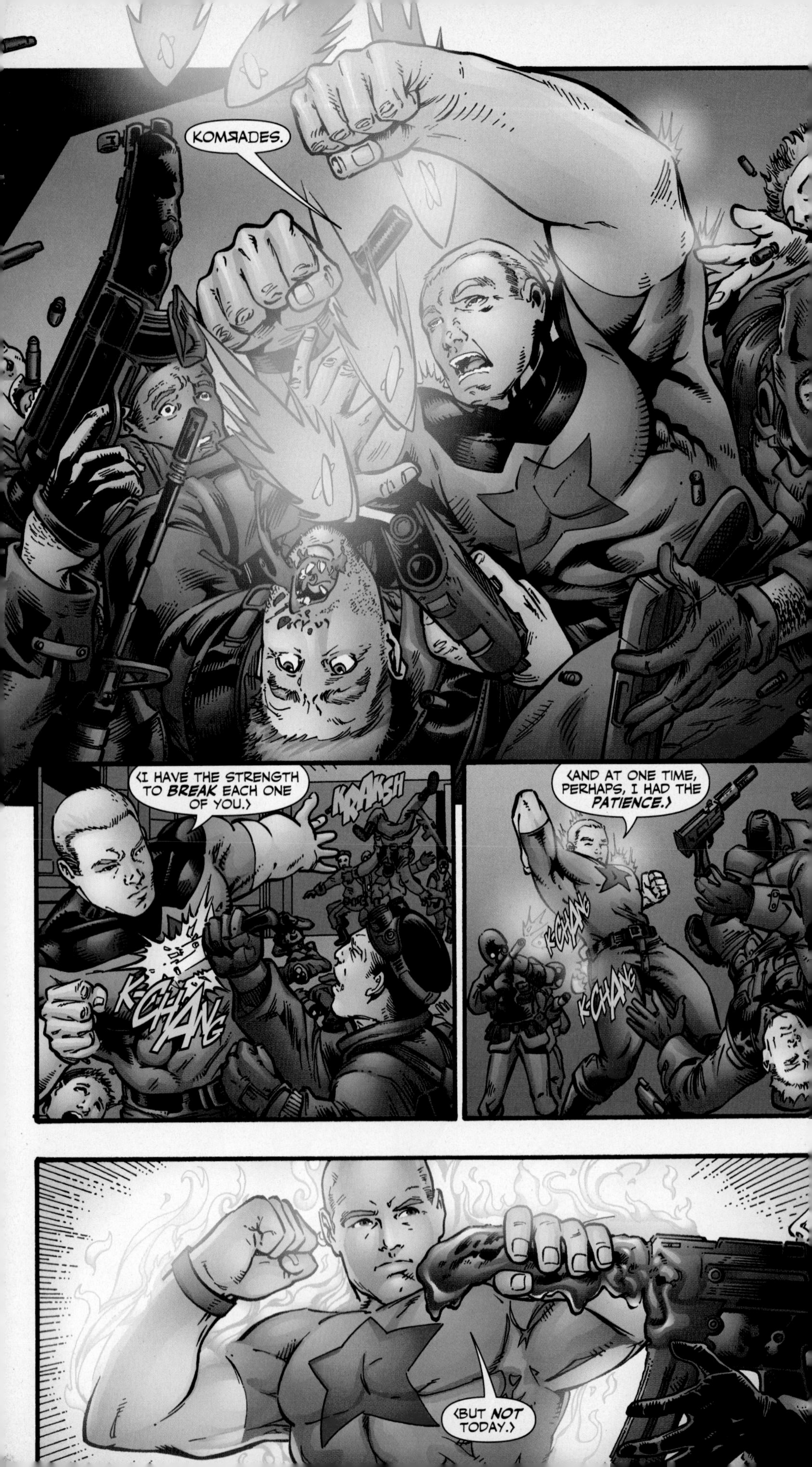
KOMЯADES.
‹I HAVE THE STRENGTH TO BREAK EACH ONE OF YOU.›
KRAASH
K-CHANG
‹AND AT ONE TIME, PERHAPS, I HAD THE PATIENCE.›
K-CHANG
K-CHANG
‹BUT NOT TODAY.›

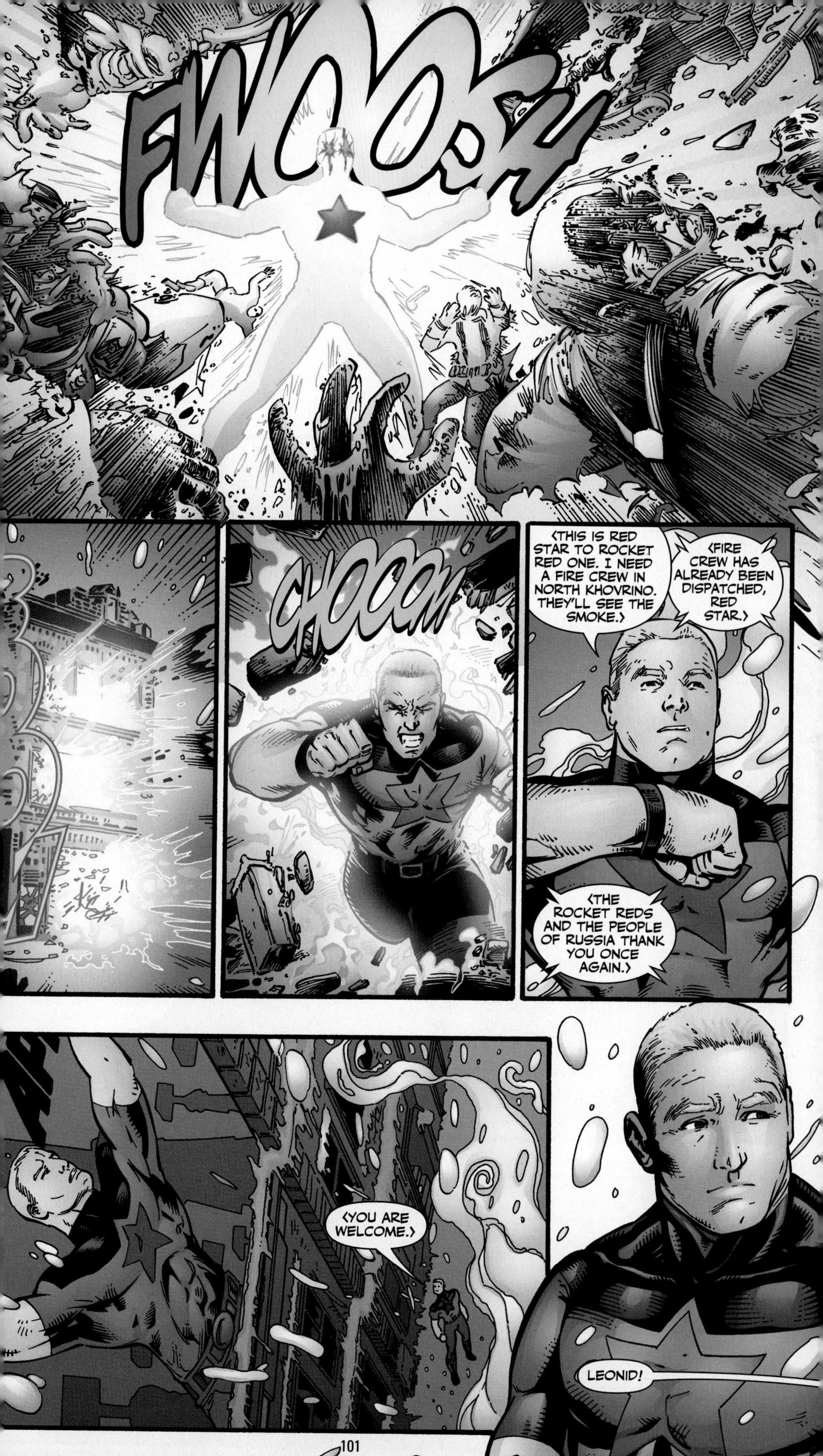
FWOOSH
CHOOM
‹THIS IS RED STAR TO ROCKET RED ONE. I NEED A FIRE CREW IN NORTH KHOVRINO. THEY'LL SEE THE SMOKE.›
‹FIRE CREW HAS ALREADY BEEN DISPATCHED, RED STAR.›
‹THE ROCKET REDS AND THE PEOPLE OF RUSSIA THANK YOU ONCE AGAIN.›
‹YOU ARE WELCOME.›
LEONID!

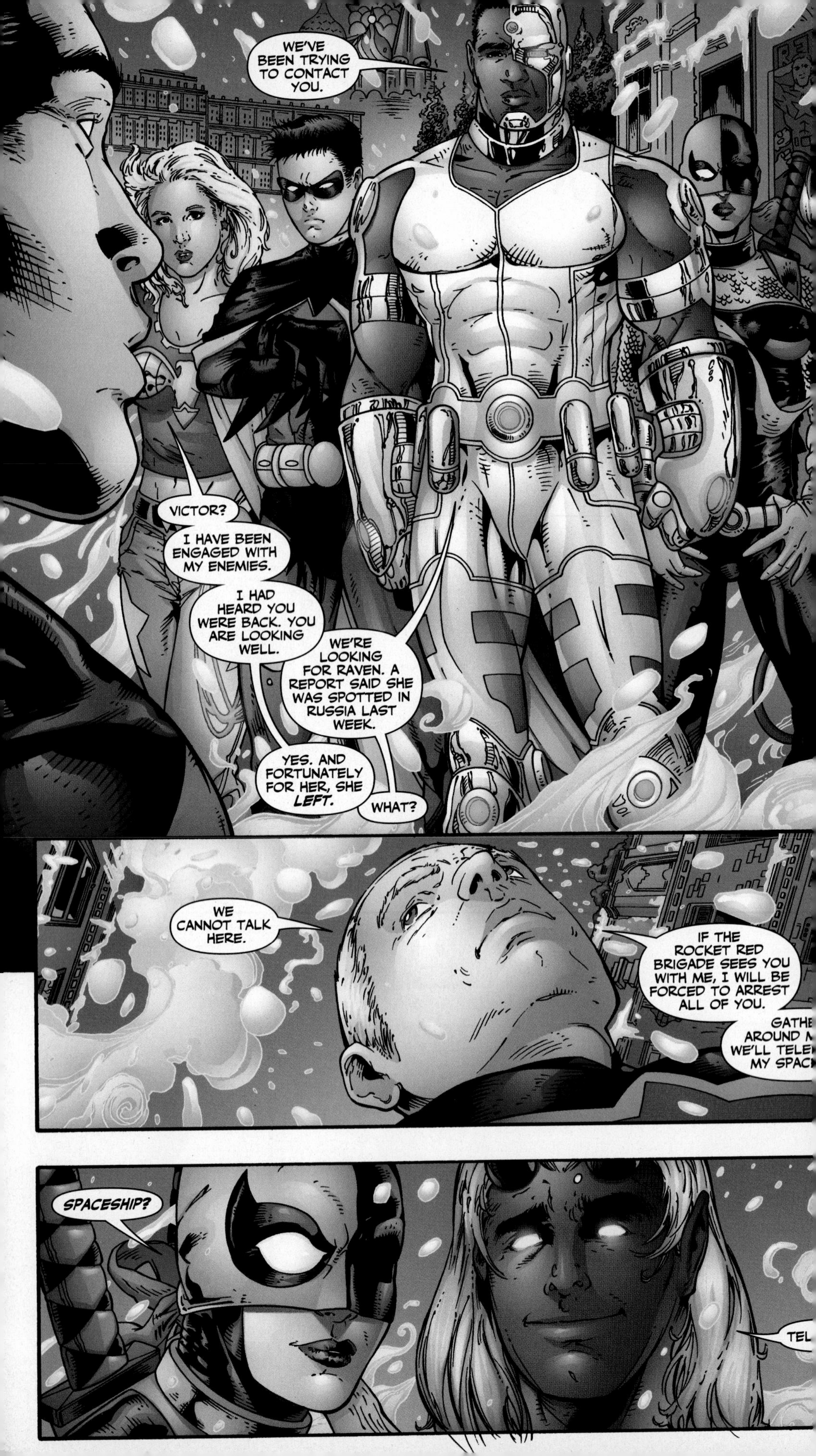
WE'VE BEEN TRYING TO CONTACT YOU.
VICTOR?
I HAVE BEEN ENGAGED WITH MY ENEMIES.
I HAD HEARD YOU WERE BACK. YOU ARE LOOKING WELL.
WE'RE LOOKING FOR RAVEN. A REPORT SAID SHE WAS SPOTTED IN RUSSIA LAST WEEK.
YES. AND FORTUNATELY FOR HER, SHE LEFT.
WHAT?
WE CANNOT TALK HERE.
IF THE ROCKET RED BRIGADE SEES YOU WITH ME, I WILL BE FORCED TO ARREST ALL OF YOU.
SPACESHIP?

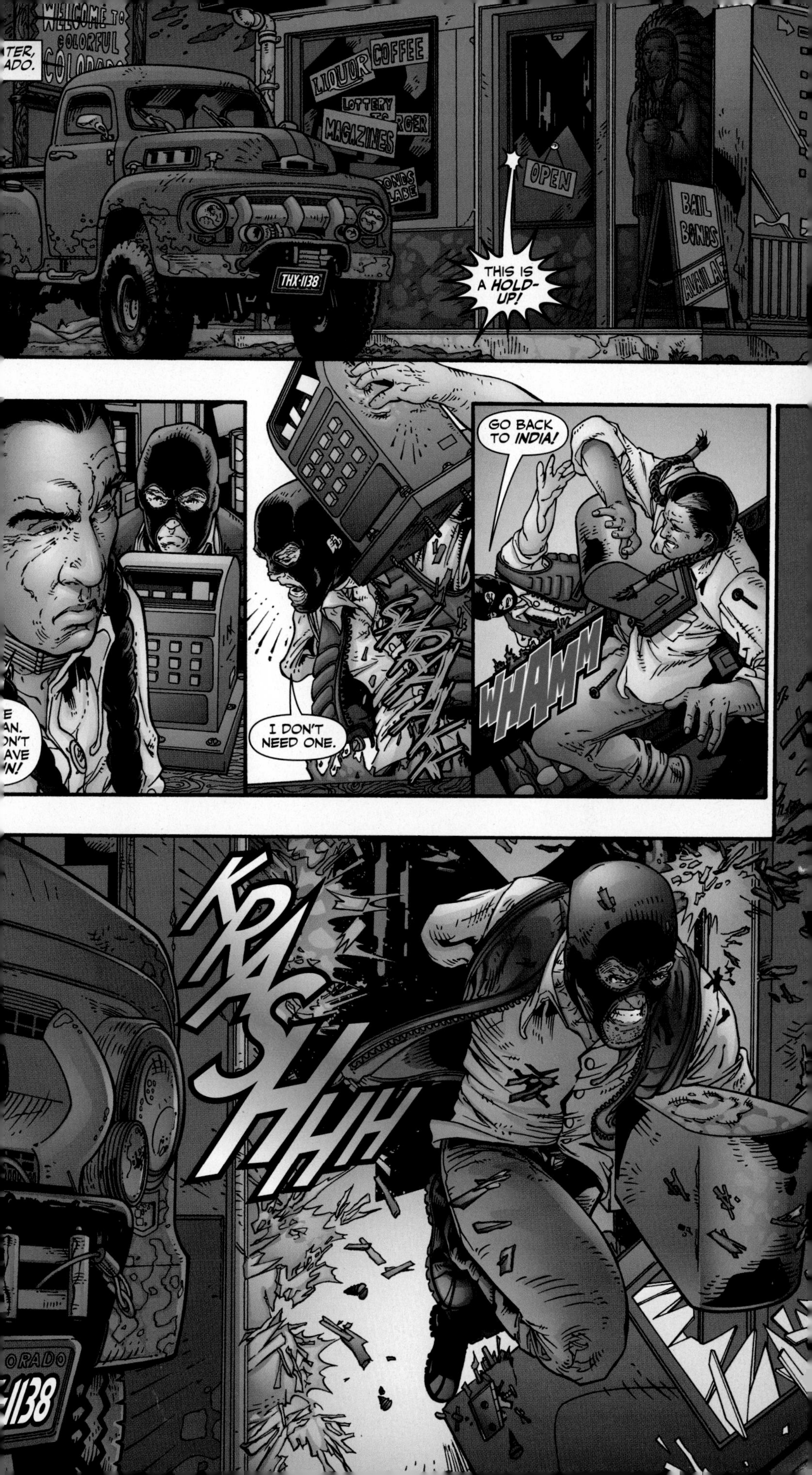

TER,
ADO.
WELCOME TO COLORFUL COLORADO
LIQUOR
COFFEE
LOTTERY
MAGAZINES
OPEN
BAIL BONDS
THX-1138
THIS IS A HOLD-UP!
I DON'T NEED ONE.
GO BACK TO INDIA!
WHAMM
KRASHHH

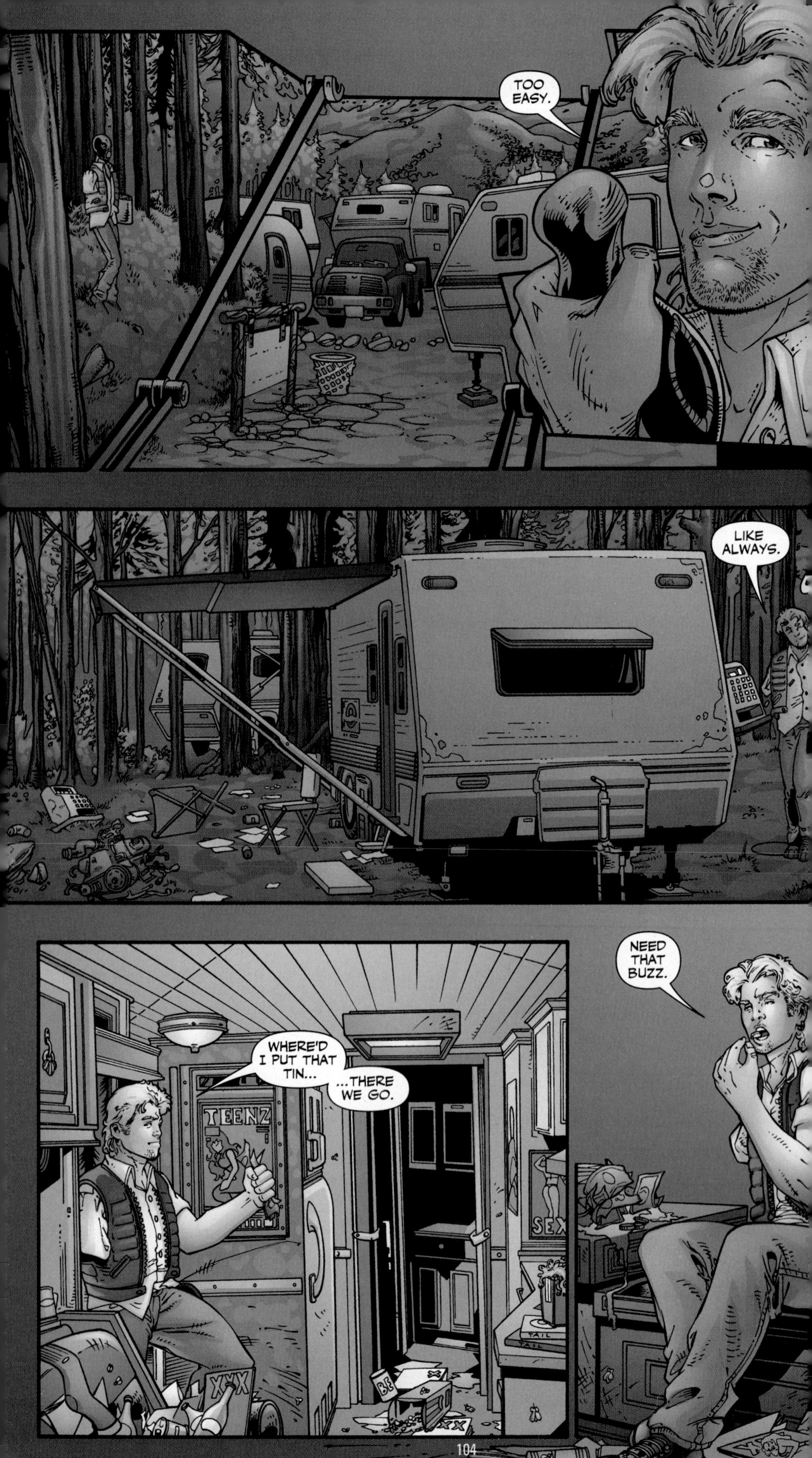
TOO EASY.
LIKE ALWAYS.
WHERE'D I PUT THAT TIN...
...THERE WE GO.
TEENZ
SEX
XXX
NEED THAT BUZZ.

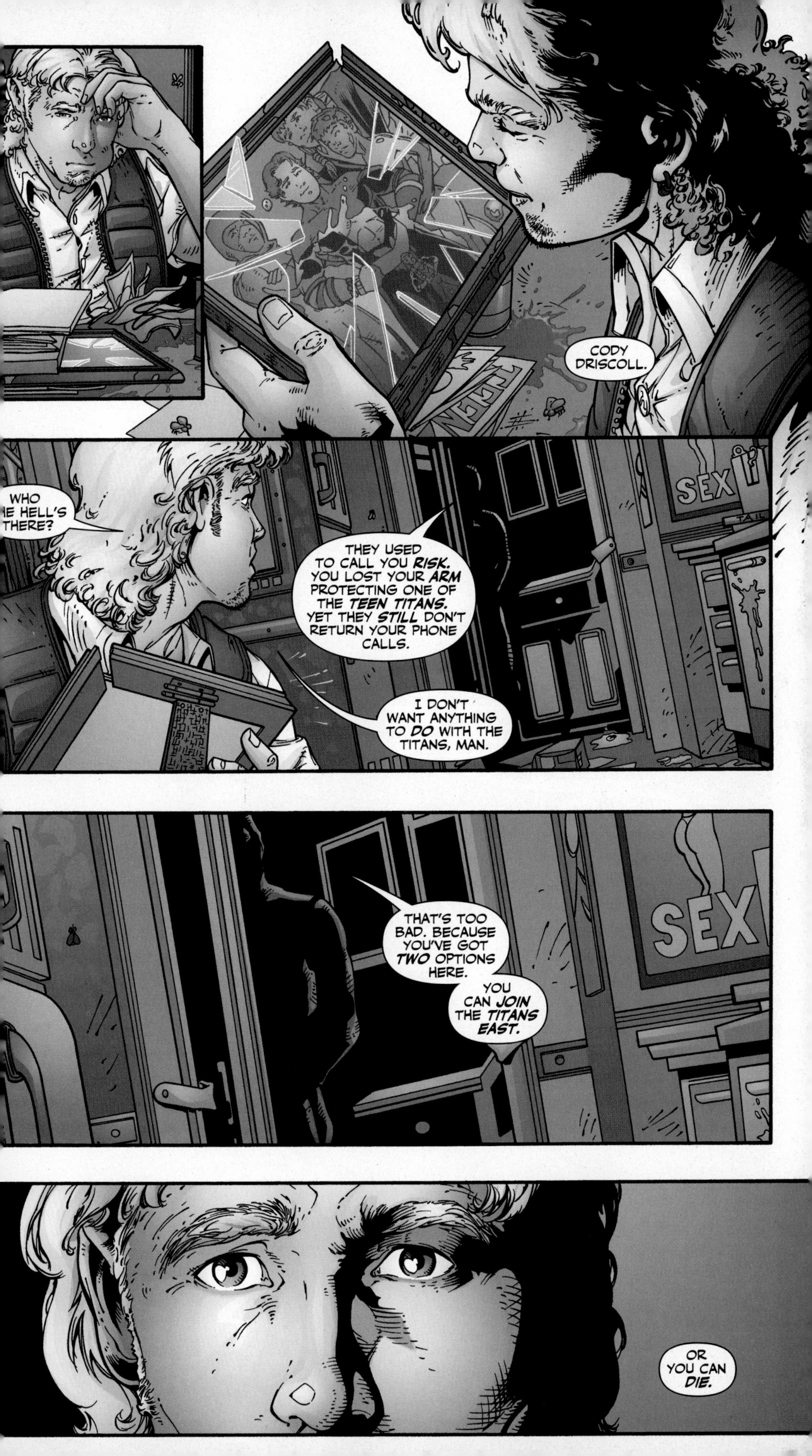
CODY DRISCOLL.
WHO THE HELL'S THERE?
THEY USED TO CALL YOU RISK. YOU LOST YOUR ARM PROTECTING ONE OF THE TEEN TITANS. YET THEY STILL DON'T RETURN YOUR PHONE CALLS.
I DON'T WANT ANYTHING TO DO WITH THE TITANS, MAN.
SEX
THAT'S TOO BAD. BECAUSE YOU'VE GOT TWO OPTIONS HERE.
YOU CAN JOIN THE TITANS EAST.
SEX
OR YOU CAN DIE.

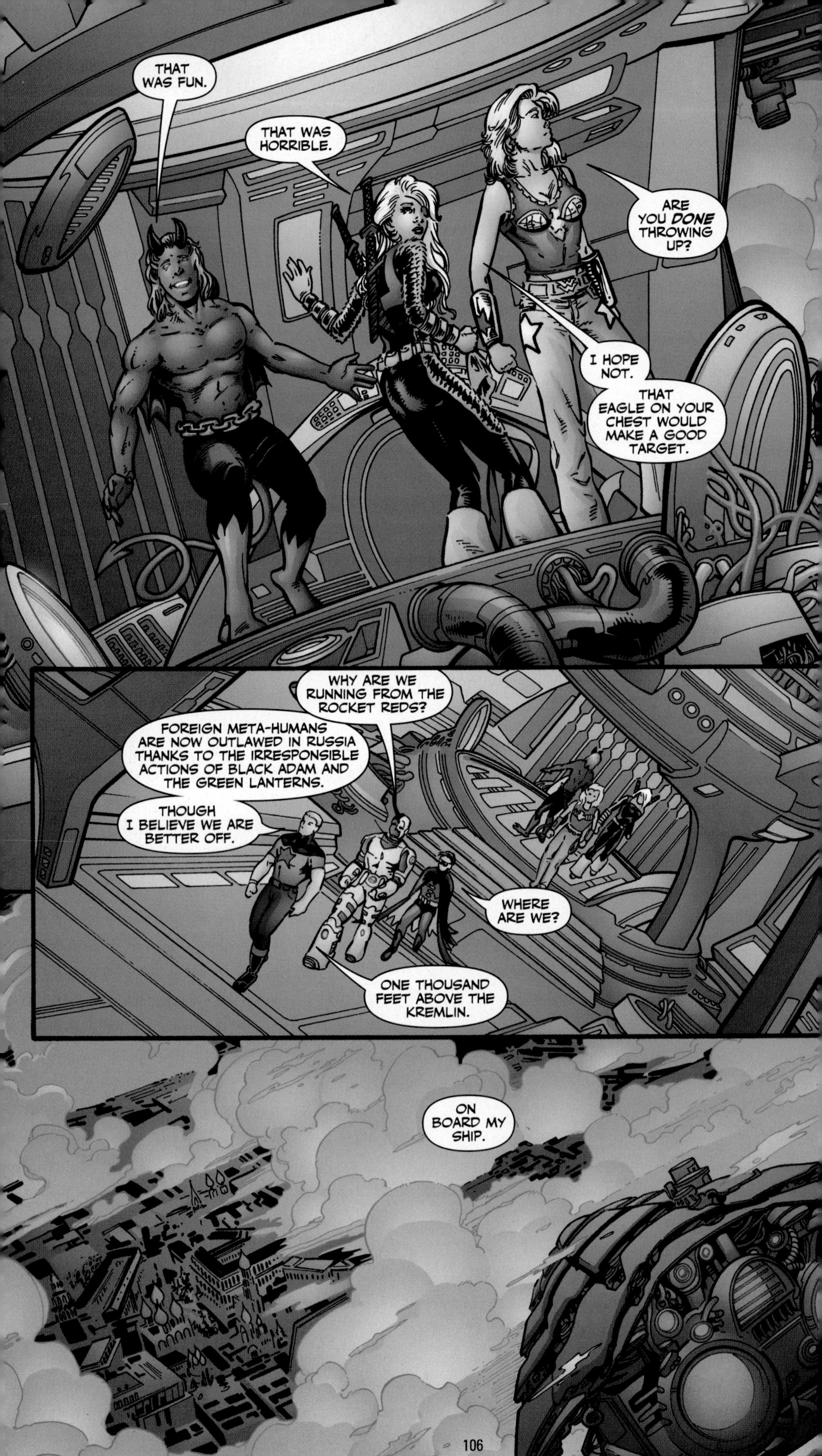
THAT WAS FUN.
THAT WAS HORRIBLE.
ARE YOU DONE THROWING UP?
I HOPE NOT.
THAT EAGLE ON YOUR CHEST WOULD MAKE A GOOD TARGET.
WHY ARE WE RUNNING FROM THE ROCKET REDS?
FOREIGN META-HUMANS ARE NOW OUTLAWED IN RUSSIA THANKS TO THE IRRESPONSIBLE ACTIONS OF BLACK ADAM AND THE GREEN LANTERNS.
THOUGH I BELIEVE WE ARE BETTER OFF.
WHERE ARE WE?
ONE THOUSAND FEET ABOVE THE KREMLIN.
ON BOARD MY SHIP.

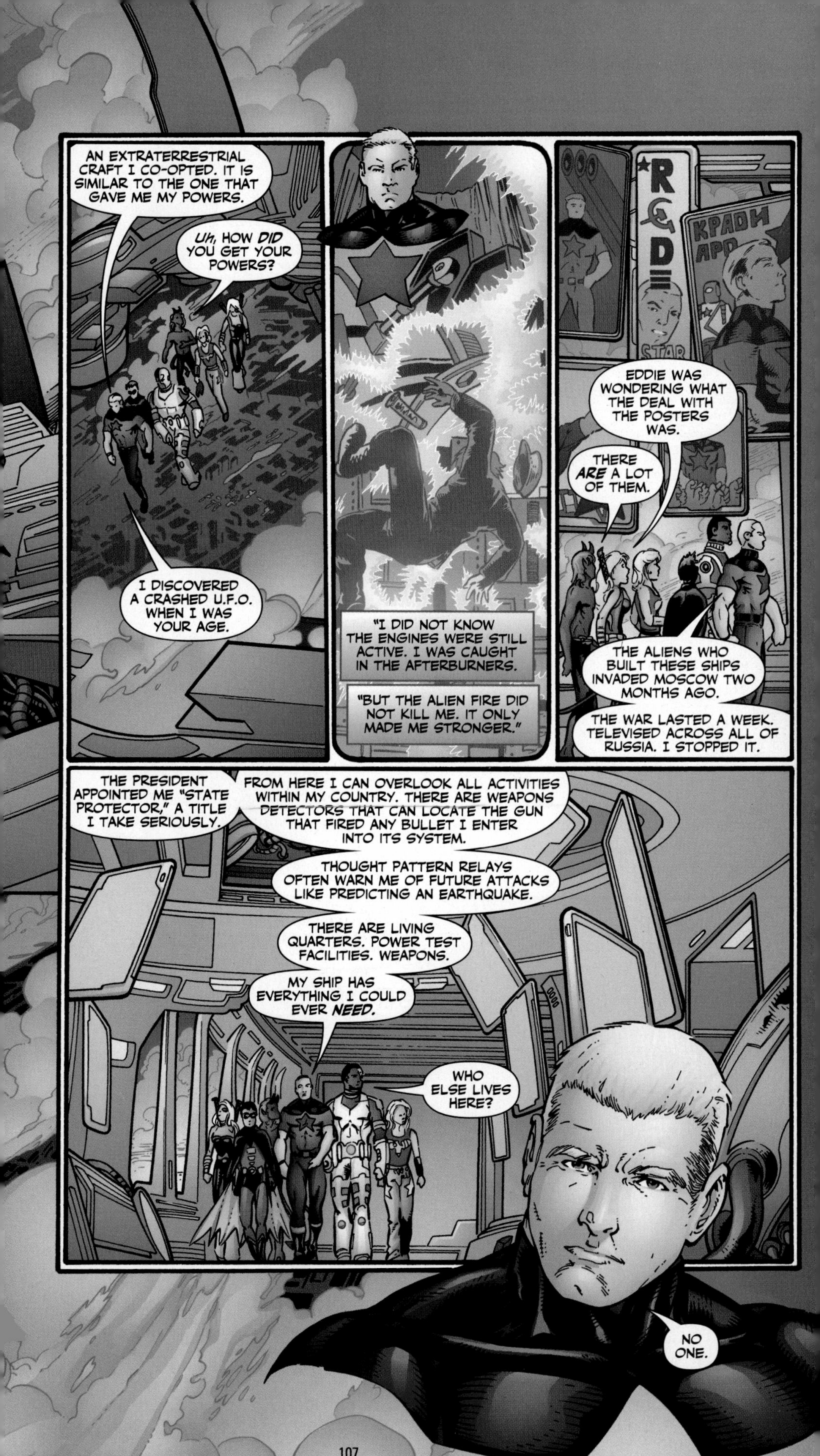

AN EXTRATERRESTRIAL CRAFT I CO-OPTED. IT IS SIMILAR TO THE ONE THAT GAVE ME MY POWERS.
Uh, HOW DID YOU GET YOUR POWERS?
I DISCOVERED A CRASHED U.F.O. WHEN I WAS YOUR AGE.
"I DID NOT KNOW THE ENGINES WERE STILL ACTIVE. I WAS CAUGHT IN THE AFTERBURNERS.
"BUT THE ALIEN FIRE DID NOT KILL ME. IT ONLY MADE ME STRONGER."
R
D
STAR
EDDIE WAS WONDERING WHAT THE DEAL WITH THE POSTERS WAS.
THERE ARE A LOT OF THEM.
THE ALIENS WHO BUILT THESE SHIPS INVADED MOSCOW TWO MONTHS AGO.
THE WAR LASTED A WEEK. TELEVISED ACROSS ALL OF RUSSIA. I STOPPED IT.
THE PRESIDENT APPOINTED ME "STATE PROTECTOR," A TITLE I TAKE SERIOUSLY.
FROM HERE I CAN OVERLOOK ALL ACTIVITIES WITHIN MY COUNTRY. THERE ARE WEAPONS DETECTORS THAT CAN LOCATE THE GUN THAT FIRED ANY BULLET I ENTER INTO ITS SYSTEM.
THOUGHT PATTERN RELAYS OFTEN WARN ME OF FUTURE ATTACKS LIKE PREDICTING AN EARTHQUAKE.
THERE ARE LIVING QUARTERS. POWER TEST FACILITIES. WEAPONS.
MY SHIP HAS EVERYTHING I COULD EVER NEED.
WHO ELSE LIVES HERE?
NO ONE.

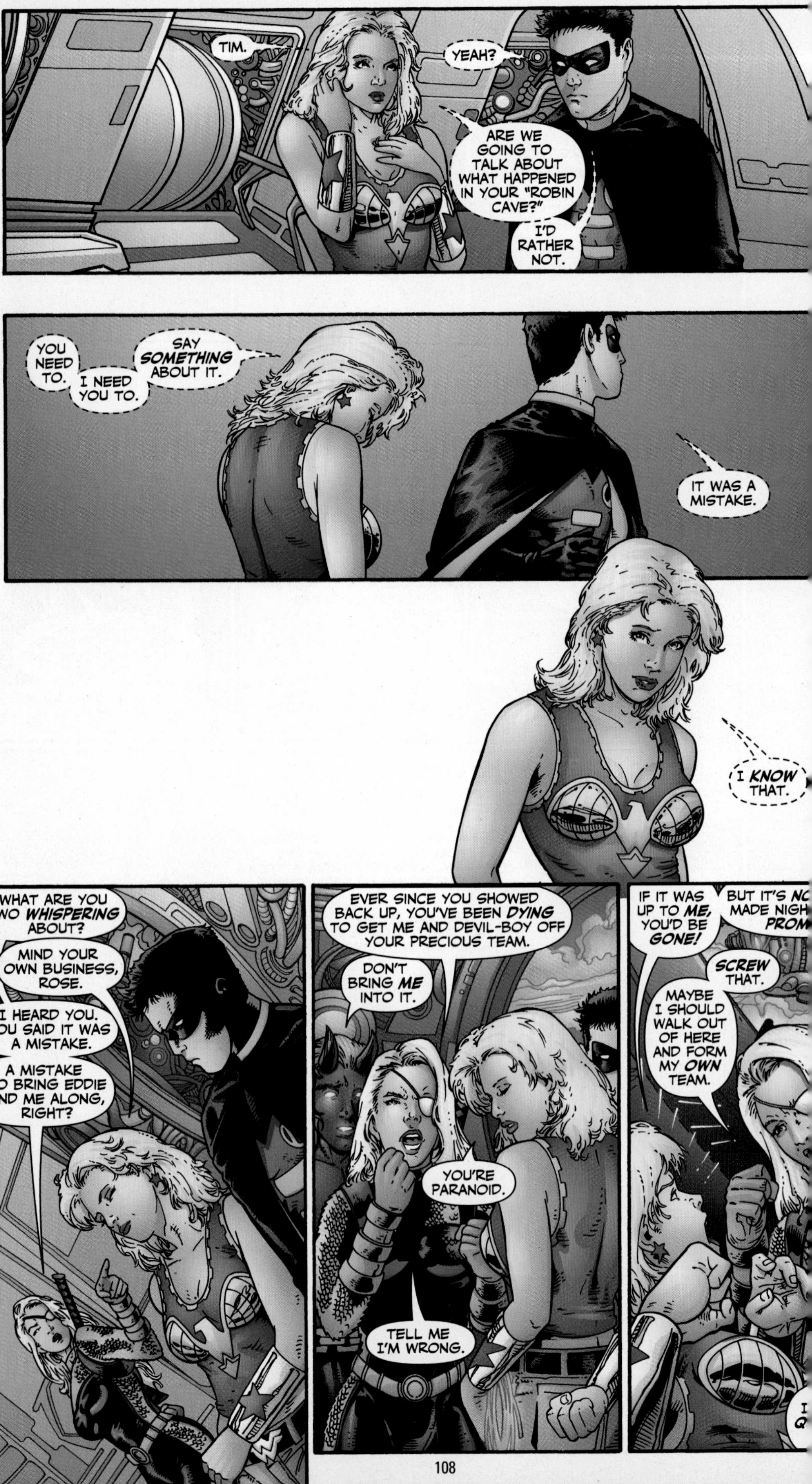
TIM.
YEAH?
ARE WE GOING TO TALK ABOUT WHAT HAPPENED IN YOUR "ROBIN CAVE?"
I'D RATHER NOT.
YOU NEED TO.
I NEED YOU TO.
SAY *SOMETHING* ABOUT IT.
IT WAS A MISTAKE.
I *KNOW* THAT.
WHAT ARE YOU TWO *WHISPERING* ABOUT?
MIND YOUR OWN BUSINESS, ROSE.
I HEARD YOU. YOU SAID IT WAS A MISTAKE.
A MISTAKE TO BRING EDDIE AND ME ALONG, RIGHT?
EVER SINCE YOU SHOWED BACK UP, YOU'VE BEEN *DYING* TO GET ME AND DEVIL-BOY OFF YOUR PRECIOUS TEAM.
DON'T BRING *ME* INTO IT.
YOU'RE PARANOID.
TELL ME I'M WRONG.
IF IT WAS UP TO *ME,* YOU'D BE *GONE!*
BUT IT'S NO
MADE NIGH
PROM
SCREW THAT.
MAYBE I SHOULD WALK OUT OF HERE AND FORM MY *OWN* TEAM.

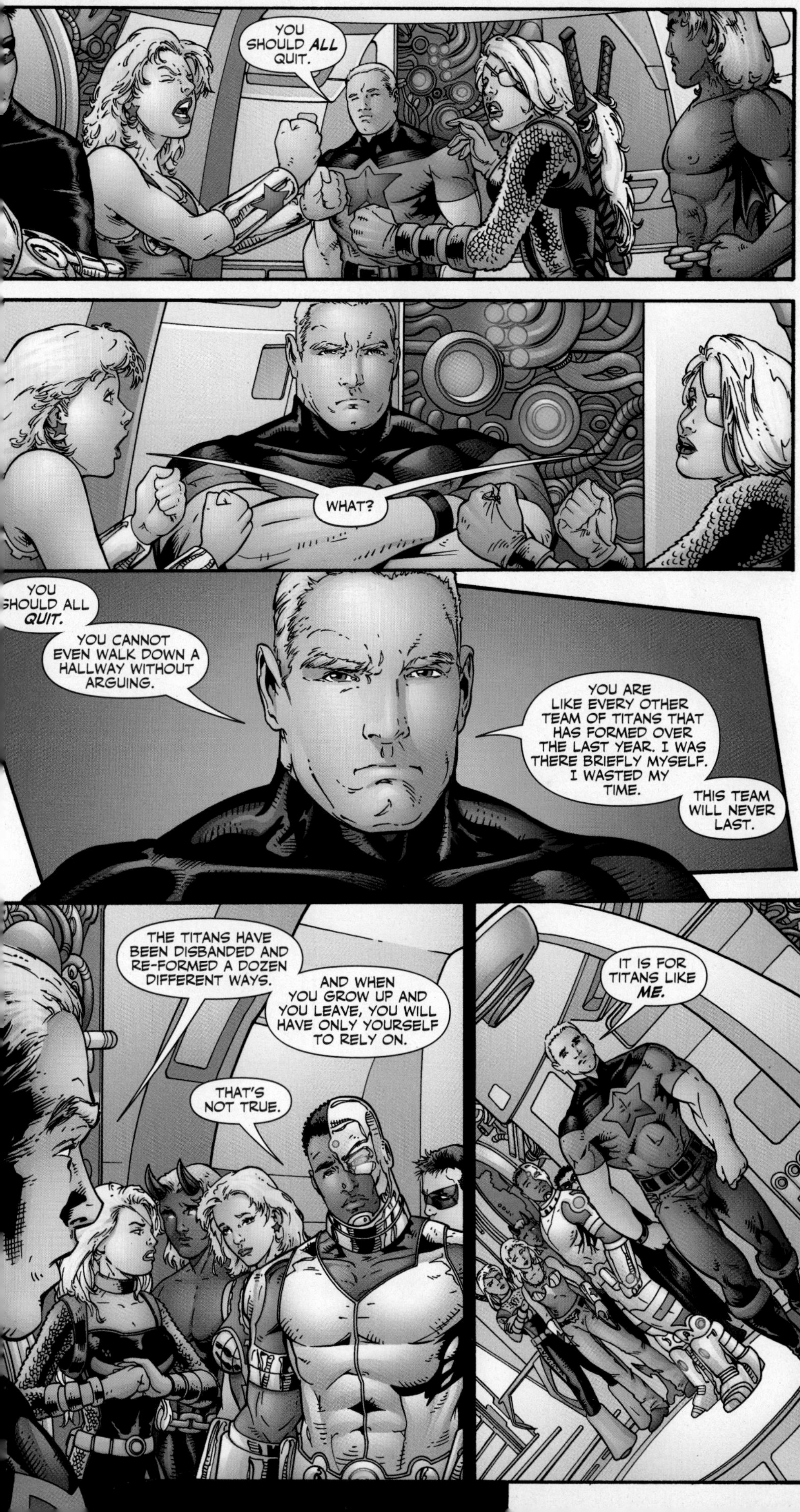
YOU SHOULD ALL QUIT.
WHAT?
YOU SHOULD ALL QUIT.
YOU CANNOT EVEN WALK DOWN A HALLWAY WITHOUT ARGUING.
YOU ARE LIKE EVERY OTHER TEAM OF TITANS THAT HAS FORMED OVER THE LAST YEAR. I WAS THERE BRIEFLY MYSELF. I WASTED MY TIME.
THIS TEAM WILL NEVER LAST.
THE TITANS HAVE BEEN DISBANDED AND RE-FORMED A DOZEN DIFFERENT WAYS.
AND WHEN YOU GROW UP AND YOU LEAVE, YOU WILL HAVE ONLY YOURSELF TO RELY ON.
THAT'S NOT TRUE.
IT IS FOR TITANS LIKE ME.

PANTHA. WILDEBEEST.

TEAMMATES THAT BECAME LIKE FAMILY.

SUPERBOY.

JERICHO.

STARFIRE.

IN THE END, WHAT DID BEING A TITAN DO FOR *ANY* OF THEM?

IT'S NOT WHAT THIS TEAM CAN DO FOR YOU--

SAVE THE SPEECH.

I HAVE ALREADY HEARD IT FROM THE *FIRST* ROBIN.

A WEEK AGO, RAVEN CAME HERE ASKING ME QUESTIONS ABOUT THE OTHER TITANS. SHE NEVER SAID WHY.

THIS IS ADDRESS APARTMENT HAD IN BE

YOU KNOW THE WAY BACK TO THE TELEPORTERS.

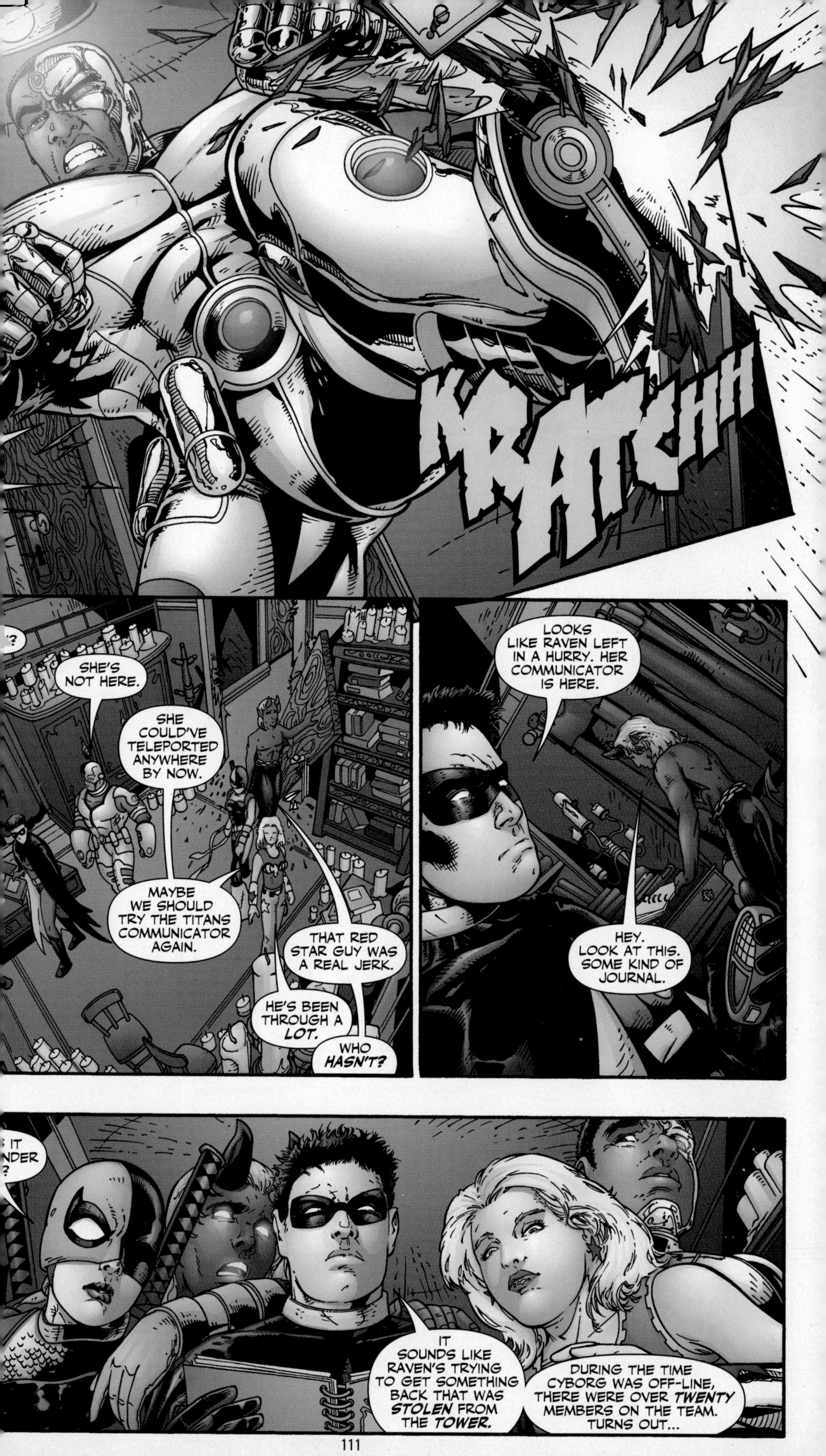
KRATCHH
SHE'S NOT HERE.
SHE COULD'VE TELEPORTED ANYWHERE BY NOW.
MAYBE WE SHOULD TRY THE TITANS COMMUNICATOR AGAIN.
THAT RED STAR GUY WAS A REAL JERK.
HE'S BEEN THROUGH A *LOT.*
WHO *HASN'T?*
LOOKS LIKE RAVEN LEFT IN A HURRY. HER COMMUNICATOR IS HERE.
HEY. LOOK AT THIS. SOME KIND OF JOURNAL.
IT SOUNDS LIKE RAVEN'S TRYING TO GET SOMETHING BACK THAT WAS *STOLEN* FROM THE *TOWER.*
DURING THE TIME CYBORG WAS OFF-LINE, THERE WERE OVER *TWENTY* MEMBERS ON THE TEAM. TURNS OUT...

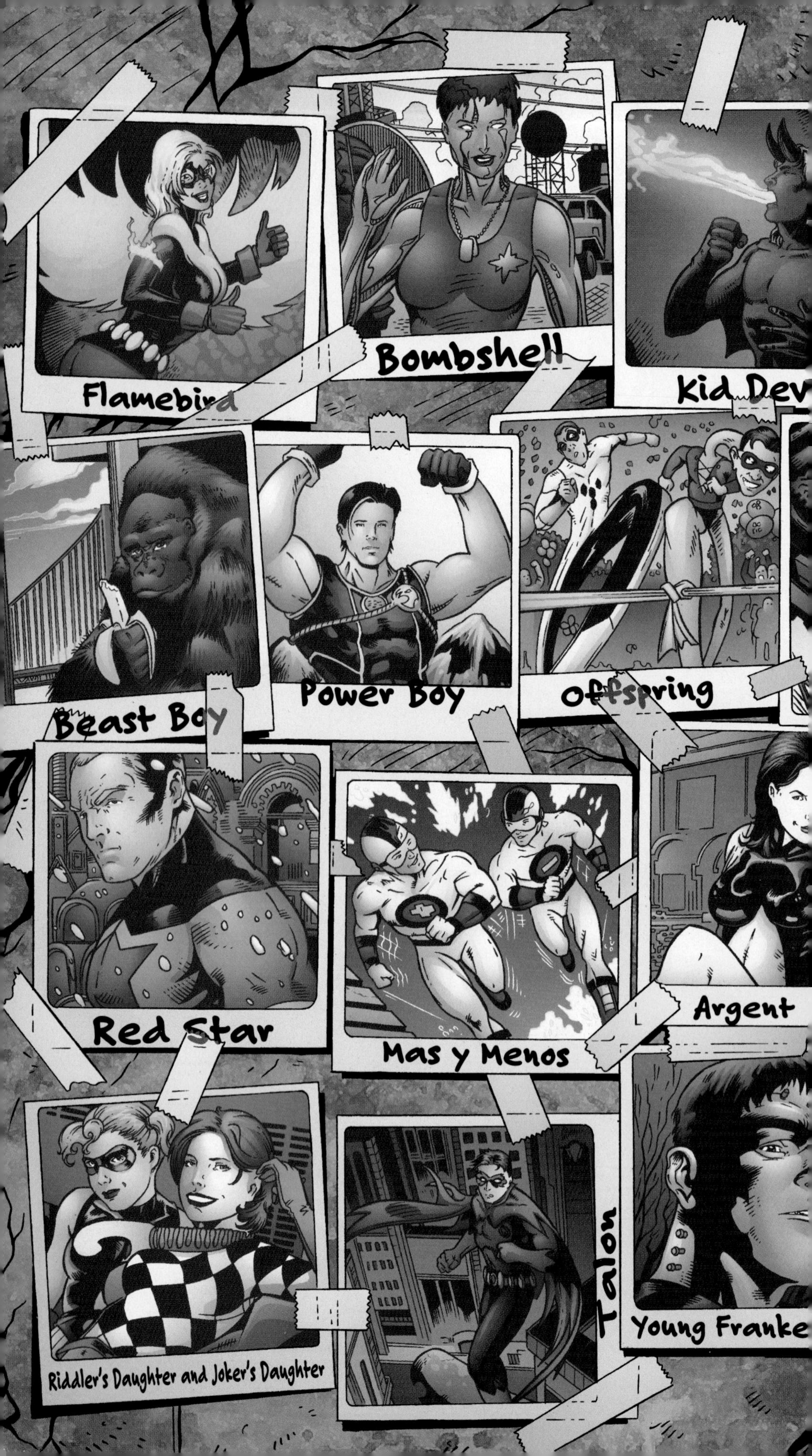
Flamebird
Bombshell
Kid Dev
Beast Boy
Power Boy
Offspring
Red Star
Mas y Menos
Argent
Riddler's Daughter and Joker's Daughter
Talon
Young Franke

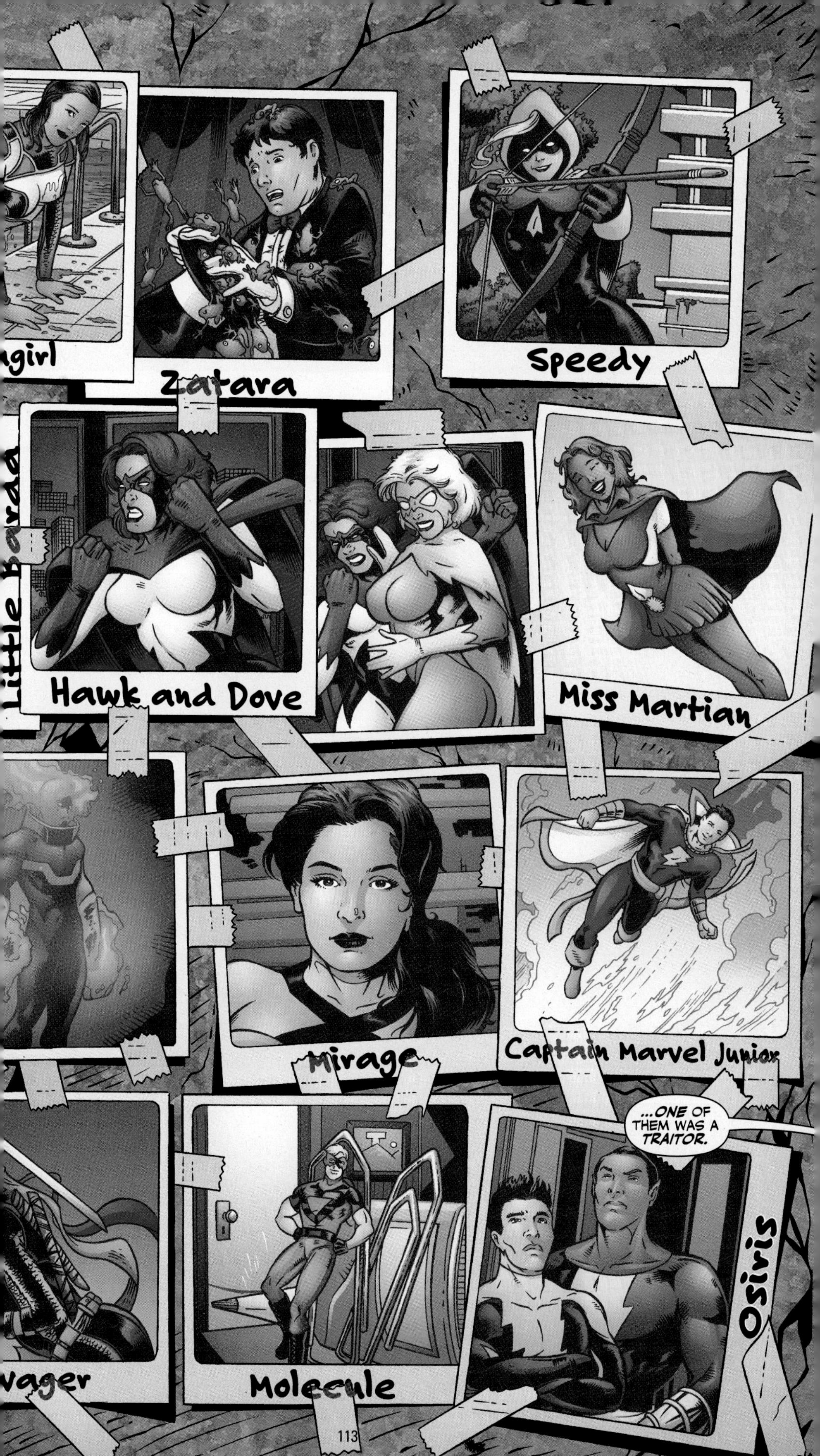
Zatara
Speedy
Little Barda
Hawk and Dove
Miss Martian
Mirage
Captain Marvel Junior
...ONE OF THEM WAS A TRAITOR.
Molecule
Osiris

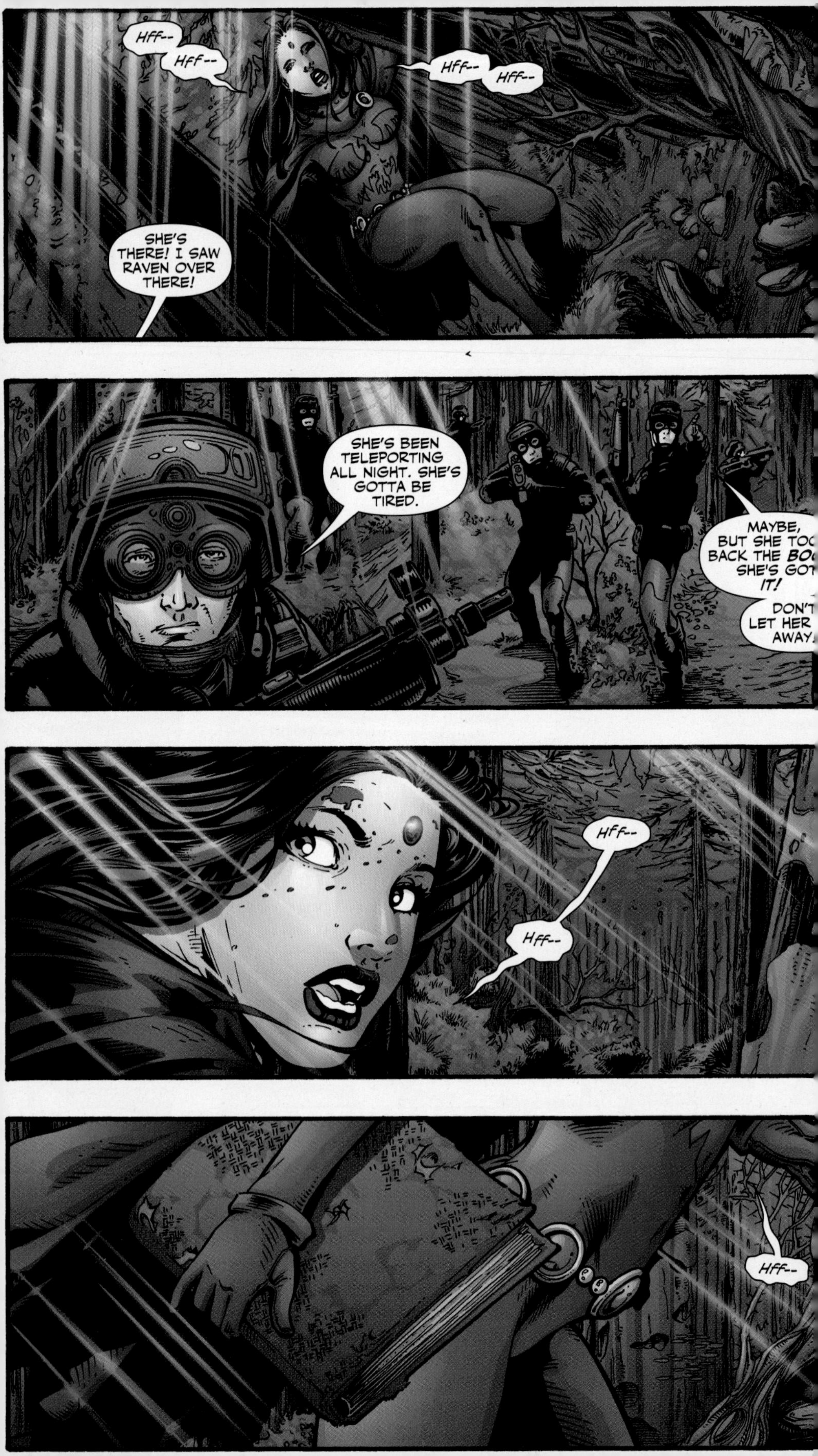
Hff-- Hff--
Hff-- Hff--
SHE'S THERE! I SAW RAVEN OVER THERE!
SHE'S BEEN TELEPORTING ALL NIGHT. SHE'S GOTTA BE TIRED.
MAYBE, BUT SHE TOO BACK THE BO SHE'S GOT IT!
DON'T LET HER AWAY.
Hff--
Hff--
Hff--

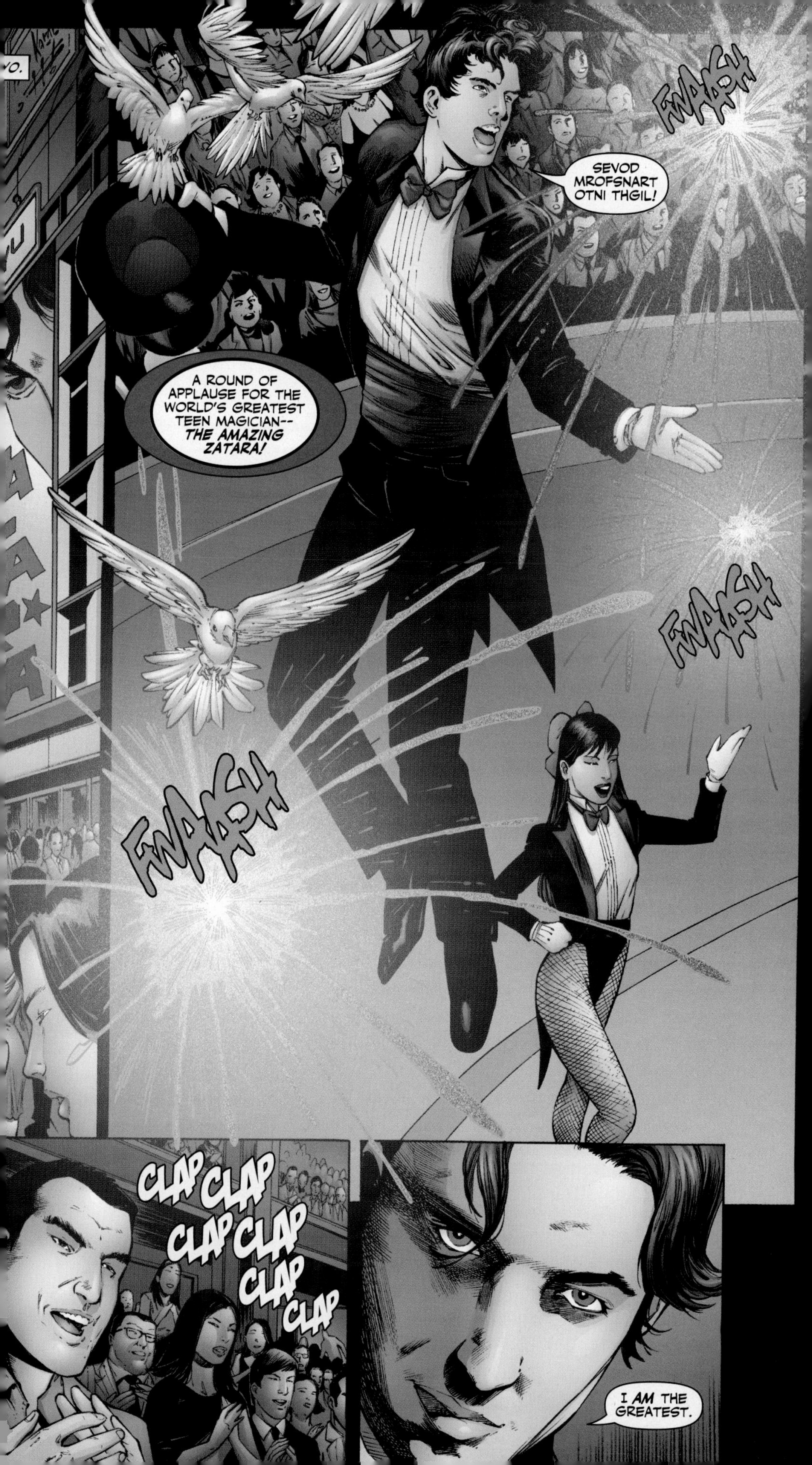
SEVOD MROFSNART OTNI THGIL!
FWASH
A ROUND OF APPLAUSE FOR THE WORLD'S GREATEST TEEN MAGICIAN-- THE AMAZING ZATARA!
FWASH
FWASH
CLAP CLAP CLAP CLAP CLAP CLAP
I AM THE GREATEST.

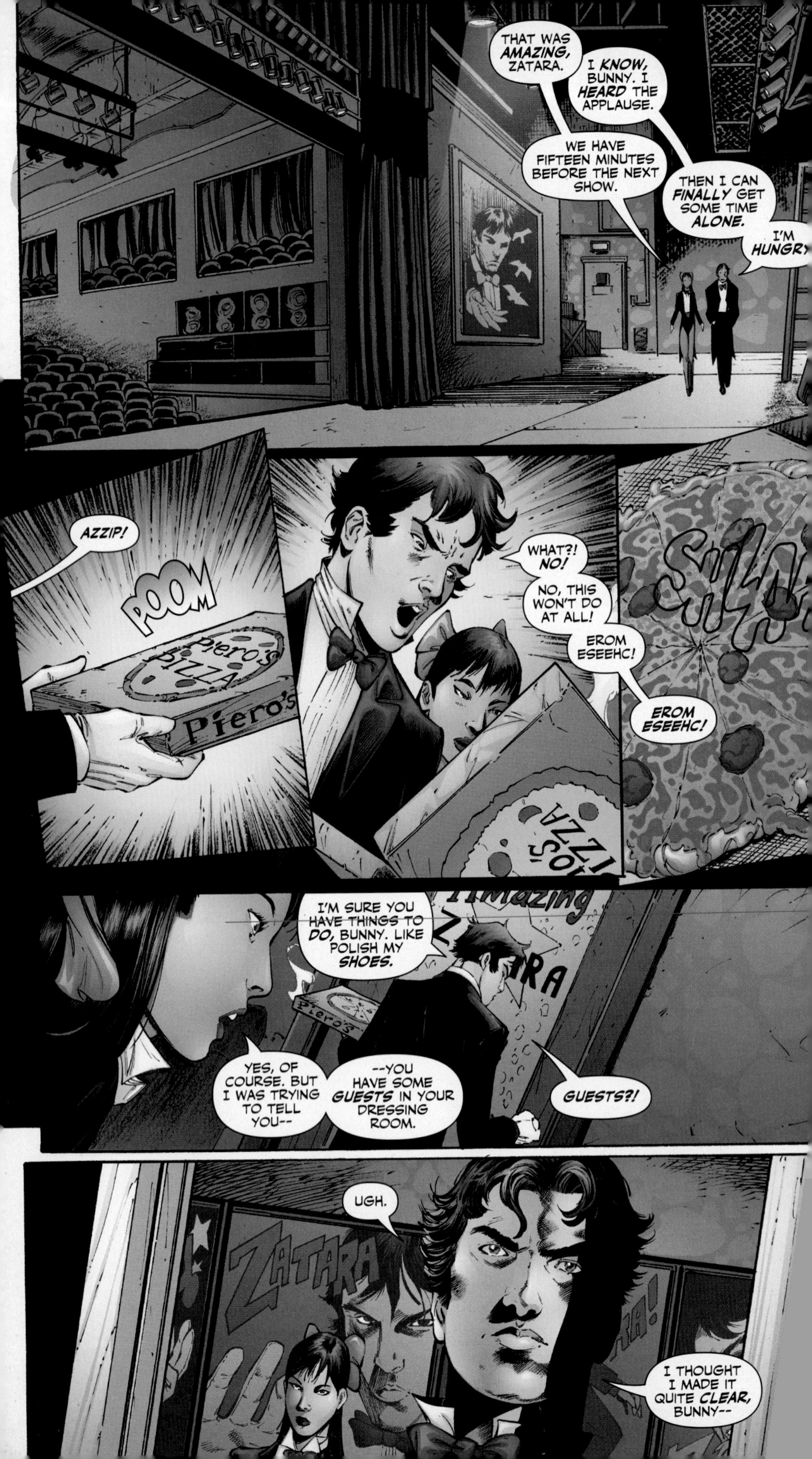

THAT WAS AMAZING, ZATARA.
I KNOW, BUNNY. I HEARD THE APPLAUSE.
WE HAVE FIFTEEN MINUTES BEFORE THE NEXT SHOW.
THEN I CAN FINALLY GET SOME TIME ALONE.
I'M HUNGRY
AZZIP!
POOM
Piero's PIZZA
Piero's
WHAT?! NO!
NO, THIS WON'T DO AT ALL!
EROM ESEEHC!
EROM ESEEHC!
I'M SURE YOU HAVE THINGS TO DO, BUNNY. LIKE POLISH MY SHOES.
Amazing
ZATARA
Piero's
YES, OF COURSE. BUT I WAS TRYING TO TELL YOU--
--YOU HAVE SOME GUESTS IN YOUR DRESSING ROOM.
GUESTS?!
UGH.
ZATARA
I THOUGHT I MADE IT QUITE CLEAR, BUNNY--

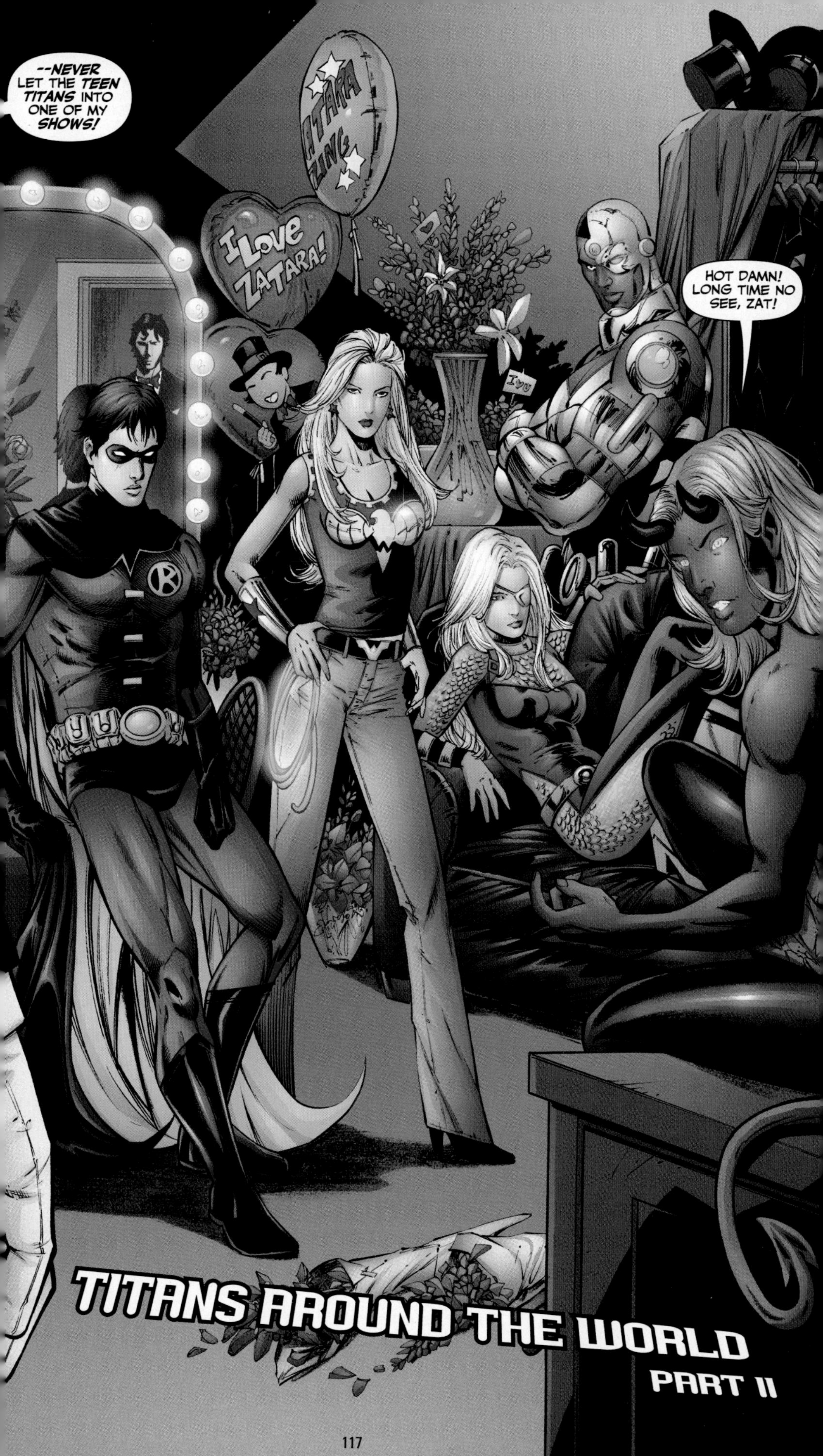
--NEVER LET THE TEEN TITANS INTO ONE OF MY SHOWS!
I LOVE ZATARA!
HOT DAMN! LONG TIME NO SEE, ZAT!
TITANS AROUND THE WORLD
PART II

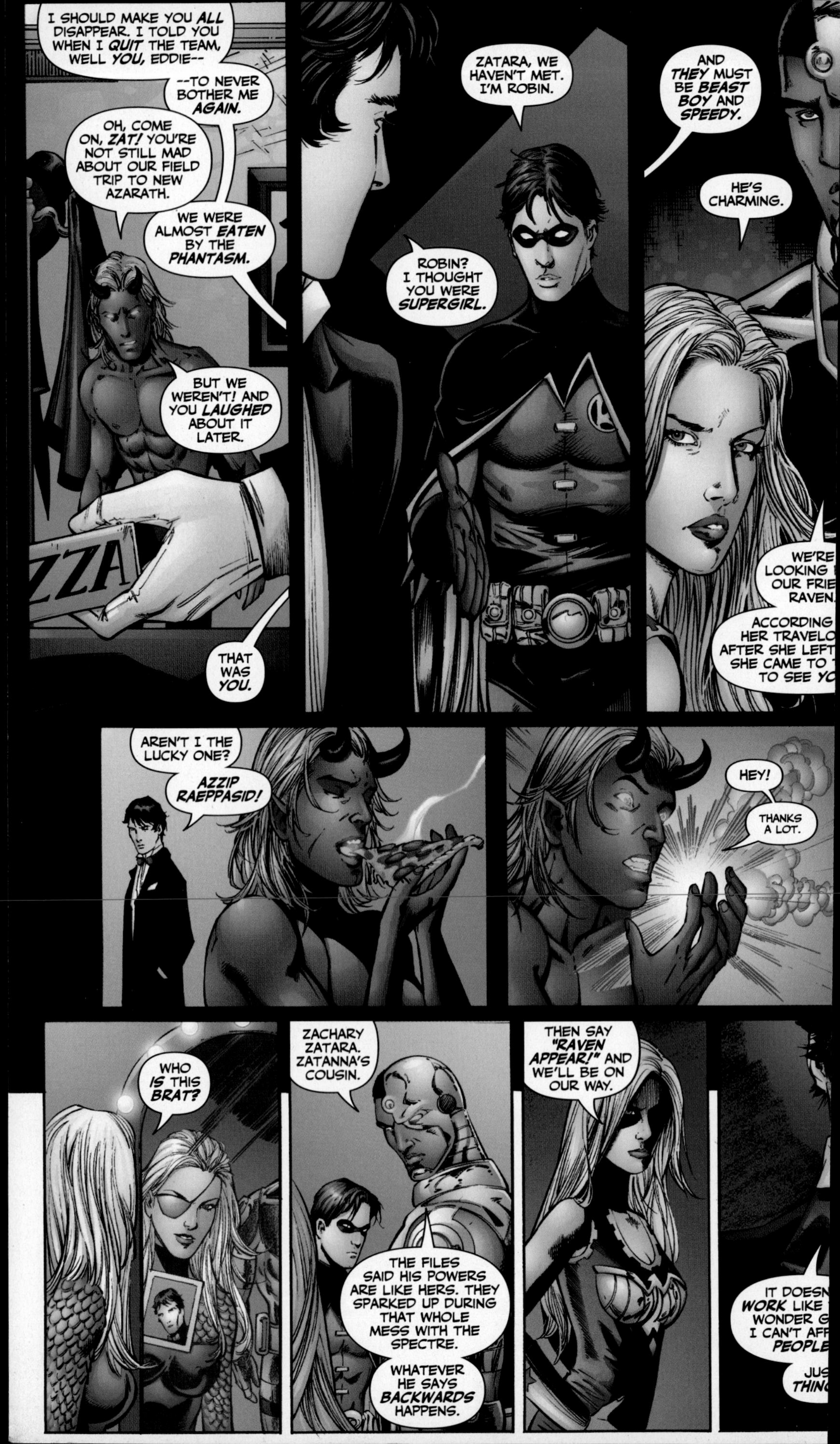

I SHOULD MAKE YOU ALL DISAPPEAR. I TOLD YOU WHEN I QUIT THE TEAM, WELL YOU, EDDIE--
--TO NEVER BOTHER ME AGAIN.
OH, COME ON, ZAT! YOU'RE NOT STILL MAD ABOUT OUR FIELD TRIP TO NEW AZARATH.
WE WERE ALMOST EATEN BY THE PHANTASM.
BUT WE WEREN'T! AND YOU LAUGHED ABOUT IT LATER.
ZZA
THAT WAS YOU.
ZATARA, WE HAVEN'T MET. I'M ROBIN.
ROBIN? I THOUGHT YOU WERE SUPERGIRL.
AND THEY MUST BE BEAST BOY AND SPEEDY.
HE'S CHARMING.
WE'RE LOOKING OUR FRIE RAVEN.
ACCORDING HER TRAVELO AFTER SHE LEFT SHE CAME TO TO SEE YO
AREN'T I THE LUCKY ONE?
AZZIP RAEPPASID!
HEY!
THANKS A LOT.
WHO IS THIS BRAT?
ZACHARY ZATARA. ZATANNA'S COUSIN.
THE FILES SAID HIS POWERS ARE LIKE HERS. THEY SPARKED UP DURING THAT WHOLE MESS WITH THE SPECTRE.
WHATEVER HE SAYS BACKWARDS HAPPENS.
THEN SAY "RAVEN APPEAR!" AND WE'LL BE ON OUR WAY.
IT DOESN WORK LIKE WONDER I CAN'T AFF PEOPLE
JUS THIN

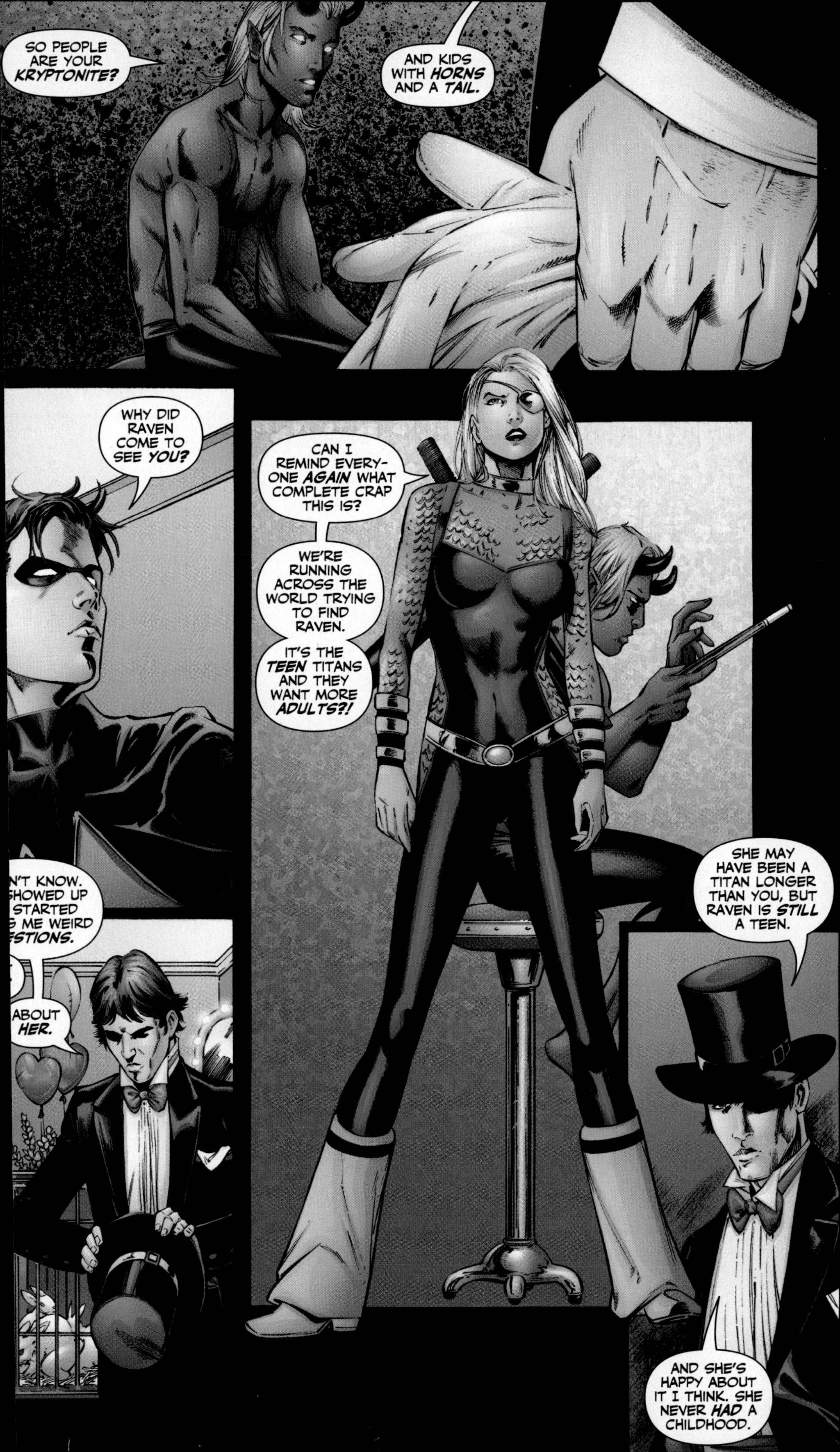
SO PEOPLE ARE YOUR KRYPTONITE?
AND KIDS WITH HORNS AND A TAIL.
WHY DID RAVEN COME TO SEE YOU?
CAN I REMIND EVERY-ONE AGAIN WHAT COMPLETE CRAP THIS IS?
WE'RE RUNNING ACROSS THE WORLD TRYING TO FIND RAVEN.
IT'S THE TEEN TITANS AND THEY WANT MORE ADULTS?!
N'T KNOW. SHOWED UP STARTED ME WEIRD ESTIONS.
ABOUT HER.
SHE MAY HAVE BEEN A TITAN LONGER THAN YOU, BUT RAVEN IS STILL A TEEN.
AND SHE'S HAPPY ABOUT IT I THINK. SHE NEVER HAD A CHILDHOOD.

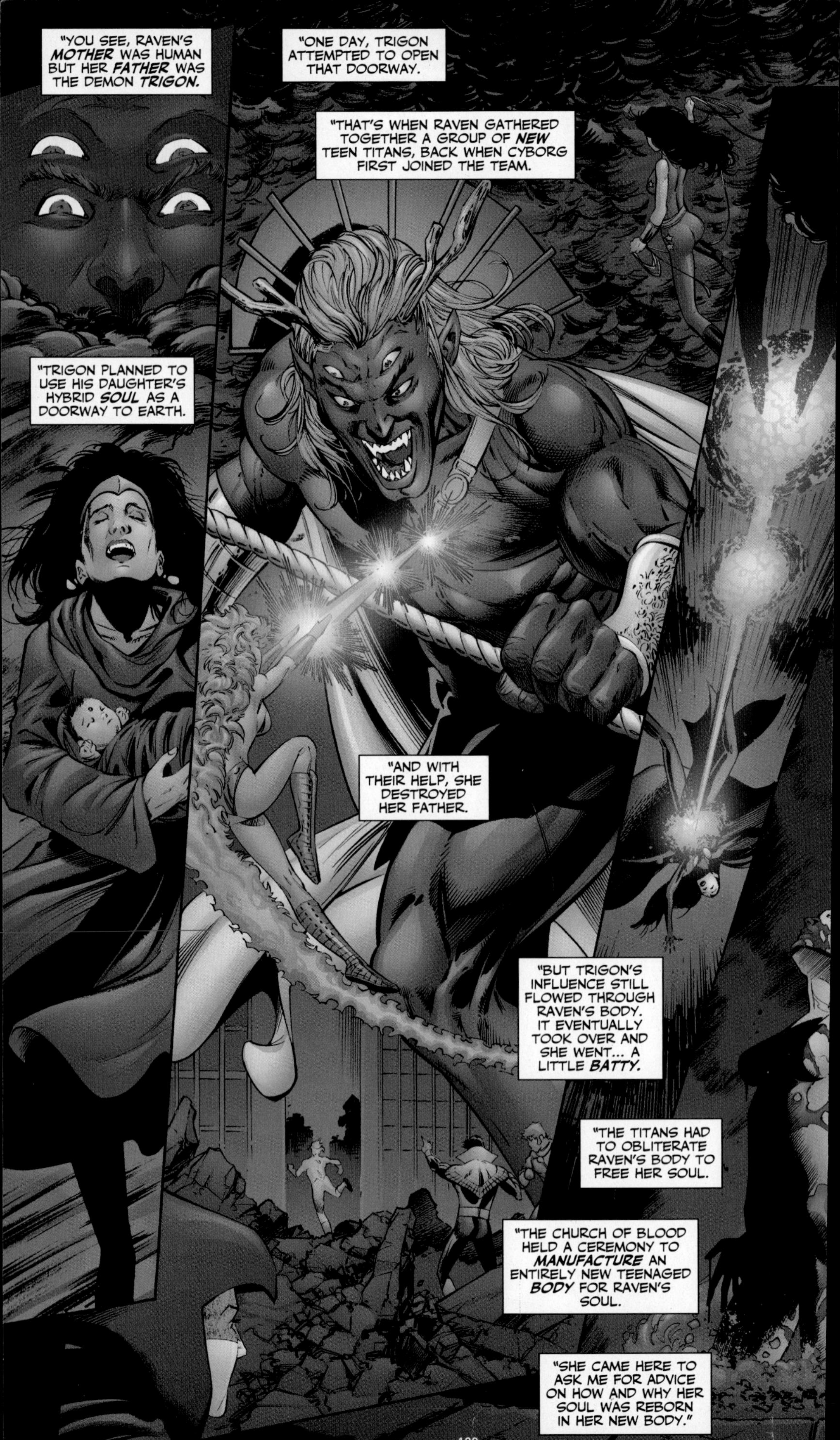
"YOU SEE, RAVEN'S MOTHER WAS HUMAN BUT HER FATHER WAS THE DEMON TRIGON.
"TRIGON PLANNED TO USE HIS DAUGHTER'S HYBRID SOUL AS A DOORWAY TO EARTH.
"ONE DAY, TRIGON ATTEMPTED TO OPEN THAT DOORWAY.
"THAT'S WHEN RAVEN GATHERED TOGETHER A GROUP OF NEW TEEN TITANS, BACK WHEN CYBORG FIRST JOINED THE TEAM.
"AND WITH THEIR HELP, SHE DESTROYED HER FATHER.
"BUT TRIGON'S INFLUENCE STILL FLOWED THROUGH RAVEN'S BODY. IT EVENTUALLY TOOK OVER AND SHE WENT... A LITTLE BATTY.
"THE TITANS HAD TO OBLITERATE RAVEN'S BODY TO FREE HER SOUL.
"THE CHURCH OF BLOOD HELD A CEREMONY TO MANUFACTURE AN ENTIRELY NEW TEENAGED BODY FOR RAVEN'S SOUL.
"SHE CAME HERE TO ASK ME FOR ADVICE ON HOW AND WHY HER SOUL WAS REBORN IN HER NEW BODY."

WAS
OU HOW
SHE WAS
RN?

IS
NG
E

I TOLD HER
E'D BEEN GIVEN A
COND CHANCE TO
PERIENCE LIFE ON
ER OWN TERMS
INSTEAD OF
TRIGON'S.

YOU KNOW A LOT ABOUT RAVEN.

WE COULD USE HELP FROM SOMEONE LIKE YOU, ZATARA. YOU UNDERSTAND MAGIC, AND RAVEN'S POWERS, PROBABLY BETTER THAN ANYONE ELSE.

COME WITH US, ZAT.

MY ACT'S A SOLO ONE. MY TIME WITH THE TITANS WAS SHORT AND, THANKFULLY FOR THE MOST PART, FORGETTABLE.

BUT ZAT--

OU
ET,

I'M EMBARRASSED I WAS EVER A PART OF YOUR TEAM!

I GUESS THAT'S OUR CUE.

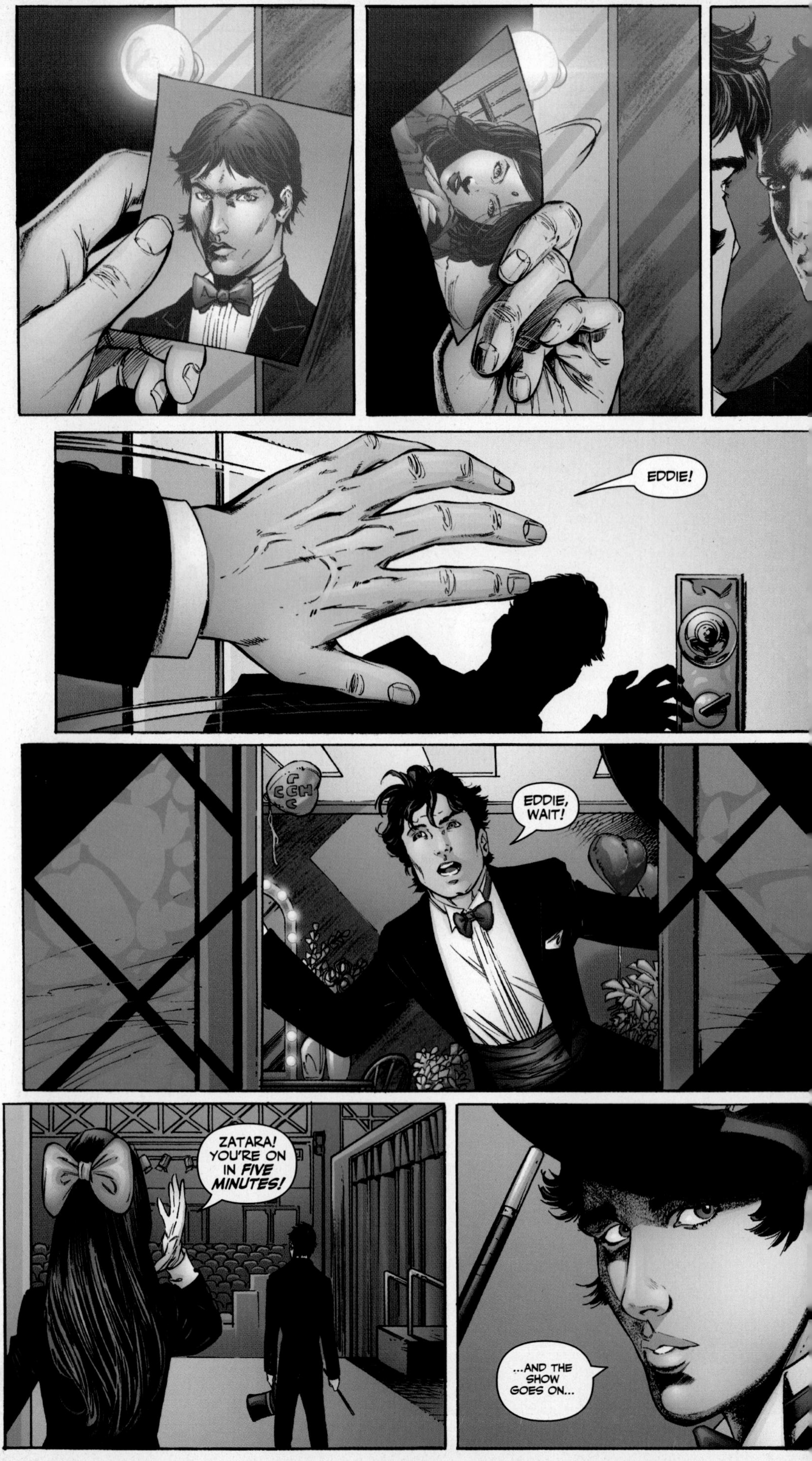

EDDIE!
EDDIE, WAIT!
ZATARA! YOU'RE ON IN *FIVE MINUTES!*
...AND THE SHOW GOES ON...

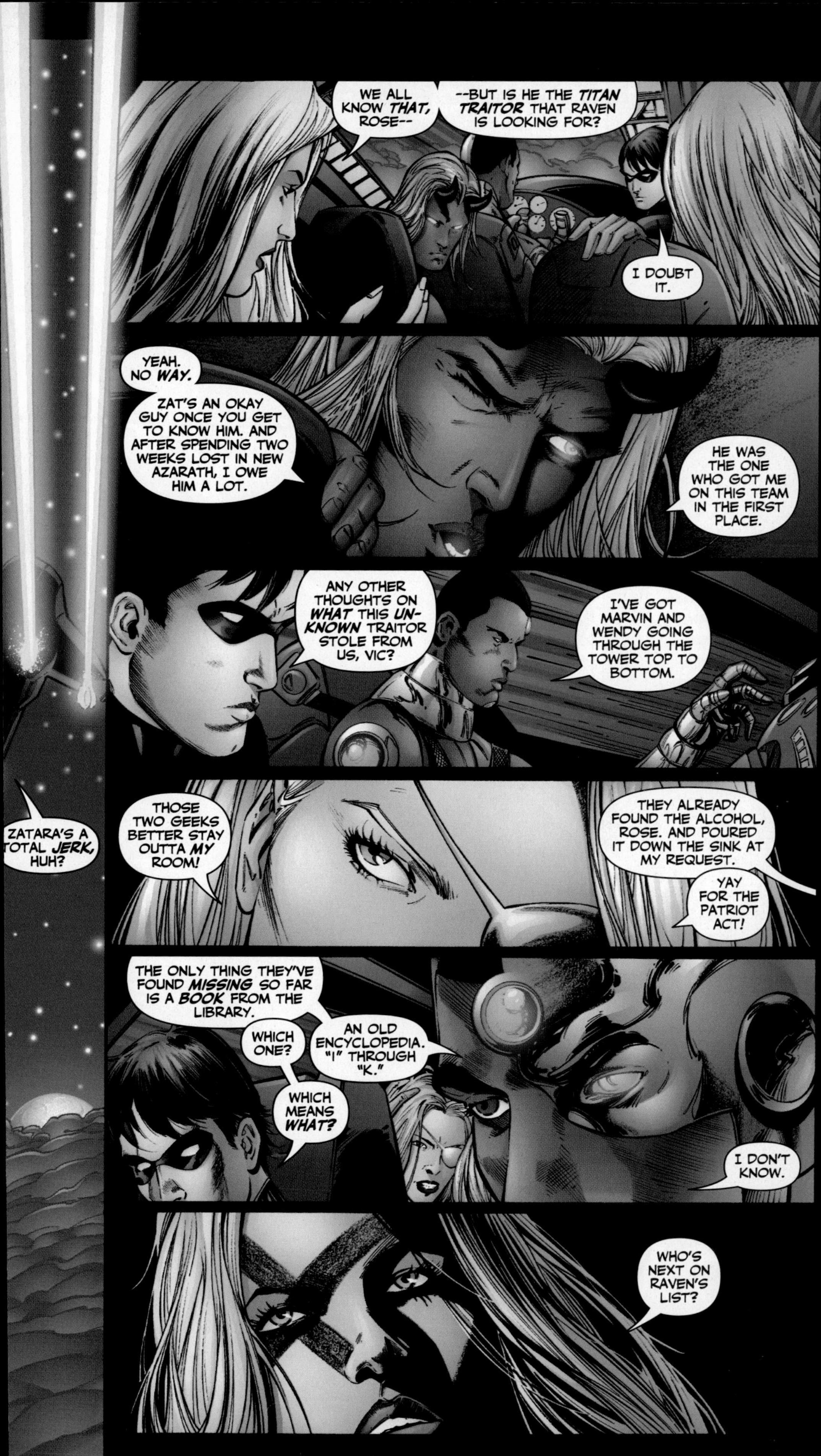
WE ALL KNOW THAT, ROSE--
--BUT IS HE THE TITAN TRAITOR THAT RAVEN IS LOOKING FOR?
I DOUBT IT.
YEAH. NO WAY.
ZAT'S AN OKAY GUY ONCE YOU GET TO KNOW HIM. AND AFTER SPENDING TWO WEEKS LOST IN NEW AZARATH, I OWE HIM A LOT.
HE WAS THE ONE WHO GOT ME ON THIS TEAM IN THE FIRST PLACE.
ANY OTHER THOUGHTS ON WHAT THIS UNKNOWN TRAITOR STOLE FROM US, VIC?
I'VE GOT MARVIN AND WENDY GOING THROUGH THE TOWER TOP TO BOTTOM.
ZATARA'S A TOTAL JERK, HUH?
THOSE TWO GEEKS BETTER STAY OUTTA MY ROOM!
THEY ALREADY FOUND THE ALCOHOL, ROSE. AND POURED IT DOWN THE SINK AT MY REQUEST.
YAY FOR THE PATRIOT ACT!
THE ONLY THING THEY'VE FOUND MISSING SO FAR IS A BOOK FROM THE LIBRARY.
WHICH ONE?
AN OLD ENCYCLOPEDIA. "I" THROUGH "K."
WHICH MEANS WHAT?
I DON'T KNOW.
WHO'S NEXT ON RAVEN'S LIST?

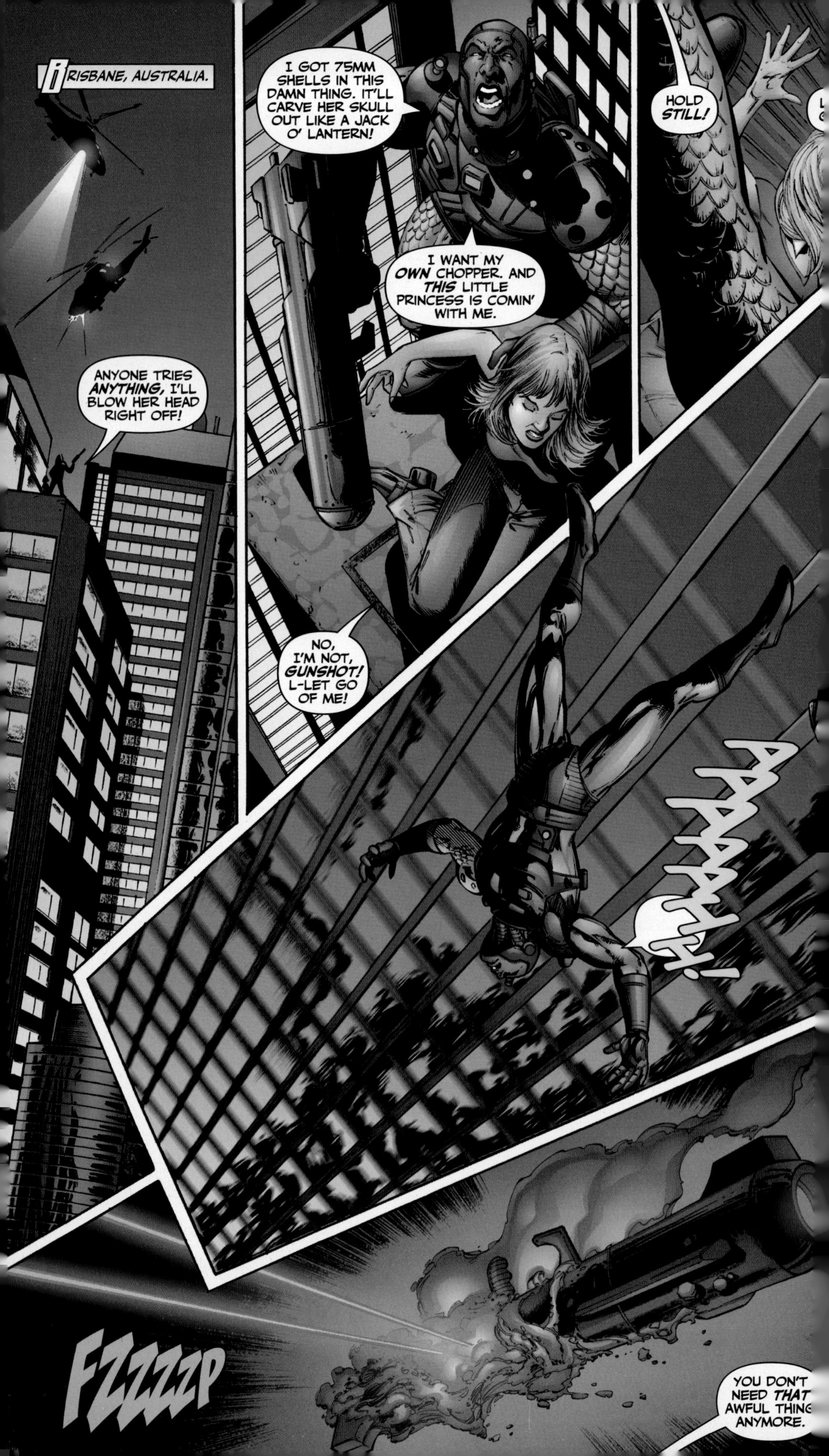

BRISBANE, AUSTRALIA.
ANYONE TRIES ANYTHING, I'LL BLOW HER HEAD RIGHT OFF!
I GOT 75MM SHELLS IN THIS DAMN THING. IT'LL CARVE HER SKULL OUT LIKE A JACK O' LANTERN!
I WANT MY OWN CHOPPER. AND THIS LITTLE PRINCESS IS COMIN' WITH ME.
NO, I'M NOT, GUNSHOT! L-LET GO OF ME!
HOLD STILL!
AAAAAAHH!
FZZZZP
YOU DON'T NEED THAT AWFUL THING ANYMORE.

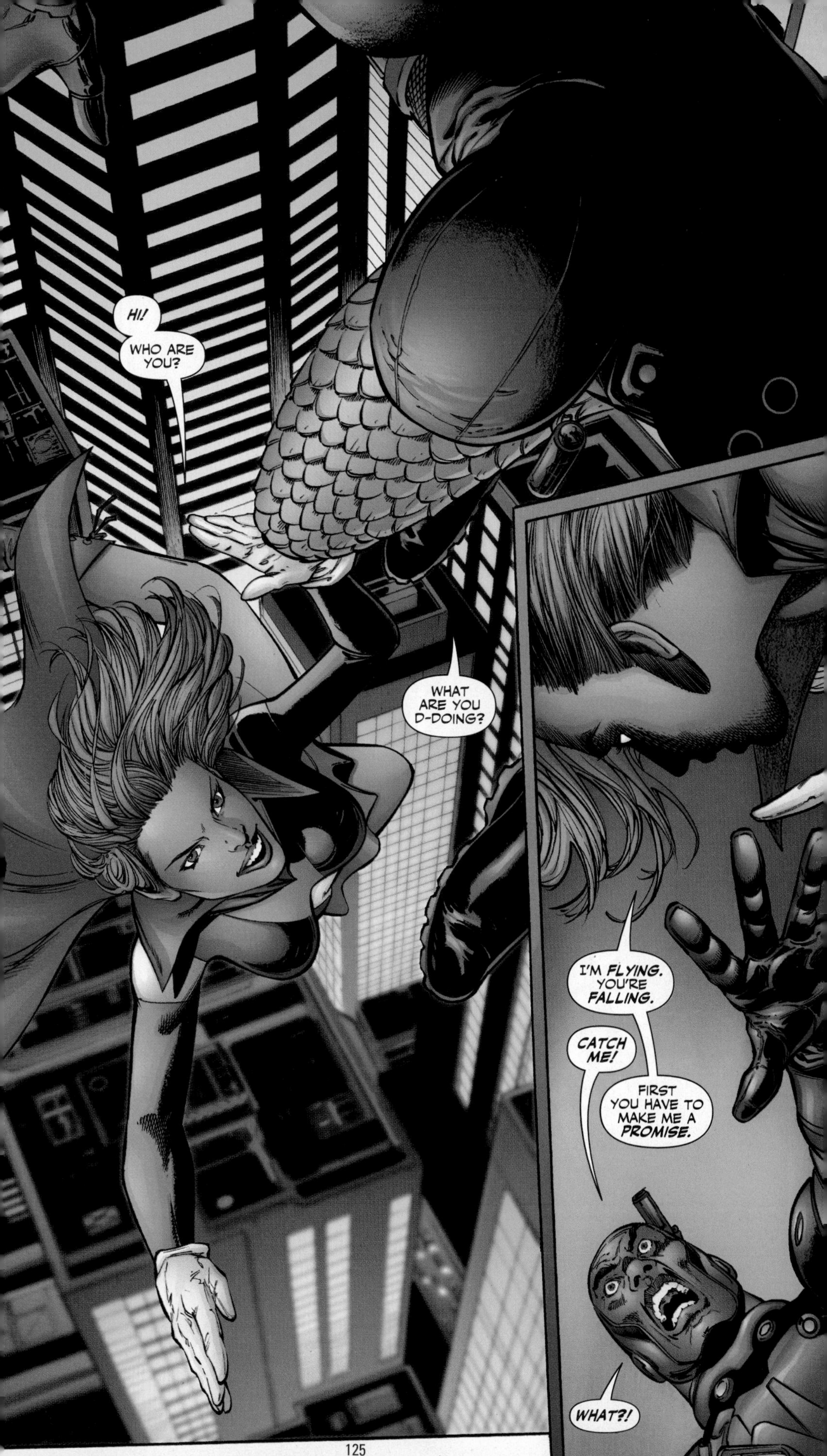
HI!
WHO ARE YOU?
WHAT ARE YOU D-DOING?
I'M FLYING. YOU'RE FALLING.
CATCH ME!
FIRST YOU HAVE TO MAKE ME A PROMISE.
WHAT?!

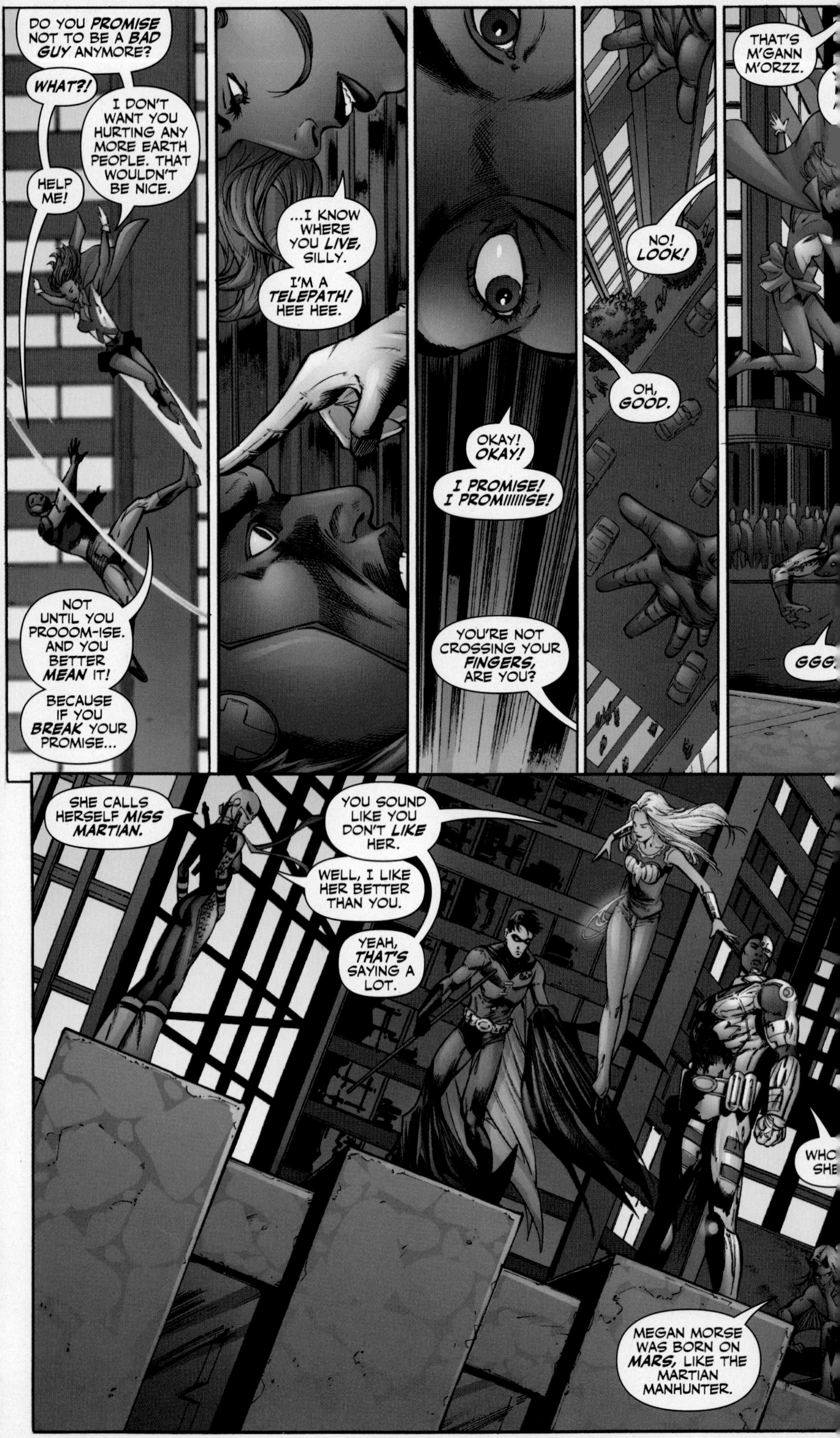
DO YOU PROMISE NOT TO BE A BAD GUY ANYMORE?
WHAT?!
I DON'T WANT YOU HURTING ANY MORE EARTH PEOPLE. THAT WOULDN'T BE NICE.
HELP ME!
NOT UNTIL YOU PROOOM-ISE. AND YOU BETTER MEAN IT!
BECAUSE IF YOU BREAK YOUR PROMISE...
...I KNOW WHERE YOU LIVE, SILLY.
I'M A TELEPATH! HEE HEE.
OKAY! OKAY!
I PROMISE! I PROMIIIIIISE!
YOU'RE NOT CROSSING YOUR FINGERS, ARE YOU?
NO! LOOK!
OH, GOOD.
THAT'S M'GANN M'ORZZ.
GGG.
SHE CALLS HERSELF MISS MARTIAN.
YOU SOUND LIKE YOU DON'T LIKE HER.
WELL, I LIKE HER BETTER THAN YOU.
YEAH, THAT'S SAYING A LOT.
MEGAN MORSE WAS BORN ON MARS, LIKE THE MARTIAN MANHUNTER.

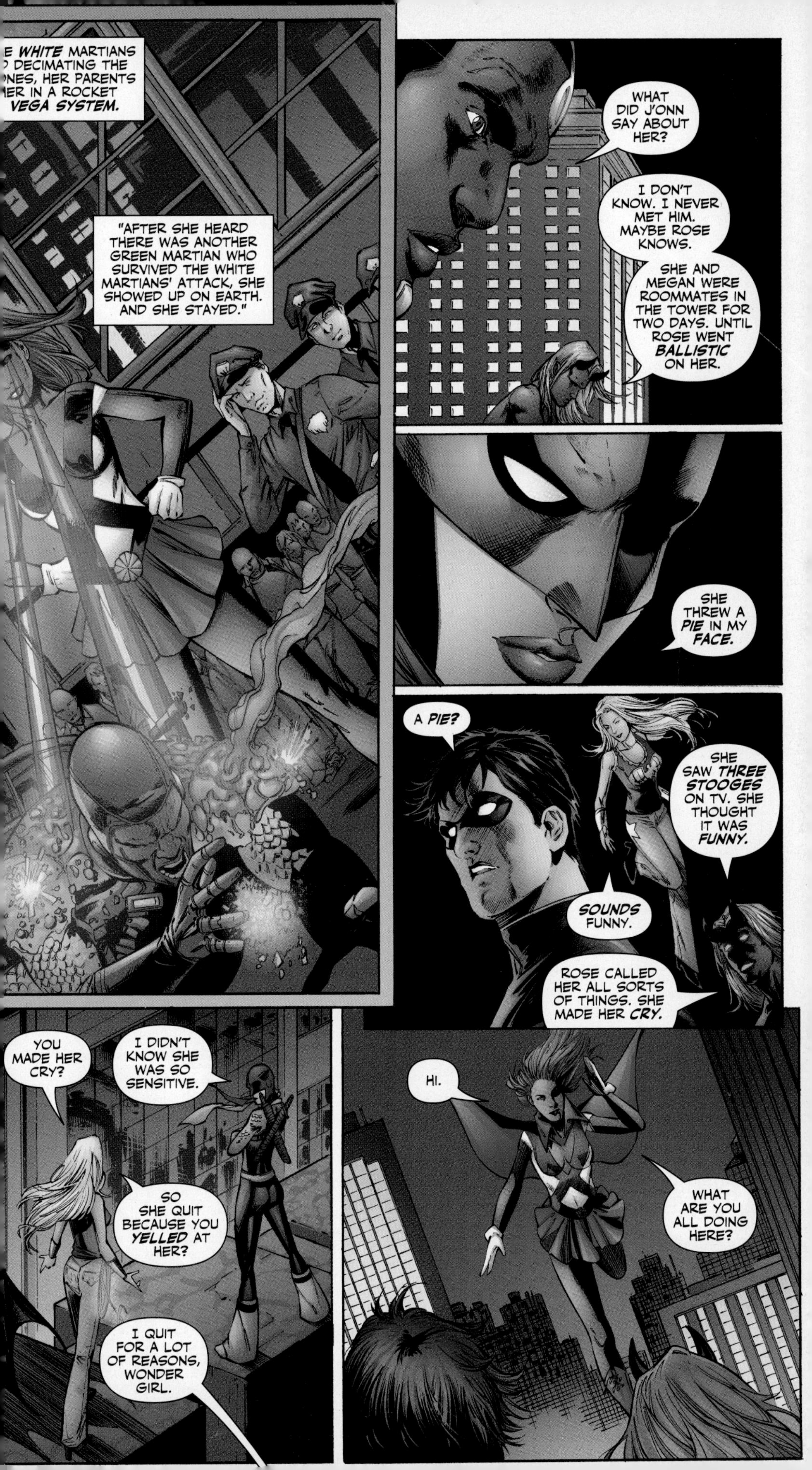

E WHITE MARTIANS
D DECIMATING THE
ONES, HER PARENTS
HER IN A ROCKET
VEGA SYSTEM.
"AFTER SHE HEARD THERE WAS ANOTHER GREEN MARTIAN WHO SURVIVED THE WHITE MARTIANS' ATTACK, SHE SHOWED UP ON EARTH. AND SHE STAYED."
WHAT DID J'ONN SAY ABOUT HER?
I DON'T KNOW. I NEVER MET HIM. MAYBE ROSE KNOWS.
SHE AND MEGAN WERE ROOMMATES IN THE TOWER FOR TWO DAYS. UNTIL ROSE WENT BALLISTIC ON HER.
SHE THREW A PIE IN MY FACE.
A PIE?
SHE SAW THREE STOOGES ON TV. SHE THOUGHT IT WAS FUNNY.
SOUNDS FUNNY.
ROSE CALLED HER ALL SORTS OF THINGS. SHE MADE HER CRY.
YOU MADE HER CRY?
I DIDN'T KNOW SHE WAS SO SENSITIVE.
SO SHE QUIT BECAUSE YOU YELLED AT HER?
I QUIT FOR A LOT OF REASONS, WONDER GIRL.
HI.
WHAT ARE YOU ALL DOING HERE?

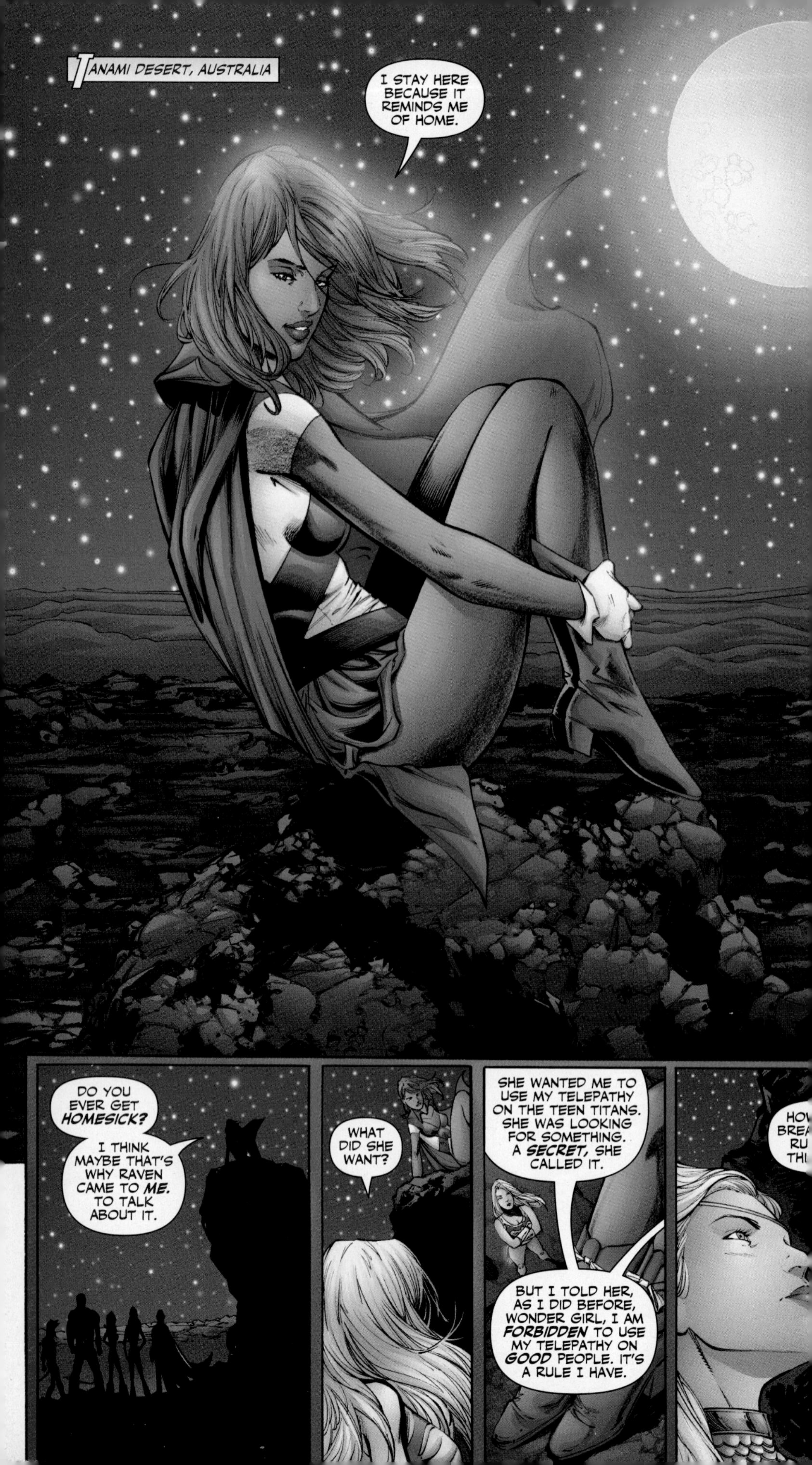
TANAMI DESERT, AUSTRALIA
I STAY HERE BECAUSE IT REMINDS ME OF HOME.
DO YOU EVER GET HOMESICK?
I THINK MAYBE THAT'S WHY RAVEN CAME TO ME. TO TALK ABOUT IT.
WHAT DID SHE WANT?
SHE WANTED ME TO USE MY TELEPATHY ON THE TEEN TITANS. SHE WAS LOOKING FOR SOMETHING. A SECRET, SHE CALLED IT.
BUT I TOLD HER, AS I DID BEFORE, WONDER GIRL, I AM FORBIDDEN TO USE MY TELEPATHY ON GOOD PEOPLE. IT'S A RULE I HAVE.

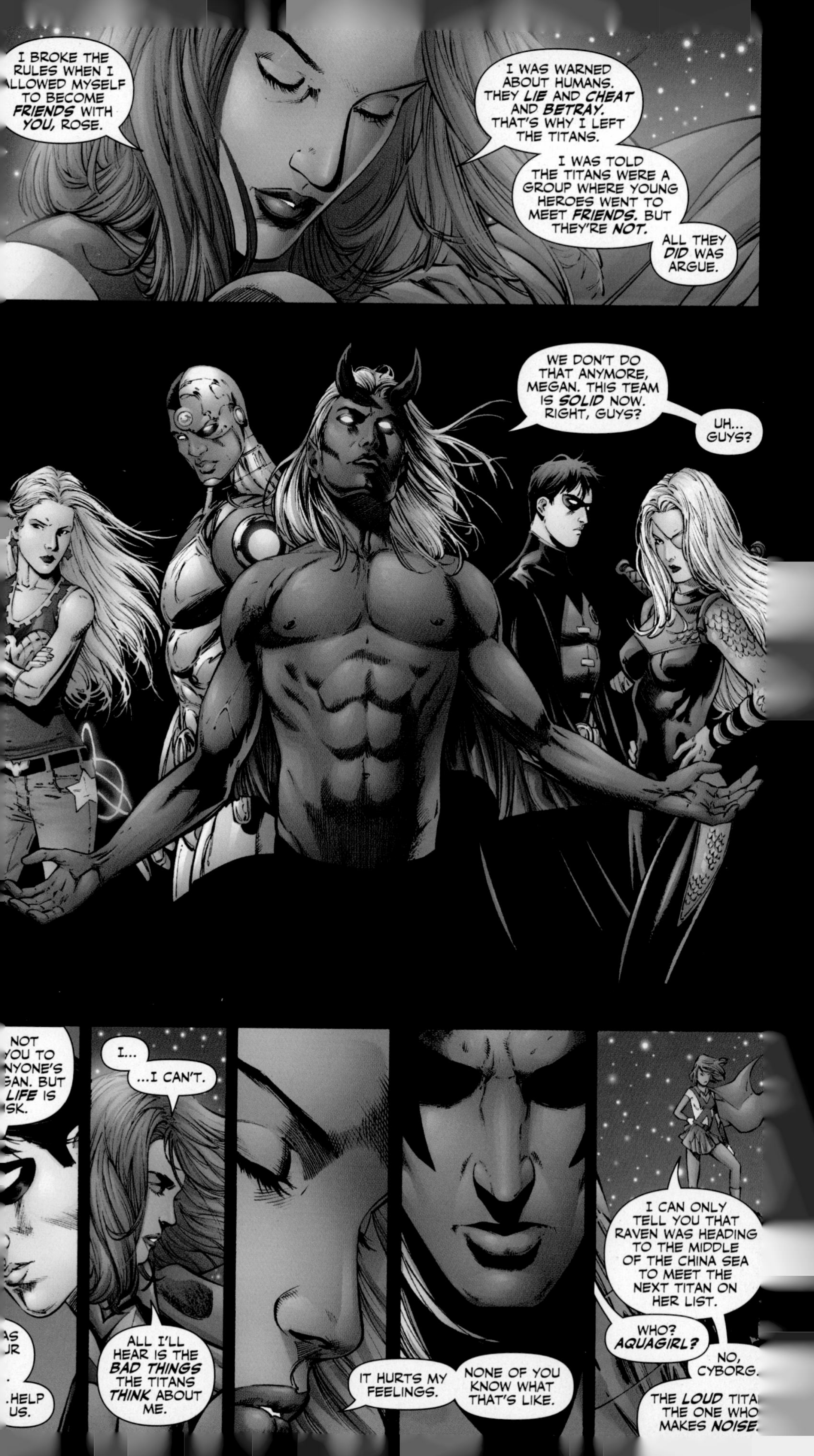

I BROKE THE RULES WHEN I ALLOWED MYSELF TO BECOME FRIENDS WITH YOU, ROSE.
I WAS WARNED ABOUT HUMANS. THEY LIE AND CHEAT AND BETRAY. THAT'S WHY I LEFT THE TITANS.
I WAS TOLD THE TITANS WERE A GROUP WHERE YOUNG HEROES WENT TO MEET FRIENDS. BUT THEY'RE NOT.
ALL THEY DID WAS ARGUE.
WE DON'T DO THAT ANYMORE, MEGAN. THIS TEAM IS SOLID NOW. RIGHT, GUYS?
UH... GUYS?
NOT YOU TO NYONE'S GAN. BUT LIFE IS SK.
.HELP US.
I...
...I CAN'T.
ALL I'LL HEAR IS THE BAD THINGS THE TITANS THINK ABOUT ME.
IT HURTS MY FEELINGS.
NONE OF YOU KNOW WHAT THAT'S LIKE.
I CAN ONLY TELL YOU THAT RAVEN WAS HEADING TO THE MIDDLE OF THE CHINA SEA TO MEET THE NEXT TITAN ON HER LIST.
WHO? AQUAGIRL?
NO, CYBORG.
THE LOUD TITA THE ONE WHO MAKES NOISE.

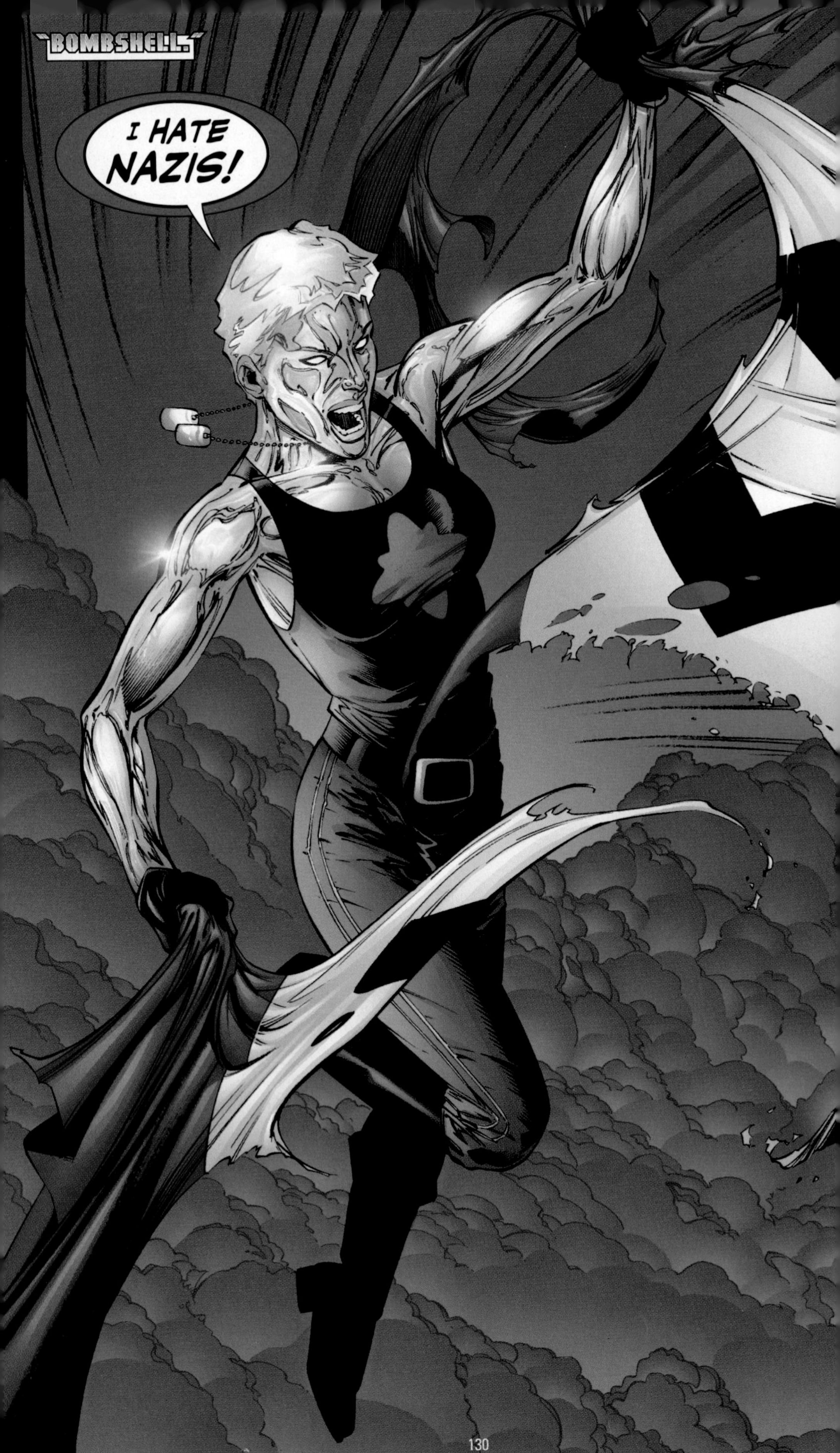
BOMBSHELL.
I HATE NAZIS!

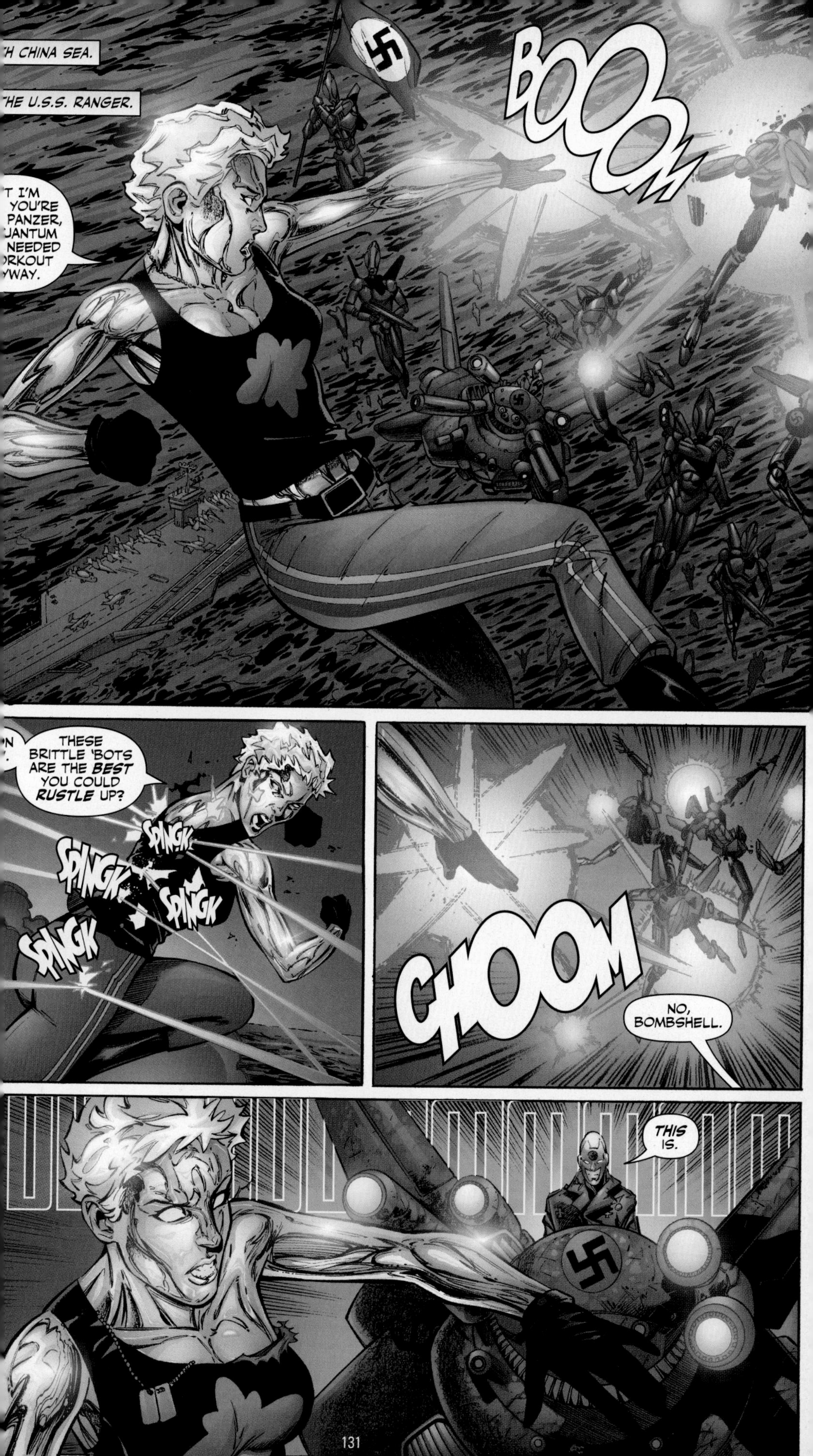

...H CHINA SEA.
...THE U.S.S. RANGER.
BOOOOM
...T I'M ...YOU'RE ...PANZER, ...UANTUM ...NEEDED ...ORKOUT ...YWAY.
THESE BRITTLE 'BOTS ARE THE *BEST* YOU COULD *RUSTLE* UP?
SPINGK
SPINGK
SPINGK
SPINGK
CHOOM
NO, BOMBSHELL.
THIS IS.

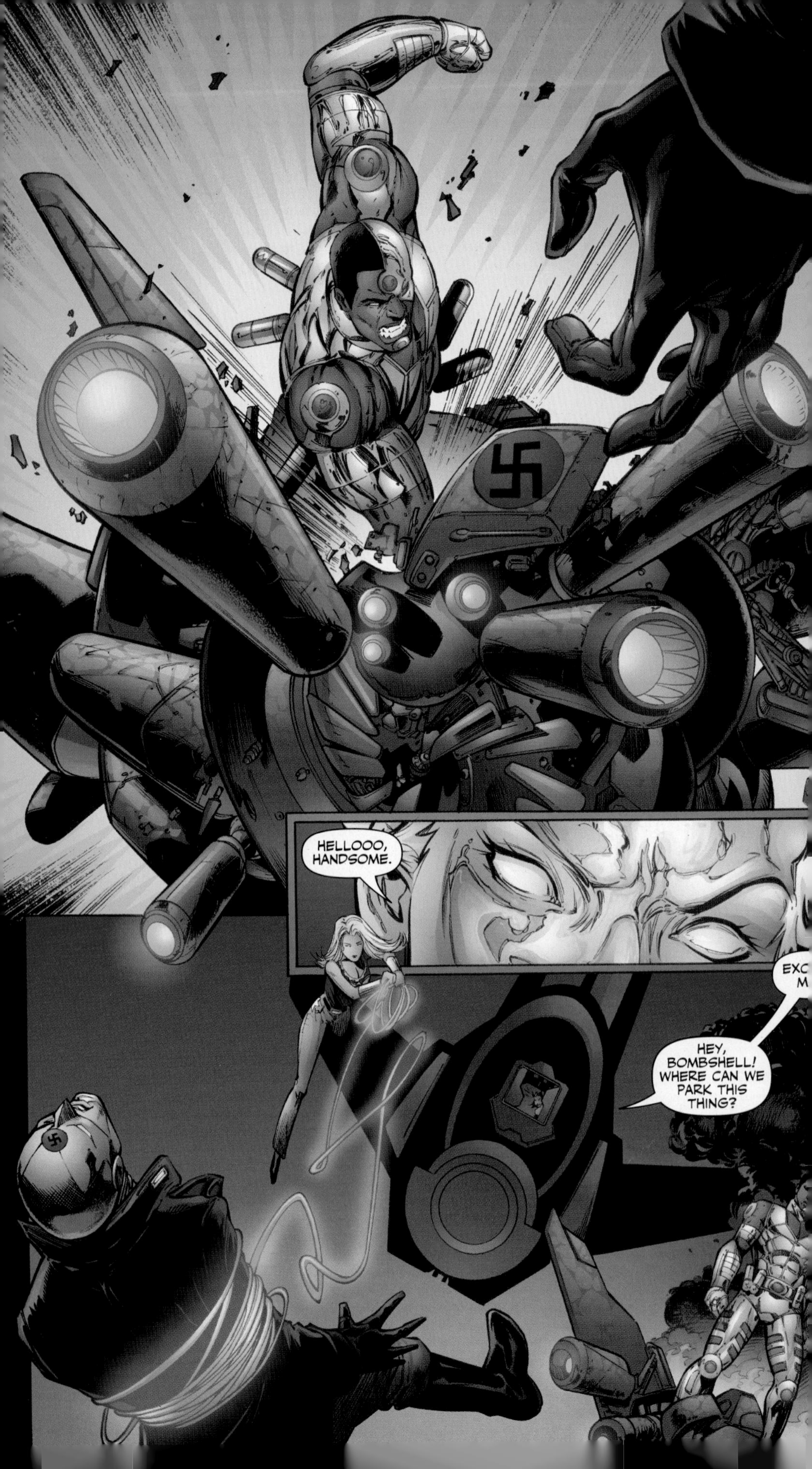
HELLOOO, HANDSOME.
HEY, BOMBSHELL! WHERE CAN WE PARK THIS THING?

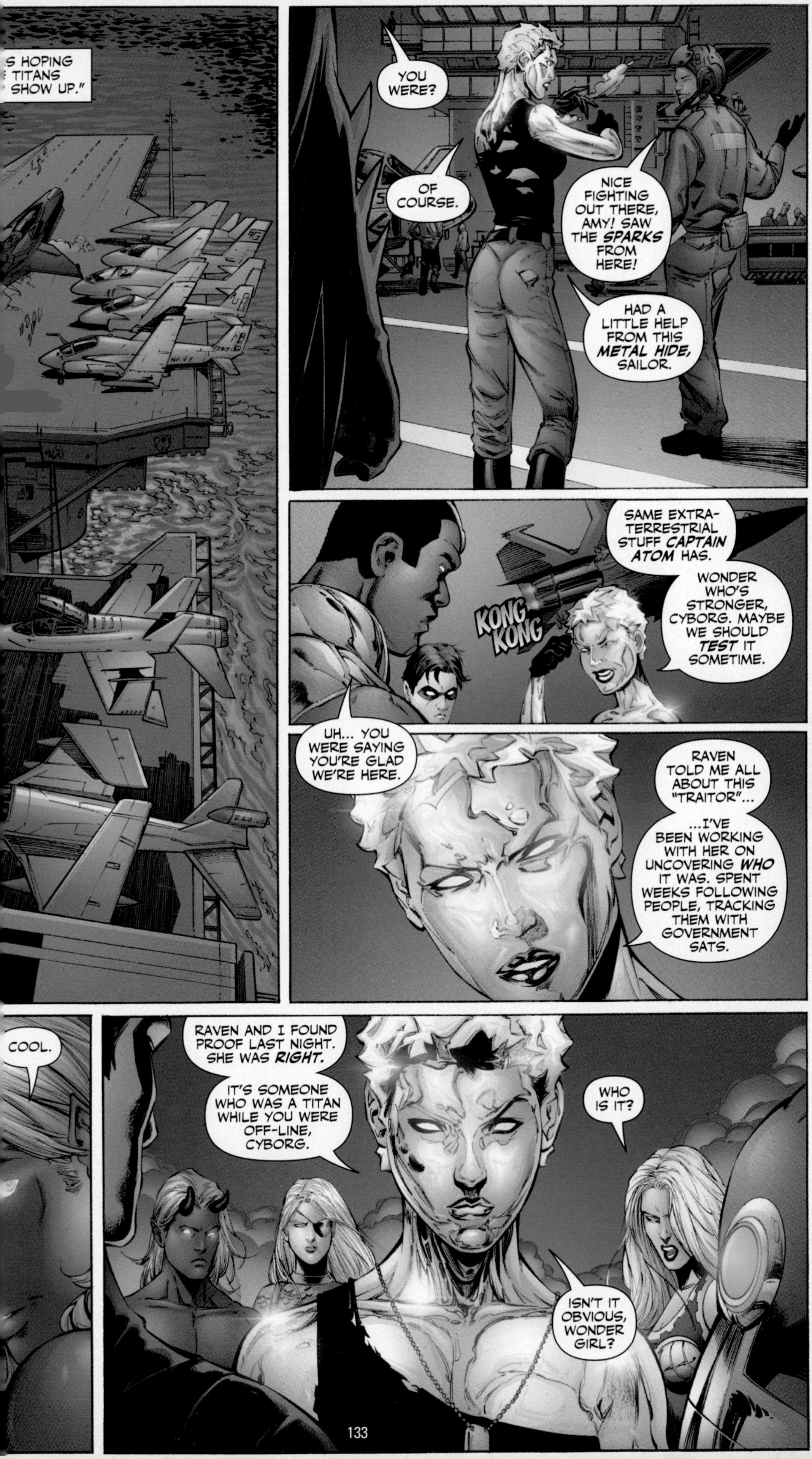

...S HOPING ...E TITANS ...SHOW UP."
YOU WERE?
OF COURSE.
NICE FIGHTING OUT THERE, AMY! SAW THE SPARKS FROM HERE!
HAD A LITTLE HELP FROM THIS METAL HIDE, SAILOR.
SAME EXTRA-TERRESTRIAL STUFF CAPTAIN ATOM HAS.
WONDER WHO'S STRONGER, CYBORG. MAYBE WE SHOULD TEST IT SOMETIME.
KONG KONG
UH... YOU WERE SAYING YOU'RE GLAD WE'RE HERE.
RAVEN TOLD ME ALL ABOUT THIS "TRAITOR"...
...I'VE BEEN WORKING WITH HER ON UNCOVERING WHO IT WAS. SPENT WEEKS FOLLOWING PEOPLE, TRACKING THEM WITH GOVERNMENT SATS.
COOL.
RAVEN AND I FOUND PROOF LAST NIGHT. SHE WAS RIGHT.
IT'S SOMEONE WHO WAS A TITAN WHILE YOU WERE OFF-LINE, CYBORG.
WHO IS IT?
ISN'T IT OBVIOUS, WONDER GIRL?

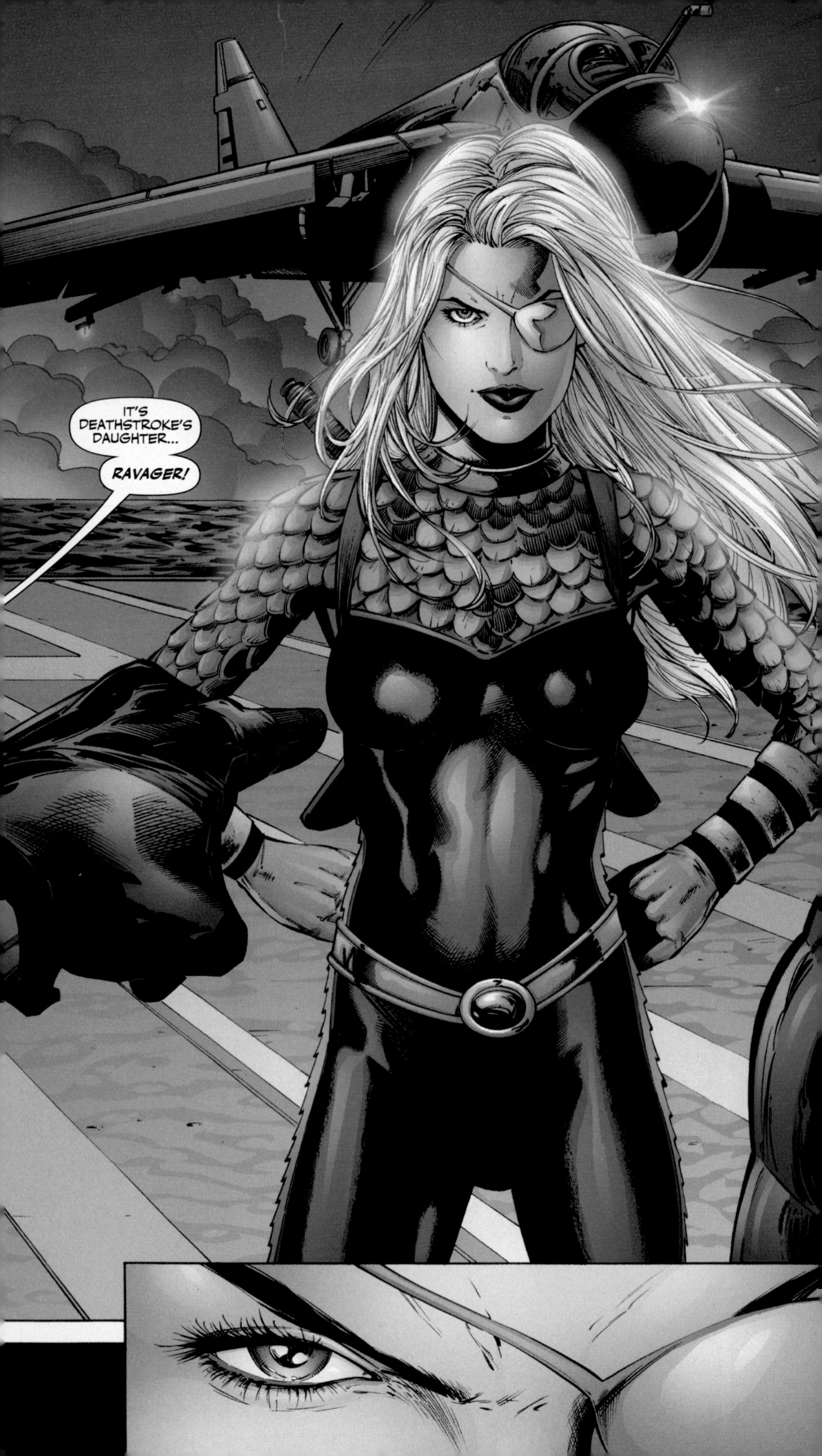
IT'S DEATHSTROKE'S DAUGHTER...
RAVAGER!

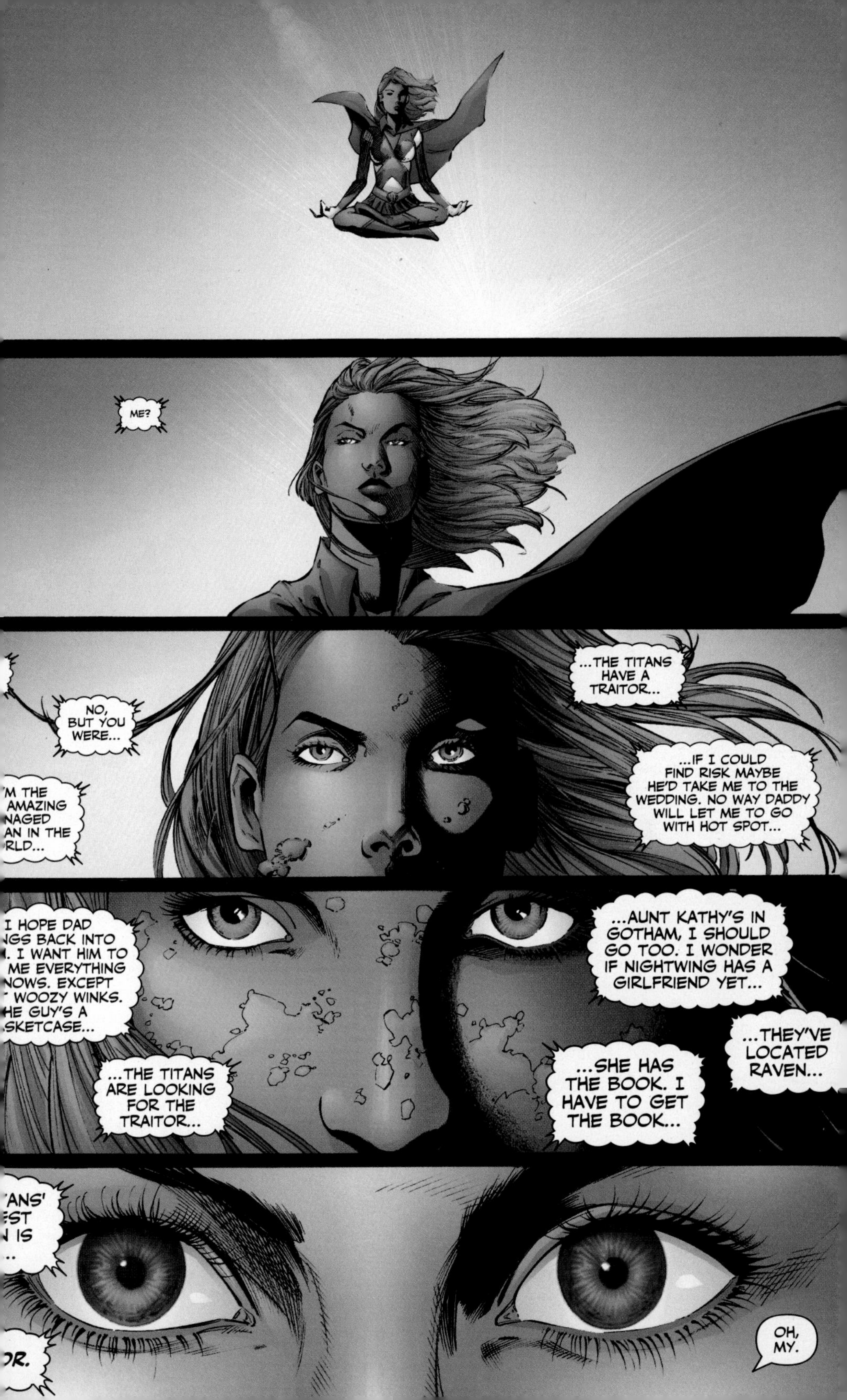
ME?
NO, BUT YOU WERE...
...THE TITANS HAVE A TRAITOR...
'M THE AMAZING NAGED AN IN THE RLD...
...IF I COULD FIND RISK MAYBE HE'D TAKE ME TO THE WEDDING. NO WAY DADDY WILL LET ME TO GO WITH HOT SPOT...
I HOPE DAD NGS BACK INTO . I WANT HIM TO ME EVERYTHING NOWS. EXCEPT WOOZY WINKS. HE GUY'S A SKETCASE...
...AUNT KATHY'S IN GOTHAM, I SHOULD GO TOO. I WONDER IF NIGHTWING HAS A GIRLFRIEND YET...
...THE TITANS ARE LOOKING FOR THE TRAITOR...
...SHE HAS THE BOOK. I HAVE TO GET THE BOOK...
...THEY'VE LOCATED RAVEN...
ANS' EST N IS ...
OR.
OH, MY.

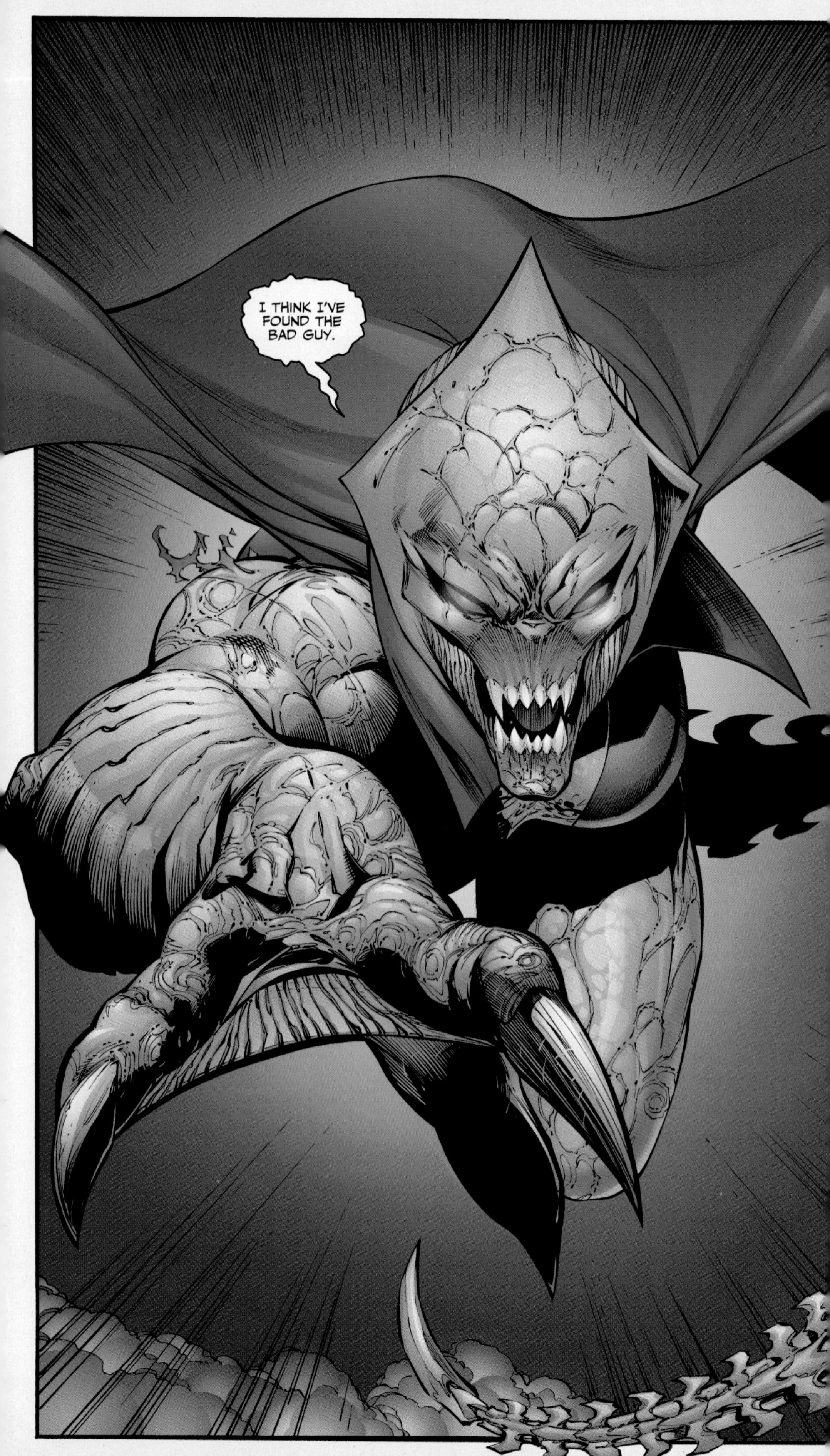
I THINK I'VE FOUND THE BAD GUY.

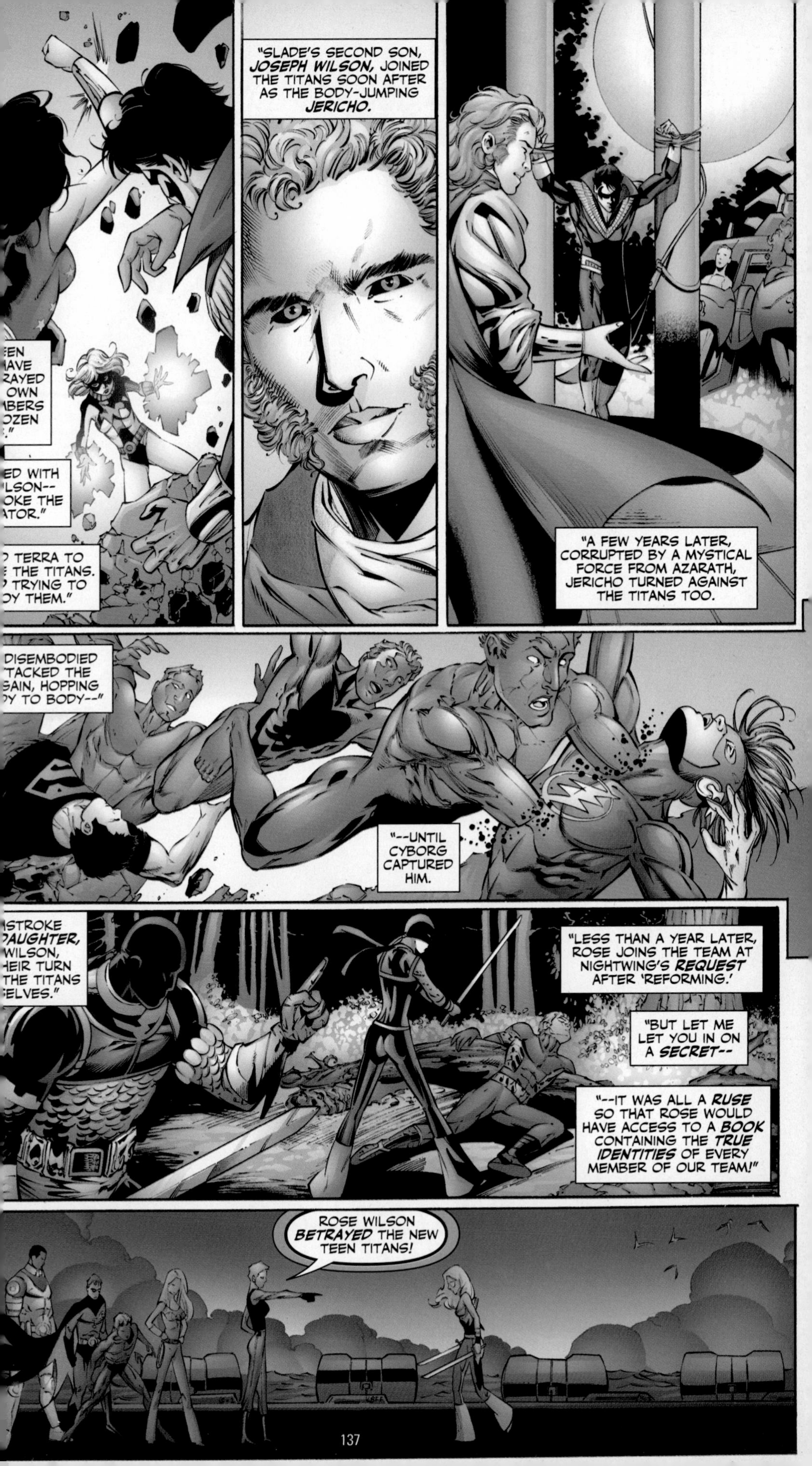

EEN
HAVE
RAYED
OWN
MBERS
OZEN
."
ED WITH
LSON--
OKE THE
ATOR."
D TERRA TO
E THE TITANS.
D TRYING TO
OY THEM."
"SLADE'S SECOND SON, JOSEPH WILSON, JOINED THE TITANS SOON AFTER AS THE BODY-JUMPING JERICHO.
"A FEW YEARS LATER, CORRUPTED BY A MYSTICAL FORCE FROM AZARATH, JERICHO TURNED AGAINST THE TITANS TOO.
DISEMBODIED
TACKED THE
GAIN, HOPPING
DY TO BODY--"
"--UNTIL CYBORG CAPTURED HIM.
ASTROKE
DAUGHTER,
WILSON,
HEIR TURN
THE TITANS
ELVES."
"LESS THAN A YEAR LATER, ROSE JOINS THE TEAM AT NIGHTWING'S REQUEST AFTER 'REFORMING.'
"BUT LET ME LET YOU IN ON A SECRET--
"--IT WAS ALL A RUSE SO THAT ROSE WOULD HAVE ACCESS TO A BOOK CONTAINING THE TRUE IDENTITIES OF EVERY MEMBER OF OUR TEAM!"
ROSE WILSON BETRAYED THE NEW TEEN TITANS!

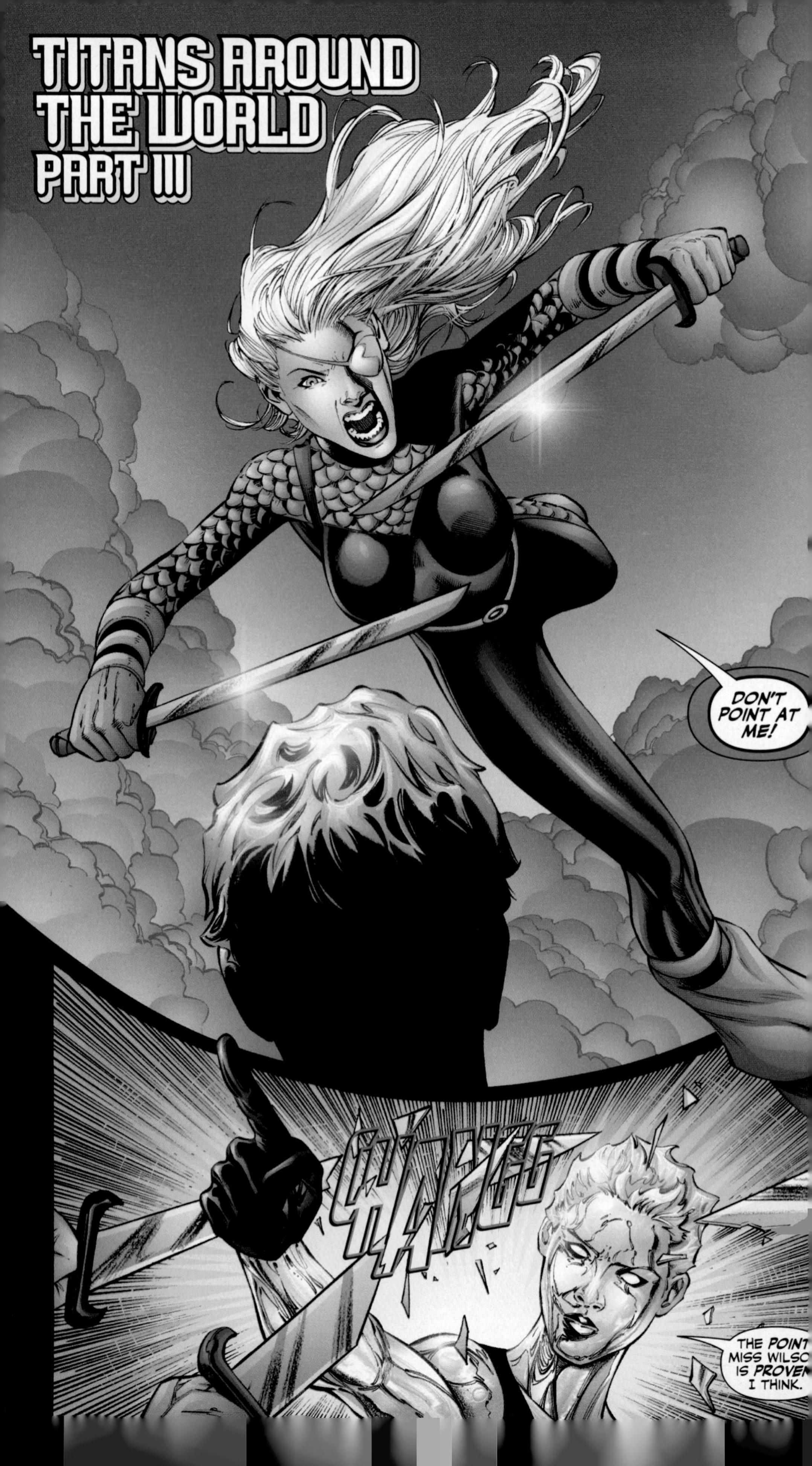

TITANS AROUND THE WORLD PART III
DON'T POINT AT ME!
CHANGG
THE POINT MISS WILSO IS PROVEN I THINK.

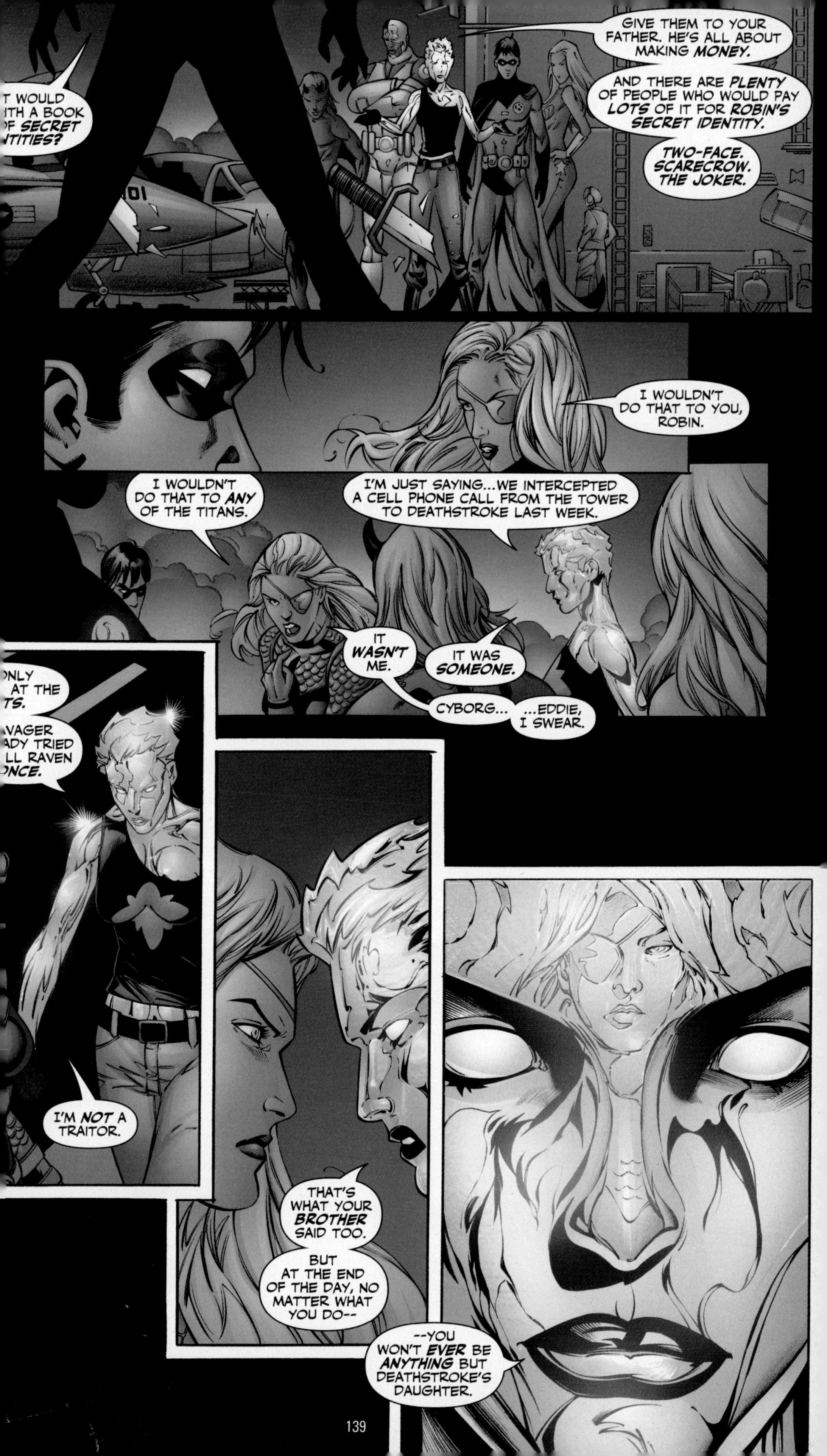
T WOULD ITH A BOOK F SECRET NTITIES?
GIVE THEM TO YOUR FATHER. HE'S ALL ABOUT MAKING MONEY.
AND THERE ARE PLENTY OF PEOPLE WHO WOULD PAY LOTS OF IT FOR ROBIN'S SECRET IDENTITY.
TWO-FACE. SCARECROW. THE JOKER.
I WOULDN'T DO THAT TO YOU, ROBIN.
I WOULDN'T DO THAT TO ANY OF THE TITANS.
I'M JUST SAYING...WE INTERCEPTED A CELL PHONE CALL FROM THE TOWER TO DEATHSTROKE LAST WEEK.
IT WASN'T ME.
IT WAS SOMEONE.
CYBORG...
...EDDIE, I SWEAR.
NLY AT THE TS.
VAGER ADY TRIED LL RAVEN NCE.
I'M NOT A TRAITOR.
THAT'S WHAT YOUR BROTHER SAID TOO.
BUT AT THE END OF THE DAY, NO MATTER WHAT YOU DO--
--YOU WON'T EVER BE ANYTHING BUT DEATHSTROKE'S DAUGHTER.

THAT'S *ENOUGH*, BOMBSHELL.

ROSE HATES HER DAD AS MUCH AS *WE* DO.

I CAN HANDLE THIS MYSELF, WONDER GIRL.

AT L LOOK OF THE ME AND GATHE RAVAG ABOA *QUA JE*

IT MIGHT BE BEST IF YOU TOOK THE T-JET AND HEADED BACK TO THE TOWER, ROSE. IT HAS AN AUTOPILOT FOR HANGAR RETURN.

WHAT?

U CLEA AND F EVE ON

FINE, ROBIN. I'M *OUT* OF HERE.

I'D TELL YOU *NOT* TO BE SURPRISED IF I'M *GONE* WHEN YOU GET BACK--

--BUT GOT A F THAT'S WH ALL WA

ROSE--

LET HER GO, RED.

GIRLS LIKE THAT ARE NOTHING BUT *BAD NEWS.*

LET'S *FLY*, TITANS!

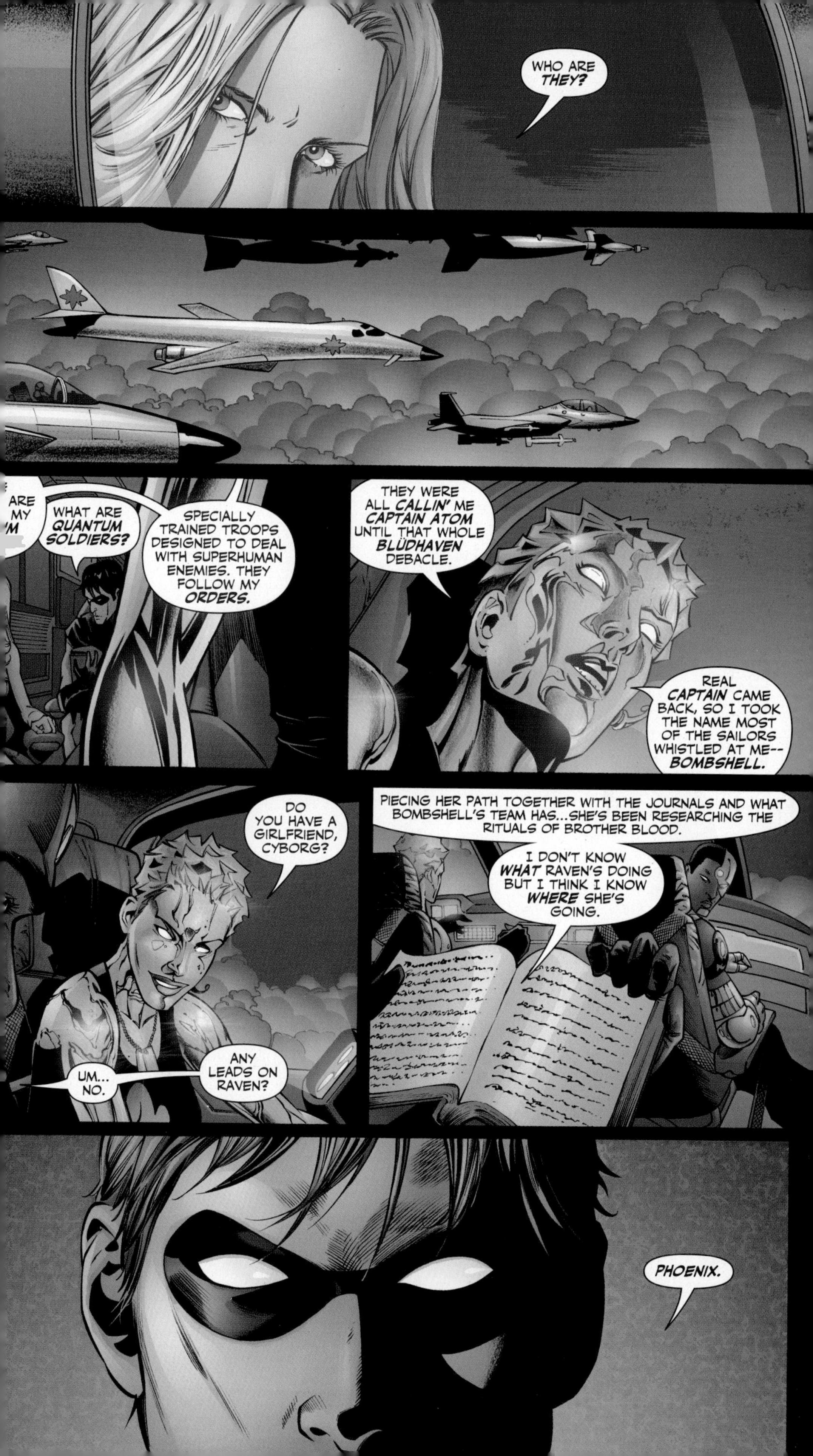
WHO ARE THEY?
WHAT ARE QUANTUM SOLDIERS?
SPECIALLY TRAINED TROOPS DESIGNED TO DEAL WITH SUPERHUMAN ENEMIES. THEY FOLLOW MY ORDERS.
THEY WERE ALL CALLIN' ME CAPTAIN ATOM UNTIL THAT WHOLE BLÜDHAVEN DEBACLE.
REAL CAPTAIN CAME BACK, SO I TOOK THE NAME MOST OF THE SAILORS WHISTLED AT ME-- BOMBSHELL.
DO YOU HAVE A GIRLFRIEND, CYBORG?
UM... NO.
ANY LEADS ON RAVEN?
PIECING HER PATH TOGETHER WITH THE JOURNALS AND WHAT BOMBSHELL'S TEAM HAS...SHE'S BEEN RESEARCHING THE RITUALS OF BROTHER BLOOD.
I DON'T KNOW WHAT RAVEN'S DOING BUT I THINK I KNOW WHERE SHE'S GOING.
PHOENIX.

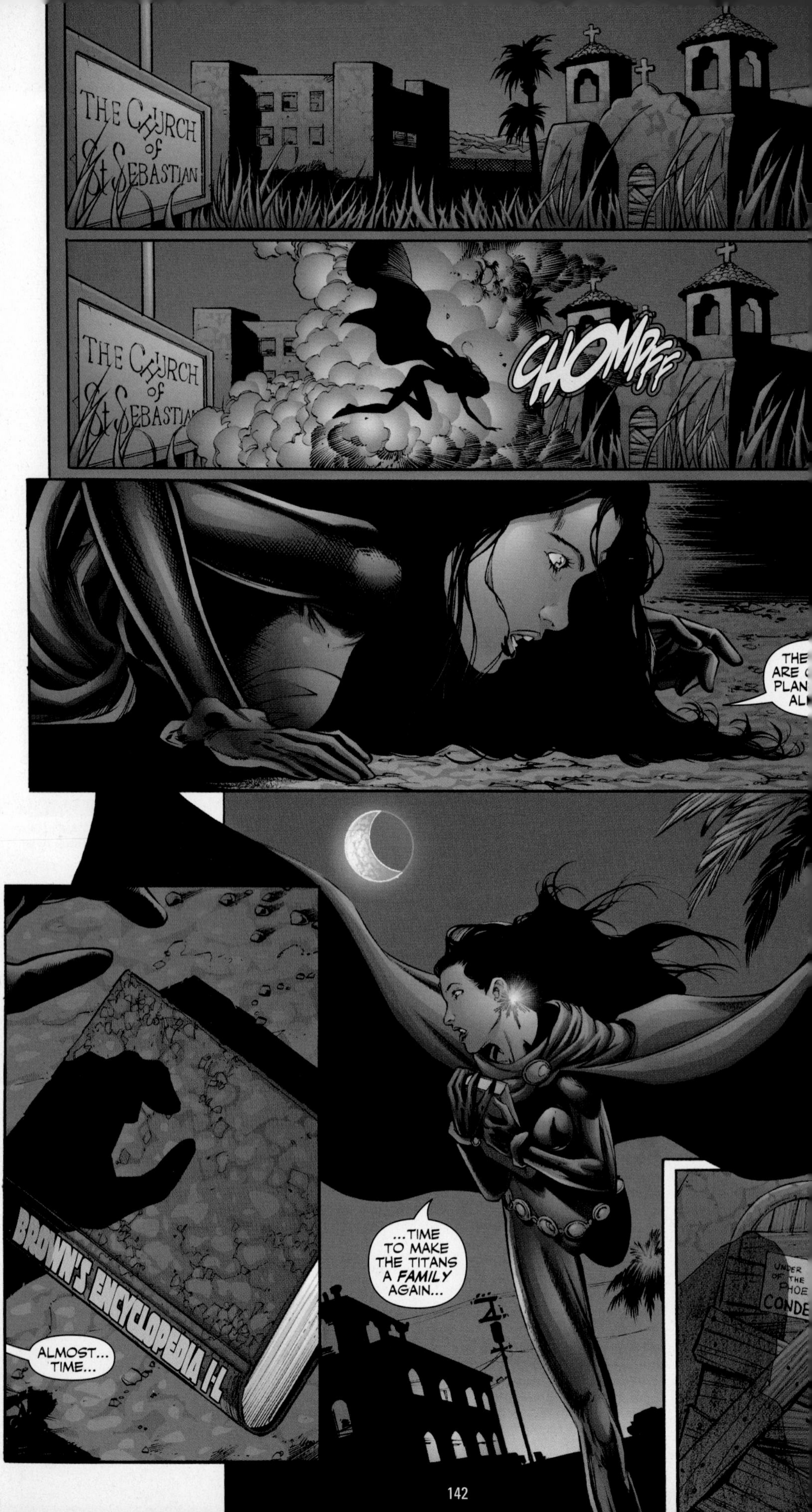
THE CHURCH of St SEBASTIAN
THE CHURCH of St SEBASTIAN
CHOMPFF
...TIME TO MAKE THE TITANS A FAMILY AGAIN...
ALMOST... TIME...
BROWN'S ENCYCLOPEDIA I-L

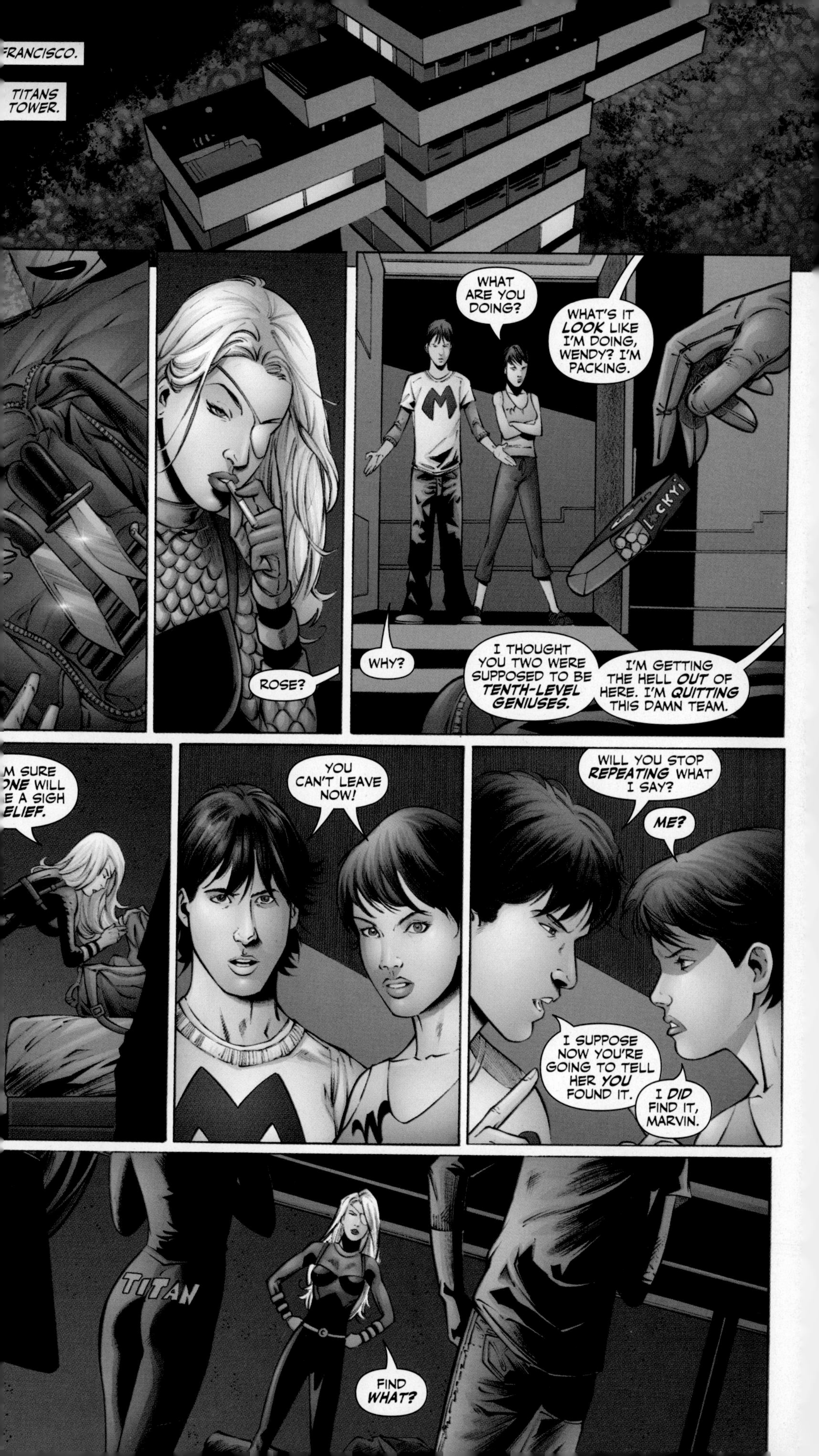

FRANCISCO.
TITANS TOWER.
ROSE?
WHAT ARE YOU DOING?
WHAT'S IT LOOK LIKE I'M DOING, WENDY? I'M PACKING.
WHY?
I THOUGHT YOU TWO WERE SUPPOSED TO BE TENTH-LEVEL GENIUSES.
I'M GETTING THE HELL OUT OF HERE. I'M QUITTING THIS DAMN TEAM.
M SURE ONE WILL E A SIGH ELIEF.
YOU CAN'T LEAVE NOW!
WILL YOU STOP REPEATING WHAT I SAY?
ME?
I SUPPOSE NOW YOU'RE GOING TO TELL HER YOU FOUND IT.
I DID FIND IT, MARVIN.
TITAN
FIND WHAT?

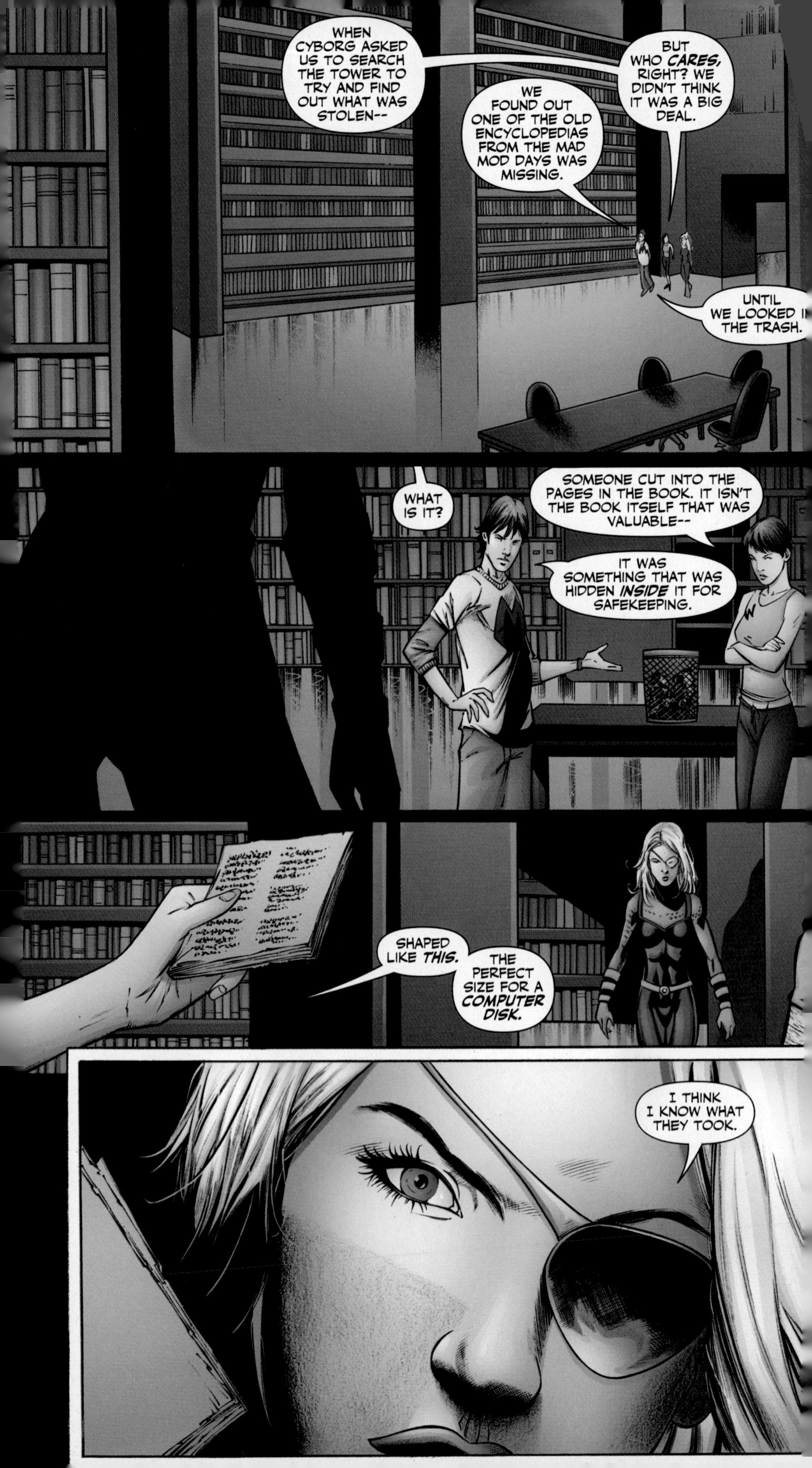
WHEN CYBORG ASKED US TO SEARCH THE TOWER TO TRY AND FIND OUT WHAT WAS STOLEN--
WE FOUND OUT ONE OF THE OLD ENCYCLOPEDIAS FROM THE MAD MOD DAYS WAS MISSING.
BUT WHO CARES, RIGHT? WE DIDN'T THINK IT WAS A BIG DEAL.
UNTIL WE LOOKED I THE TRASH.
WHAT IS IT?
SOMEONE CUT INTO THE PAGES IN THE BOOK. IT ISN'T THE BOOK ITSELF THAT WAS VALUABLE--
IT WAS SOMETHING THAT WAS HIDDEN INSIDE IT FOR SAFEKEEPING.
SHAPED LIKE THIS.
THE PERFECT SIZE FOR A COMPUTER DISK.
I THINK I KNOW WHAT THEY TOOK.

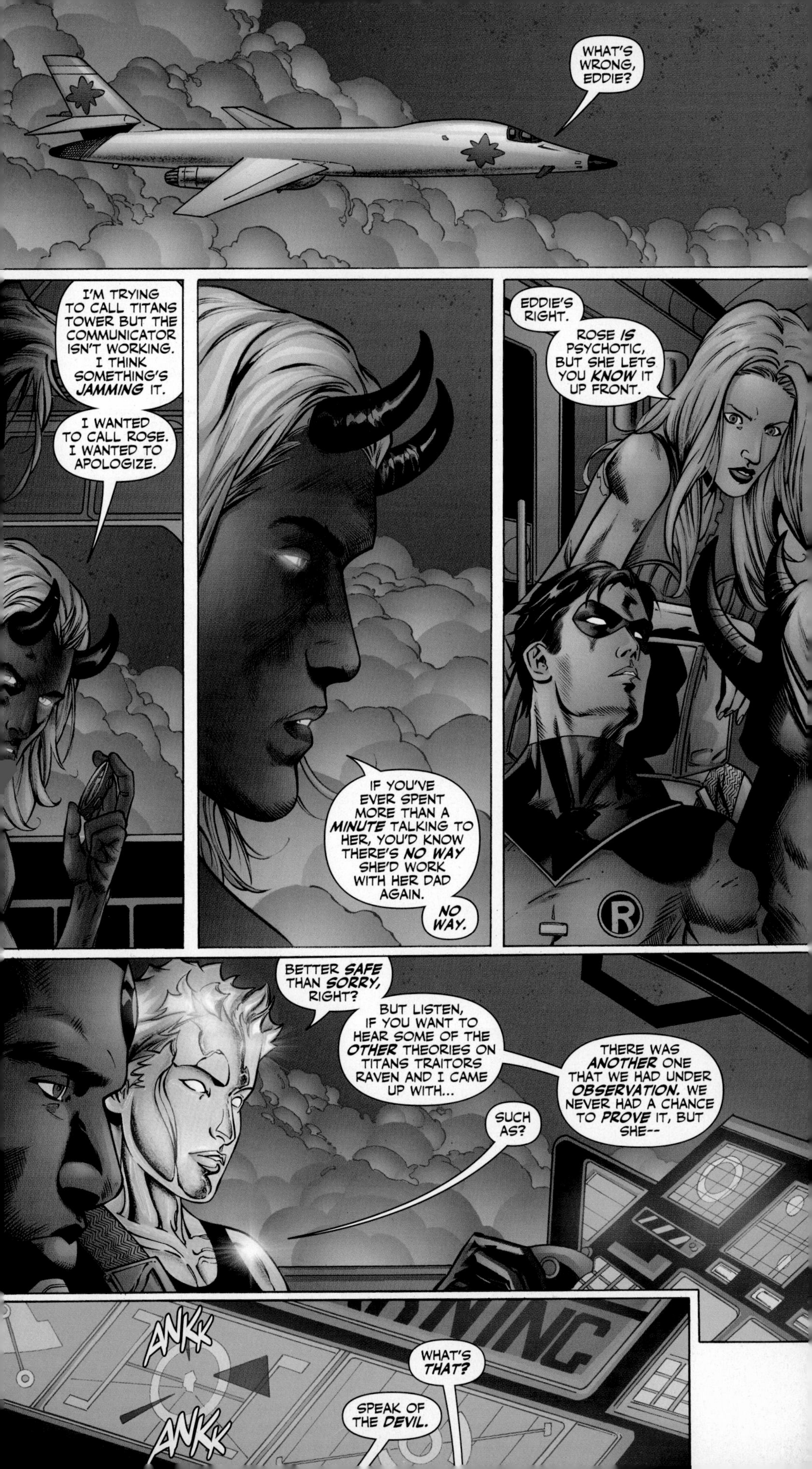
WHAT'S WRONG, EDDIE?
I'M TRYING TO CALL TITANS TOWER BUT THE COMMUNICATOR ISN'T WORKING. I THINK SOMETHING'S JAMMING IT.
I WANTED TO CALL ROSE. I WANTED TO APOLOGIZE.
IF YOU'VE EVER SPENT MORE THAN A MINUTE TALKING TO HER, YOU'D KNOW THERE'S NO WAY SHE'D WORK WITH HER DAD AGAIN.
NO WAY.
EDDIE'S RIGHT.
ROSE IS PSYCHOTIC, BUT SHE LETS YOU KNOW IT UP FRONT.
BETTER SAFE THAN SORRY, RIGHT?
BUT LISTEN, IF YOU WANT TO HEAR SOME OF THE OTHER THEORIES ON TITANS TRAITORS RAVEN AND I CAME UP WITH...
SUCH AS?
THERE WAS ANOTHER ONE THAT WE HAD UNDER OBSERVATION. WE NEVER HAD A CHANCE TO PROVE IT, BUT SHE--
ANKK
ANKK
WHAT'S THAT?
SPEAK OF THE DEVIL.

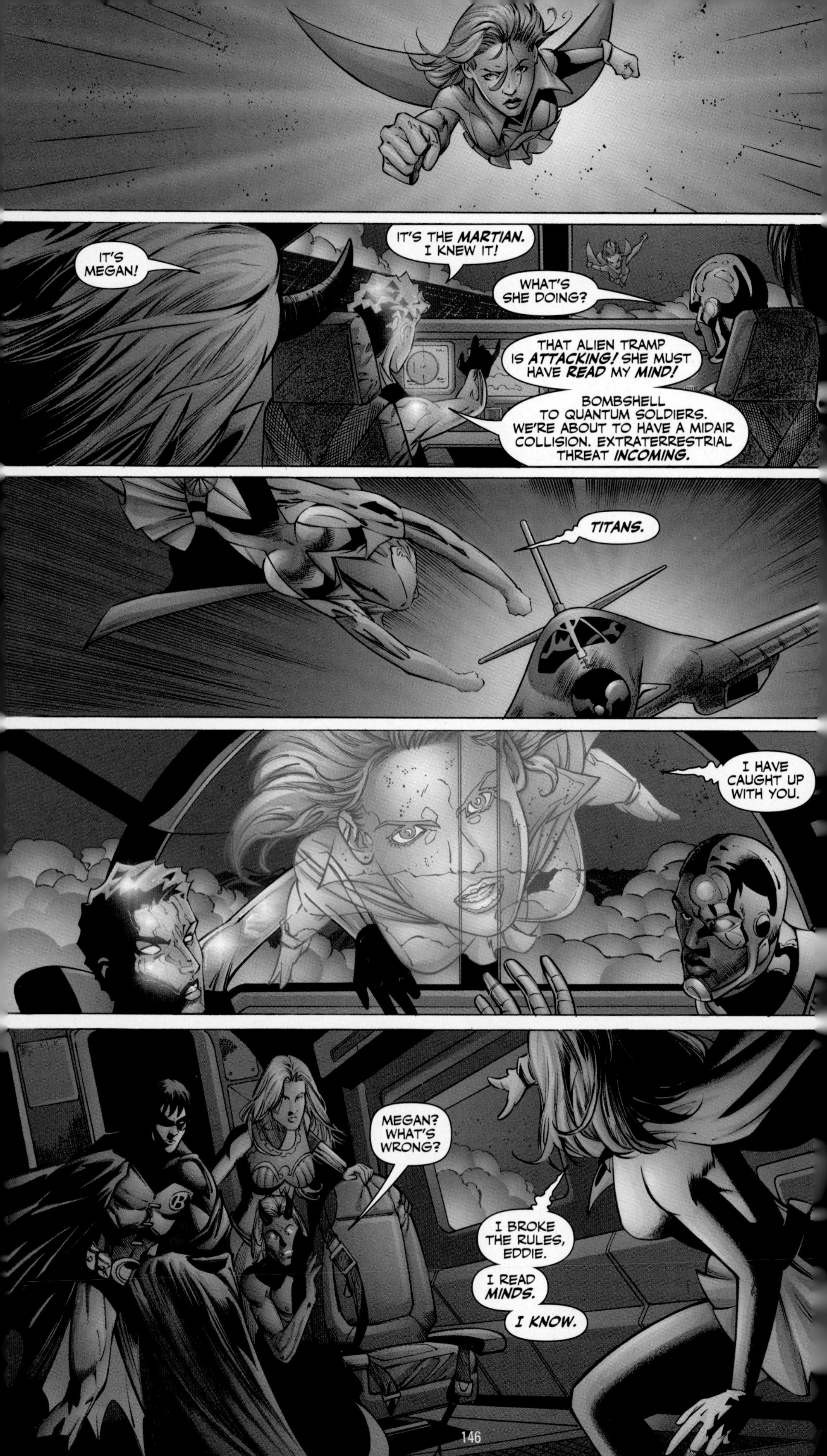
IT'S MEGAN!
IT'S THE MARTIAN. I KNEW IT!
WHAT'S SHE DOING?
THAT ALIEN TRAMP IS ATTACKING! SHE MUST HAVE READ MY MIND!
BOMBSHELL TO QUANTUM SOLDIERS. WE'RE ABOUT TO HAVE A MIDAIR COLLISION. EXTRATERRESTRIAL THREAT INCOMING.
TITANS.
I HAVE CAUGHT UP WITH YOU.
MEGAN? WHAT'S WRONG?
I BROKE THE RULES, EDDIE.
I READ MINDS.
I KNOW.

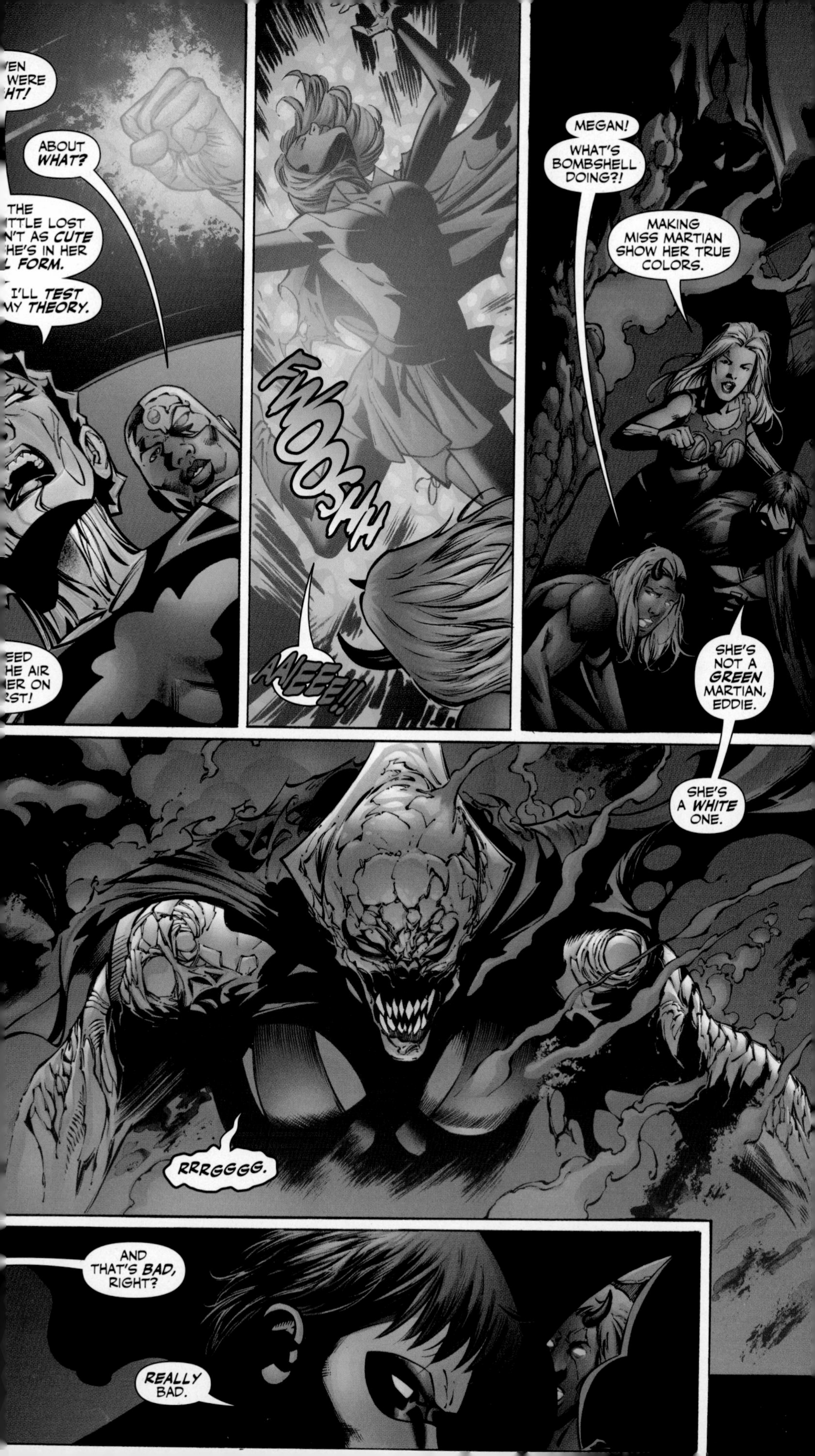

'EN WERE GHT!
ABOUT WHAT?
THE TTLE LOST N'T AS CUTE HE'S IN HER L FORM.
I'LL TEST MY THEORY.
EED HE AIR ER ON RST!
FWOOSHH
AAIEEEE!!
MEGAN! WHAT'S BOMBSHELL DOING?!
MAKING MISS MARTIAN SHOW HER TRUE COLORS.
SHE'S NOT A GREEN MARTIAN, EDDIE.
SHE'S A WHITE ONE.
RRRGGGG.
AND THAT'S BAD, RIGHT?
REALLY BAD.

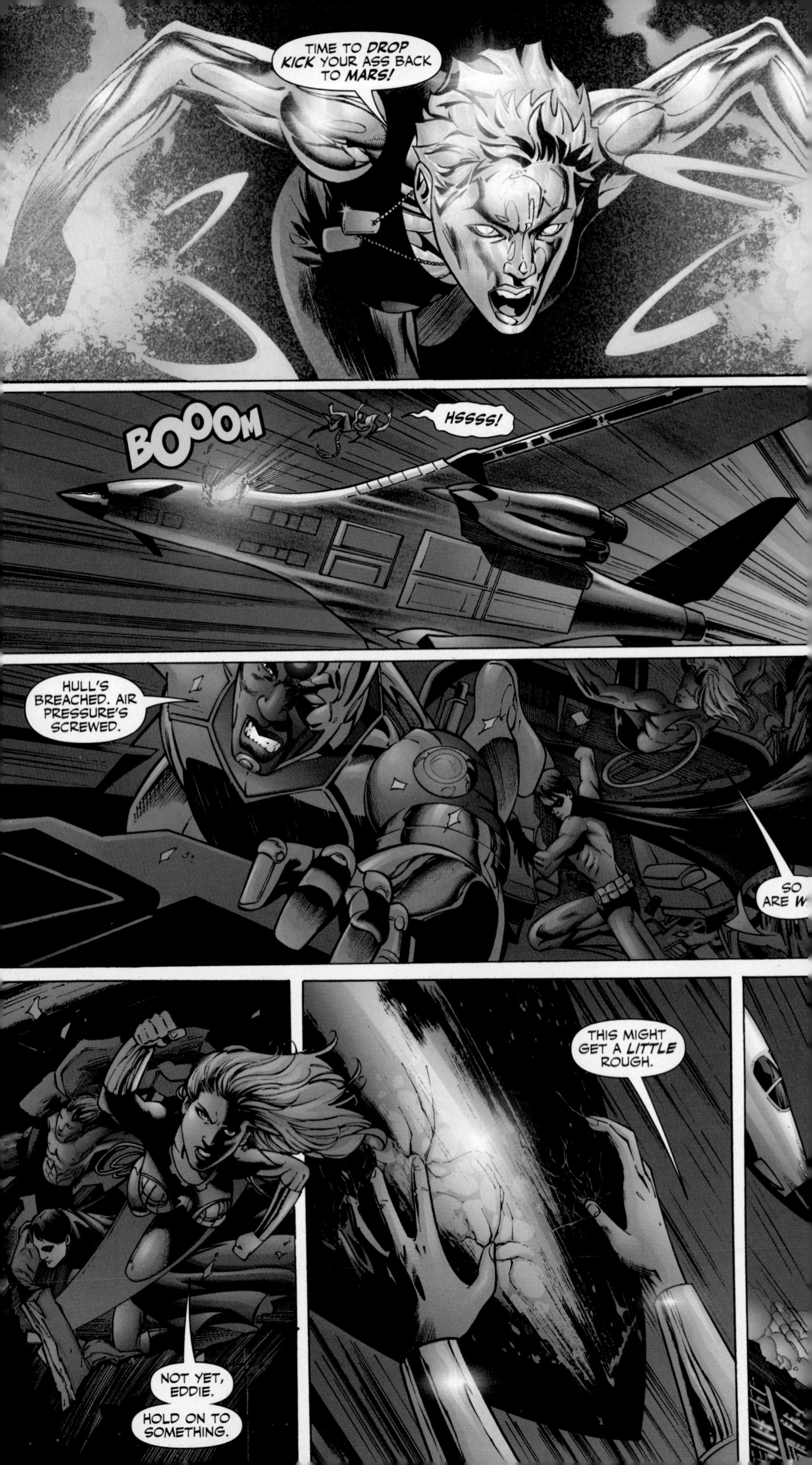
TIME TO DROP KICK YOUR ASS BACK TO MARS!
BOOOM
HSSSS!
HULL'S BREACHED. AIR PRESSURE'S SCREWED.
SO ARE W
NOT YET, EDDIE.
HOLD ON TO SOMETHING.
THIS MIGHT GET A LITTLE ROUGH.

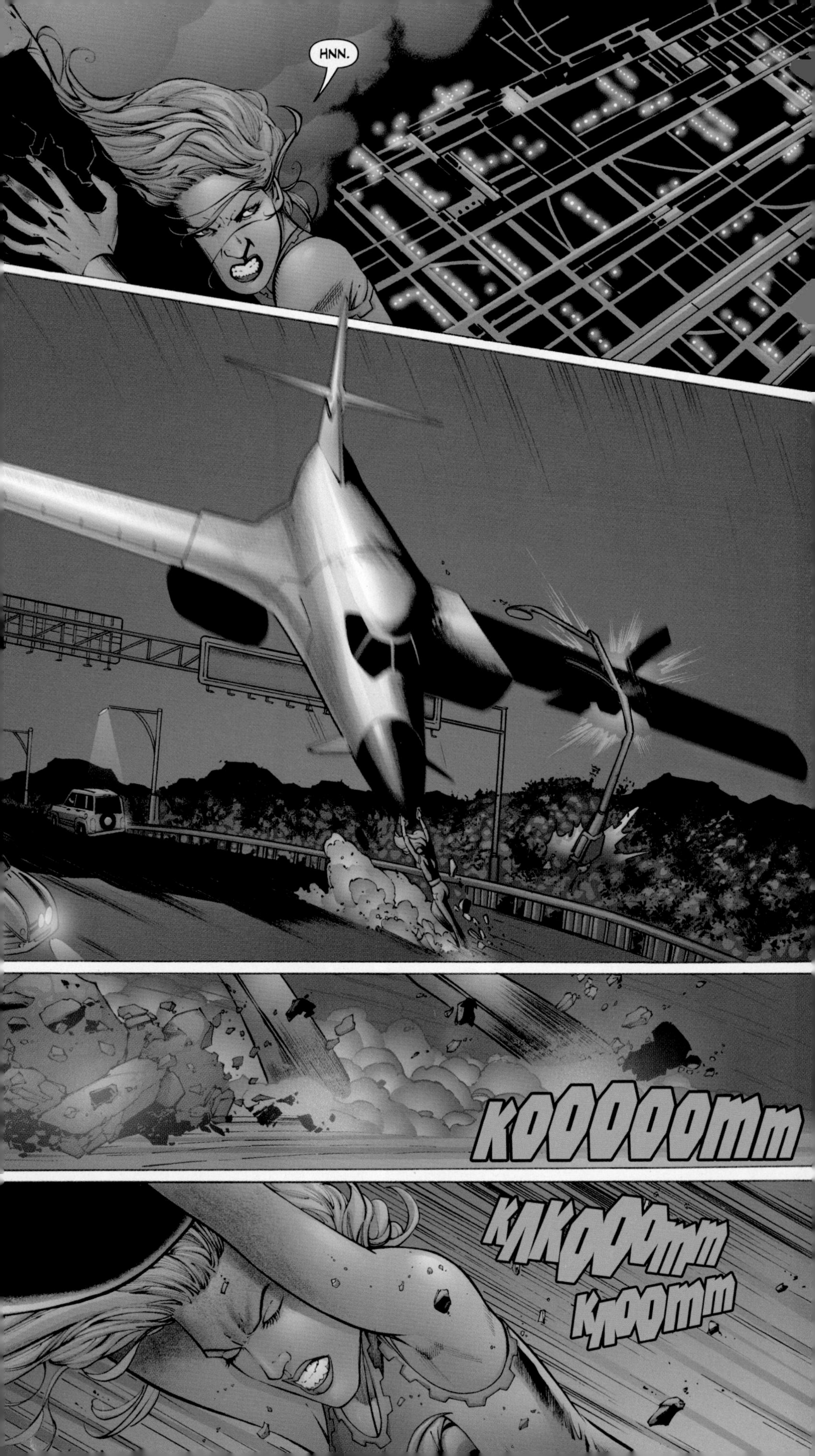
HNN.
KOOOOOMM
KAKOOOMM
KAOOMM

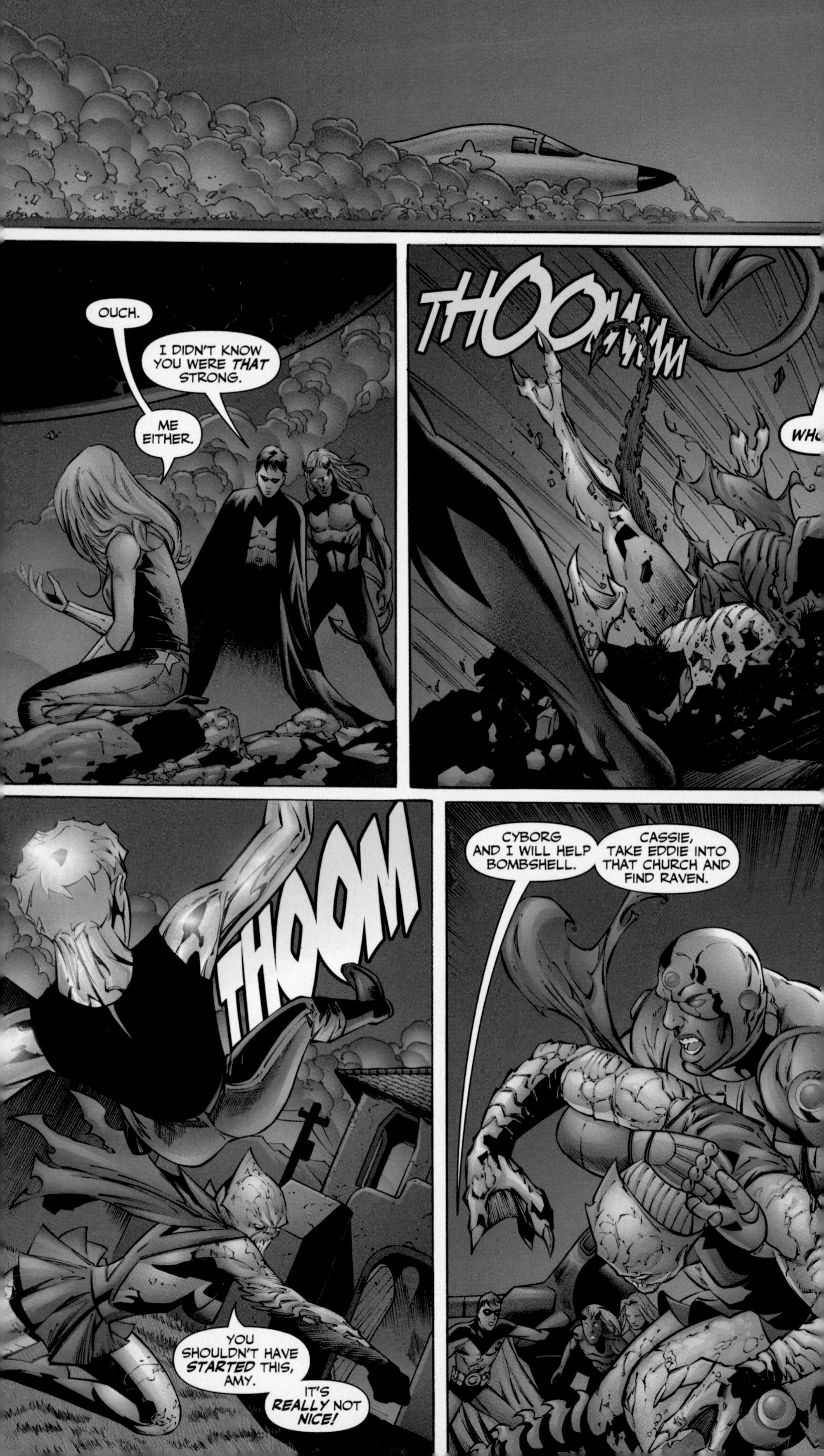
OUCH.
I DIDN'T KNOW YOU WERE THAT STRONG.
ME EITHER.
THOOMM
WHO
THOOM
YOU SHOULDN'T HAVE STARTED THIS, AMY.
IT'S REALLY NOT NICE!
CYBORG AND I WILL HELP BOMBSHELL.
CASSIE, TAKE EDDIE INTO THAT CHURCH AND FIND RAVEN.

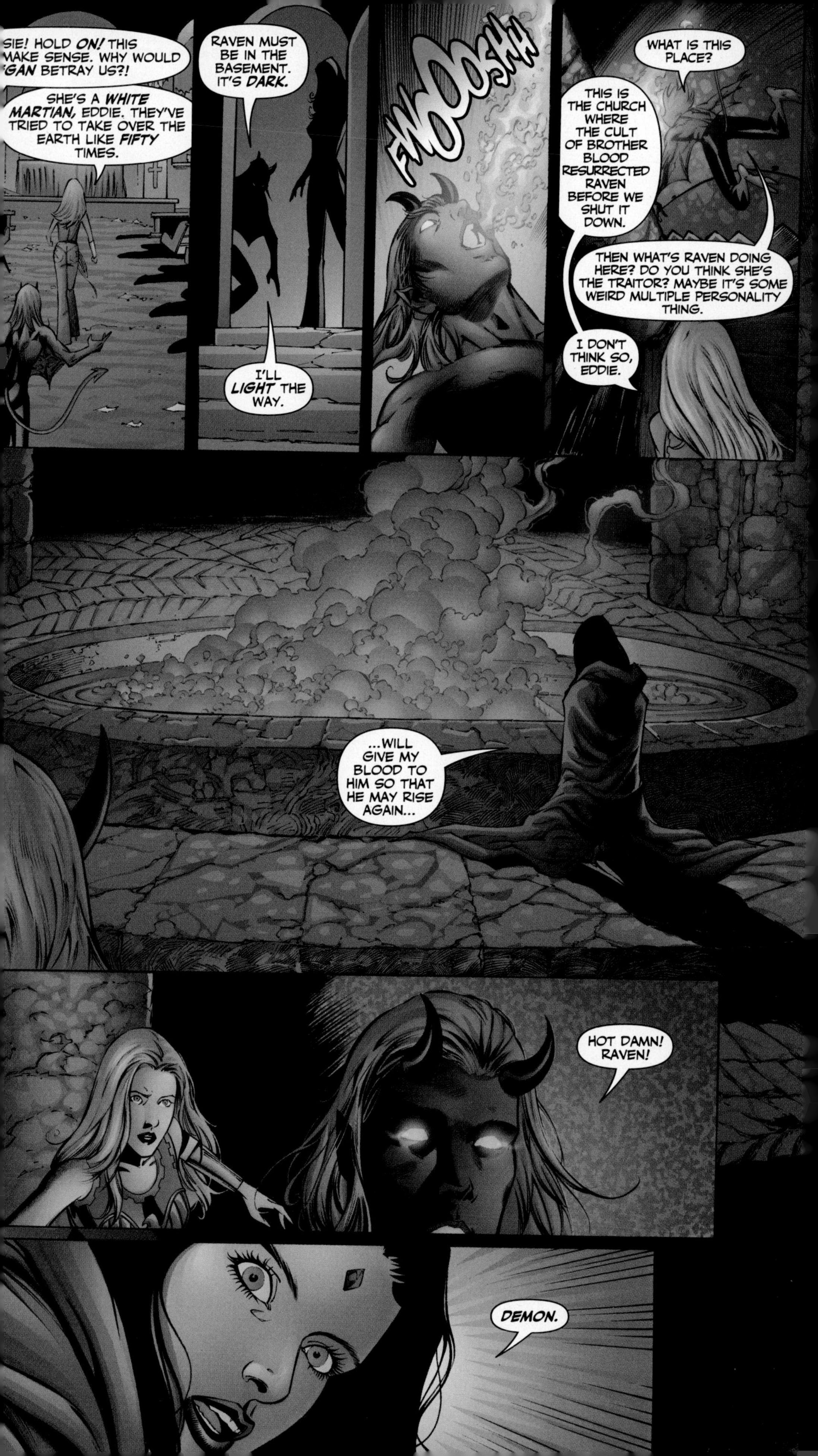

SIE! HOLD ON! THIS
MAKE SENSE. WHY WOULD
GAN BETRAY US?!
SHE'S A WHITE MARTIAN, EDDIE. THEY'VE TRIED TO TAKE OVER THE EARTH LIKE FIFTY TIMES.
RAVEN MUST BE IN THE BASEMENT. IT'S DARK.
I'LL LIGHT THE WAY.
FWOOSH!
WHAT IS THIS PLACE?
THIS IS THE CHURCH WHERE THE CULT OF BROTHER BLOOD RESURRECTED RAVEN BEFORE WE SHUT IT DOWN.
THEN WHAT'S RAVEN DOING HERE? DO YOU THINK SHE'S THE TRAITOR? MAYBE IT'S SOME WEIRD MULTIPLE PERSONALITY THING.
I DON'T THINK SO, EDDIE.
...WILL GIVE MY BLOOD TO HIM SO THAT HE MAY RISE AGAIN...
HOT DAMN! RAVEN!
DEMON.

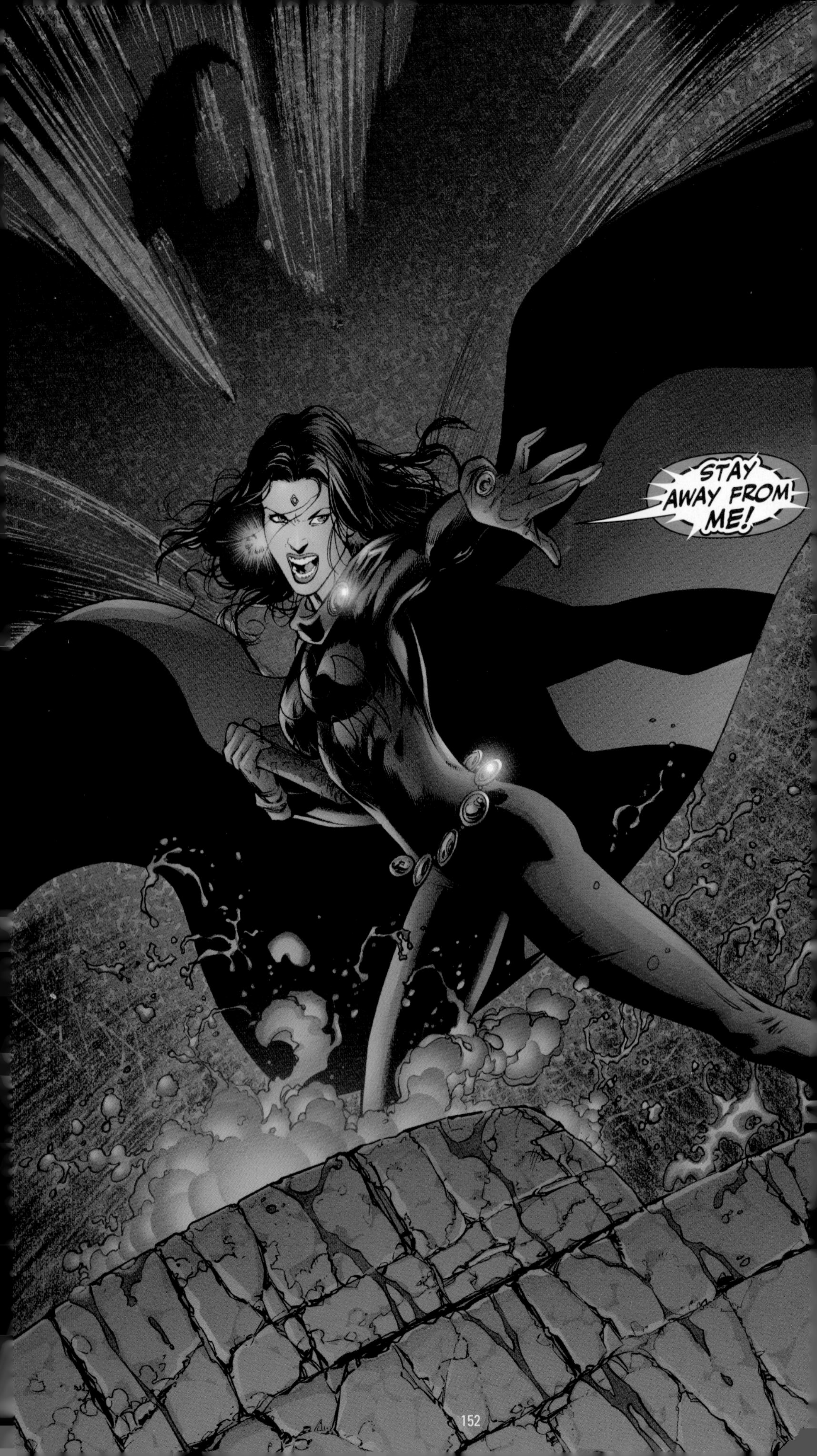
STAY AWAY FROM ME!

NNFFF.

KRAK

CASSIE?

UM, YEAH-- --THIS IS *KID DEVIL.* HE'S A *TEEN TITAN.*

N THE MIDDLE CANTATION. IN 3ESS...KID DEVIL KE MY *FATHER.* OKED LIKE RIGON.

I DIDN'T MEAN TO *HURT* HIM.

WANT YONE, E.

YOU SHOULDN'T HAVE LEFT THE TITANS. WE *NEEDED* YOU.

I KNOW YOU DON'T.

ME?! I *DIDN'T* LEAVE. ROBIN DID--

AND THEN *YOU* DID. WITHOUT HIM OR CONNER OR BART AROUND, YOU THOUGHT YOU DIDN'T HAVE ANY *FRIENDS* LEFT.

YOU WERE *WRONG.*

I NEED TO GET YOU OUT OF HERE. MISS MARTIAN IS HERE.

MISS MARTIAN?!

THE TITAN YOU'VE BEEN TRACKING. THE ONE WHO'S *BETRAYING* THIS TEAM.

OH, *NO.* NO, NO, NO.

THE *TRAITOR* IS *NOT* MISS MARTIAN, CASSIE. IT'S--

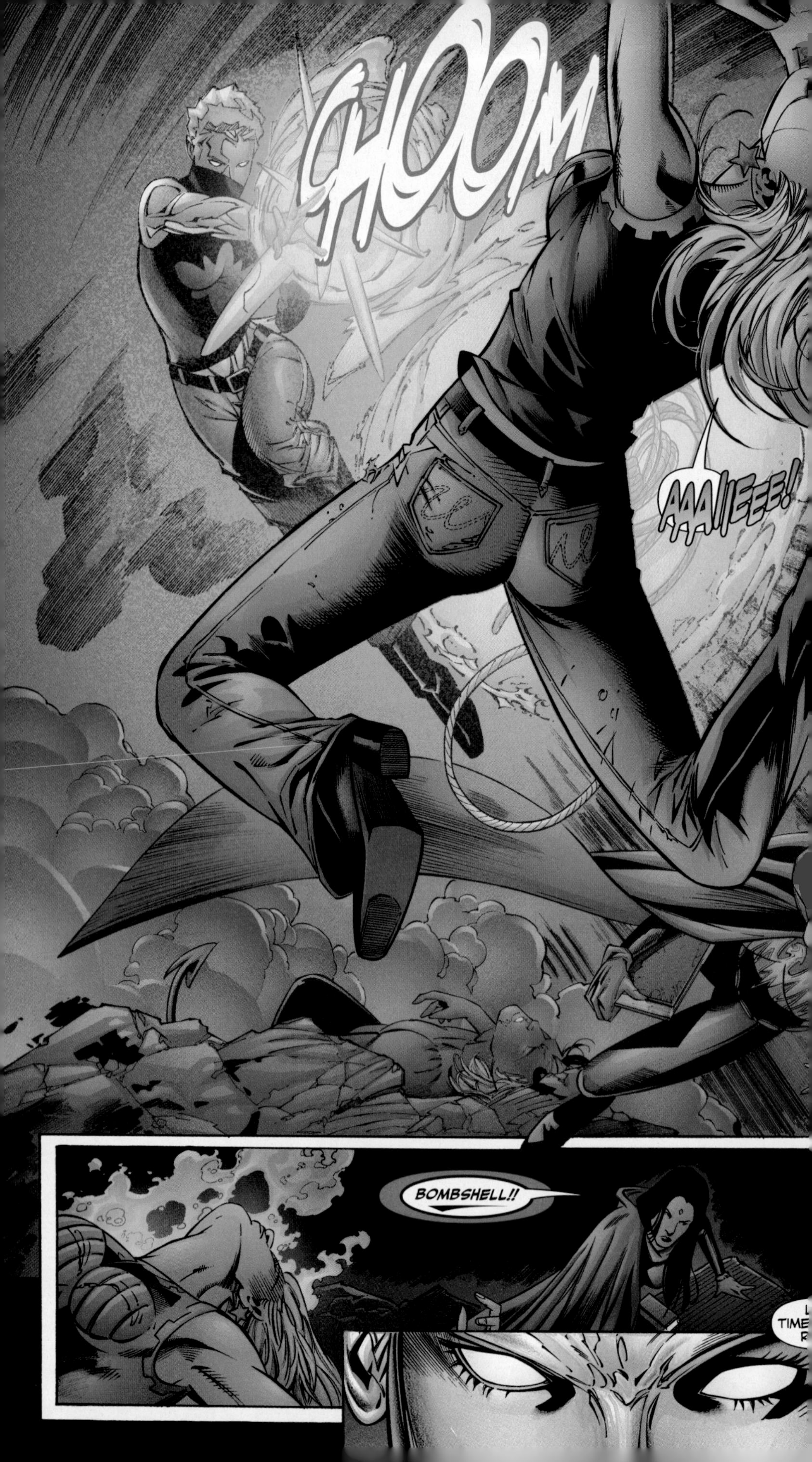
CHOOM
AAAIIEEE!
BOMBSHELL!!

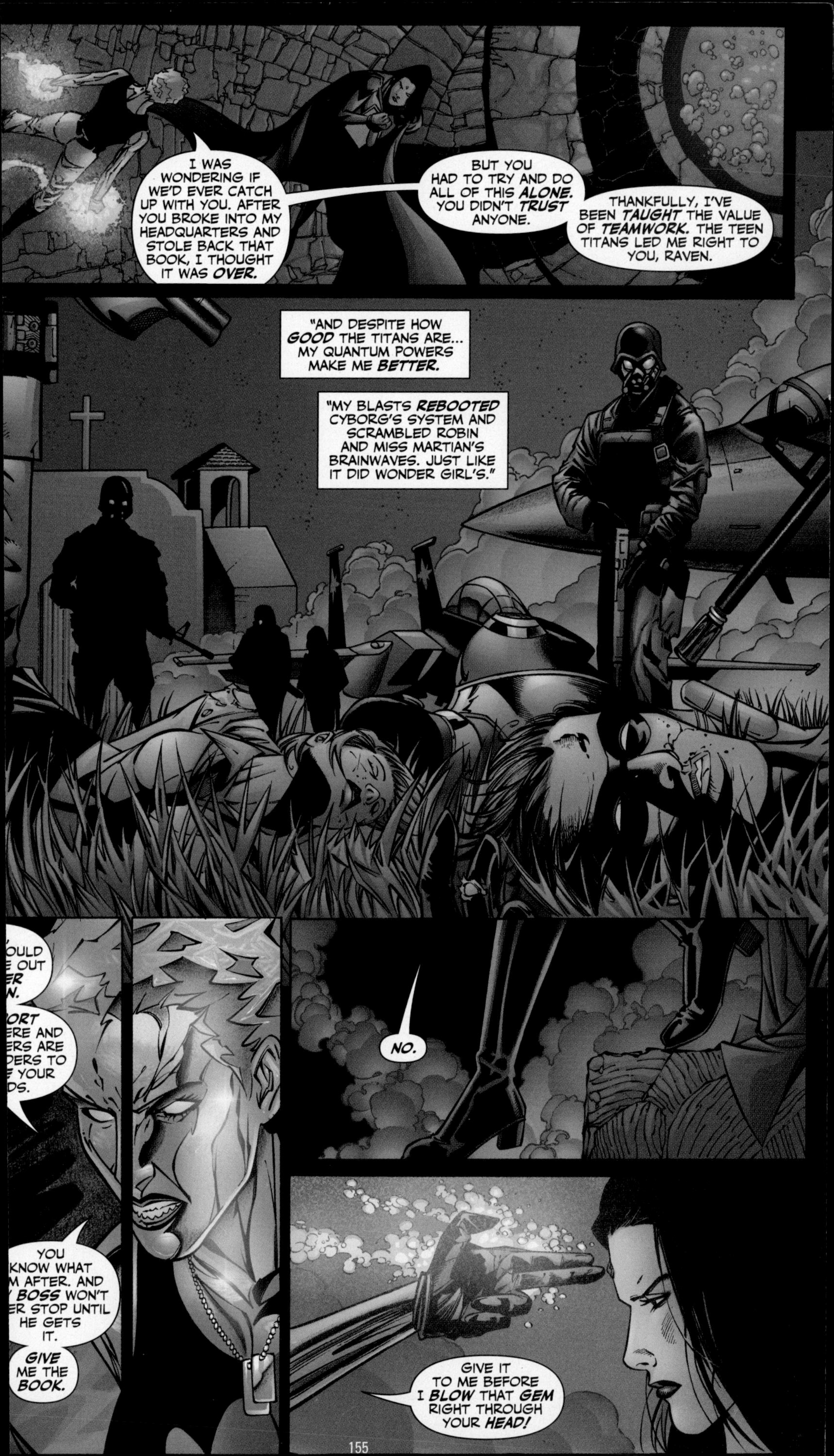
I WAS WONDERING IF WE'D EVER CATCH UP WITH YOU. AFTER YOU BROKE INTO MY HEADQUARTERS AND STOLE BACK THAT BOOK, I THOUGHT IT WAS OVER.
BUT YOU HAD TO TRY AND DO ALL OF THIS ALONE. YOU DIDN'T TRUST ANYONE.
THANKFULLY, I'VE BEEN TAUGHT THE VALUE OF TEAMWORK. THE TEEN TITANS LED ME RIGHT TO YOU, RAVEN.
"AND DESPITE HOW GOOD THE TITANS ARE... MY QUANTUM POWERS MAKE ME BETTER.
"MY BLASTS REBOOTED CYBORG'S SYSTEM AND SCRAMBLED ROBIN AND MISS MARTIAN'S BRAINWAVES. JUST LIKE IT DID WONDER GIRL'S."
OULD E OUT ER N. ORT ERE AND ERS ARE DERS TO E YOUR DS.
NO.
YOU KNOW WHAT M AFTER. AND BOSS WON'T ER STOP UNTIL HE GETS IT.
GIVE ME THE BOOK.
GIVE IT TO ME BEFORE I BLOW THAT GEM RIGHT THROUGH YOUR HEAD!

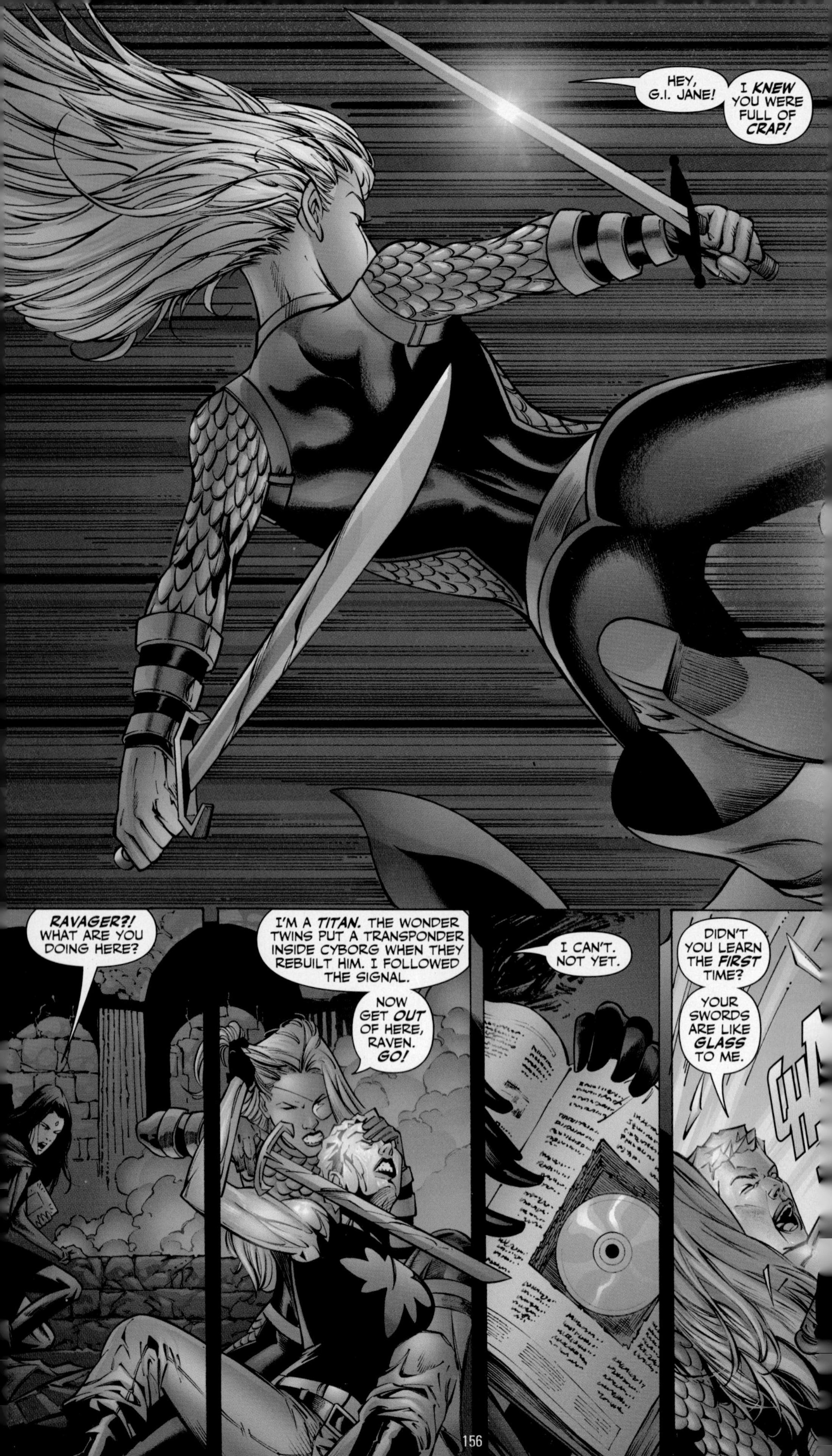
HEY, G.I. JANE!
I KNEW YOU WERE FULL OF CRAP!
RAVAGER?! WHAT ARE YOU DOING HERE?
I'M A TITAN. THE WONDER TWINS PUT A TRANSPONDER INSIDE CYBORG WHEN THEY REBUILT HIM. I FOLLOWED THE SIGNAL.
NOW GET OUT OF HERE, RAVEN. GO!
I CAN'T. NOT YET.
DIDN'T YOU LEARN THE FIRST TIME?
YOUR SWORDS ARE LIKE GLASS TO ME.

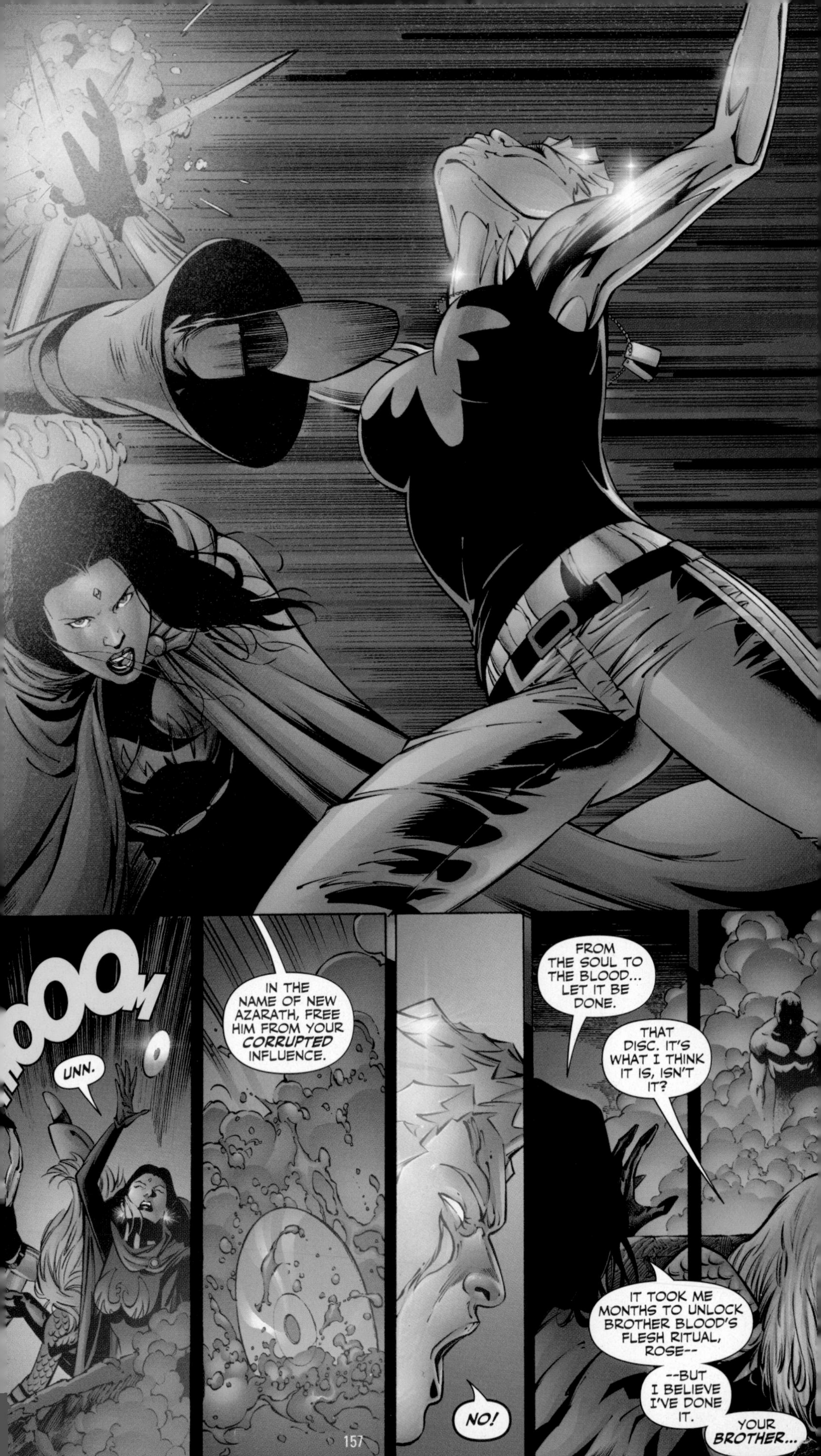

OOOM
UNN.
IN THE NAME OF NEW AZARATH, FREE HIM FROM YOUR CORRUPTED INFLUENCE.
NO!
FROM THE SOUL TO THE BLOOD... LET IT BE DONE.
THAT DISC. IT'S WHAT I THINK IT IS, ISN'T IT?
IT TOOK ME MONTHS TO UNLOCK BROTHER BLOOD'S FLESH RITUAL, ROSE--
--BUT I BELIEVE I'VE DONE IT.
YOUR BROTHER...

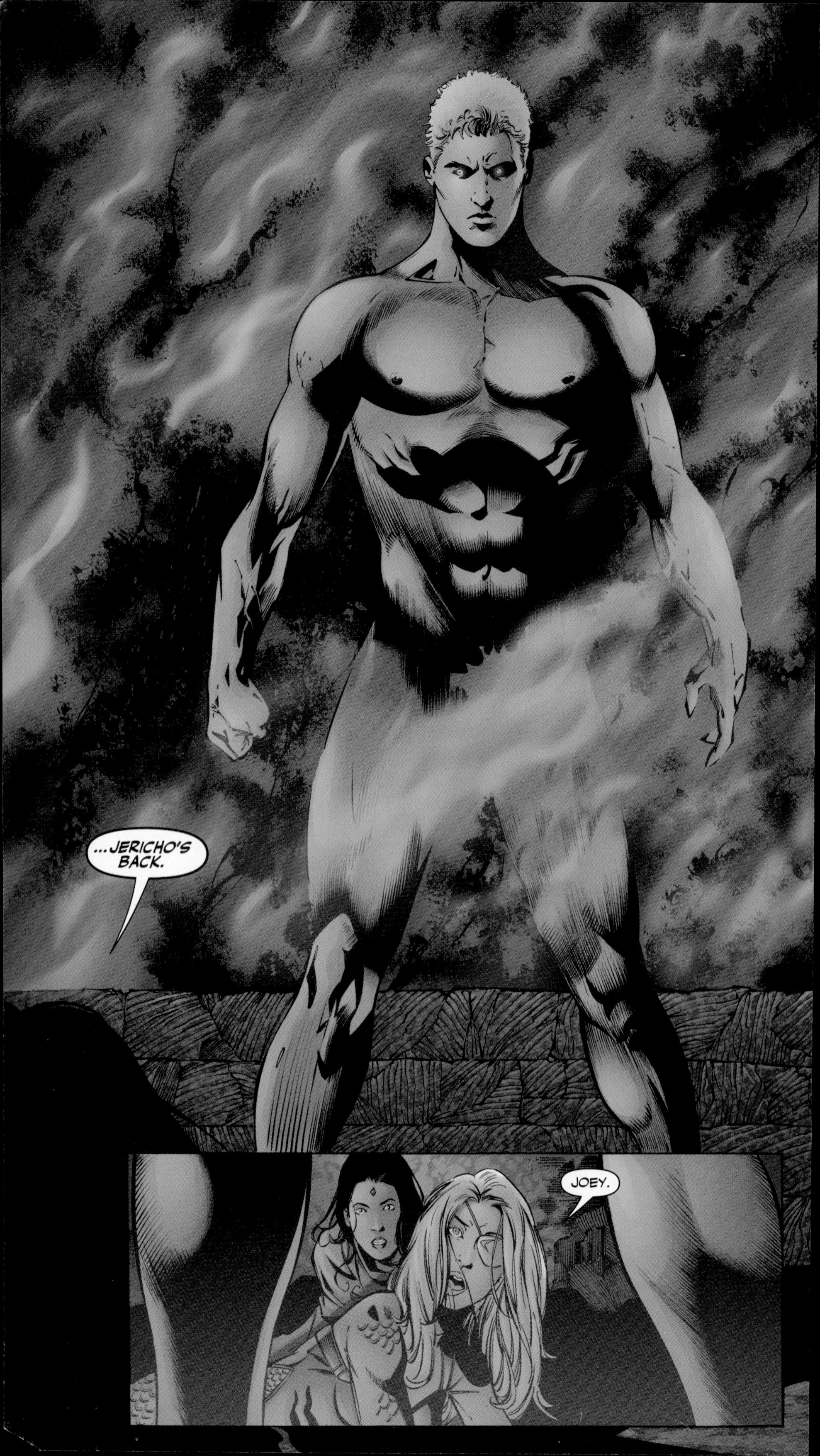
...JERICHO'S BACK.
JOEY.

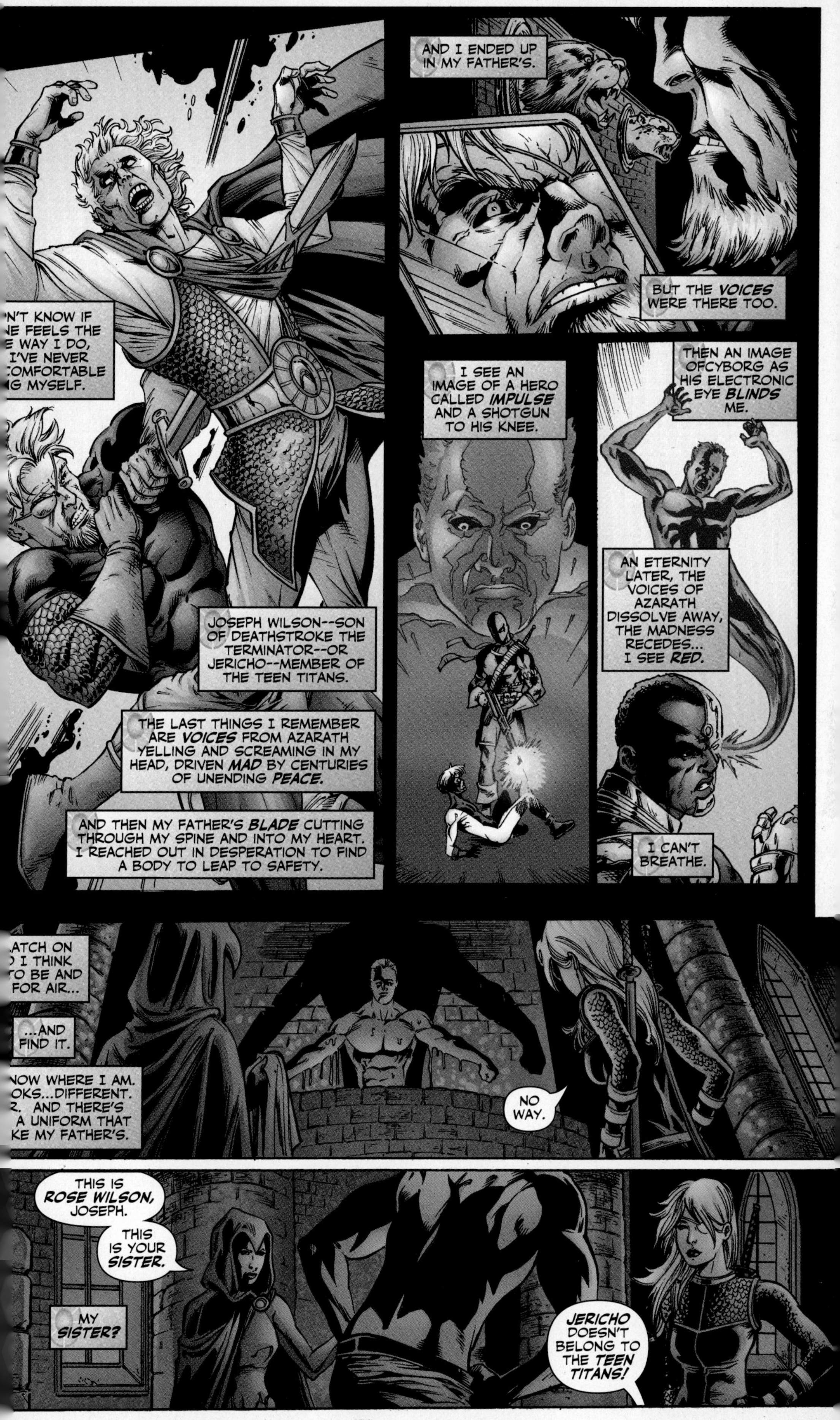

N'T KNOW IF
NE FEELS THE
E WAY I DO,
I'VE NEVER
COMFORTABLE
G MYSELF.
JOSEPH WILSON--SON OF DEATHSTROKE THE TERMINATOR--OR JERICHO--MEMBER OF THE TEEN TITANS.
THE LAST THINGS I REMEMBER ARE *VOICES* FROM AZARATH YELLING AND SCREAMING IN MY HEAD, DRIVEN *MAD* BY CENTURIES OF UNENDING *PEACE.*
AND THEN MY FATHER'S *BLADE* CUTTING THROUGH MY SPINE AND INTO MY HEART. I REACHED OUT IN DESPERATION TO FIND A BODY TO LEAP TO SAFETY.
AND I ENDED UP IN MY FATHER'S.
BUT THE *VOICES* WERE THERE TOO.
I SEE AN IMAGE OF A HERO CALLED *IMPULSE* AND A SHOTGUN TO HIS KNEE.
THEN AN IMAGE OFCYBORG AS HIS ELECTRONIC EYE *BLINDS* ME.
AN ETERNITY LATER, THE VOICES OF AZARATH DISSOLVE AWAY, THE MADNESS RECEDES... I SEE *RED.*
I CAN'T BREATHE.
ATCH ON
D I THINK
TO BE AND
FOR AIR...
...AND FIND IT.
NOW WHERE I AM.
OKS...DIFFERENT.
R. AND THERE'S
A UNIFORM THAT
KE MY FATHER'S.
NO WAY.
THIS IS *ROSE WILSON,* JOSEPH.
THIS IS YOUR *SISTER.*
MY *SISTER?*
JERICHO DOESN'T BELONG TO THE *TEEN TITANS!*

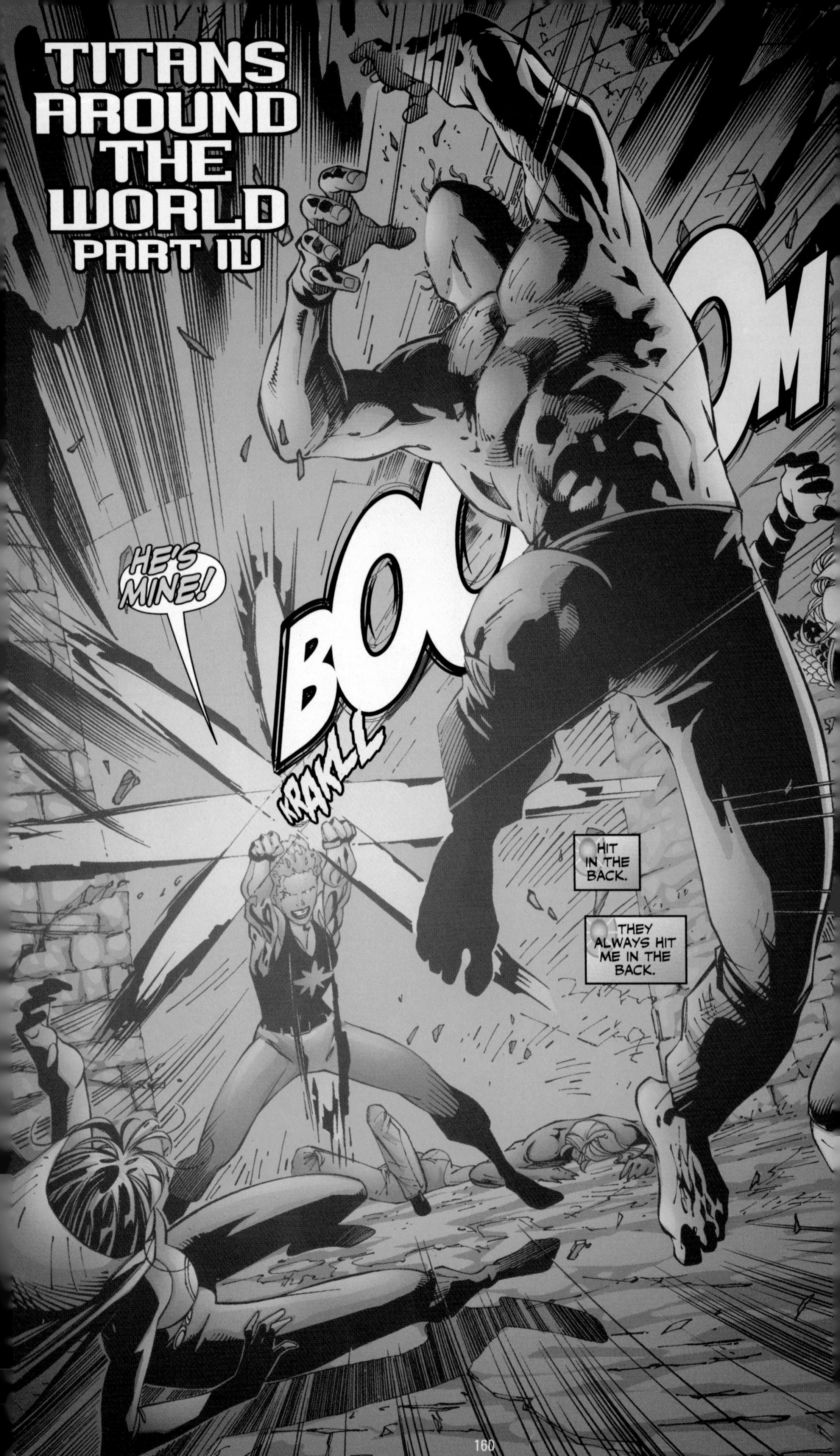

TITANS AROUND THE WORLD PART IV
HE'S MINE!
BOOM
KRAKLL
HIT IN THE BACK.
THEY ALWAYS HIT ME IN THE BACK.

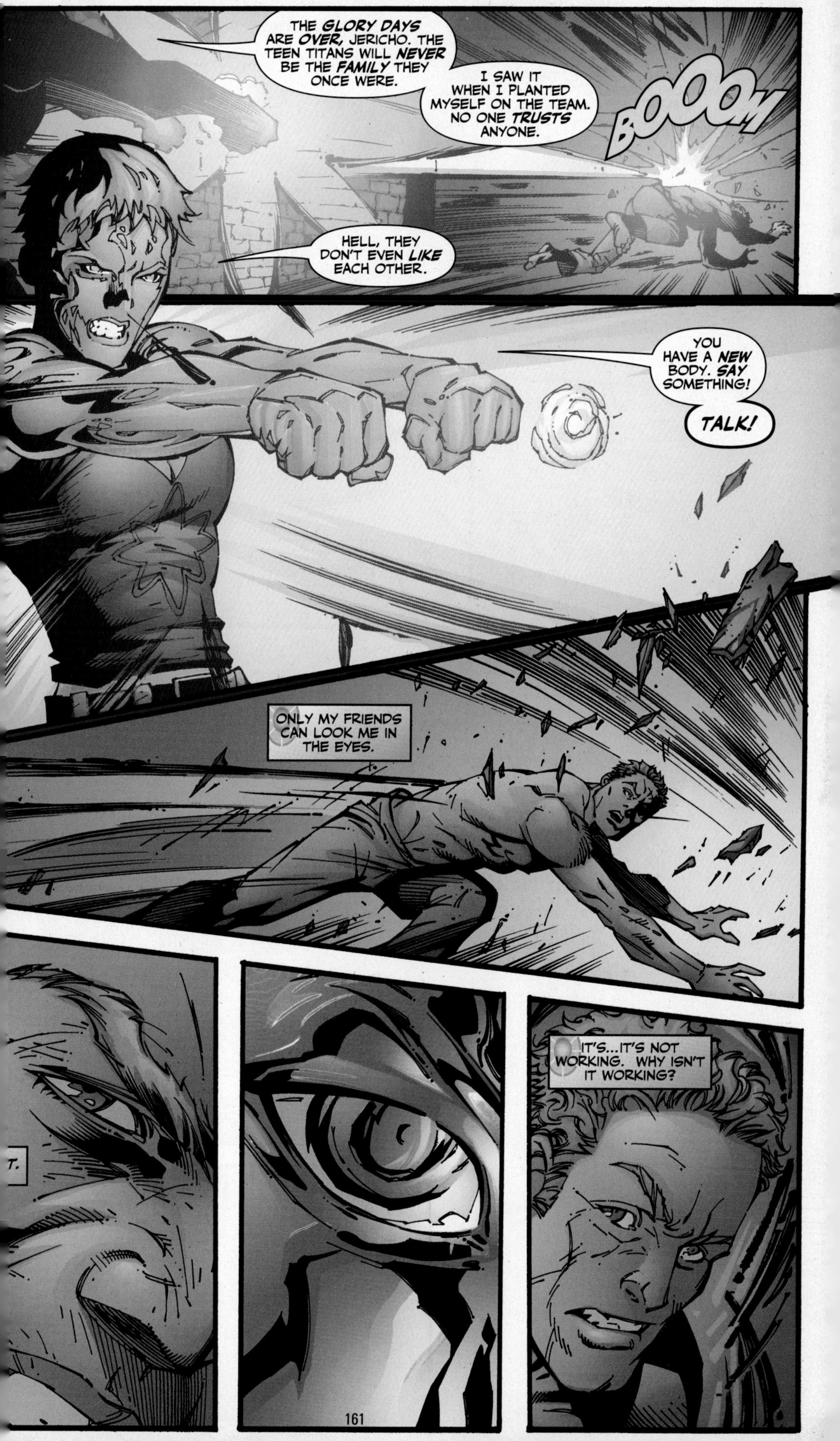

THE GLORY DAYS ARE OVER, JERICHO. THE TEEN TITANS WILL NEVER BE THE FAMILY THEY ONCE WERE.
I SAW IT WHEN I PLANTED MYSELF ON THE TEAM. NO ONE TRUSTS ANYONE.
BOOOOM
HELL, THEY DON'T EVEN LIKE EACH OTHER.
YOU HAVE A NEW BODY. SAY SOMETHING!
TALK!
ONLY MY FRIENDS CAN LOOK ME IN THE EYES.
T.
IT'S...IT'S NOT WORKING. WHY ISN'T IT WORKING?

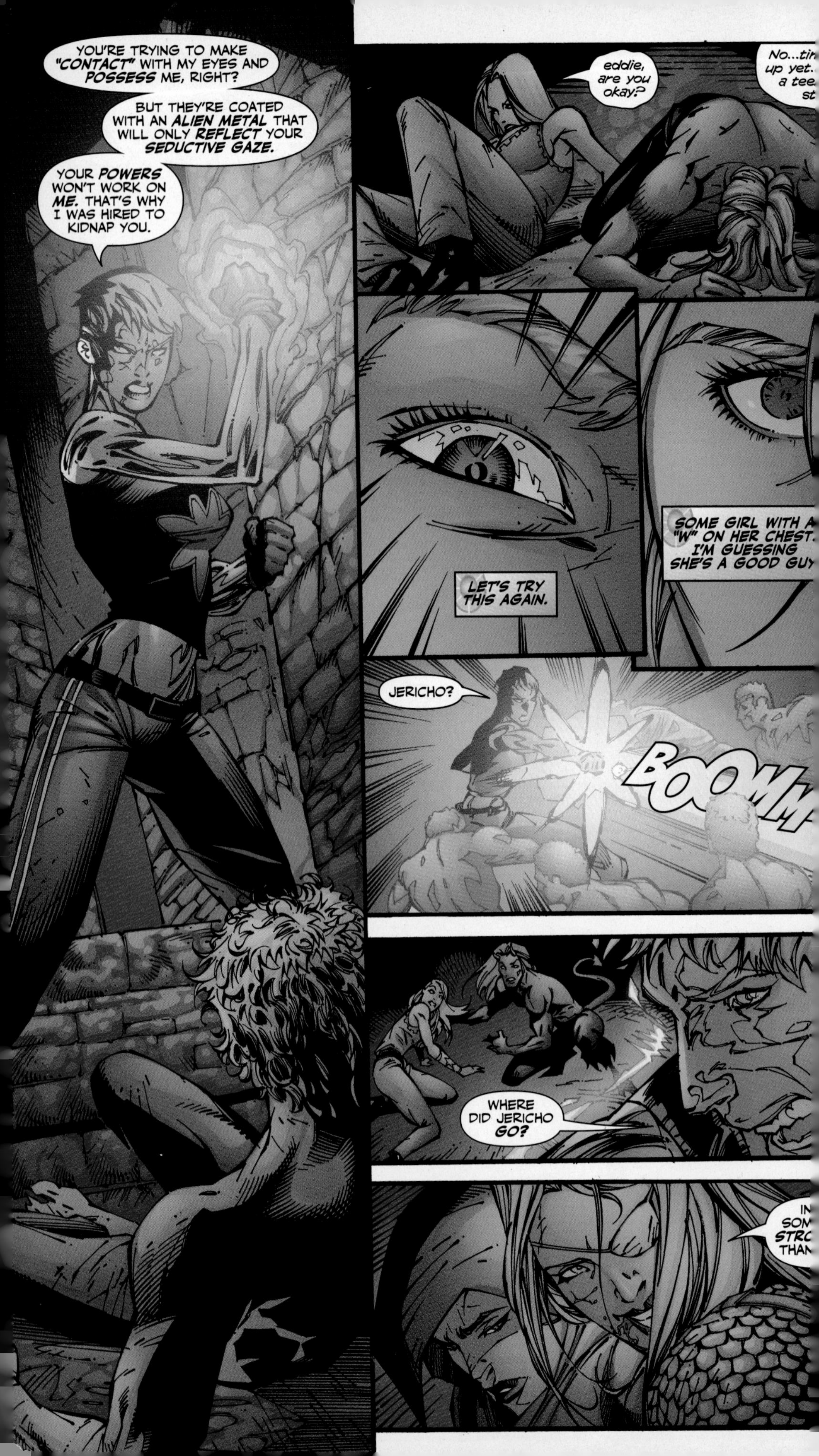
YOU'RE TRYING TO MAKE "CONTACT" WITH MY EYES AND POSSESS ME, RIGHT?
BUT THEY'RE COATED WITH AN ALIEN METAL THAT WILL ONLY REFLECT YOUR SEDUCTIVE GAZE.
YOUR POWERS WON'T WORK ON ME. THAT'S WHY I WAS HIRED TO KIDNAP YOU.
eddie, are you okay?
LET'S TRY THIS AGAIN.
SOME GIRL WITH A "W" ON HER CHEST. I'M GUESSING SHE'S A GOOD GUY
JERICHO?
WHERE DID JERICHO GO?

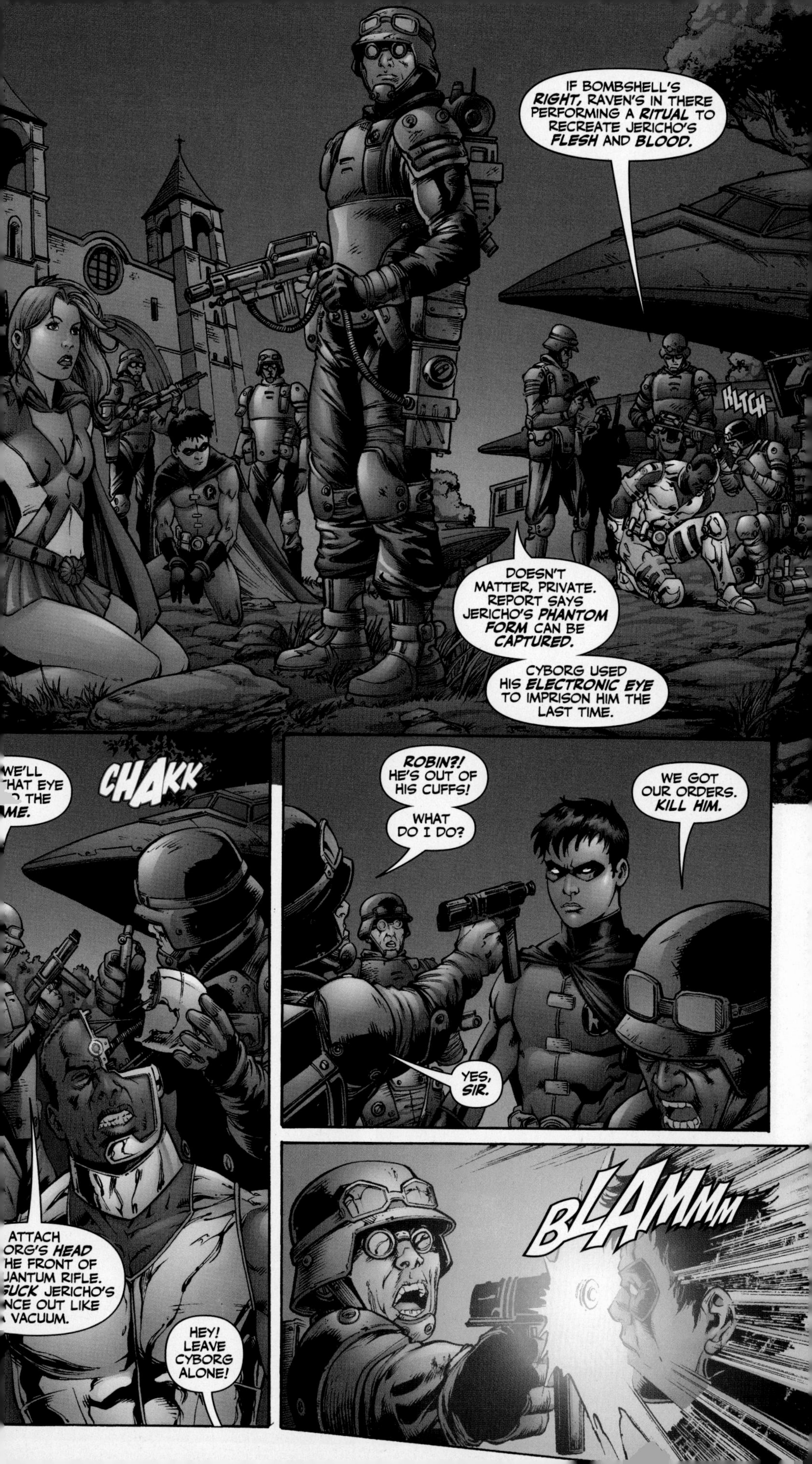
IF BOMBSHELL'S RIGHT, RAVEN'S IN THERE PERFORMING A RITUAL TO RECREATE JERICHO'S FLESH AND BLOOD.
DOESN'T MATTER, PRIVATE. REPORT SAYS JERICHO'S PHANTOM FORM CAN BE CAPTURED.
CYBORG USED HIS ELECTRONIC EYE TO IMPRISON HIM THE LAST TIME.
KLTCH
WE'LL THAT EYE THE
CHAKK
ATTACH HEAD FRONT OF RIFLE. JERICHO'S OUT LIKE VACUUM.
HEY! LEAVE CYBORG ALONE!
ROBIN?! HE'S OUT OF HIS CUFFS!
WHAT DO I DO?
WE GOT OUR ORDERS. KILL HIM.
YES, SIR.
BLAMMM

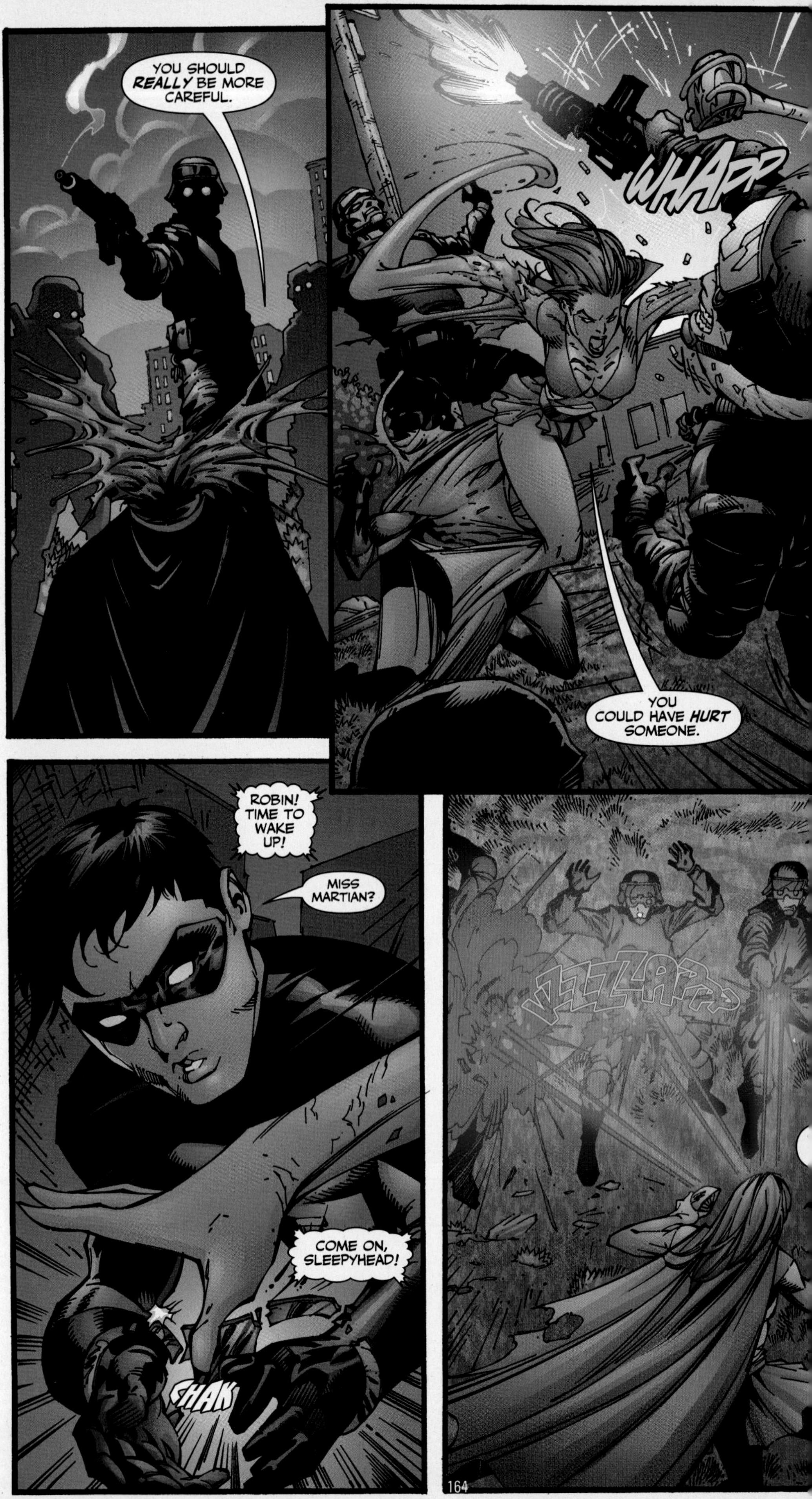
YOU SHOULD REALLY BE MORE CAREFUL.
WHAPP
YOU COULD HAVE HURT SOMEONE.
ROBIN! TIME TO WAKE UP!
MISS MARTIAN?
COME ON, SLEEPYHEAD!
CHAK

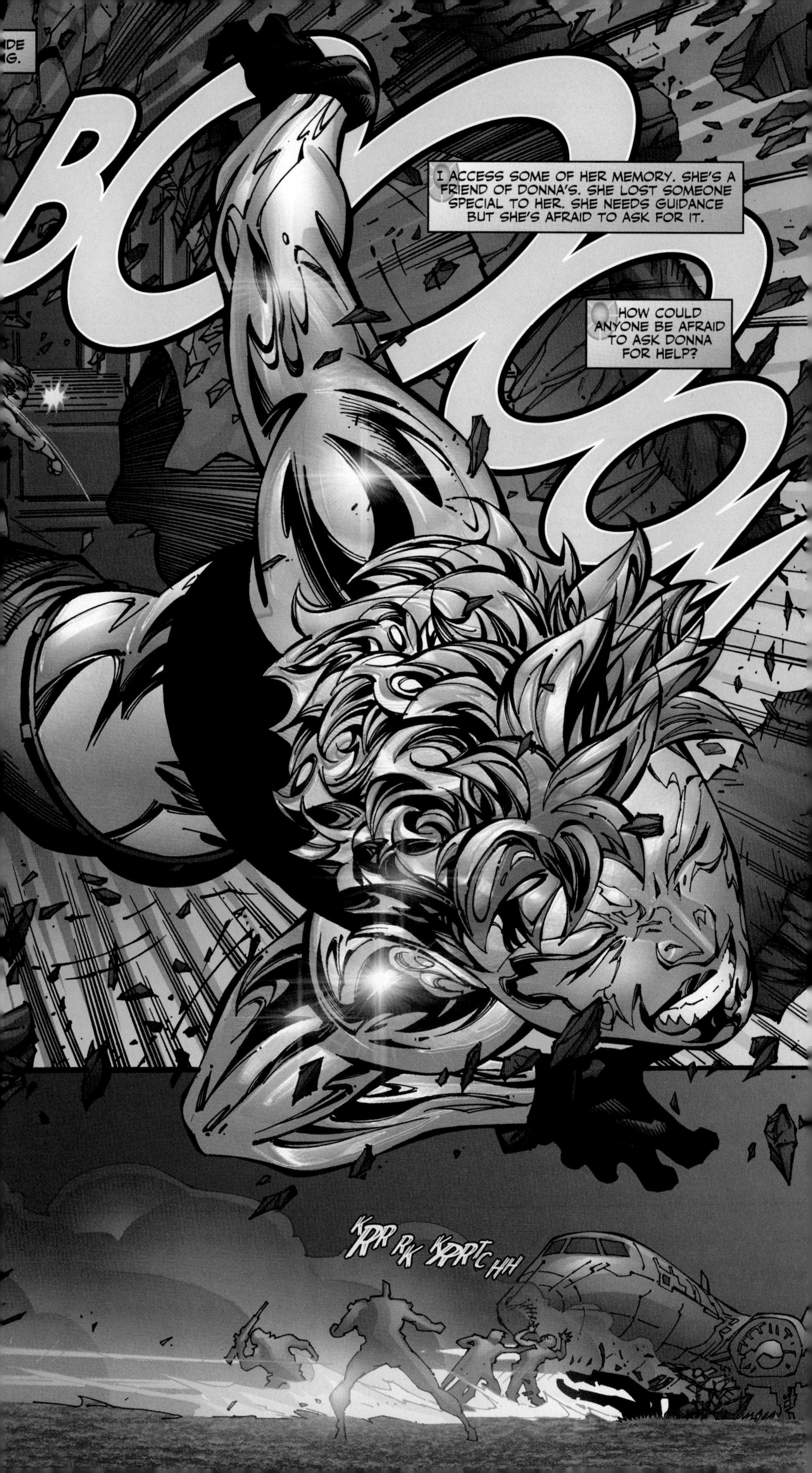
DE
G.
BOOOM
I ACCESS SOME OF HER MEMORY. SHE'S A FRIEND OF DONNA'S. SHE LOST SOMEONE SPECIAL TO HER. SHE NEEDS GUIDANCE BUT SHE'S AFRAID TO ASK FOR IT.
HOW COULD ANYONE BE AFRAID TO ASK DONNA FOR HELP?
KRPR RK KRPRTCHH

SHE'S FIGHTING ME. BUCKING LIKE A WILD BULL.

ROBIN?! WHAT'S...WHAT'S WRONG WITH ME?

I CAN'T CONTROL MY BODY. SOMETHING'S--

JERICHO?

CASS GET Y LASS AROU HIM

WHER WHERE

WHAT'S HAPPENED TO THE TEEN TITANS?

ROBIN, WAIT. JOSEPH IS HIMSELF AGAIN. HE'S BACK.

SO IS ROSE.

I TOLD EVERYONE I WASN'T THE TRAITOR.

IT'S BOMBSHELL?

YEAH. SHE'S A TOTAL SILVER SKANK.

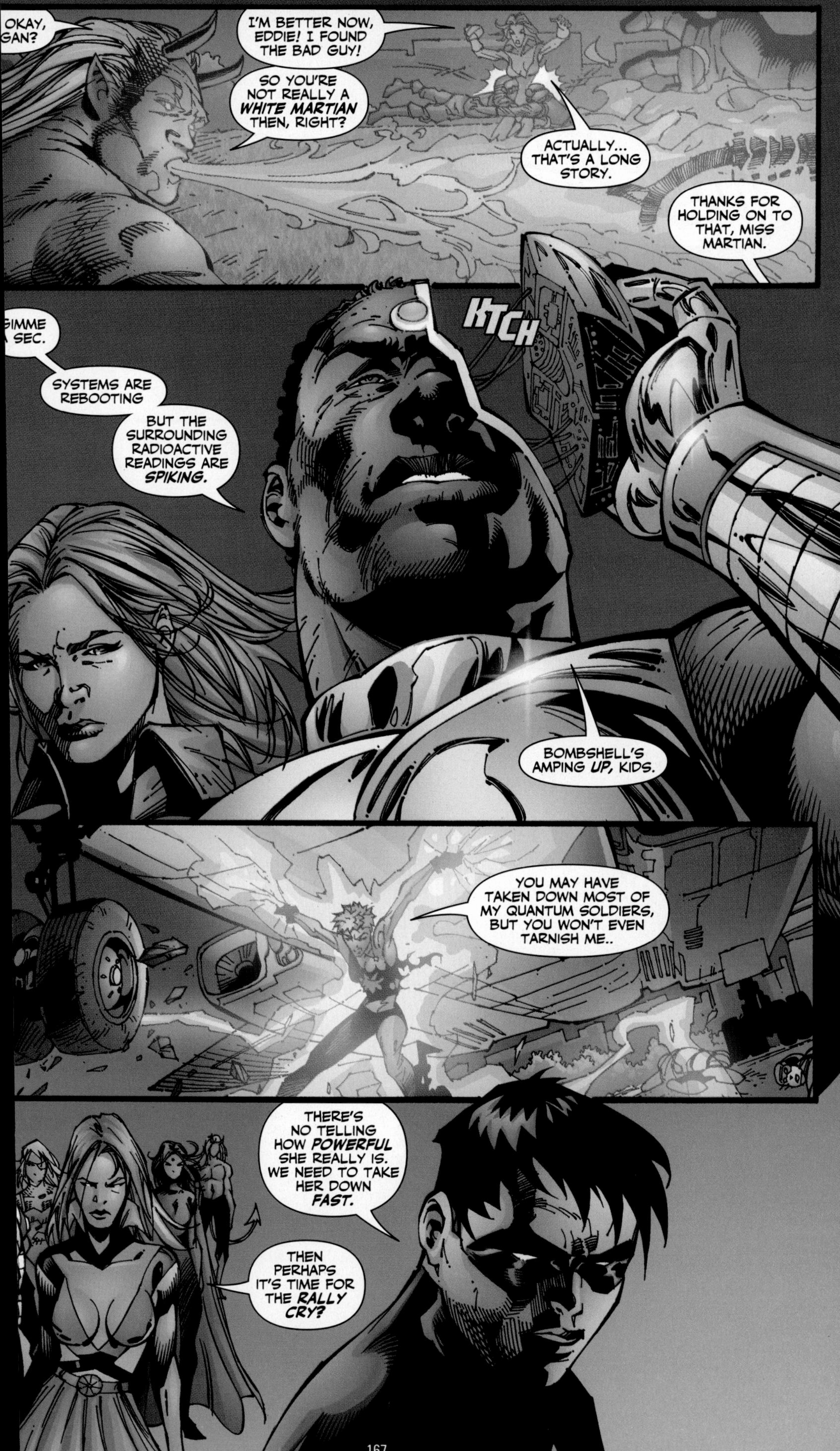
OKAY, GAN?
I'M BETTER NOW, EDDIE! I FOUND THE BAD GUY!
SO YOU'RE NOT REALLY A WHITE MARTIAN THEN, RIGHT?
ACTUALLY... THAT'S A LONG STORY.
THANKS FOR HOLDING ON TO THAT, MISS MARTIAN.
KTCH
GIMME A SEC.
SYSTEMS ARE REBOOTING
BUT THE SURROUNDING RADIOACTIVE READINGS ARE SPIKING.
BOMBSHELL'S AMPING UP, KIDS.
YOU MAY HAVE TAKEN DOWN MOST OF MY QUANTUM SOLDIERS, BUT YOU WON'T EVEN TARNISH ME..
THERE'S NO TELLING HOW POWERFUL SHE REALLY IS. WE NEED TO TAKE HER DOWN FAST.
THEN PERHAPS IT'S TIME FOR THE RALLY CRY?

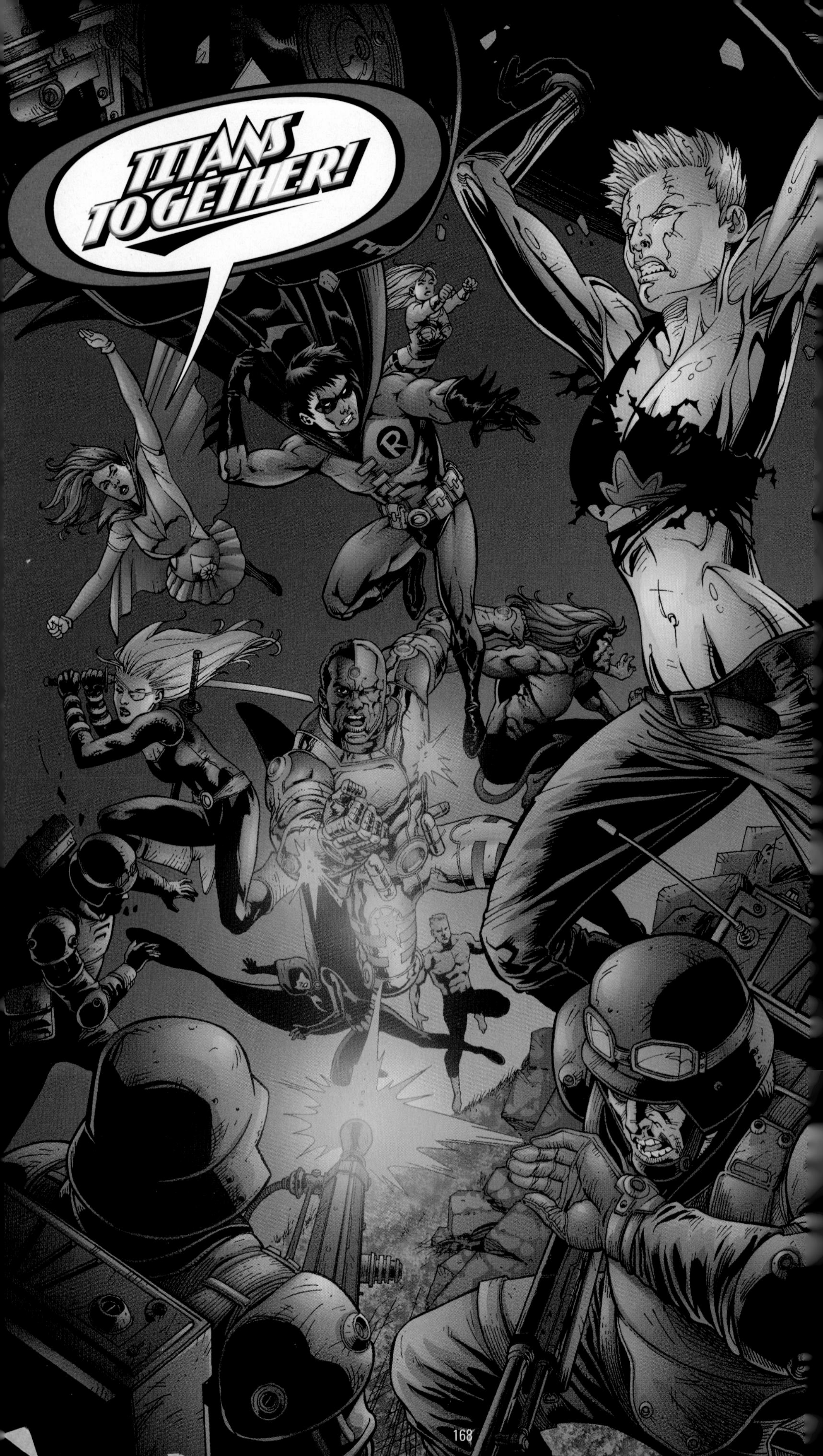
TITANS TOGETHER!

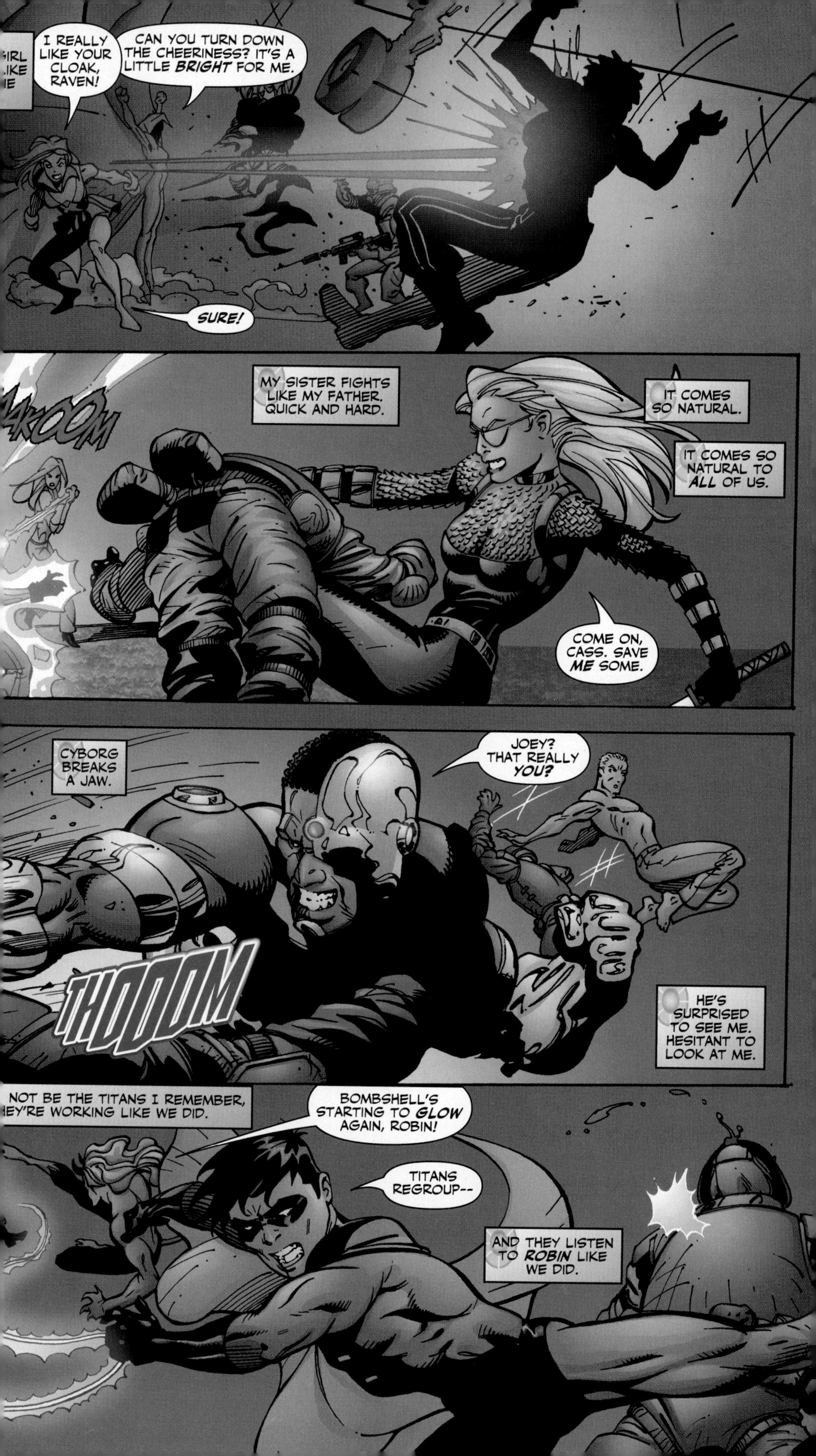

GIRL
LIKE
IE
I REALLY LIKE YOUR CLOAK, RAVEN!
CAN YOU TURN DOWN THE CHEERINESS? IT'S A LITTLE BRIGHT FOR ME.
SURE!
MY SISTER FIGHTS LIKE MY FATHER. QUICK AND HARD.
IT COMES SO NATURAL.
IT COMES SO NATURAL TO ALL OF US.
COME ON, CASS. SAVE ME SOME.
CYBORG BREAKS A JAW.
JOEY? THAT REALLY YOU?
THOOOM
HE'S SURPRISED TO SEE ME. HESITANT TO LOOK AT ME.
NOT BE THE TITANS I REMEMBER,
HEY'RE WORKING LIKE WE DID.
BOMBSHELL'S STARTING TO GLOW AGAIN, ROBIN!
TITANS REGROUP--
AND THEY LISTEN TO ROBIN LIKE WE DID.

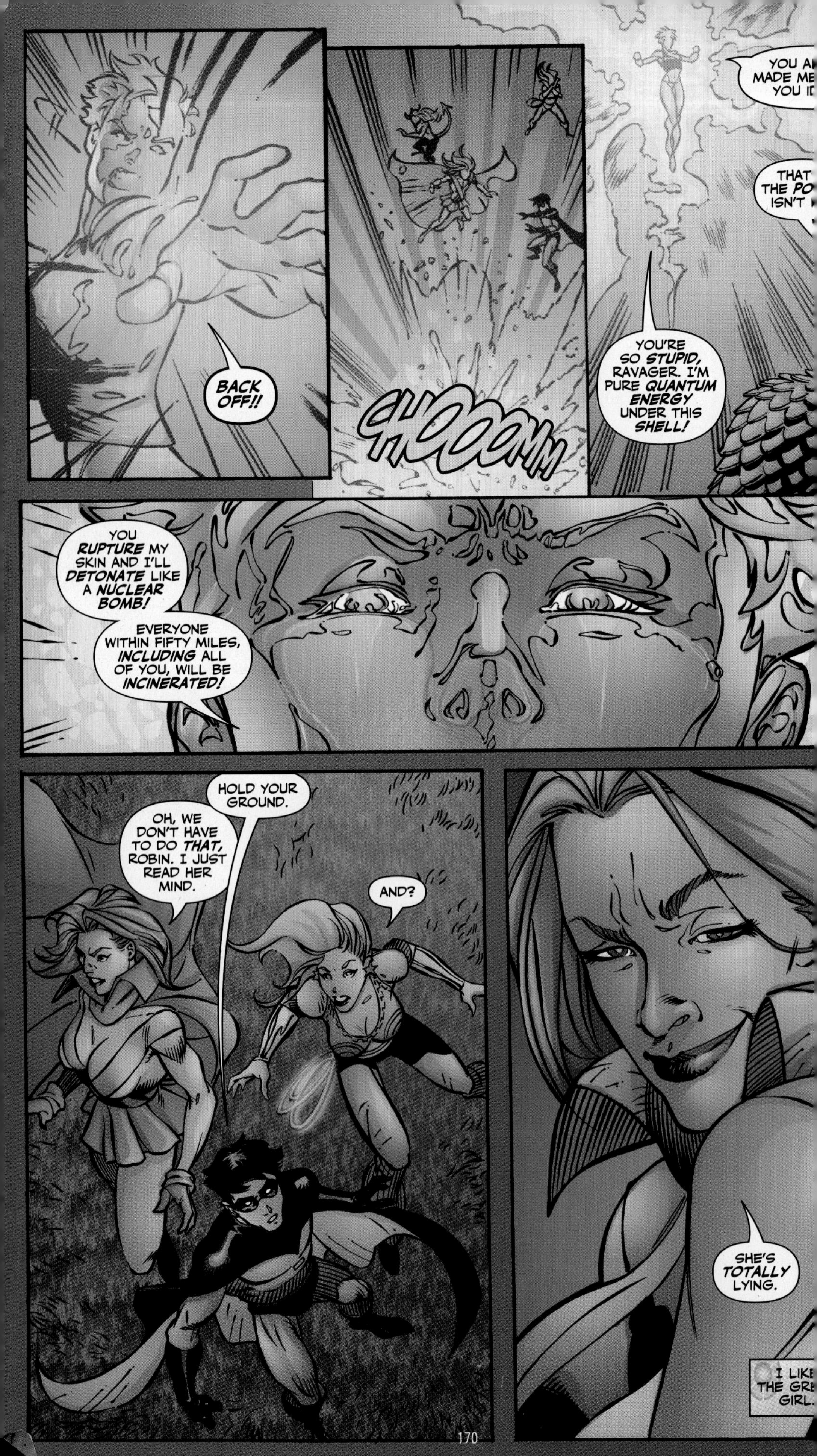
BACK OFF!!
SHOOOMM
YOU A
MADE ME
YOU I
THAT
THE PO
ISN'T
YOU'RE SO STUPID, RAVAGER. I'M PURE QUANTUM ENERGY UNDER THIS SHELL!
YOU RUPTURE MY SKIN AND I'LL DETONATE LIKE A NUCLEAR BOMB!
EVERYONE WITHIN FIFTY MILES, INCLUDING ALL OF YOU, WILL BE INCINERATED!
HOLD YOUR GROUND.
OH, WE DON'T HAVE TO DO THAT, ROBIN. I JUST READ HER MIND.
AND?
SHE'S TOTALLY LYING.
I LIK
THE GR
GIRL.

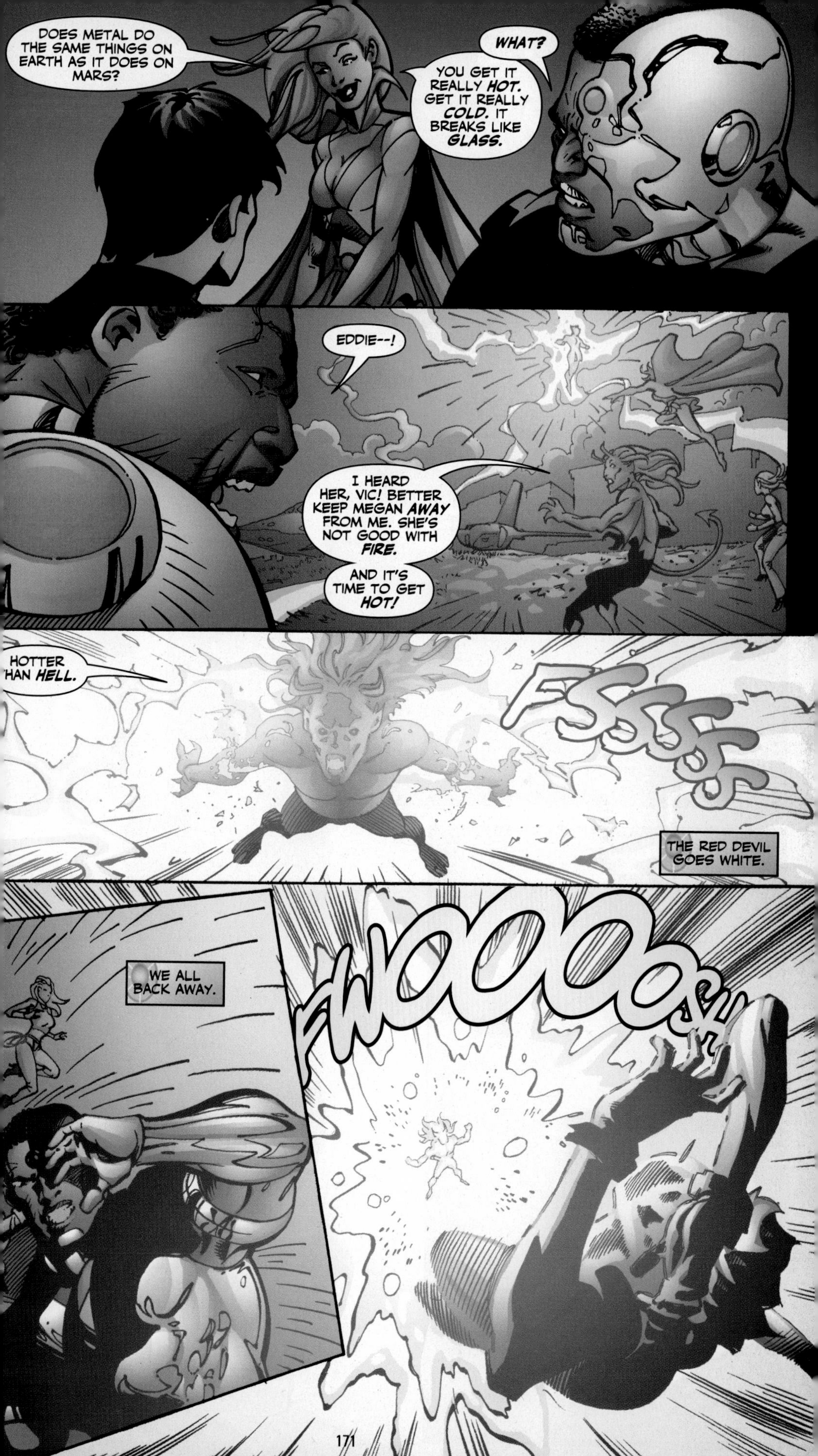
DOES METAL DO THE SAME THINGS ON EARTH AS IT DOES ON MARS?
WHAT?
YOU GET IT REALLY HOT. GET IT REALLY COLD. IT BREAKS LIKE GLASS.
EDDIE--!
I HEARD HER, VIC! BETTER KEEP MEGAN AWAY FROM ME. SHE'S NOT GOOD WITH FIRE.
AND IT'S TIME TO GET HOT!
HOTTER THAN HELL.
FSSSSS
THE RED DEVIL GOES WHITE.
WE ALL BACK AWAY.
FWOOOOSH

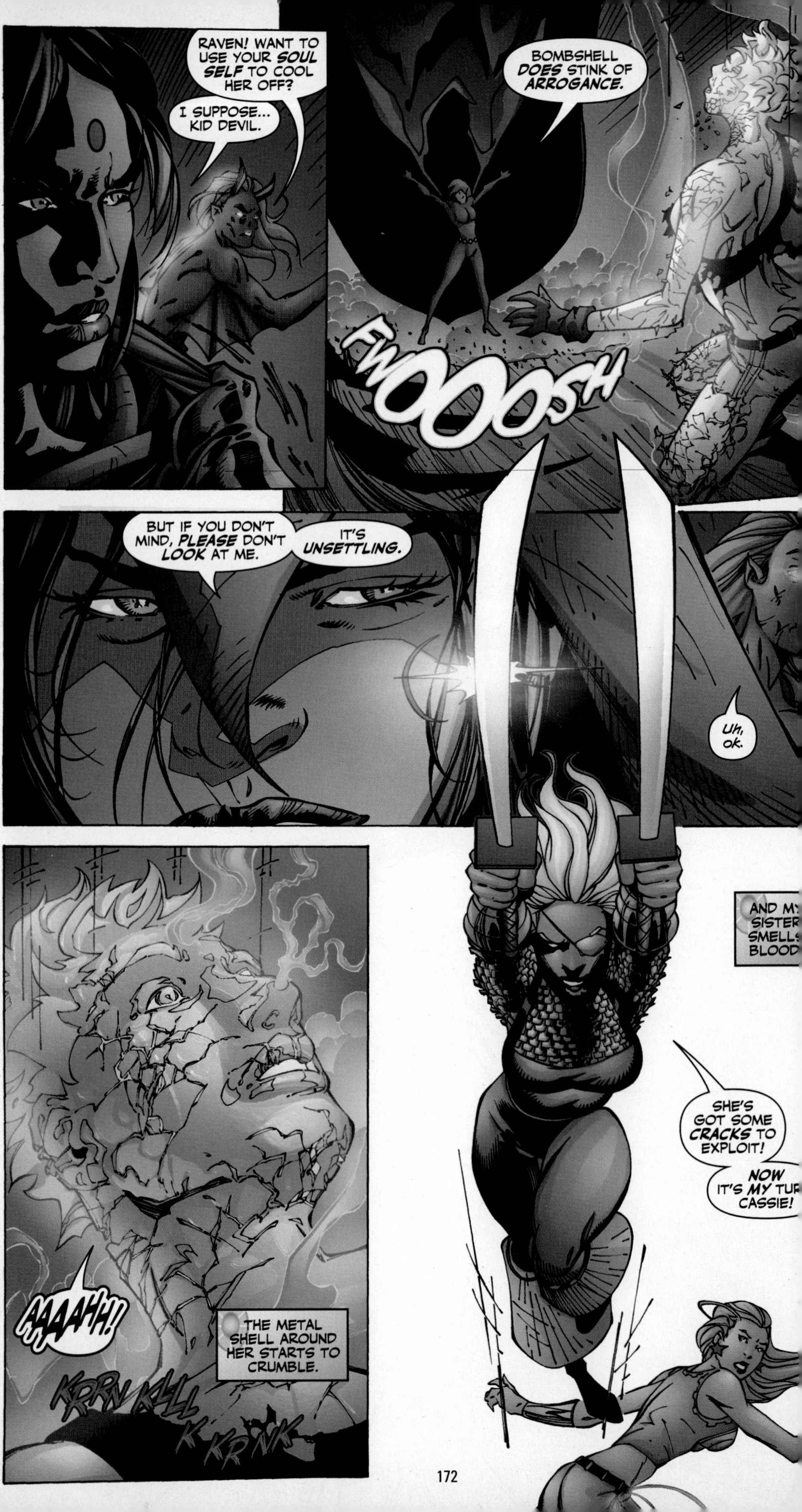
RAVEN! WANT TO USE YOUR SOUL SELF TO COOL HER OFF?
I SUPPOSE... KID DEVIL.
BOMBSHELL DOES STINK OF ARROGANCE.
FWOOOSH
BUT IF YOU DON'T MIND, PLEASE DON'T LOOK AT ME.
IT'S UNSETTLING.
Uh, ok.
AAAAHH!
THE METAL SHELL AROUND HER STARTS TO CRUMBLE.
KRRN KLLL K KRNK
AND MY SISTER SMELLS BLOOD
SHE'S GOT SOME CRACKS TO EXPLOIT!
NOW IT'S MY TU CASSIE!

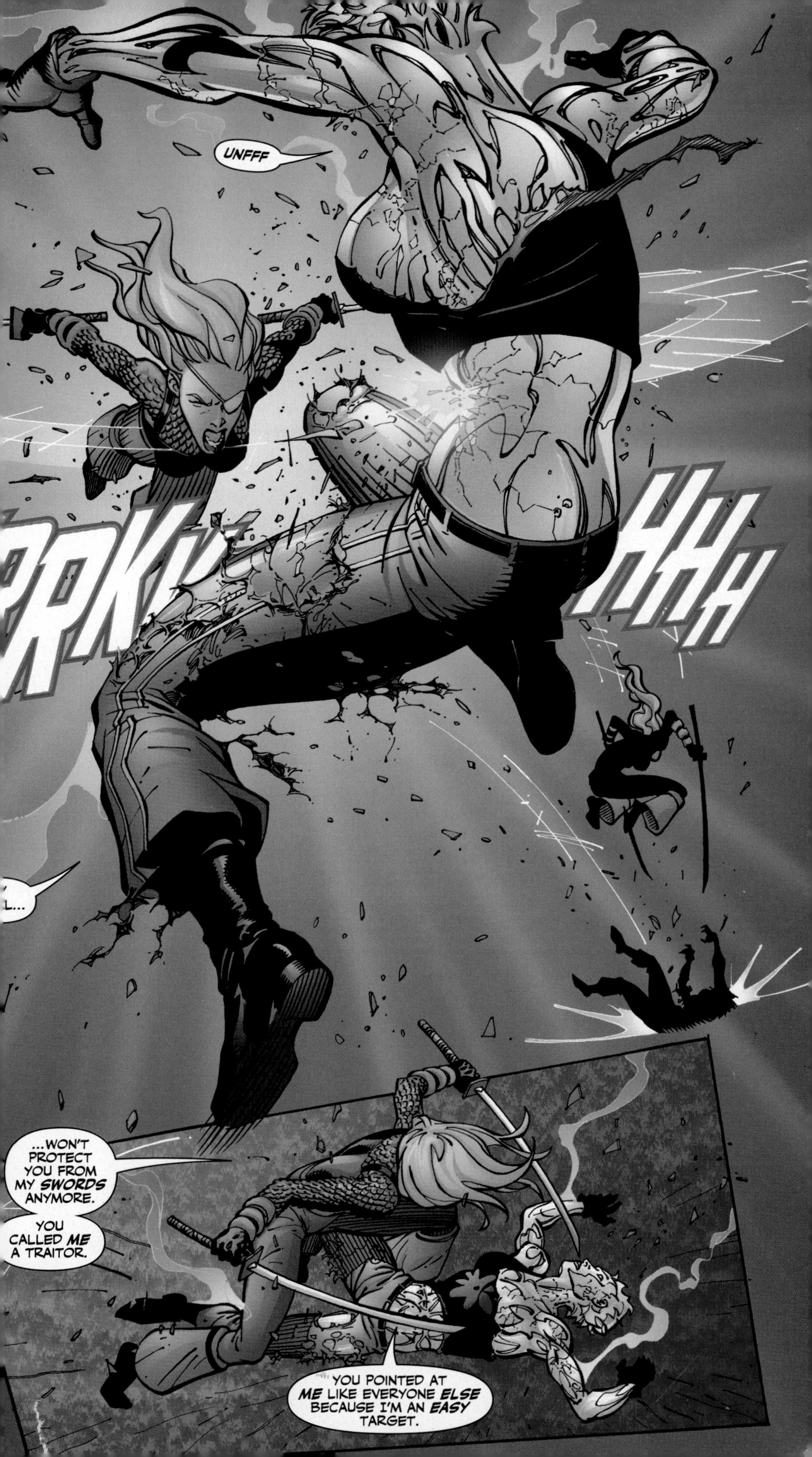
UNFFF
...WON'T PROTECT YOU FROM MY **SWORDS** ANYMORE.
YOU CALLED **ME** A TRAITOR.
YOU POINTED AT **ME** LIKE EVERYONE **ELSE** BECAUSE I'M AN **EASY** TARGET.

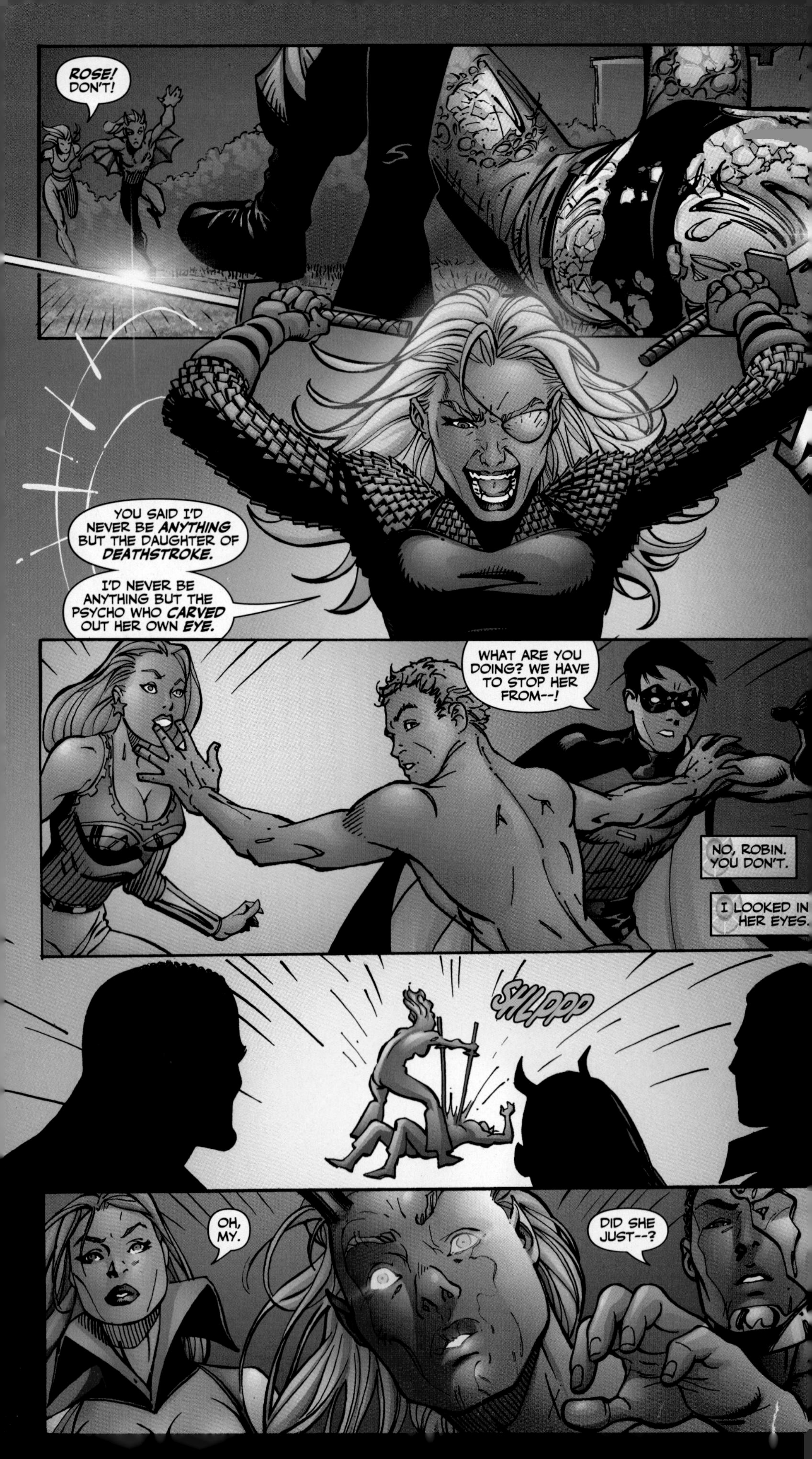
ROSE! DON'T!
YOU SAID I'D NEVER BE ANYTHING BUT THE DAUGHTER OF DEATHSTROKE.
I'D NEVER BE ANYTHING BUT THE PSYCHO WHO CARVED OUT HER OWN EYE.
WHAT ARE YOU DOING? WE HAVE TO STOP HER FROM--!
NO, ROBIN. YOU DON'T.
I LOOKED IN HER EYES.
SHLPPP
OH, MY.
DID SHE JUST--?

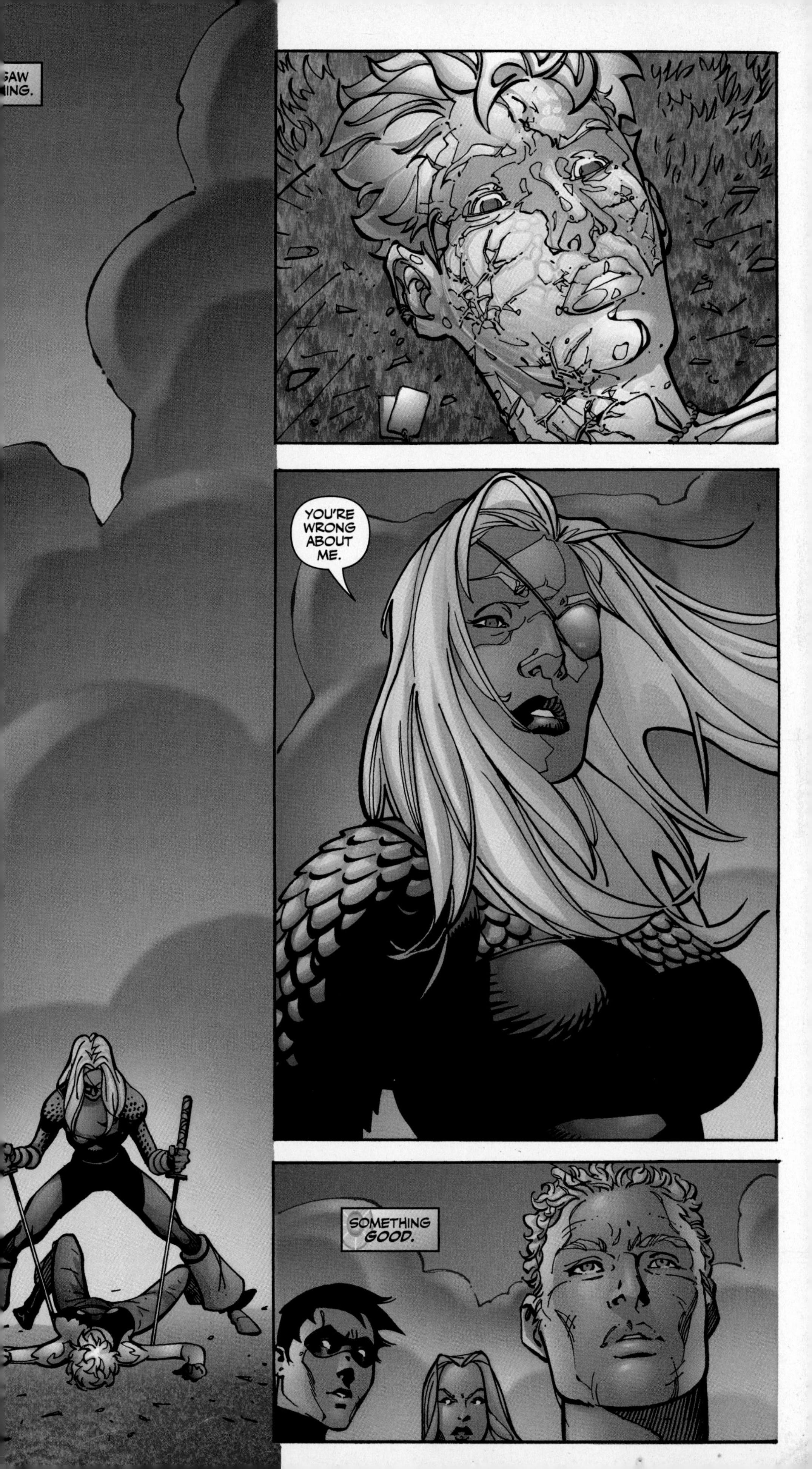
YOU'RE WRONG ABOUT ME.
SOMETHING *GOOD.*

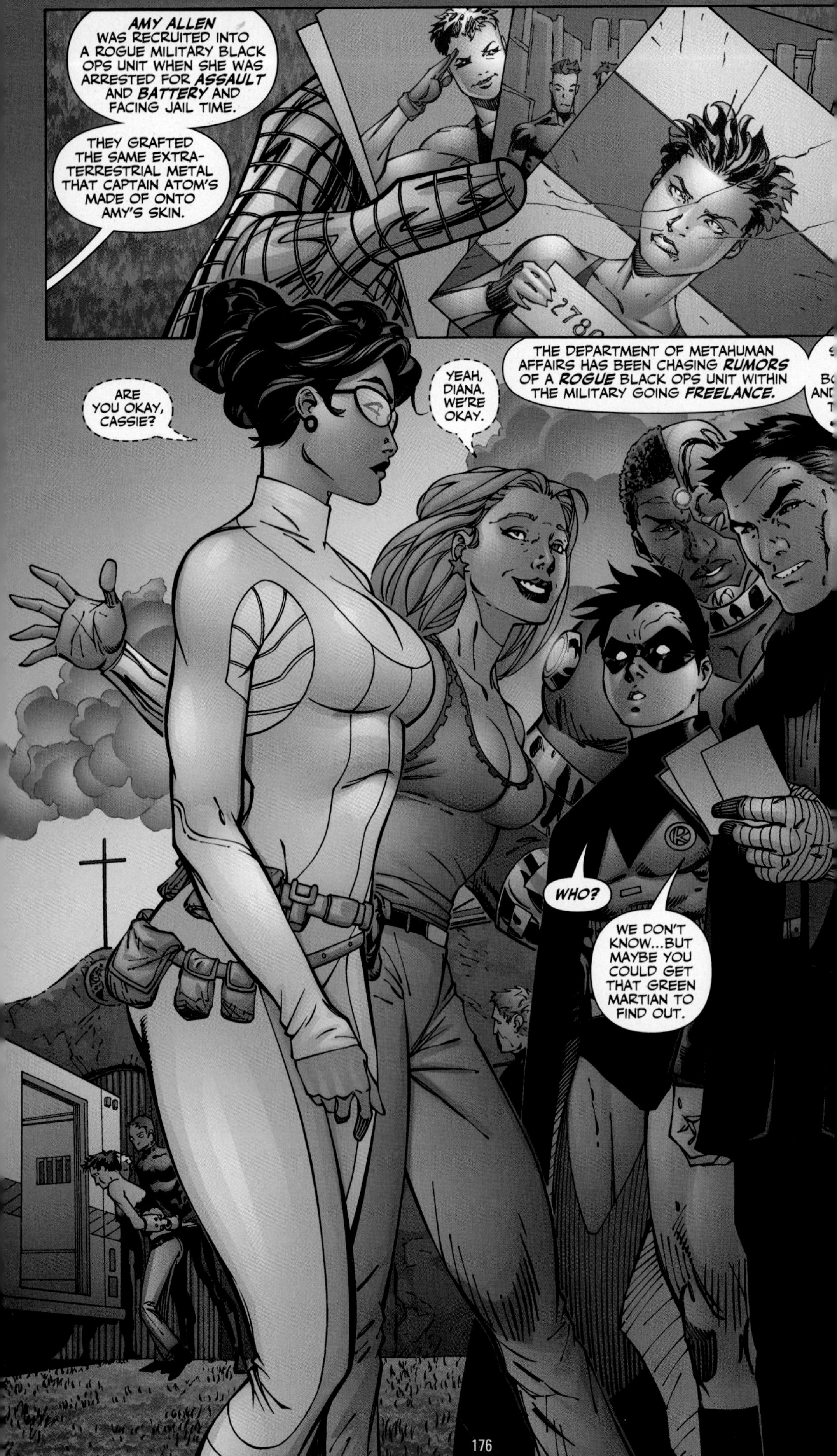

AMY ALLEN WAS RECRUITED INTO A ROGUE MILITARY BLACK OPS UNIT WHEN SHE WAS ARRESTED FOR ASSAULT AND BATTERY AND FACING JAIL TIME.
THEY GRAFTED THE SAME EXTRA-TERRESTRIAL METAL THAT CAPTAIN ATOM'S MADE OF ONTO AMY'S SKIN.
ARE YOU OKAY, CASSIE?
YEAH, DIANA. WE'RE OKAY.
THE DEPARTMENT OF METAHUMAN AFFAIRS HAS BEEN CHASING RUMORS OF A ROGUE BLACK OPS UNIT WITHIN THE MILITARY GOING FREELANCE.
WHO?
WE DON'T KNOW...BUT MAYBE YOU COULD GET THAT GREEN MARTIAN TO FIND OUT.

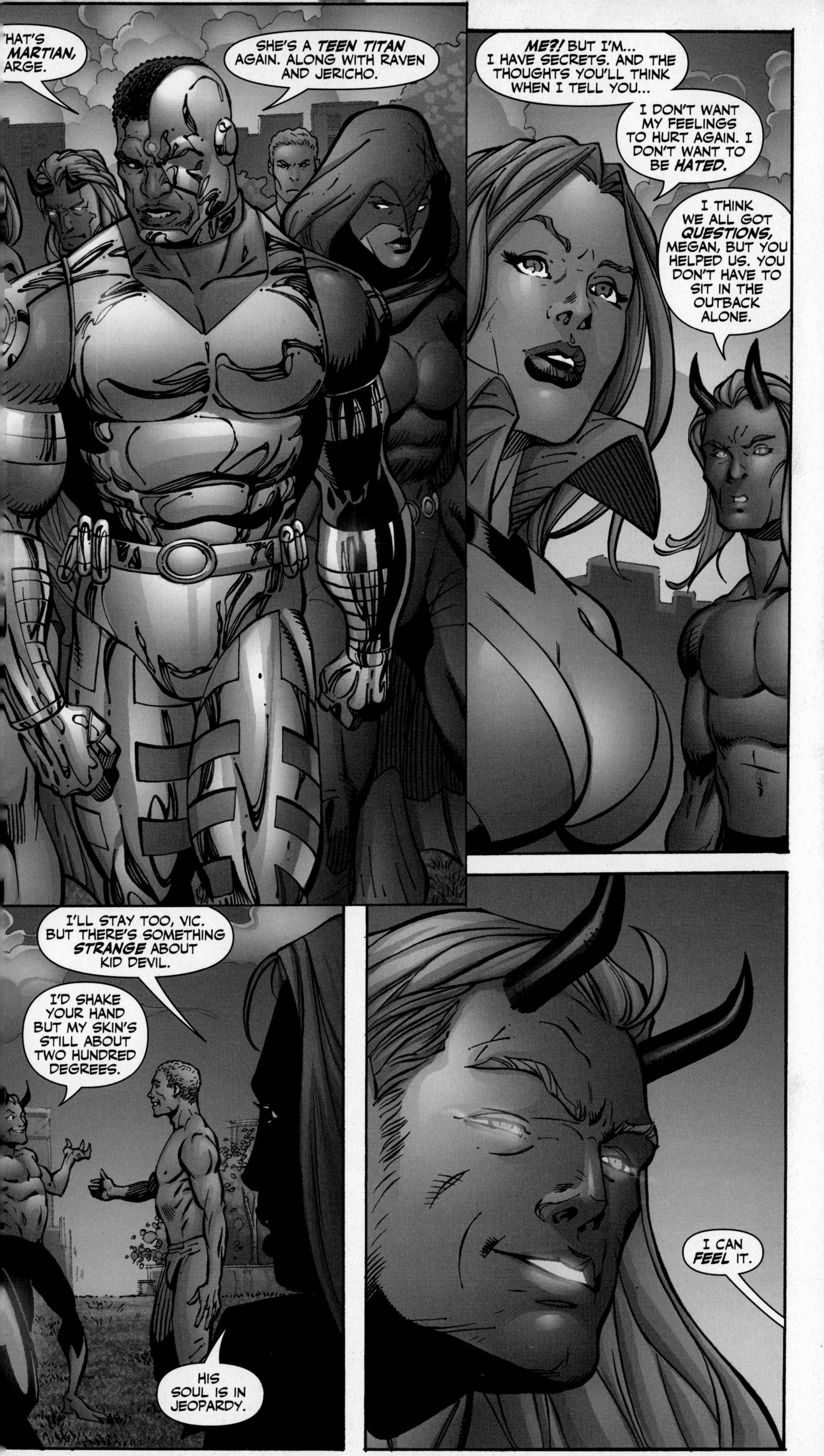
'HAT'S MARTIAN, ARGE.
SHE'S A TEEN TITAN AGAIN. ALONG WITH RAVEN AND JERICHO.
ME?! BUT I'M... I HAVE SECRETS. AND THE THOUGHTS YOU'LL THINK WHEN I TELL YOU...
I DON'T WANT MY FEELINGS TO HURT AGAIN. I DON'T WANT TO BE HATED.
I THINK WE ALL GOT QUESTIONS, MEGAN, BUT YOU HELPED US. YOU DON'T HAVE TO SIT IN THE OUTBACK ALONE.
I'LL STAY TOO, VIC. BUT THERE'S SOMETHING STRANGE ABOUT KID DEVIL.
I'D SHAKE YOUR HAND BUT MY SKIN'S STILL ABOUT TWO HUNDRED DEGREES.
HIS SOUL IS IN JEOPARDY.
I CAN FEEL IT.

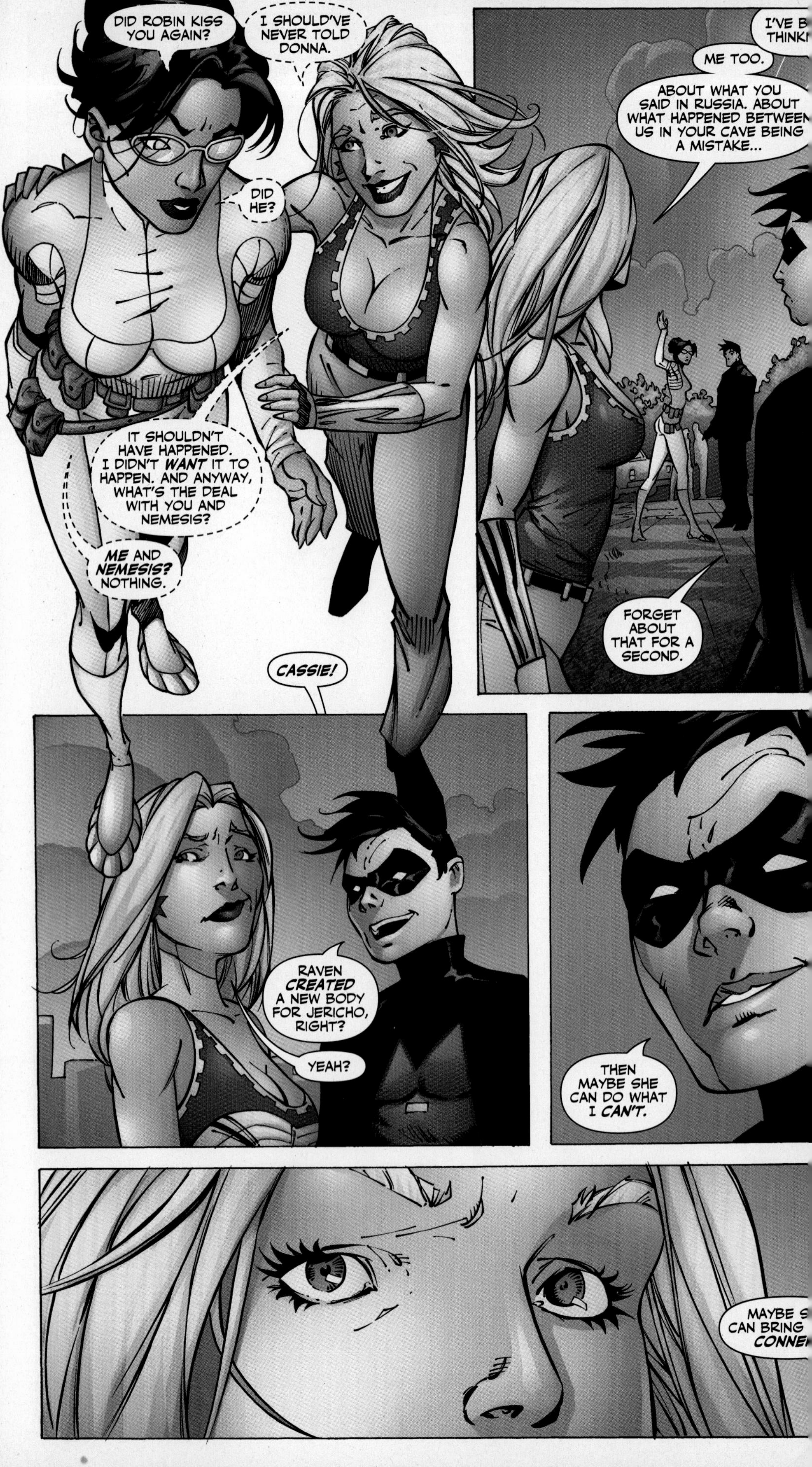
DID ROBIN KISS YOU AGAIN?
I SHOULD'VE NEVER TOLD DONNA.
DID HE?
IT SHOULDN'T HAVE HAPPENED. I DIDN'T *WANT* IT TO HAPPEN. AND ANYWAY, WHAT'S THE DEAL WITH YOU AND NEMESIS?
ME AND *NEMESIS?* NOTHING.
I'VE B THINKI
ME TOO.
ABOUT WHAT YOU SAID IN RUSSIA. ABOUT WHAT HAPPENED BETWEEN US IN YOUR CAVE BEING A MISTAKE...
FORGET ABOUT THAT FOR A SECOND.
CASSIE!
RAVEN *CREATED* A NEW BODY FOR JERICHO, RIGHT?
YEAH?
THEN MAYBE SHE CAN DO WHAT I *CAN'T.*
MAYBE S CAN BRING *CONNE*

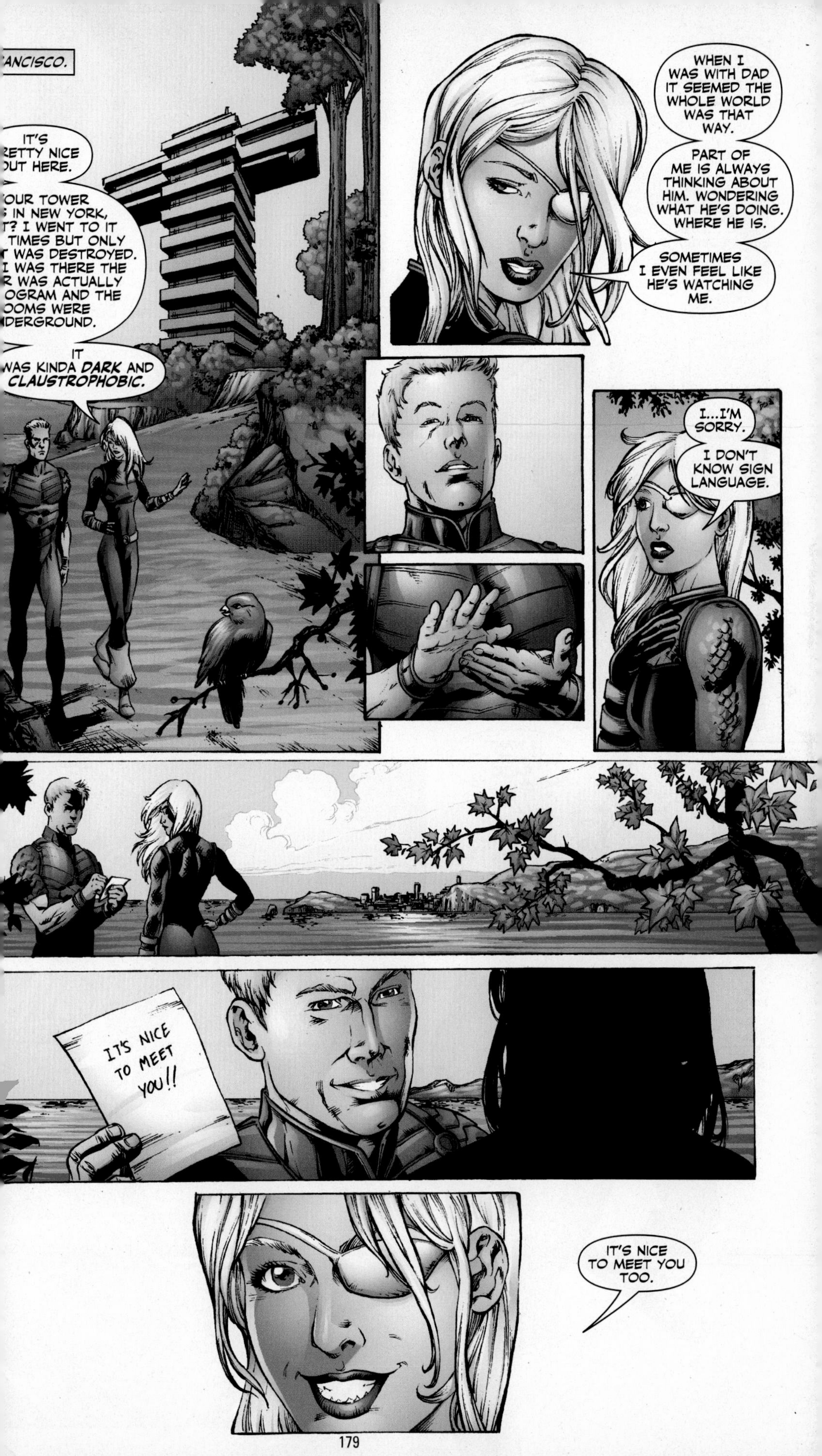

ANCISCO.
IT'S
RETTY NICE
OUT HERE.
OUR TOWER
S IN NEW YORK,
T? I WENT TO IT
TIMES BUT ONLY
T WAS DESTROYED.
I WAS THERE THE
R WAS ACTUALLY
OGRAM AND THE
OOMS WERE
DERGROUND.
IT WAS KINDA DARK AND CLAUSTROPHOBIC.
WHEN I WAS WITH DAD IT SEEMED THE WHOLE WORLD WAS THAT WAY.
PART OF ME IS ALWAYS THINKING ABOUT HIM. WONDERING WHAT HE'S DOING. WHERE HE IS.
SOMETIMES I EVEN FEEL LIKE HE'S WATCHING ME.
I...I'M SORRY.
I DON'T KNOW SIGN LANGUAGE.
IT'S NICE TO MEET YOU!!
IT'S NICE TO MEET YOU TOO.

NEW YORK.

TITANS ISLAND.

...CYBORG IS GOING TO TAKE MISS MARTIAN AND INTERROGATE BOMBSHELL.

WE'LL FIND OUT WHO WAS TRYING TO HURT YOU, JOEY.

HURT HIM? I HIRED BOMBSHELL AND HER CREW TO BRING YOUR BROTHER BACK.

I WANT BOTH OF YOU BACK.

BAT GIRL

RISK

MATCH

SUN GIRL

AND I KNOW JUST HOW TO DO IT.

INERTIA

JOKER'S DAUGHTER

KIND CRU

JOKER'S DAUGHTER

Issue #34
Inked by
Kevin Conrad

Issue #35

Issue #36

Issue #37

Issue #38
Inked by
Kevin Conrad

Issue #39

Issue #40
Colored by
Moose Baumann

Issue #41

Covers by
Tony Daniel with
Tanya and **Richard Horie**

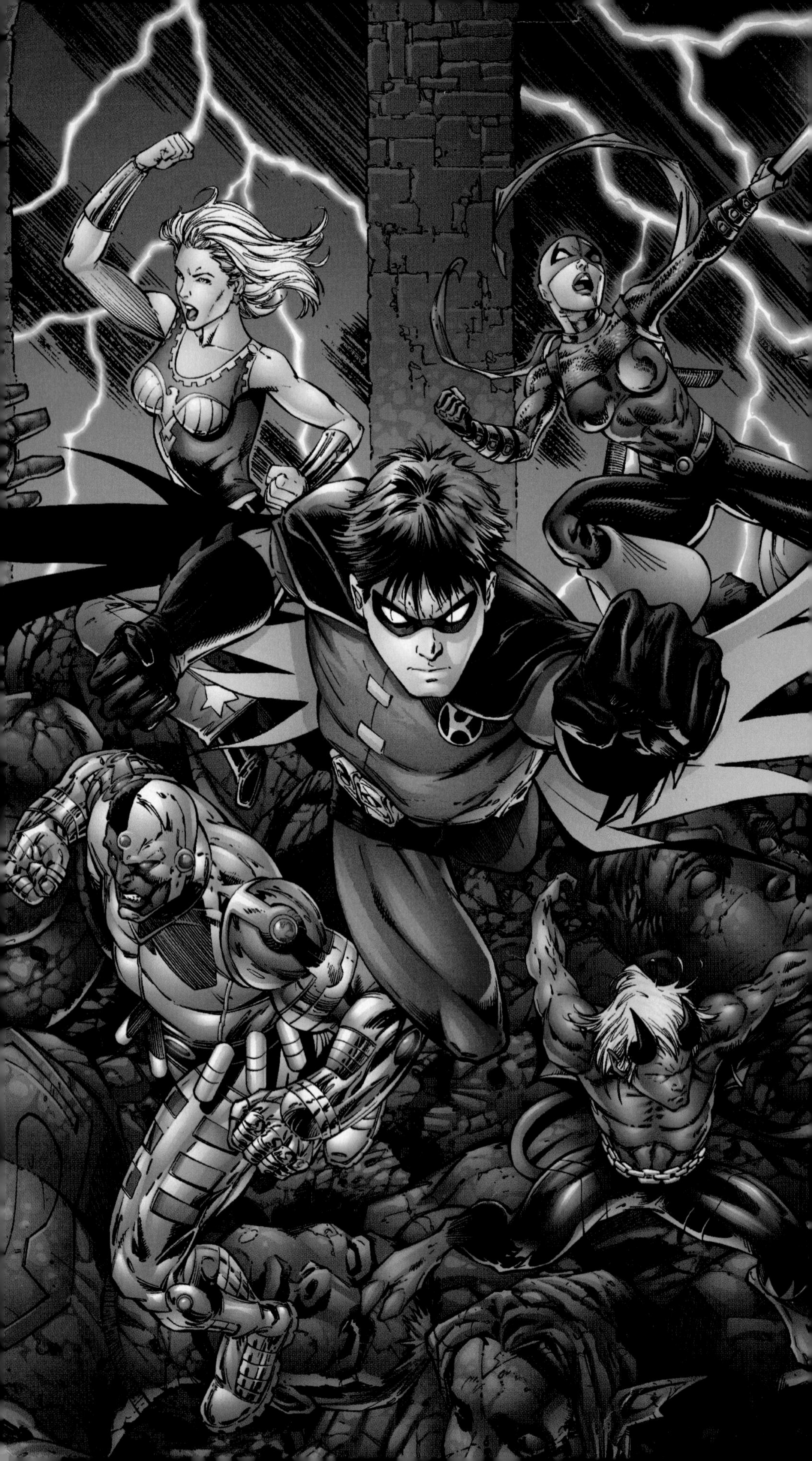

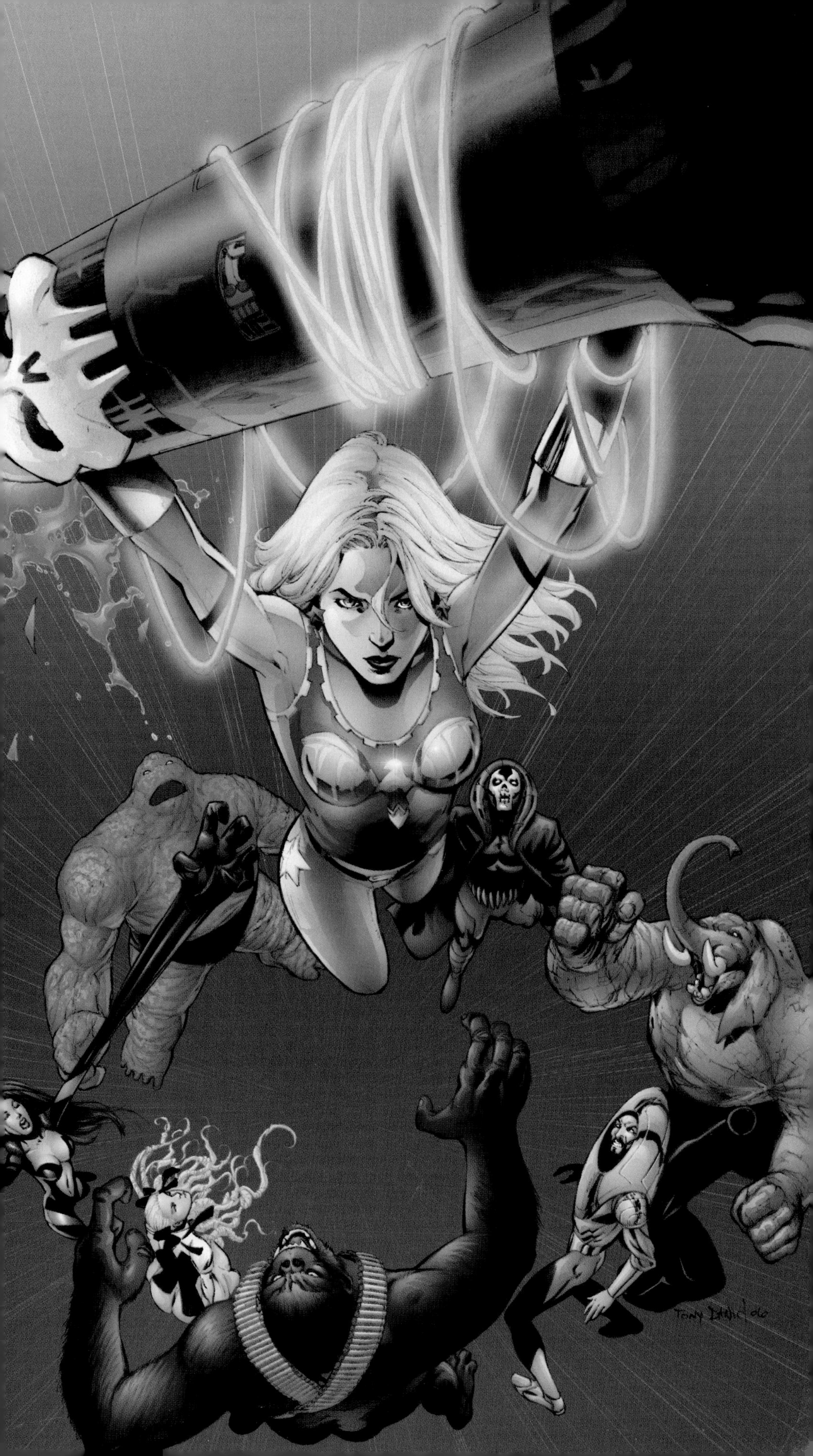

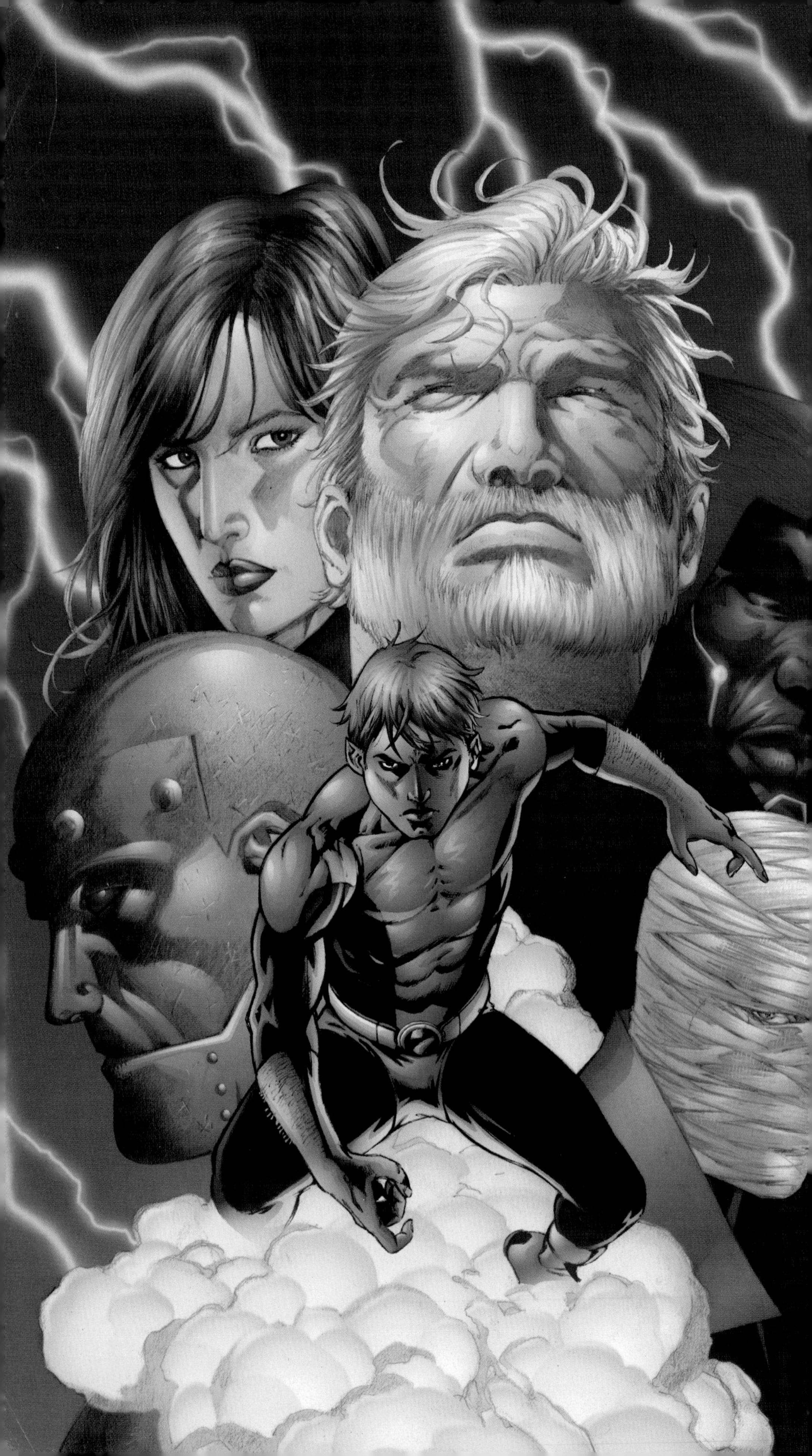

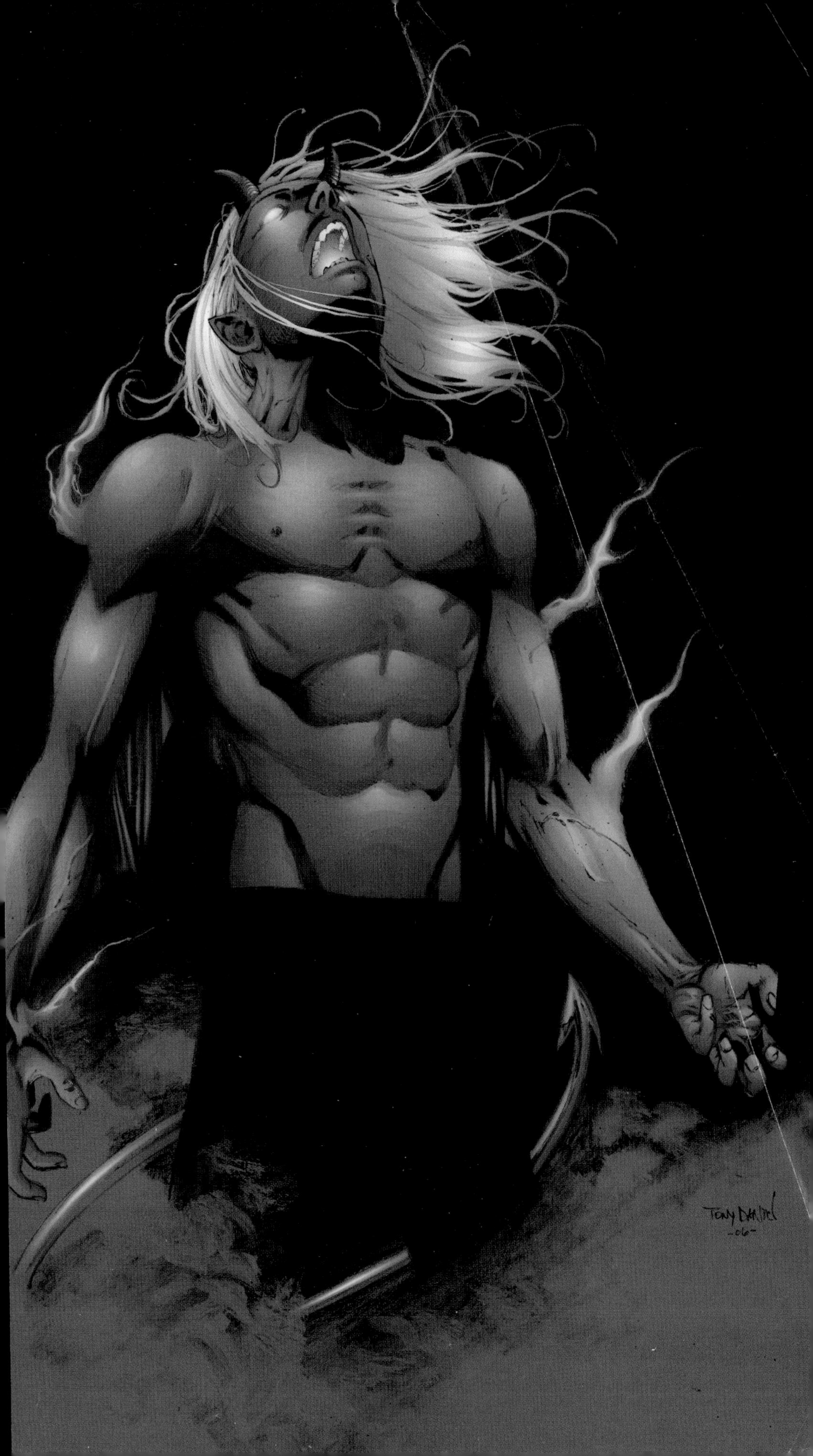
TONY DANIEL
-06-

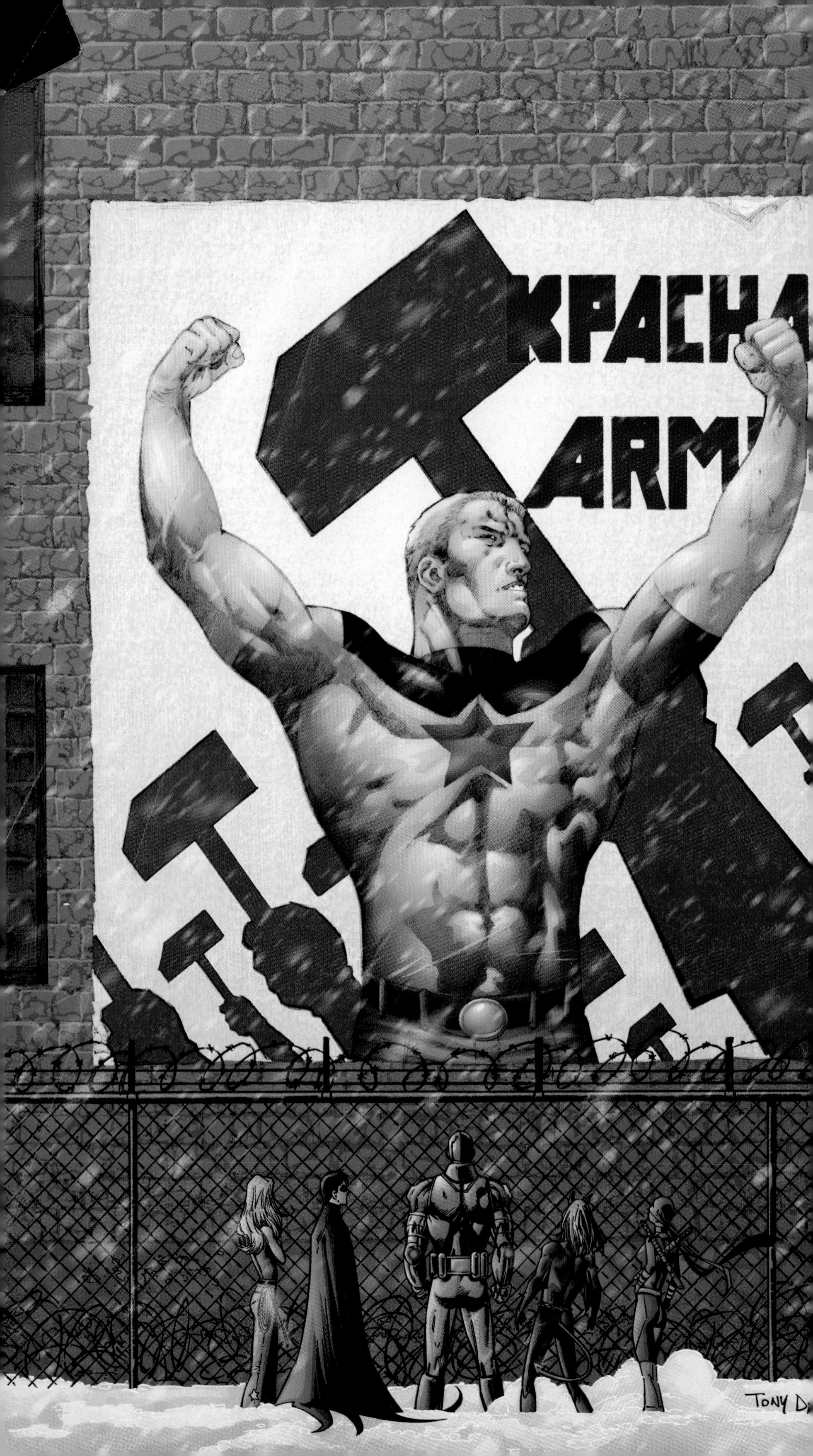
KPACHA
ARMI
TONY D.

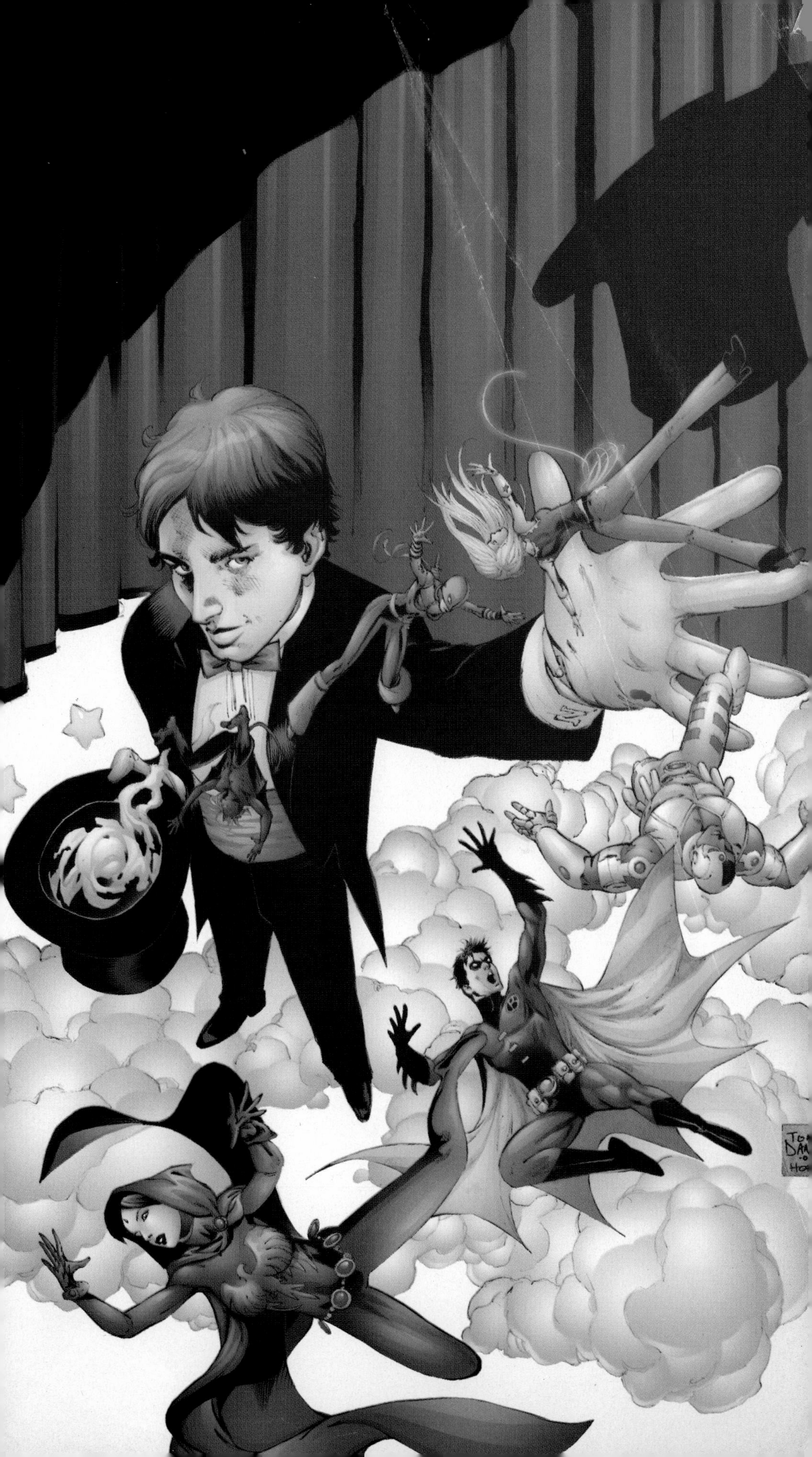

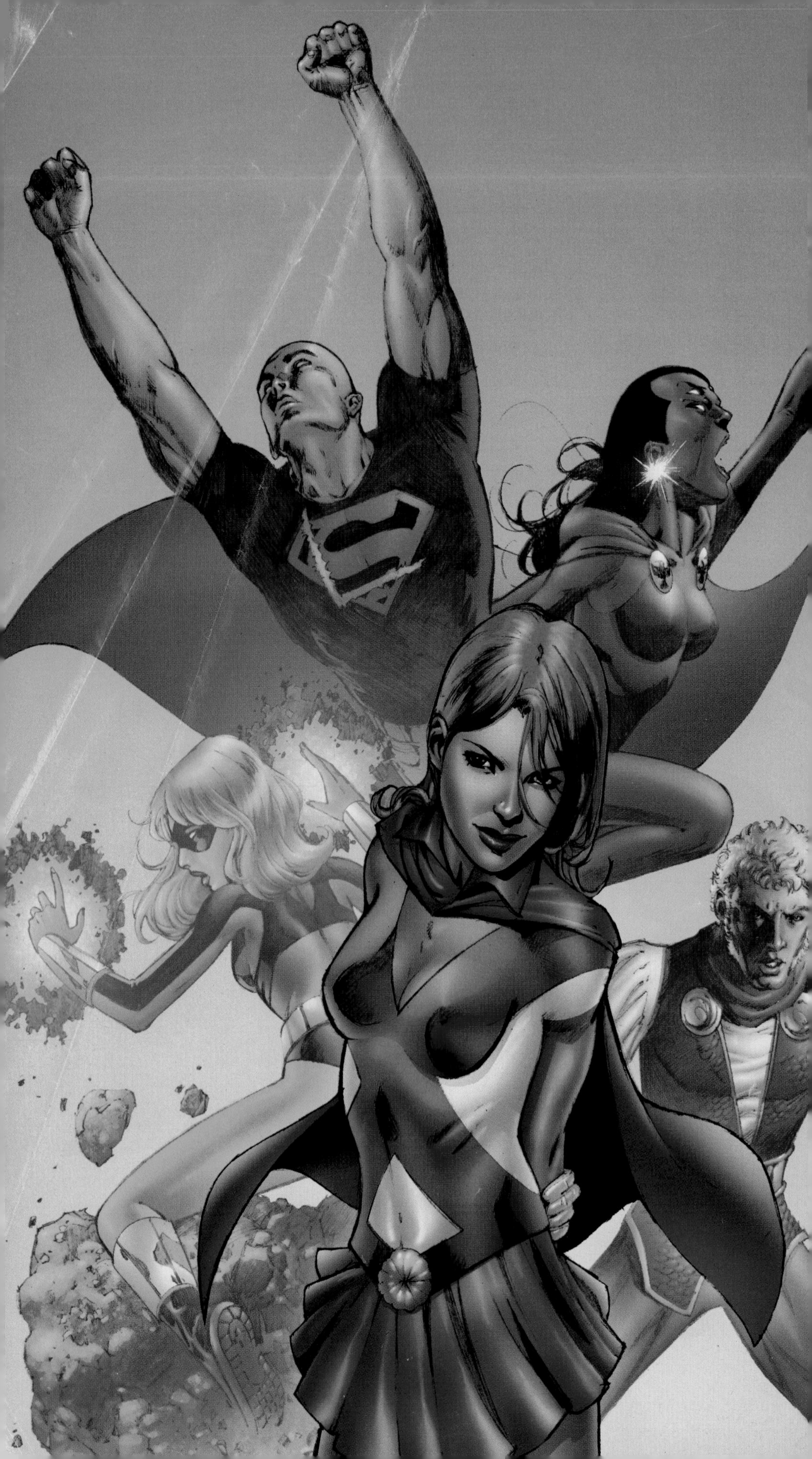

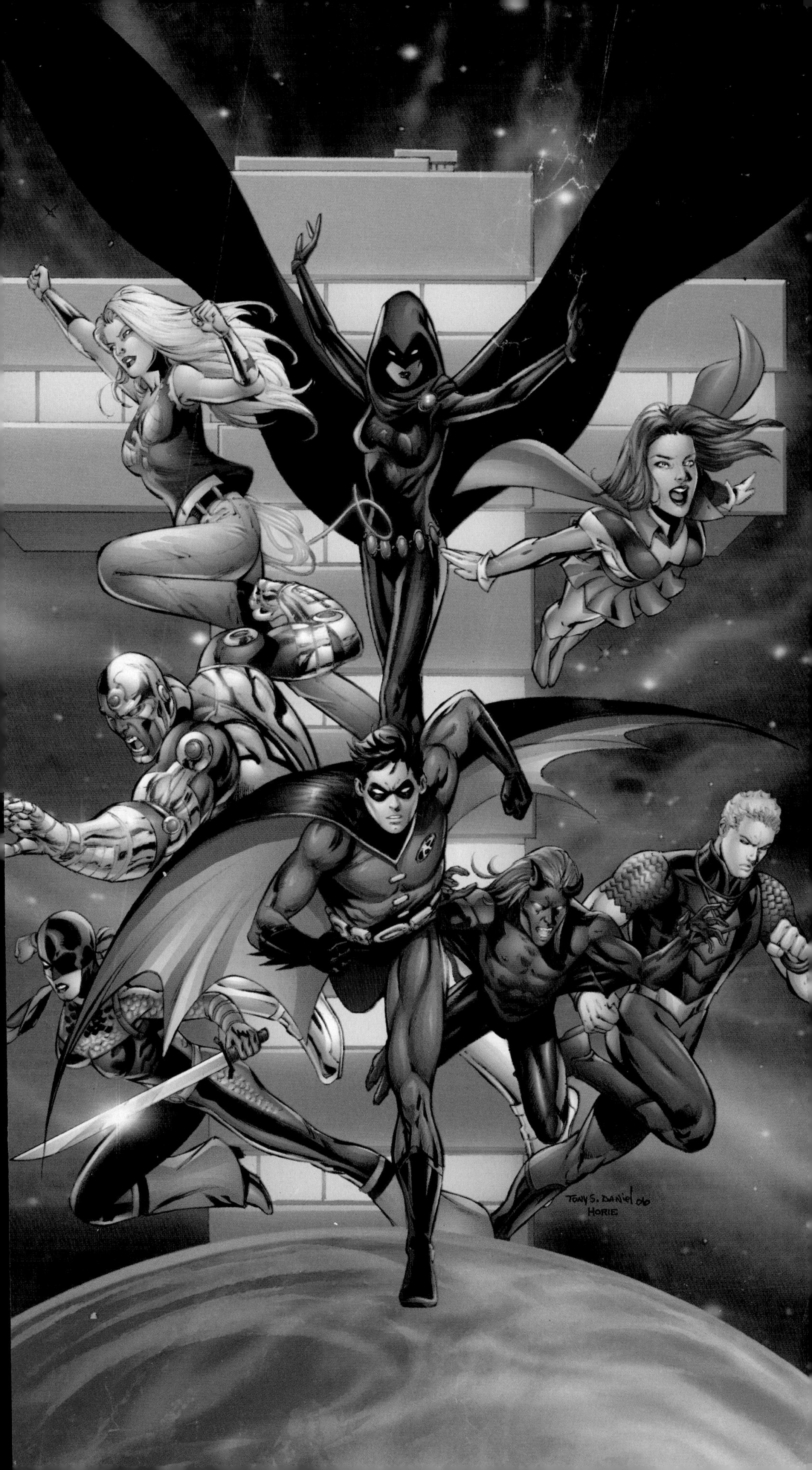
TONY S. DANIEL '06
HORIE

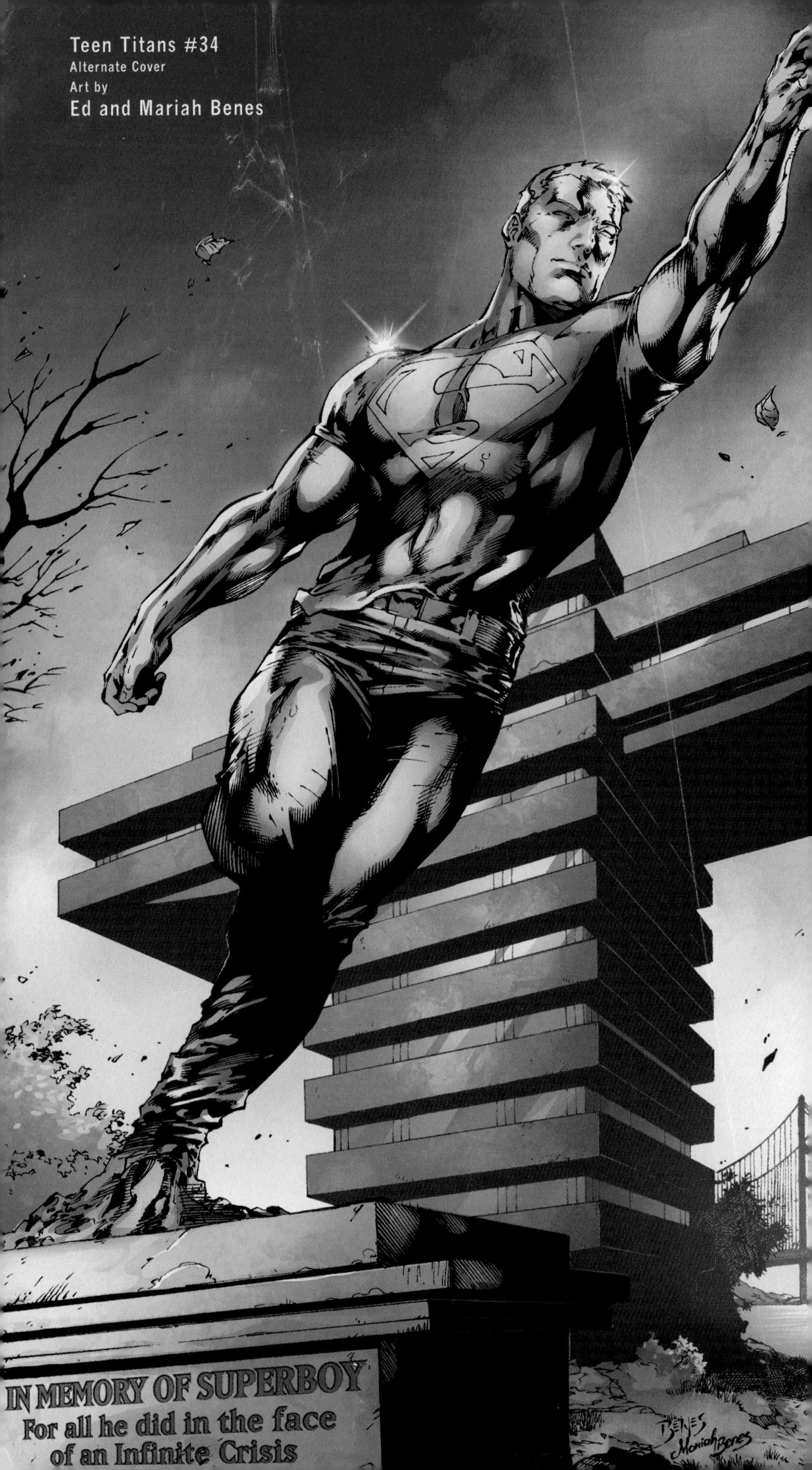
IN MEMORY OF SUPERBOY
For all he did in the face
of an Infinite Crisis

Teen Titans #34
Alternate Cover
Art by
Ed and Mariah Benes

INGDOM
OME

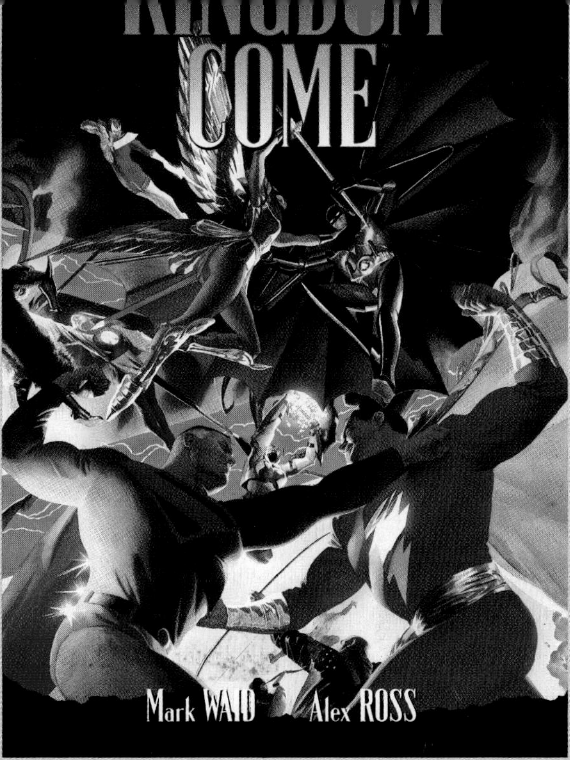
COME
Mark WAID
Alex ROSS

Vaid and **Alex Ross** deliver a
le of youth versus experience,
n versus change and what
a hero. KINGDOM COME is
ng story pitting the old guard —
nan, Batman, Wonder Woman
eir peers — against a new
promising generation.

R OF FIVE EISNER AND
Y AWARDS, INCLUDING
IMITED SERIES
ST ARTIST

IDENTITY CRISIS

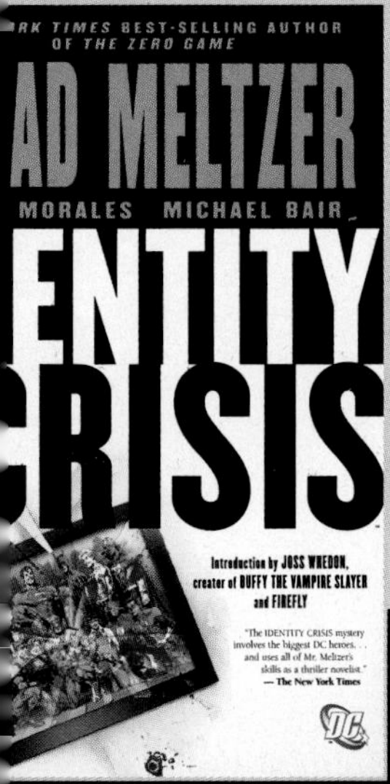
RK TIMES BEST-SELLING AUTHOR OF THE ZERO GAME
AD MELTZER
MORALES MICHAEL BAIR
ENTITY
CRISIS
Introduction by JOSS WHEDON, creator of BUFFY THE VAMPIRE SLAYER and FIREFLY
"The IDENTITY CRISIS mystery involves the biggest DC heroes... and uses all of Mr. Meltzer's skills as a thriller novelist."
— The New York Times

BRAD MELTZER

CRISIS ON
INFINITE EARTHS

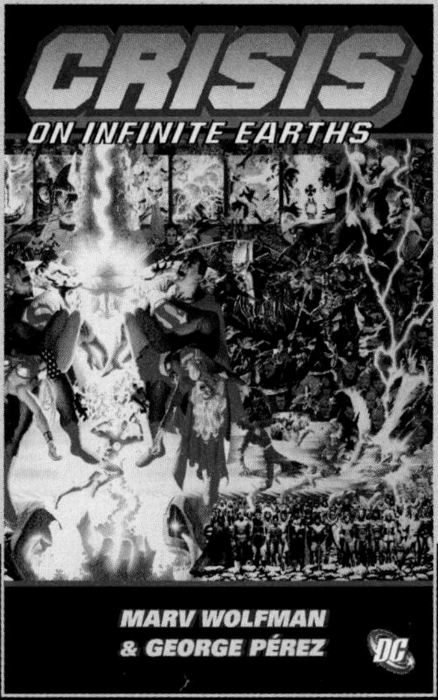
CRISIS
ON INFINITE EARTHS
MARV WOLFMAN
& GEORGE PÉREZ

MARV WOLFMAN

DC: THE NEW FRONTIER
VOLUME 1

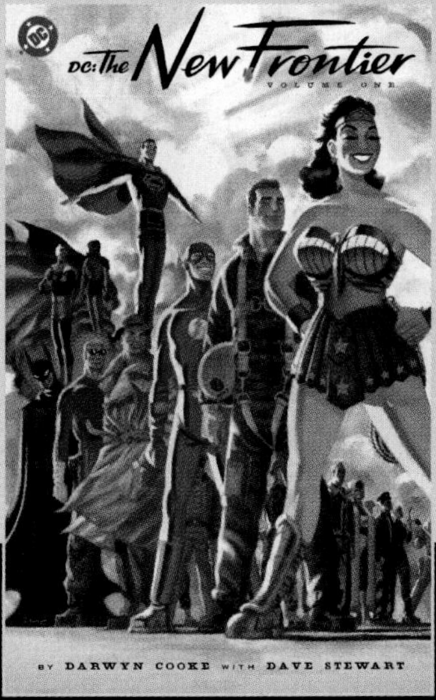
DC: The New Frontier
VOLUME ONE
BY DARWYN COOKE WITH DAVE STEWART

DARWYN COOKE

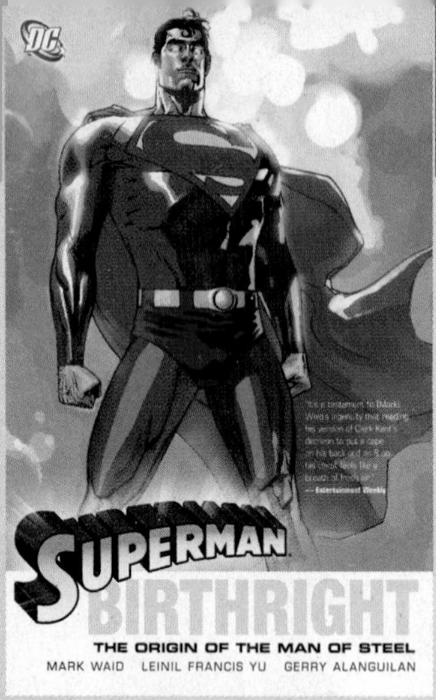
SUPERMAN
BIRTHRIGHT
THE ORIGIN OF THE MAN OF STEEL
MARK WAID LEINIL FRANCIS YU GERRY ALANGUILAN

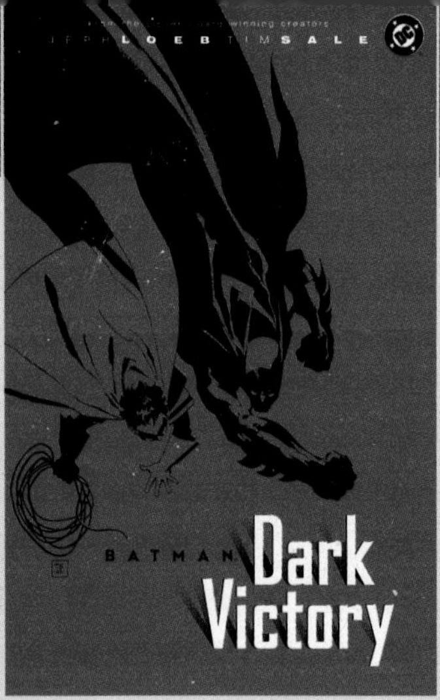
JEPH LOEB TIM SALE
BATMAN
Dark Victory

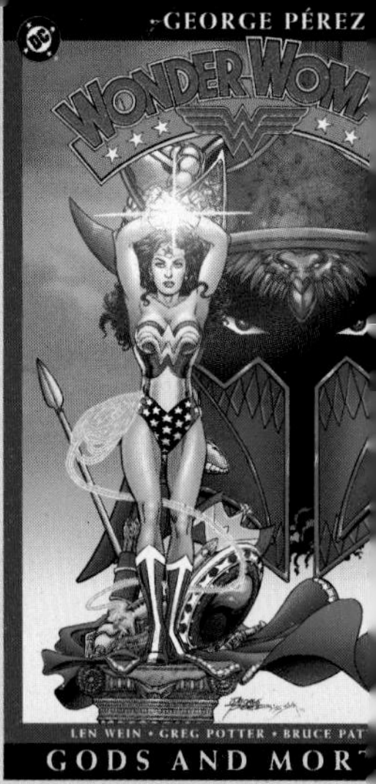
GEORGE PÉREZ
LEN WEIN • GREG POTTER • BRUCE PAT
GODS AND MORT

MARK WAID
LEINIL FRANCIS YU
GERRY ALANGUILAN

JEPH LOEB
TIM SALE

GEORGE PÉREZ
LEN WEIN/GREG PO
BRUCE PATTERSC

GREEN LANTERN:
NO FEAR

GREEN ARROW:
QUIVER

TEEN TITANS:
A KID'S GAME

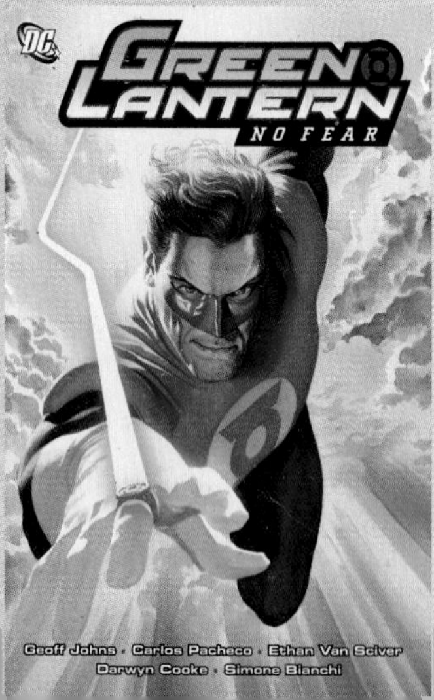
GREEN LANTERN
NO FEAR
Geoff Johns · Carlos Pacheco · Ethan Van Sciver
Darwyn Cooke · Simone Bianchi

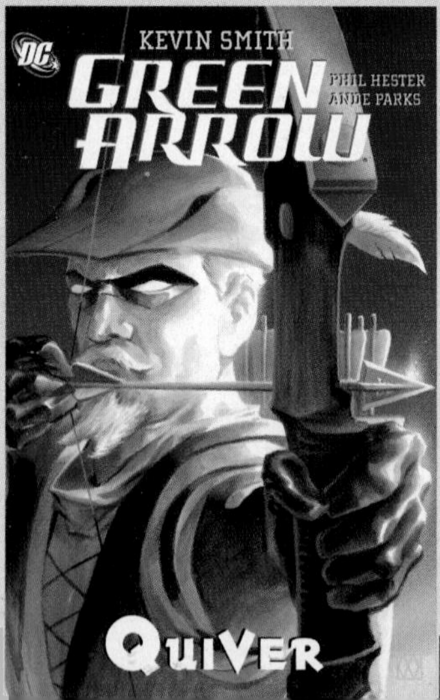
KEVIN SMITH
GREEN ARROW
PHIL HESTER
ANDE PARKS
QUIVER

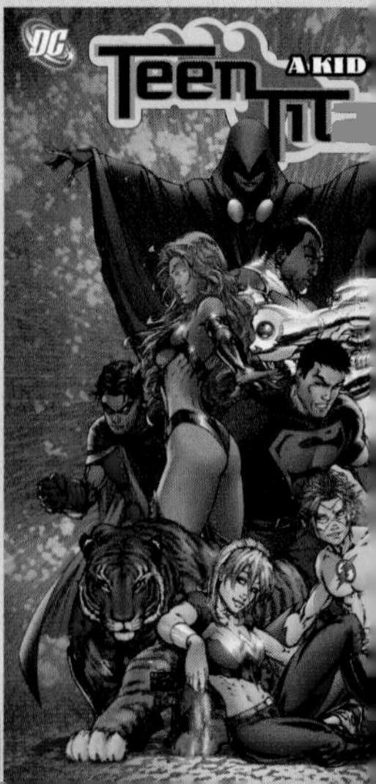
Teen
A KID